ADVANCE PRAISE FOR *THE OHIO STATE UNIVERSITY IN THE SIXTIES*

"The book is a comprehensive and in-depth narrative of events that unfolded at Ohio State in the turbulent decade of the 1960s. Shkurti captures the broad issues and themes that characterized this era as well as their specific manifestation on the Ohio State campus. Readers who know Ohio State today will gain insight into how and why their university changed over the past five decades. And readers with a more general national interest in the politics and turmoil of the 1960s will be fascinated to discover how these political conflicts and social changes played out in a specific setting: The Ohio State University. Shkurti tells a compelling story."

—Herb Asher, Professor Emeritus, The Ohio State University

THE OHIO STATE UNIVERSITY IN THE SIXTIES

THE OHIO STATE UNIVERSITY IN THE SIXTIES

THE UNRAVELING OF THE OLD ORDER

William J. Shkurti

TRILLIUM, AN IMPRINT OF
THE OHIO STATE UNIVERSITY PRESS
COLUMBUS

Trillium, an imprint of The Ohio State University Press.

Library of Congress Cataloging-in-Publication Data
Names: Shkurti, William J., author.
Title: The Ohio State University in the sixties : the unraveling of the old order / William J. Shkurti.
Description: Columbus : Trillium, an imprint of The Ohio State University Press, [2016] | "2016" | Includes bibliographical references and index.
Identifiers: LCCN 2016011762 | ISBN 9780814213070 (hardcover ; alk. paper) | ISBN 0814213073 (hardcover ; alk. paper)
Subjects: LCSH: Ohio State University—History—20th century.
Classification: LCC LD4228 .S55 2016 | DDC 378.771/5709046—dc23
LC record available at http://lccn.loc.gov/2016011762

Cover design by Regina Starace
Text design by Juliet Williams
Type set in Adobe Sabon

Cover image: A Columbus police officer tries to relax during riot duty at Ohio State in May of 1970 (University Archives)

♾ The paper used in this publication meets the minimum requirements of the American National Standard for Information Sciences—Permanence of Paper for Printed Library Materials. ANSI Z39.48-1992.

9 8 7 6 5 4 3 2 1

CONTENTS

ILLUSTRATIONS

PREFACE

At 5:30 p.m. on May 6, 1970, Ohio State president Novice G. Fawcett took the unprecedented step of closing down the university. Despite the presence of more than 1,500 armed highway patrol officers, Ohio National Guardsmen, deputy sheriffs, and Columbus city police, university and state officials feared they could not maintain order in the face of student protests. Students, faculty, and staff were told to leave. Offices, classrooms, and laboratories were closed. The campus was sealed off.

Never in the first one hundred years of Ohio State's existence had student protests made such a drastic step necessary. Nor would it be necessary again in the nearly 50 years since.

Student unrest swept over many college campuses that spring, but what set Ohio State apart was the intensity and scope of protests on a heretofore conservative campus. The events reflected more than just a clash between protestors and police. Student opposition to the Vietnam War and the shootings at Kent State University contributed, but tell only part of the story. The unrest at Ohio State began with a contentious student strike on April 29, before the Cambodia-related protests began on other campuses. Indeed, the roots of the Ohio State disturbances of May 1970 trace back at least a decade.

This story is about more than just protests or protestors. It's about the so-called silent majority of students and faculty who weren't political activists by nature, but ended up being reluctant participants. It's also about how a large institution struggled with rapid growth while being buffeted by the shifting demands of a society experiencing traumatic change.

My association with Ohio State began when I was a freshman in the fall of 1964. By the time I graduated four years later, campus unrest had grown significantly but remained within some sort of generally recognized boundaries. I left Columbus for three years in the army in January 1969 and was on active duty in West Germany when the campus shut down in May 1970. I remember wondering what had happened to precipitate such a dramatic series of events, and I felt that I had missed out on something important by not being there.

When I returned to pursue a master's degree in the spring of 1972, I was stunned by how much the campus had changed. Gone was the activism of the sixties. A few upperclassmen spoke in almost reverential tones of the protests two years earlier, but most people simply wanted to put them behind them. The Vietnam War and the draft, which had intruded so forcefully into our lives in 1968, were history. Younger students seemed more interested in drugs, sex, and rock 'n' roll. I wondered how things could have changed so quickly.

Like many other baby boomers, I came to terms with this in my own way and moved on. After I returned to Ohio State in 1990 as vice president for finance, I witnessed the impact of many of the changes that came out of the activism of the 1960s and early 1970s. On September 11, 2001, I inherited the direct reporting line for campus safety as part of a previously approved reorganization. I spent the final nine years of my career worrying about such things as potential terrorists and swine flu outbreaks. From time to time I thought about what it must have been like to be responsible for campus safety and security during the tumult of the sixties. My sympathies remained with the students, but I also became more curious about the challenges faced by those responsible for maintaining some semblance of order.

Shortly after I retired in 2010, I visited the Kent State campus on the anniversary of the events of May 1970. It left me wondering if the mythology of what had happened 40 years ago had already begun to overtake reality. This book is an effort to address those questions.

The story of Ohio State in the 1960s includes an array of groups and individuals, all with a cause to advance. It includes protests against the hypocrisy of the existing order. It includes defenders of the existing order against what they saw as the hypocrisy of protestors. It includes administrators whose decisions sometimes defused dangerous situations, but at other times inflamed them. It also includes the often overlooked amorphous center—the people who were caught in the crossfire between ideologues and who coalesced to fight back against being steamrolled by either side. And it played out on one of the nation's largest campuses, a once tranquil community that found itself caught in the growing imbalance between what it wanted to be and what it was.

The Ohio State University in the Sixties is organized chronologically. It begins with a look at the university at the end of the 1950s, a period when order and conformity seemed to be the rule of the day. The next 12 chapters are devoted to the cascading effects of changes in each of the school years of the 1960s. It concludes with an epilogue that attempts to sort out the transformational effects of the tumult of the decade. Each chapter is divided into three sections that parallel the forces that wrestled for control throughout the 1960s: the students, the university, and society.

The changing relationship between student activists who sought to promote change and the mass of less engaged students is the primary focus of the first theme. It addresses the well-known protests—such as the 1961 Rose Bowl uproar, the 1965 Speakers Rule sit-ins, the 1968 takeover of the Administration Building, and the 1965–70 antiwar demonstrations—and the reactions of previously less involved students to them. This section also traces student efforts to end in loco parentis and to improve the treatment of women and black students, as well as the attempts of student government leaders to adapt to their changing constituency.

The second theme explores how university officials confronted exploding enrollments and a growing research portfolio, while students demanded that change occur more quickly and elected officials demanded tougher measures to preserve order. This section goes behind closed doors to examine how major decisions were made and their impact on instruction, research, academics, and relations with state officials.

The impact of changes in society at large is part of the third theme. This includes how the campus community responded to events such as the Cuban Missile Crisis; the assassinations of John F. Kennedy, Martin Luther King Jr., and Robert F. Kennedy; the civil rights movement; the Vietnam War; and the rise of the counterculture. It also looks into the changing dynamics between the university and the surrounding community.

Many of the descriptions of events are drawn from the pages of Ohio State's student newspaper, the *Lantern*. As a student laboratory, the *Lantern* has its limitations, but there is no substitute for the richness of detail it provides from an army of reporters who were present at nearly every significant event of the decade. What they lacked in experience they made up for in enthusiasm. I have also made use of other publications of the period, including local newspapers; material in University Archives, some of which has not been made public until now; and the recollections of those who were there.

Condensing 10 turbulent years of events at an institution as complex as Ohio State into one volume was a difficult task, and I would like to acknowledge the contributions of many people. Tamar Chute and her staff at University Archives were indispensable to the collection and interpretation of source material. Special thanks goes to Kevlin Haire, who located documents and diligently checked the accuracy of sources, and Michelle Drobik, who helped find key photographs. Former university archivist Raimund Goerler gave generously of his time to review the manuscript and make many useful suggestions. The reference staff at the Upper Arlington Public Library, headed by Mark Mangini, tracked down many obscure but important pieces of information. Leslie Flesch helped pull together the segments into a consistent electronic format. Herb Asher, Kevin Boyle, Mike Curtin, Emily Foster, David Steigerwald, Sharon West, and Chris Zacher read portions of the manuscript and offered suggestions. My editor, Lynne Bonenberger, deserves special recognition for her tireless diligence in making this a much more presentable manuscript. I appreciate the faith Tony Sanfilippo and his staff at OSU Press showed in this manuscript and their efforts to bring it into print.

Finally, I want to thank the more than 40 former Ohio State students, faculty, and administrators who consented to be interviewed. Their viewpoints added an element that news reports and official documents alone could not.

Any errors of omission or commission are my sole responsibility.

William J. Shkurti
February 1, 2016

PROLOGUE

OHIO STATE IN THE FIFTIES

During the 1950s Ohio State thrived under a philosophy of modulated, businesslike conservatism. University leaders embraced gradual growth. Students had fun while obeying the rules. There were disagreements, but even dissent was channeled within accepted boundaries. But by the end of that decade, signs of the coming ruptures in the postwar consensus were already beginning to emerge.

P.1. Ohio State cheerleaders, 1960. As the fifties segued into the sixties, traditions were still honored and students were expected to obey the rules. (*Makio*)

THE UNIVERSITY: BIG IS BEAUTIFUL

The Ohio State University was founded in 1870 as one of the country's original 29 land grant universities, the only one of its kind in Ohio. These universities were a product of the 1862 Morrill Act, which sought to broaden access to higher education across the country. In exchange for the coveted federal and state designation, land grant universities would seek to create and broadly disseminate knowledge useful to society, especially in agriculture and the mechanical arts.[1]

Prior to the 1960s Ohio State thrived under this mandate. It grew steadily, emerging as a modern research university after World War II. First, war-related research brought an influx of federal dollars. After the war thousands of veterans flocked to campuses under the GI Bill. Ohio State's enrollment doubled from a wartime low of 6,500 in the fall of 1943 to more than 13,000 in 1945, then nearly doubled again before peaking at 25,400 in 1947. The rapid growth strained people and facilities, but produced a generation of educated Americans who, after more than 20 years of economic depression, war, and postwar adjustment, were ready for a period of stability. Americans at all levels of society, but particularly the growing middle class, knew they were better off than their parents had been and that their children's future was even brighter.

No place better represented the aspirations of the growing middle class than the nation's great public universities. Relatively accessible and inexpensive, they offered a quality education that proved the surest path to a good life. Ohio State had the nation's 10th largest enrollment at the end of the 1950s. Located in the middle of the country, in the capital of the fifth most populous state, it represented a commitment to middle-class values of hard work and orderly progress.

Columbus's population of nearly 500,000 made it the 28th largest city in the country in 1960. Bigger than the likes of Ann Arbor, Bloomington, or Madison, Columbus was not overwhelmed by the university's size. Yet the city was not so big that it was hard to control. The conservative business establishment ran a tight ship that didn't tolerate much in the way of dissenting viewpoints.

Ohio State's board of trustees—seven men nominated by the governor and approved by the Ohio Senate—served as the university's ultimate governing authority. The trustees hired and fired the president and

P.2. Most students in the late 1950s were not inclined to rock the boat, a situation that would soon change dramatically. (*Makio*)

KEY UNIVERSITY OFFICIALS: 1960–70

President	Novice Fawcett (1956–72)
Vice president for instruction	Frederic W. Heimberger (1951–64) John C. Weaver (1964–66)
Vice president for academic affairs and provost	John E. Corbally (1966–69) James A. Robinson (1969–71)
Vice president for administration	John E. Corbally (1964–66)
Vice president for administrative operations	Edward Q. Moulton (1969–71)
Executive dean for student relations	William S. Guthrie (1957–61) John T. Bonner Jr. (1961–68)
Vice president for student affairs	John T. Mount (1968–70) Ted R. Robinson (1970–73)

Source: Weisenburger, *Fawcett Years*, 13–26

approved the budget, all major hires, and major policy changes. They delegated to the president responsibility for day-to-day operations of the university. He in turn was assisted by an eight-member cabinet that included the vice president for instruction and faculty, vice president for business and finance, executive dean for student relations, and other experts. In this sense the structure of the university was similar to that of large corporations and government organizations of the time.

The university also included 1,300 full-time tenure-track faculty members who expected to make academic policy and—to some degree, both by tradition and legislation—be deferred to in academic matters by the president and the board.

As the 1960s began Novice Gail Fawcett had been Ohio State's president for three years. Born in 1909 on a farm near the small town of Gambier, Ohio, Fawcett was conservative in outlook and reserved in demeanor. He was a physically imposing 6-foot-2 and played center on his high school basketball team. Fawcett had planned to go into business after graduating from nearby Kenyon College. With his options limited by the Great Depression, however, he returned to Gambier High School as a teacher. By age 25 he was superintendent of the Gambier school system. He earned a master's degree from Ohio State in 1937.

P.3. Ohio State president Novice G. Fawcett. (University Archives)

After a succession of administrative positions in other Ohio city school districts, Fawcett returned to Columbus in 1949 to head its rapidly growing system. At age 40 he became the youngest superintendent of a large public school system in the country. In Columbus he solidified his reputation as an effective administrator and skillful politician. He guided the district through rapid growth while avoiding many of the problems facing others in similar circumstances. When Howard Bevis stepped down in 1956 after more than 16 years as Ohio State president, the board of trustees selected the 47-year-old Fawcett to succeed him.

One credential Fawcett did not have was a Ph.D. Even though none of his predecessors had achieved that distinction, some members of the faculty grumbled about hiring a president of a large research university who lacked not only a doctorate but administrative experience at that level. The trustees, however, saw in Fawcett two things they believed were more important: he was a capable administrator who knew how to manage growth, and he was a known quantity to the Columbus power structure. He would get things done but not openly challenge the existing order.[2]

Under Fawcett Ohio State continued to grow—carefully, thoughtfully, and without drama.

STUDENTS: DON'T ROCK THE BOAT

Ohio State boasted seven campuses at the end of the 1950s, with branches in Dayton, Lima, Marion, Mansfield, Newark, and Lakewood, near Cleveland. The Columbus campus, with all but a thousand of the 23,000 students, was the heart and soul of the university. Bordered by the Olentangy River to the west and residential neighborhoods to the east, north, and south, the campus retained a small-town feel. The Oval, a grassy area the size of four football fields, was both the geographic and spiritual center of campus. On warm afternoons dog walkers, ballplayers, and sunbathers would dot the landscape. The Oval also provided a rallying point for political gatherings that became more intense as the decade progressed.

Ohio State students of the time looked forward to careers as accountants, engineers, lawyers, physicians, or schoolteachers. By the time the last World War II veterans graduated in June 1960, their place had been taken by 1,500 Korean War veterans and their younger brothers and sisters. They brought with them a commitment to the same values and a desire to succeed, but also found time for parties, concerts, and dances. Traditions such as football games and Homecoming in the fall, Greek Week in the winter, and May Week in the spring defined each quarter on

P.4. The Ohio State campus in the early 1960s, facing west. High Street runs across the bottom of the photo. The large building at the center front is Mershon Auditorium. The building to the left of it is the Ohio Historical Society, now Sullivant Hall. The Main Library sits at the west end of the Oval. The hospital complex is at the upper left, and Ohio Stadium is at the upper right. The agricultural fields are at the top of the photo across the Olentangy River. (*Makio*)

the academic calendar. For the most part students accepted the rules of conduct established by their elders.

Under a 1914 state law all public universities were required to admit any graduate of an Ohio high school. Not all of these students proved capable of doing college-level work, and a third of the freshmen admitted each fall flunked out or dropped out after their first year. Only a little more than a third persisted to graduation.[3]

This led to unusually large freshman classes; in a typical year in the late 1950s freshmen accounted for almost a third of the entire student body on the Columbus campus. Ohio State was also much more of a commuter campus than many of its Big Ten counterparts. Ohio's network of community colleges and branches was in its infancy, so many Ohio State students called Franklin County and the six surrounding counties home.

Although the student body did include about 600 international students (largely graduate students) and 2,500 students from out of state, it was not representative of the country, or the state, as a whole. Women, who comprised half of the general population, were outnumbered by men two to one. Franklin County and surrounding counties represented only 6 percent of the state population but accounted for almost 40 percent of the student enrollment.[4]

Such a large number of freshmen and commuters meant the 4,500 students who were members of fraternities and sororities exerted an influence far in excess of their numbers alone. They lived on or near campus, were well organized, and participated much more in campus activities. They also tended to be more affluent and more conservative than other students. Although Greeks would lose some of their influence as enrollment soared in the second half of the sixties, at the beginning of the decade they still shaped a big part of the student culture.

SOCIETY: A TIME OF TRANSITION

In the larger world outside of Ohio State, some of the big changes that would characterize the sixties had already begun. The summer of 1960 saw TV images of the first sit-ins by black college students in the south—a means of protest that would empower the otherwise powerless to challenge the established order. Also that summer the Food and

Drug Administration approved the first birth control pills, an event that would allow women to take more control over their lives.

Technology and demographics also conspired to bring a new order. In 1950 only 9 percent of Americans had a television set in their home. By 1960 television was part of nearly 90 percent of all homes, transmitting images that could divide as well as unify. The baby boomers born in the prosperous years between 1946 and 1957, who grew up with television, were now approaching young adulthood. The first phalanx of this generation marched into ninth grade in the fall of 1960. Anxious university officials were already fretting about how they would handle the influx of students headed their way.[5]

These students shared a connection unlike that of any generation before them. Nurtured by a media-drenched affinity for the same language, music, and dress, they would seek to find their own identity. The older generation had conquered the Great Depression and won the Second World War, but many of their sons and daughters would question, mock, and defy what their parents had worked so hard to create. And nowhere would the struggle play out more forcefully than at the nation's great universities.

At Ohio State small groups of individuals had begun to raise issues that challenged the status quo, including expectations of women students, the role of military training, the treatment of minority students, and the boundaries of free speech. None of these controversies erupted into a major confrontation in the late 1950s, but each would serve as a flash point for campus unrest at some point during the coming decade.

CHAPTER 1

NEW FRONTIERS (1960–61)

During the 1960–61 school year student activists pushed onto Ohio State's agenda many of the issues of conscience that would dominate public discourse in the years to come. Meanwhile, the university embraced growth as the best path to greatness, and optimistic visions of the decade ahead clashed with the lingering realities of the one just ended.

1.1. Cadets join a May 1961 protest against compulsory ROTC. (*Makio*)

STUDENTS: TESTING THE SYSTEM

A surge in student activism challenged long-standing university policies involving expectations of female students, compulsory military training, treatment of African Americans, and limits of free speech. All would be resolved to some degree by working "within the system."

The system at that time consisted of a labyrinth of offices and committees that governed Ohio State with varying degrees of success. The students occupied the lowest level of the hierarchy. In the late 1950s they were expected to get an education and move on. The nearly 24,000 students on the Columbus campus—including 18,100 undergraduates and 5,700 graduate and professional students—had formal representation through the Student Senate and other organizations. But the senate could only advise, not legislate, and students often would find one of their biggest obstacles was disagreement among themselves.

"ABOUT BUCKEYE COEDS"

Upon admission to Ohio State each woman received a booklet titled "About Buckeye Coeds," produced by the Women's Self Government Association (WSGA), a group that dated to 1908. "Friendships are the principal aspects of a Buckeye Coed's social life," the booklet began. "Gradually her friendships increase to include those in activities and organizations of which she has become a part. Many of these activities such as record dances, open houses, and fraternity parties give her ample opportunity to meet many nice fellows—perhaps even that special fellow."

By the fourth paragraph it got around to academics: "Here at Ohio State, a Buckeye Coed realizes the importance of devoting time and energy to her studies. In return for the opportunity to get an education granted her by her parents, she naturally does the best in all her subjects." "About Buckeye Coeds" went on for 72 pages, but the core of the booklet was seven pages of single-spaced dos and don'ts called "Things We Live By"—a list of rules covering every aspect of a woman's conduct. For example, Rule 9.2 stated: "Any woman student who visits a man's apartment without university approved chaperones will be subject to suspension from the university."[1]

Such strictures flowed from two widely accepted concepts: in loco parentis and the so-called double standard. In loco parentis, Latin for "in place of parents," was a legal doctrine with its roots in common law. In this case it meant Ohio State had not only the right but the responsibility to fulfill the role of the parents when their children were under the university's control.

The double standard, which was not a formal legal doctrine, was based on the belief that a woman's primary role in society was to be a good wife and mother. "Nice" girls were to be seen but not heard and did not engage in sex before marriage. Rules at Ohio State, and at most other campuses at the time, defined how women should act, how they should dress (both in class and outside of class), where they could live, when they had to be in for the night, and where they could visit and with whom. College men were given much more leeway. For example, men also were forbidden to have members of the opposite sex in their rooms, but sanctions were described as "university disciplinary actions," while women committing the same violation faced dismissal.[2]

WSGA was not only a service organization for Ohio State's 7,800 female students but also helped enforce regulations and could recommend changes to the dean of women. The WSGA standards commission, which consisted of representatives (mostly elected) of the women's housing areas, served as the chief judicial arm. The associate dean of women was the group's principal adviser. The two most common rule violations involved alcohol and unchaperoned visits to men's apartments.

As might be expected, the standards commission was not popular among all students, some of whom referred to it as the "Girl Gestapo." WSGA saw it differently. Vice president and commission chair Mary Kennedy described its role this way: "The idea . . . is not to punish women students because they have done something wrong. We want the women to know why there is a rule and why we must all live with it. Our main purpose is to understand them and have them understand us."[3]

Although in theory they represented the same people, the Student Senate and WSGA did not always see eye to eye. And they wouldn't in the case of the Apartment Rule. By 1961 even the standards commission thought the rule was too strict, so it recommended it be changed to permit any woman not a freshman to visit a man's apartment without a chaperone as long as she had written permission from her parents

1.2. According to the Women's Self Government Association, only the student on the left is properly attired for attending class in the fall of 1960. (*Lantern*)

and had another woman accompany her. The WSGA board voted its approval on January 4.

The Student Senate approved its own recommendation a week later. The senate at that time consisted of 40 members and was supposed to be the legislative body representing all students. Members included presidents of key campus organizations, including WSGA, as well as elected representatives of the 10 colleges and 21 elected representatives of the sophomore, junior, and senior classes.

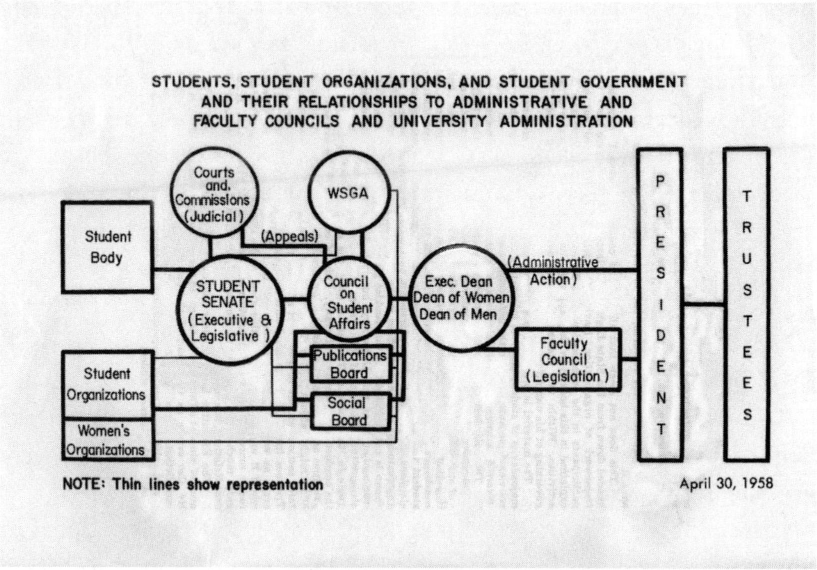

1.3. Ohio State governance structure circa early 1960s. (1960 Student Handbook)

Senate administrative vice president Mary Linn Horn introduced the resolution to liberalize the Apartment Rule further by allowing a junior or senior woman to enter a man's room or apartment without any escort, as long as she had written parental approval on file with her living unit. The senate passed Horn's version, and the *Lantern* signed on the next day with an editorial supporting it. But when WSGA would not budge, senate leaders circulated a petition in support of its version. Within two weeks they claimed to have the signatures of 1,053 women students.

The proposal moved next to the Council on Student Affairs (CSA), which served as a kind of super appeals body and traffic cop for process. Chaired by William S. Guthrie, the executive dean for student relations, it included the dean of men and dean of women, three faculty members, and six students, including the presidents of the Student Senate and WSGA. The university liked to brag there was only one committee like it in the Big Ten with more student members, but the administration, specifically the executive dean, still made the ultimate decisions, as the students would find out.

After four months of deliberation the CSA adopted a rule closer to the WSGA version in that it required juniors and seniors under 21 to have another woman present. The requirement for parental permission was dropped, due to enforcement problems. Even though three of the four student representatives present voted against the less liberal proposal, it was approved by a vote of seven to three. WSGA vice president Mary Kennedy was the lone student to vote for Guthrie's proposal. She was joined by the three administrators and three faculty members.[4] The revised Apartment Rule became effective that fall, but the contest was far from over.

THE END OF COMPULSORY ROTC

While women chafed under the likes of the Apartment Rule, men were growing restless over compulsory military training.

The concept of military training as part of the curriculum dated to the 1862 Morrill Act, which established land grant universities. Ohio State created its military science department in 1876. President William Oxley Thompson, along with George Converse of the faculty and alumnus Ralph Mershon, were leaders in drafting and passing the 1916 National Defense Act, which established the Reserve Officers Training Corps on campuses across the country. The first ROTC unit at Ohio State was established shortly thereafter to address the need for more officers to serve in the army as it expanded to meet the threat of war in Europe.

At Ohio State, as at most universities, ROTC enrollment was mandatory for freshmen and sophomores. Juniors and seniors who voluntarily enrolled and completed the program received commissions as second lieutenants in the army reserve upon graduation. The United States, which did not want a large peacetime army, could then call on reserves and mobilize quickly if needed. World War I ended before the first officers graduated, but ROTC programs nationwide provided many of the junior officers who led the army in World War II.

Ohio State's program expanded in 1945 to include navy officers and in 1946 to include the air force. When war broke out in Korea in 1950, ROTC again contributed a large number of officers. By 1960 Ohio State had produced 6,219 ROTC graduates, the fourth most of any university in the country. Nevertheless, the program was not without controversy. Student and faculty opposition to the idea of mandatory military training on a college campus dated back to at least the 1880s. It became a major issue in the 1930s as war clouds gathered in Europe. In the early 1950s it surfaced again when students unsuccessfully petitioned for an end to mandatory training in the middle of the Korean War.[5]

As Cold War tensions eased in the midfifties, the issue of compulsory training surfaced again. This time, proposed changes had more widespread support. Even some members of the military, particularly the air force and navy, which relied exclusively on volunteers, wanted to stop requiring all male freshmen and sophomores to take basic military science. In early 1959 the Student Senate voted to recommend a change to voluntary ROTC. The action required faculty approval because it involved a change in curriculum. After more than a year of deliberations, the appropriate faculty committees endorsed the recommendation to make ROTC voluntary in the spring of 1960. Ohio State administrators, however, were reluctant to move quickly. Because only three of the 41 ROTC programs at land grant universities were voluntary at the time, they feared a backlash from the army and from veterans groups, which still supported compulsory training.[6]

Supporters felt double-crossed, and the first controversy of the 1960s was under way. The *Lantern* started the ball rolling with an editorial supporting the change in its first issue of the school year. "We are very concerned about some students who could make their contribution to national security without taking ROTC," the editors wrote. "They are the students who will be the 'soldiers' in the battle already being fought so fiercely in the science laboratories. . . . And let's clear up once and for all the notion that those students who do not wish to take ROTC are any less patriotic than those enrolled in the program."[7]

Student Senate president Robert Young made ending compulsory ROTC a major part of his State of the Senate address, accusing the university administration of dragging its feet. Young and the *Lantern* had widespread support from the faculty and the student body. President Novice Fawcett responded by saying that Ohio State and other land grant institutions had requested clarification from the Department of Defense.

Things remained relatively quiet until the following spring. When new Student Senate president Phil Moots laid out his goals for his term, he included making ROTC voluntary. Then on April 11 a group called the Student Peace Committee threatened a protest at the ROTC review on the Oval scheduled for May 4, also known as Corps Day. Fawcett pulled the item from the agenda of the May board of trustees meeting, prompting senate leaders to announce they would lead protests on Corps Day themselves.[8]

With only a week to go the Pentagon rode to the rescue. On April 24 Roswell Gilpatric, the deputy secretary of defense, responded to the request from the land grant universities by saying the Defense Department had no objection to voluntary ROTC. Fawcett met with the Student Senate leaders four days later. They agreed to call off the Corps Day demonstrations with the understanding that Fawcett would present his recommendations for voluntary ROTC to the trustees at their June meeting. Corps Day festivities went on as planned. About 30 pickets from the Student Peace Committee showed up but did not interfere with the proceedings.

On June 8 the trustees adopted the recommendation to make ROTC voluntary. Effective for students entering fall quarter, those who chose not to enroll in ROTC would instead have to take at least 10 additional hours of lower-level math and foreign language, or six hours of more advanced math and language.[9] The potential confrontation had come to a peaceful resolution.

BLACK STUDENTS: NOT SEPARATE, BUT NOT EQUAL

African American students did not receive any special consideration from the university in 1960, nor did they expect to. Officially, Ohio State practiced a policy of nondiscrimination. Black students had been admitted since at least 1888 and had been graduating since 1892. A strong network of black fraternities and sororities helped bolster students' success. By 1960 five of Ohio State's 53 social fraternities and sororities were predominantly black. Over the preceding year the university had gotten the remainder to eliminate discriminatory clauses from their constitutions, with the exception of two fraternities that were told to get into compliance or face the loss of university recognition.[10]

In the fall of 1960 students elected Marlene Owens Homecoming Queen, marking the first time the honor was bestowed upon an African American. Owens was a senior from Chicago and the daughter of 1930s track star and Ohio State alumnus Jesse Owens. It fell to John T.

Mount, Fawcett's administrative assistant, to make sure everything went smoothly. First, Mount had to find a place for Marlene's parents to stay during Homecoming weekend. The university normally housed VIPs at Columbus's premier hotel, the Neil House. But the Neil House had a reputation for not being welcoming to black people. A few discreet phone calls got the hotel management on board.

Next was the challenge of who would kiss the Homecoming Queen in front of 80,000 football fans. Normally that duty was performed by the president of the Alumni Association, but having an older white man kiss a young black woman was more than Columbus, or Ohio State, was ready for in 1960. So Mount worked out an alternative arrangement: the queen's trophy would be presented to Marlene's father, who in turn would kiss her.[11] The event was duly celebrated, and Jesse Owens played his part flawlessly. "And remember, darling, it could only happen in America," he told his daughter.[12]

Ohio State did not track the racial composition of its students until required to do so by the 1964 Civil Rights Act, so it is difficult to determine how many black students were enrolled in the fall of 1960. It appears the number was no more than 2 or 3 percent, even though African Americans comprised 8 percent of the state's population at the time.[13] No African Americans held senior administrative positions at the university, and few held any faculty rank.

Although statutory segregation was not legal in Ohio and the rest of the states outside the old Confederacy, de facto segregation—segregation by practice rather than law, especially in housing—was very much the rule.[14] As recently as 1957 Ohio State did not allow black and white students to room together in dormitories unless they had written permission from their parents. The majority of African American students—those who could not afford to live in university housing or a black fraternity or sorority—had to live in the traditionally black neighborhoods on Columbus's east side and take public transportation to campus.

After years of complaints the Student Senate prodded the administration to address discrimination in off-campus housing. In July 1960 Ohio State adopted a policy of nondiscrimination that called for campus-area rooming houses to have their university registration revoked if they were found to discriminate against a student on the basis of race, creed, or national origin. Of the 347 landlords who had been contacted by the university earlier, only 71 had pledged not to discriminate. Some

1.4. Marlene Owens is crowned the first black Homecoming Queen. Her father, Ohio State track star and Olympian Jesse Owens, is at the microphone. (*Makio*)

landlords had said that if they allowed black tenants, then white ones would not want to live in their properties. Because of a housing shortage on campus, the university depended on landlords to house nearly 6,000 students, and was therefore reluctant to take them on en masse.[15] The situation continued to fester.

PICKET AT YOUR OWN RISK

On April 6, 1961, scientist Wernher von Braun enthralled a capacity crowd at Mershon Auditorium with a discussion of rocket travel to the moon. For three students von Braun's appearance was an opportunity to raise concerns about the militarization of space exploration. They stood in front of Mershon carrying placards with slogans such as "We are buying a multibillion dollar monument to Mars—the God of War" and "Millions for the Moon, pennies for people." Columbus city police appeared and questioned the students. They were then led into a paddy wagon for what they were told was their "own protection," because it looked like they might incite a riot.[16]

The students later told the *Lantern* there was no threat of a riot and not even a crowd until the police showed up. They also claimed the officers told them they were being picked up because "we [the police] just don't go for this stuff" and because they needed to display an American flag before they could demonstrate. The students were hauled off to the campus police station, where they were released but told to report the next day for questioning.

When the students returned they were accompanied by Gordon Grigsby, an instructor in the English department and chair of the central Ohio chapter of the American Civil Liberties Union. Grigsby and the students were told they could not picket without university approval, and that approval would not be forthcoming. They were then released without charges being filed. Grigsby complained that the process was an attempt to discourage the students from exercising their constitutional rights. Various elements of the university community immediately spoke out in support. The *Lantern* printed an editorial the next morning, and the University Senate unanimously passed a resolution later that day calling on the administration to "reprimand the university police for their misconduct and educate them as to the role of the state in protecting free speech."[17]

The senate received a reply from President Fawcett on April 19, two weeks later. Fawcett maintained the police "acted in the absence of any regular and defined procedure, but in what they believed at the time to be clearly [their line of duty]," which included "to provide protection" for students. Fawcett went on to say: "The university respects different points of view when convictions are sincere and honestly motivated. It is our conviction that for the good of the university we must continue to provide for the suitable enforcement of university rules and regulations and still respect the honest rights of all parties concerned." In fact, university officials privately acknowledged the case was mishandled.[18]

Six days later Ohio State announced campus police were participating in a training program to acquaint them with the "correlative rights and responsibilities" of various segments of the university community in possible future picketing situations. It was described as being done at the request of Gordon B. Carson, the vice president to whom campus police reported, with Fawcett's "concurrence." This came after three students picketed the annual Military Ball on April 13 and others announced plans to picket the annual ROTC review on Corps Day, May 4.[19]

On May 1 William Guthrie, the executive dean for student relations, announced an agreement on a new set of guidelines for student pickets. The guidelines were the product of an all-day meeting involving student leaders, faculty representatives, administrators, and experts from the College of Law. This seemed to settle the issue for the time being, but other free speech controversies would not be so easy to resolve.

NO SUBVERSIVES NEED APPLY

Who should have the right to decide who could speak on campus became a major flash point in the first half of the 1960s. Many faculty and students believed a publicly supported campus was obliged to permit a variety of speakers and viewpoints. The established power structure, as represented by elected officials and the university's trustees, said a taxpayer-supported university should not be allowed to provide a forum for subversives who advocated the violent overthrow of the government.

The outbreak of the Cold War between the United States and the Soviet Union gave rise to fears of a worldwide communist conspiracy. In 1948 Ohio State's trustees adopted a rule prohibiting the fostering of doctrines "favoring the overthrow of government by force." It would become known as the Speakers Rule or Gag Rule.[20]

In July 1951, at the height of the Korean War, Harold O. Rugg, a Columbia University professor whom some, including the Columbus media, considered a communist, spoke at a campus conference at the invitation of the College of Education. At their September meeting the trustees voted to condemn Rugg's appearance and enacted a rule requiring President Howard Bevis to pre-screen speakers. Many of the faculty and students objected to what they believed was an unwarranted prior restraint on free speech, but the board held firm.

By the time Novice Fawcett became president in 1956, Cold War tensions had eased somewhat, and the issue remained dormant for several years. But in the spring of 1961 it came forward again, sparking a standoff that would take four years to resolve. Students for Liberal Action, a university-recognized group, invited William Mandel to speak on campus on April 13. Mandel was a former Stanford professor who had been fired for alleged communist ties. He then became a radio commentator and regularly attacked the U.S. House Un-American Activities Committee. Ohio State refused to allow Mandel to speak on campus on the grounds he was a subversive under the Speakers Rule. Henry St. Onge, an assistant instructor in the English department, then invited Mandel to speak in the backyard of his home on East Woodruff Avenue.

"The issue here is not whether we agree on our ideas, but whether you have a right to hear those ideas and to [make up] your own minds about these ideas," Mandel told a crowd estimated at about 200. He went on to say that war with the Soviet Union would be "insane" and that government committees such as the HUAC represented "a movement towards fascism in America." He also described the Communist Party in America as "ineffective" and urged students to read the U.S. Constitution and follow it, because "We must be free to vote."[21]

The controversy over Mandel sparked expressions of opposition to the Speakers Rule from the *Lantern,* the Student Senate, and many members of the faculty. But the university remained firm in its resolve to ban speakers it considered subversive, setting the stage for a conflict that would intensify during the next four years.

A NEW ACTIVISM?

By the end of the school year those close to campus recognized that student attitudes were changing. William Guthrie, the executive dean for student relations, laid out his thoughts at the annual meeting of the National Association of Student Personnel Administrators in April. "The pendulum has undoubtedly swung over from the days of student apathy and privatism of some past years," Guthrie told his colleagues. He warned that people with ulterior motives would attempt to hijack popular causes for their own purposes, but advised university administrators to be open to change. He said that by helping to encourage "responsible actions of student bodies," administrators could preempt the alternative of "irresponsible student rioting as already seen in various forms around the world."[22]

Ohio State's alumni magazine picked up the theme in an article in its May edition: "Today's students, definitely not the Silent Generation of a few years ago, are concerned with, of all things: principles." The piece quoted heavily from Guthrie's speech, then pointed out what had happened at normally placid Bowling Green State University just before spring break. Students boycotted classes, held mass meetings, and blocked downtown traffic to protest what they believed was the authoritarian style of their administration. The Ohio Highway Patrol had to be called in to restore order.[23]

Even the *Columbus Dispatch,* which seldom had anything good to say about student activism, noticed something had changed. Education reporter William Fulwider wrote: "Like a bolt of lightning, and in some ways almost as potent, student opinion on the Ohio State University campus has been something with which to reckon." Fulwider credited the Student Senate and the *Lantern,* both of which were willing to question the administration's positions, as the "fulcrum" of student activism. He described how the senate prodded the administration into doing more about housing, for example.

Fulwider characterized the administration as "reasonably happy" with the situation. "It is better that issues be discussed in the open and explored with reasonable objectivity under responsible guidance than under cover," President Fawcett had told him.[24]

University officials clearly thought they could channel student energy toward constructive input into the governance system. The system had resolved the compulsory ROTC issue to everyone's satisfaction and had produced guidelines to allow picketing to proceed in an orderly manner. For the remaining issues, the outcome was less benign from a student point of view. The administration had watered down changes in the hated Apartment Rule. It paid only lip service to eliminating housing discrimination, and it drew a line in the sand regarding long-standing concerns about the Speakers Rule.

Bearcat Ambush

Ohio State's 1959–60 basketball team under second-year coach Fred Taylor stunned the sports world with a dominant season that led to the Buckeyes' first national championship. The next year's squad was even better.

While the 1960 national champs went 21–3 in regular-season contests, the 1960–61 team went 22–0, becoming the first Ohio State basketball squad to go undefeated in the regular season and the first Big Ten team to do so since Minnesota in 1919. The members played so well together, one New York columnist described them as "almost inhuman."[1]

The Buckeyes were unanimous picks in the United Press International Coaches Poll at the season's end and the first team in the history of the poll to receive all 35 votes for No. 1 team in the country. Taylor was named Coach of the Year, and Jerry Lucas was named Player of the Year. Lucas, Larry Siegfried, and John Havlicek made both the All-Big Ten and All-American squads. Mel Nowell won honorable mention for the All-American squad and Richie Hoyt honorable mention for the All-Big Ten team. Their superb team play as well as their demeanor off the court made them heroes across the country. Going into the NCAA playoffs in Kansas City, they were heavily favored. *Sports Illustrated* featured them on its cover the week of March 27, 1961.

The Buckeyes quickly dispatched Louisville, Kentucky, and St. Joseph's in the opening rounds. The only team standing between them and Ohio State's second-straight championship was the No. 2–ranked Cincinnati Bearcats, whose best player, Oscar Robertson, had departed the year before for the NBA.

The stubborn Bearcats hung on to a 61–61 tie in regulation time. The teams then traded points back and forth until, with 28 seconds left, the Bearcats sank two free throws to make the score 68–65. Cincinnati's Tom Thacker then hit a jump shot with four seconds remaining, making the final score of 70–65 one of the biggest upsets in NCAA history.

The Buckeyes returned to the finals the following year, but again lost to the Bearcats in the final game. They would not play in the national finals again until 1997.

1. "1961 Buck Basketball Team Wins Unparalleled Honors," *Makio*, 1961, 254–56.

These issues would remain points of contention for years. Administrators knew the students weren't about to give up. But what they did not foresee, nor did anyone else, was that before the end of the decade students would challenge not only these specific policies but the legitimacy of the governance system itself.

THE UNIVERSITY: THE GOLDEN AGE OF RESEARCH

Academic historians would later refer to the 1960s as the golden age of federally funded research. Stunned by the apparent Soviet scientific edge in launching the first man-made satellite in October 1957, the U.S. government responded with a crash program to expand research. The nation's top research universities were the immediate beneficiaries. Between 1958 and 1968 federally funded research jumped 523 percent.[25]

Bernard Berelson's work was the most widely accepted source of rankings at the time. Berelson, a behavioral scientist at Columbia University, published the landmark *Graduate Education in the United States* in 1960. He divided all 92 national universities with graduate programs into four categories. The categories were based on a reputational survey of graduate programs conducted in 1957–58, with additional material Berelson provided. He ranked 12 universities—including Harvard, the University of California at Berkeley, and the University of Michigan—in the top category. Ohio State was in the next tier along with nine others, including Indiana, Northwestern, and Minnesota.[26]

The university's ranking in the top 20 gave it leverage in attracting dollars. In 1957 Ohio State's research foundation recorded grants totaling $3.9 million, spread over 216 projects. By 1960–61 funding had nearly doubled to $7.6 million and projects had increased to 450. About 2,000 faculty, staff, and students were supported on these grants. Eighty percent of the money came from the federal government (particularly the Department of Defense), the rest from private industry and state appropriations.[27]

Ohio State researchers achieved national and international distinction in areas of research that spanned human activity, including transportation systems, polar mapping and exploration, cancer detection and treatment, and food production. Impact ranged from the mundane to the cosmic. For example, William Heintz, associate professor in the College of Dentistry, developed the plastic mouth guard still used today to protect the teeth of young athletes. But it would be the race into space that would capture the nation's attention more than any other endeavor.

NEW FRONTIERS IN SPACE

Radio astronomer John Kraus, who joined the faculty of the College of Engineering in 1946, was the most well-known space scientist at Ohio State. Kraus specialized in using radio waves to map uncharted areas of space. In 1950 he published *Antenna,* which quickly became known as the bible of the field. Working with graduate students, he built up the university's Antenna Lab on west campus. When the Soviets launched Sputnik in 1957, Ohio State's was the only facility in world able to accurately track it in its first orbit around the earth. By 1961 Kraus was looking forward to the opening of the Big Ear, a 340-foot-long radio telescope in Delaware, Ohio. When completed it would allow the tracking of previously invisible stars and aid in the search for extraterrestrial life.[28]

The university's rocket and antenna facilities attained national prominence in the space program. Much of the work of the Rocket Lab was classified for security purposes. The lab, located at the northeast corner of Lane Avenue and Olentangy River Road (near where Longaberger Alumni House now stands), worked closely with the Air Force Power Plant Laboratory at Wright-Patterson Air Force Base in Dayton. Rudolph Edse, a professor of aeronautical and astronautical engineering, headed the lab, which he had helped establish in 1946. It specialized in research on rocket fuel, particularly liquid hydrogen; rocket engines could be fired and evaluated under measured conditions in its three test pits.

The Antenna Lab did research into communications. In October 1960 an antenna and small receiver built by the lab's Ronald K. Long and Robert C. Taylor traveled 600 miles into space inside the nose cone of an Atlas missile. Its purpose was to measure the properties of the atmosphere as the cone descended to earth. The instrument functioned flawlessly. The following year, a 10-pound aluminum box built

1.5. The Antenna Lab on west campus helped scientists probe outer space. It remains active today as the ElectroScience Laboratory. (*Makio*)

by Dean E. Svoboda and Robert C. Taylor traveled 5,000 miles in the cone of another Atlas missile fired from Cape Canaveral, Florida. The instrument, consisting of a small receiver and antenna, measured "cosmic noise" in order to help scientists improve communications in space.

The Laboratory of Molecular Spectroscopy and Infrared Studies joined the roster of space-oriented research facilities when it opened in October 1960. Its goal was to capitalize on Ohio State's international reputation for work in infrared imaging to explore better guidance systems in space.

THE GOLDEN AGE OF TEACHING?

Ohio State's influence in teaching was also significant, especially if enrollment was the measure. Fall quarter 1960 began with 23,813 full- and part-time students on main campus, plus another 1,338 at branches. This represented the university's second-highest enrollment ever, eclipsed only by the 25,400 students on campus at the height of the postwar GI Bill influx in 1947. According to a survey by the journal *School and Society,* Ohio State was the seventh-largest university in the country in terms of full-time enrollment. If just full-time single-campus enrollment was counted, it ranked fifth.[29]

Its size gave Ohio State the leverage to invest in academic programs in both teaching and research. In January 1961 the trustees approved a new major in Russian and Slavic languages. The program would offer 28 courses in Russian language, including three in scientific Russian. Leon Twarog, who had been recruited from Boston University to lead the initiative, pointed out that Russian was the second-most important language in the world, and interest had soared since the launch of Sputnik several years earlier.

The university also announced a new graduate program in geodetic science, the study of measuring the earth through maps and charts. Acting department chair Robert A. Oetjen explained the program would develop tools to take advantage of new satellite technology for both military and civilian applications.

Beyond counting heads and courses, defining success in teaching was more elusive. The *Lantern* ran a series in November on what constituted good teaching. Each segment consisted of interviews with a set of stakeholders: department heads, college deans, faculty members, and undergraduates. The department chairs and deans agreed the foundation of good teaching was scholarship (research). The faculty emphasized the importance of allowing students to be actively engaged in their learning. The students, many of whom asked to remain anonymous for fear of retaliation, complained faculty members were more concerned about their research than what their students learned.[30]

Meanwhile, the numbers showed the university continued to struggle with the effects of Ohio's open admissions law. Major research universities in other states, such as the University of Michigan and the University of California at Berkeley, used high school grades and standardized test scores to limit admissions, theorizing that the better students were the most likely to succeed. Under Ohio's policy any graduate of an Ohio high school could attend any public university in the state. The weaker students would be weeded out as they went along. In fall quarter 1960 alone, 951 students were dismissed for low grades, including 507 freshmen, 195 sophomores, 104 juniors, and 36 seniors.[31]

Many critics saw this as wasteful, the *Columbus Dispatch* included: "The increase in dismissals is partially the result of higher academic standards, of which we heartily approve. The point is, however, that many of the dismissed students might have been weeded out by entrance examinations, thus saving the universities thousands of dollars in administrative and instructional costs, not to mention the embarrassment and in some instances, emotional upsets to many of the young people who failed to make the grade."[32]

Four years earlier President Fawcett had convinced the board of trustees to approve a series of proposals from the Faculty Council designed to upgrade the university's academic standing. The cumulative point hour ratio necessary for graduation was raised from 1.8 to 2.0 out of 4.0. Additional steps were taken to make sure weaker students received early warning that they were at risk. By the fall of 1960 it looked like the changes were paying off. Academic dismissals jumped from just under 1,600 annually before the change in 1955–56 to nearly 2,800 for the 1959–60 school year. At the same time the university seemed to be successful in attracting better students. The proportion of incoming freshmen in the upper third of their high school class increased from 45 percent in 1955–56 to 54 percent in 1959–60, while the proportion coming from the lower third fell from 21 percent to 15 percent.[33]

The faculty and administration believed more needed to be done, so in October the trustees approved a proposal to limit fall quarter enrollment on the Columbus campus to high school students in the upper two-thirds of their class. Students in the lower third could still attend, but only by starting another quarter or attending one of the branches. The policy became effective June 1, 1961. Officials estimated that had it been in place the preceding fall, 800 students would have been denied admission at that time.

An even bigger instructional challenge was looming. The large numbers of children born in the years immediately following World War II were nearing college age. The university's projections showed enrollment would double before the end of the decade. Ronald B. Thompson, the executive dean for special services, predicted a series of crises in finding places for these students when they began arriving in 1964.[34]

In February 1960 the *Lantern* did a story on what Ohio State might look like 10 years later. Reflecting the optimism of the day, university officials said they could manage the projected growth in enrollment and still provide a quality teaching environment. Arts and sciences dean J. Osborn Fuller said universities were up to the challenge because they were more independent than public school systems. Donald P. Cottrell, dean of the College of Education, suggested that they "focus on the instructor problem on an imaginative basis. . . . The university should not be run like a factory."[35] Fuller and Cottrell both overestimated the ability of universities to respond. Before the end of the decade, student discontent would boil over.

SOCIETY: NEW FRONTIERS AND OLD REALITIES

SWING STATE

The tight presidential race between Senator John F. Kennedy and Vice President Richard M. Nixon turned out to be one of the signature events of the 1960s. Both Nixon and Kennedy operatives worked hard to capture Ohio's 25 electoral votes. On September 29, 1960, Democratic vice presidential candidate Lyndon B. Johnson spoke to an estimated crowd of 8,000 on the steps of the Ohio Historical Society (now Sullivant Hall). Kennedy and Nixon made multiple stops in Ohio, including one each in Columbus. Kennedy drew a crowd of 40,000 to the Statehouse on October 17, and Nixon spoke to 80,000 at the Statehouse on October 26 with Woody Hayes at his side. Hayes and Nixon met in 1957 at a dinner at the home of trustee John Bricker, a former Ohio governor and U.S. senator, and had remained friends since.

As part of a presidential straw poll across the Big Ten, more than 6,000 Ohio State students cast ballots on October 19. Nixon easily carried the voting, 4,055 to 2,303. Results were similar at the five other Big Ten schools that participated (Illinois, Indiana, Iowa, Michigan, and Northwestern).[36] Why Kennedy did better among voters as a whole than with the college students who voted in the mock elections is open to speculation. Most likely it is because the voters Kennedy appealed to most—Catholics, African Americans, and members of union households—were not as well represented on Big Ten campuses as they were in the population at large.

The *Lantern* staff was split. Editor Myron Belkind told readers he supported Nixon but did not feel it was proper to speak for the entire *Lantern* staff, so the paper remained officially neutral.

On October 27 Kennedy supporters in the Student Senate introduced a resolution calling on Columbus's two daily papers, the *Dispatch* and the *Citizen-Journal,* to be more even-handed in their election coverage. Both papers supported Nixon editorially. As evidence of bias, Student

Government Commission chair Benson Wolman pointed out how both papers put news of Nixon's visit on the front page but Kennedy's on the back page. Opposition leader Dennis Burns, president of the Council of Fraternity Presidents, argued that the press should be free to print whatever it believed was appropriate. Wolman's resolution failed by a vote of 19–18.[37]

On election night, November 8, a capacity crowd jammed into the Ohio Union ballroom to view the results. Women students were granted special permission to stay out until midnight, as opposed to the usual 11 p.m. curfew, but it wasn't until the early hours of the next day that a winner was declared. Nixon carried Franklin County and the state of Ohio, but Kennedy narrowly won the national popular vote and easily won the all-important Electoral College.

Shortly after the election the *Lantern* asked 17 faculty members about the implications of Kennedy's victory for their respective fields. The majority said that despite the bold rhetoric of the campaign, Kennedy's slim margin and the unaltered composition of Congress meant a change in style, perhaps, but not in policy. Economics professor Paul Craig summed it up this way: "Open under new management. Some new appetizers and desserts. Entrees unchanged. Prices about as usual."[38]

THE PSEUDO-EVENT IS THE MESSAGE

An array of notable individuals visited campus in 1960–61, including two participants in a conference on popular and mass culture sponsored by the graduate school in late October. Marshall McLuhan, professor of English at the University of Toronto, would go on to fame as the major media guru of the decade and the coiner of the phrases "the global village" and "the medium is the message." McLuhan talked about the start of the "post-literate era," where technology had advanced to such a degree that images overpowered the written word.

Daniel J. Boorstin, professor of American history at the University of Chicago, argued that the need to fill the public's appetite for images would create what he called "pseudo-events" or "contriv[ed] situations which are of importance because they have been brought to the attention of the public, but would not have had any significance if left alone." He cited as an example the first televised presidential debates, which had

What You Can Do For Your Country

President John F. Kennedy's proposal for young men and women to serve in the Peace Corps generated an enthusiastic response at Ohio State. Just three days after Kennedy's inauguration on January 20, 1961, a group of students announced the formation of a committee to explore the concept. The campus YMCA and YWCA supported the action, as did the Student Senate and the *Lantern.*

The initiative attracted national attention. *Life* magazine sent a reporter and photographer who spent two days on campus for a story that appeared in the March 17 edition. On May 26, 29 Ohio State students took the first Peace Corps entrance exam.

The Peace Corps became one of the most enduring legacies of the Kennedy administration. On March 1, 2011, Ohio State commemorated its 50th anniversary with a program that included Steven Honore, the first volunteer from the university. Honore was a master's student at the time he enrolled in the Peace Corps; his undergraduate degree was from Capital University, where he had been the first African American to serve as student body president. Honore spent two years in Columbia as a volunteer and then two years in the Dominican Republic as a staff member. He later became a municipal judge in Houston, Texas.

At the time of the anniversary, Ohio State had contributed nearly 1,600 volunteers over a half century and ranked 10th among all colleges and universities. In addition, 35 faculty members were former Peace Corps volunteers.[1]

1. Encarnacion Pyle, "OSU Marks Peace Corps' 50th Anniversary," *Dispatch,* March 2, 2011, 1A.

occurred recently.[39] Public interest focused not on the substance of what the candidates said, but on the performance aspects. At the dawn of a decade when iconic images on TV screens would define reality, Boorstin's observations could not have been timelier.

PARANOIA ON PARADE

Cold War paranoia asserted itself in full force as the 1960–61 school year came to an end. At a time when many people feared communist aggression abroad and communist subversion at home, the debate over enemies imagined and real filled public discourse. A discussion of the merits of the film *Operation Abolition,* which purported to reveal a plot to undermine the House Un-American Activities Committee, drew a thousand people to the University Hall auditorium in late May. Fulton Lewis III, a researcher for the HUAC, defended the committee. He described the Communist Party in America as not a traditional political party but a "fifth-column Trojan horse, a conspiracy" that hoped to destroy the nation from within. David Kettler, an associate professor of political science at Ohio State who had emigrated from Nazi-occupied Europe, took the opposing point of view. He argued the HUAC itself was un-American because it routinely violated constitutional safeguards, including freedom of speech and due process.[40]

The following evening more than 200 students and faculty witnessed what the *Lantern* described as a "tension-packed" debate between Albert B. Gregg, a local member of the virulently anti-communist John Birch Society, and William W. Van Alstyne, assistant dean of the College of Law. Van Alstyne got his biggest applause when he chided Gregg: "If the local branch of the John Birch Society divorces itself from the national [organization's philosophy], it is a commendable offspring of a regrettable parent."[41]

On July 25 President Kennedy made a televised address to the nation on the deepening crisis over Berlin. The president said escalating Soviet threats over the Allied presence in Berlin made it necessary to be prepared to go to war to defend the city if necessary. He also announced he would ask Congress for $207 million to step up civil defense preparedness throughout the United States. The *Lantern* decided to do a story on civil defense preparations at Ohio State for its last issue of summer quarter on August 24.

Campus police chief W. L. Parker refused to give the *Lantern* any information, but Gordon Carson, vice president for business and finance, and university relations director Frederick Stecker confirmed there were no plans for civil defense and no fallout shelters on campus. They explained that the university instead would follow Franklin County's plan. The *Lantern* dutifully followed up with Russ Pennell of the Columbus civil defense department, who explained that the plan centered on an air raid siren on the roof of Hagerty Hall. A steady blast of three to five minutes would alert citizens to tune their radios to a certain station and wait for further instructions, which might be to evacuate the city, if time permitted, or seek shelter. No one explained how the 24,000 students on the Columbus campus, most of whom lacked transportation, as well as 10,000 faculty and staff members would be evacuated, or to where. Nor was it explained where students, faculty, staff, and visitors could seek shelter on campus.

Pennell did say that his department was "urging everyone to be prepared," and that a home shelter could be built for about $1,500 and stocked with food, water, and other supplies for $200. The department would supply building plans free of charge. Tests had proven shelters effective, Pennell said, adding that although millions of persons would die in a nuclear attack, millions would survive if proper precautions were taken.[42]

CHAPTER 2

GOING NUCLEAR

(1961–62)

It seemed as if everyone was going nuclear in 1961–62, at least metaphorically. The Faculty Council exercised the nuclear option when it took the unprecedented step of turning down an invitation for Ohio State to play in the Rose Bowl, setting off protests by students and alumni. President Novice Fawcett exercised the nuclear option when he locked out a controversial speaker, sparking protests from students and faculty. The university tried to prepare for an impending explosion in enrollment with mixed results. Researchers explored peaceful uses of nuclear energy, while the people who controlled actual nuclear weapons threatened to use them.

2.1. Students gather on the Oval to protest the Rose Bowl decision. (*Makio*)

STUDENTS: ACTIVISM AND APATHY

THE ROSE BOWL THAT WASN'T

Normally, a Rose Bowl invitation is cause for the Buckeye faithful to celebrate. In 1961 it became a cause for civil war, leaving the Ohio State community bruised, embarrassed, and divided.

The Rose Bowl had developed a reputation as the premier postseason football game. The gala event, which originated in 1902, was played in Pasadena, California, on New Year's Day. Since the end of World War II it featured the winner of the Big Ten Conference (then known as the Western Conference) against the winner of the Pacific Coast Conference. Its allure continued to increase as it attracted a growing TV audience.

But when Ohio State received a Rose Bowl invitation in November 1961, the Faculty Council took the unprecedented step of declining it. The sequence of events involved a dispute dating back to the expiration of the Big Ten Conference's Rose Bowl contract in 1959. At that time five of the conference's schools, including Ohio State, voted against renewal because they thought the contract was too one-sided in favor of the California sponsors, and also because of concerns about the growing influence of athletics on their campuses. While negotiations dragged on, the Big Ten agreed to let each institution decide for itself whether to accept an invitation, as long as the faculty approved.[1]

CLASH OF THE TITANS: FULLEN VERSUS HAYES

The 1961 Rose Bowl controversy would draw in the entire university community, but would be personified by two Ohio State legends: football coach Woody Hayes and alumni secretary Jack Fullen.

One of Woody Hayes's biographers described him as a humble, small-town man firm in the belief that "all that was right with the world came from rural America, where love of country, hard work, and loyalty made America great."[2] Wayne Woodrow Hayes was born in rural Clifton, Ohio, and graduated from Denison University in 1935. After four years in the navy during World War II, where he rose to the rank of lieutenant commander, Hayes returned to Denison to coach the football team. His winning record there, and then at Miami University in Ohio, caught the attention of Ohio State officials, who awarded him the head coaching job in 1951. Hayes started off slowly, but before long he showed he knew how to win consistently. In the next seven years he would win three conference titles and two Rose Bowls, in 1954 and 1957.

While Woody Hayes was on his way to becoming a legend, Jack Fullen already was one. By 1961 the 61-year-old Fullen had been secretary of the Alumni Association for 33 years. Fullen had been a swimming champion and ROTC boxing champ at Ohio State, and also editor of the *Lantern.* He received his journalism degree in 1925 and worked as a reporter and secretary of a chamber of commerce in Florida before being named alumni head in 1928.

Fullen had amassed an impressive list of accomplishments. He helped found Ohio Staters, the university's leading student/faculty service organization. He also helped create the Research Foundation and the Development Fund. By 1961 he was regarded as the most influential alumni director in the country. Not only did he head the second-oldest alumni association, he edited its award-winning magazine, with 31,000 paid subscribers, and directed the country's third-largest development fund.

Fullen also harbored a deep-seated concern about the influence of intercollegiate football on Ohio State's academic programs. "The tail is wagging the dog," he was fond of saying.[3] Fullen did support Woody Hayes when he took over as football coach in 1951. He even defended Hayes against critics who argued he should be fired at the end of the 1952 season for not winning enough games. But a 1955 recruiting scandal raised Fullen's concerns about the integrity of the program. Hayes admitted loaning money to financially needy players and finding them part-time jobs. He said he found nothing wrong with the practice. The Western Conference disagreed and suspended Ohio State after an investigation. The university then appointed a faculty committee to review the matter. After 30 months of study, it recommended a number of changes, including closer oversight by the faculty. The university quickly followed up by establishing the Athletic Council. The council in turn was accountable to the Faculty Council, which included 44 members elected by faculty in the various colleges and 13 administrators, such as deans and vice presidents.

Hayes believed Fullen had leaked the recruiting story to *Sports Illustrated.* The relationship between the two men deteriorated quickly after that, and they clashed regularly. Observers who knew them both said

2.2. Alumni Association secretary Jack Fullen, second from left, and colleagues celebrate a successful fund-raising effort in 1964. (University Archives)

they were too much alike—stubborn, opinionated, and unwilling to concede an inch.[4]

In the fall of 1960, the Big Ten proposed to change its policy regarding athletics scholarships. That served as the opening skirmish in the campuswide hostilities to follow. Up to that point scholarships had been limited to students with financial need. The Big Ten leadership wanted to extend full-ride scholarships to all varsity athletes, regardless of need. The scholarships averaged $1,200 to $1,500 annually (between $9,400 and $11,700 in 2015 prices), which would cover tuition and room and board. Hayes supported the change. "These boys come back from the summer three weeks early," he said. "They practice every day and most of their weekend is taken up. The scholarship money comes out to about $1 an hour. . . . People don't realize the sacrifice some of these boys make; there's no free ride about it."[5]

Jack Fullen was among the first to come out against the proposal. He found the idea that an athlete could keep his scholarship by retaining a C average, while a student on a need-based scholarship had to maintain at least a B average, particularly offensive. Student Senate president Phil Moots agreed, expressing concern about the availability of need-based scholarships for all students. Marvin Fox, an associate professor of philosophy, spoke for many of his colleagues when he told the Faculty Council: "We are going off the deep end by admitting these athletes are professionals, being paid to play football so that we can fill up the stadium and draw huge sums of money from football attendance." The showdown came at the Faculty Council meeting on October 10. In this case supporters of the Big Ten proposal carried the day when the council voted 31–13 to approve the plan, but the controversy over the proper place for athletics in an academic institution was far from over.[6]

The 1961 football season began with a disappointing tie against Texas Christian University. But aided by outstanding sophomore halfbacks Paul Warfield and Matt Snell, the team came to life in its second game and went on to reel off seven straight victories, including a 50–20 humiliation of Michigan at Ann Arbor. That clinched the Big Ten title and generated the invitation to play the University of Southern California in the Rose Bowl. The Athletic Council voted 6–4 to recommend approval to the Faculty Council.

THE DECISION

Reporters and photographers jammed into the Faculty Club the afternoon of November 28 to report on the Faculty Council's decision. Roy M. Kottman, dean of the College of Agriculture and Home Economics, moved to approve the Athletic Council's recommendation to accept the invitation. Two hours of debate followed. Marvin Fox led the faculty critics. "What educational objectives would be served by a Rose Bowl trip?" he asked. Fox also questioned the timing of the game, one day before winter quarter classes started. Others said the safety of students would be compromised as they raced back to Columbus for the first day of classes.

Richard H. Armitage, associate dean of the graduate school and a member of the Athletic Council, attacked the way the Rose Bowl proceeds were divided, pointing out that Ohio State had collected only $15,000 of the million dollars of revenue generated by its participation in the 1958 bowl game. Bruce Bennett, an associate professor of physical education, attacked the game itself, calling it a "mismatch in which Ohio State has everything to lose and nothing to win." Others, including athletics director Dick Larkins and engineering professor Mars G. Fontana, spoke in favor of approval. Finally, after voting in a secret ballot, the council came out 28–25 against accepting the invitation.[7]

That evening about 2,000 students gathered at the corner of High Street and 15th Avenue with signs proclaiming "If OSU can't go to the Rose Bowl, the faculty can go to Hell" and "Roses for the Bucks, Poison for the Faculty." The protestors decided to head downtown to complain to Ohio governor Michael V. DiSalle in what was believed to be the first march ever to the Statehouse. When they learned DiSalle was out of town, the students marched back up High Street.

Woody Hayes was in Cleveland when he got the news. After taking an hour-long walk to collect himself, he told reporters the decision was wrong, "but they [the Faculty Council] make the rules, and the football team must abide by rules off the field as well as on. I've thought this thing over and decided that it would be a real shame if this would cause a cleavage in the university. No football team is worth that."[8] His comments were widely reported that evening on TV and radio and in newspapers across the state the next morning, but that wasn't enough for some.

The next afternoon a surly crowd of about 1,500 students gathered on the Oval. After marching on the Faculty Club and breaking the glass in a door, they moved downtown to Broad and High Streets and blocked traffic. They headed back to campus after hearing a rumor of a potential re-vote, tearing down street signs and tipping over vehicles on the way. About 500 lingered at a bonfire at the corner of High and 15th. Extra police and highway patrolmen were called in. The university administration threatened disciplinary action. At around 11:30 p.m. Mike Ingram, co-captain of the football team, used a loudspeaker on a sheriff's car to tell the crowd to disperse. "We've been defeated. Woody has accepted this," he said. The protestors reluctantly left.[9] Four students were subsequently disciplined by the university.

That same day the trustees discussed the issue with President Fawcett. Many were inclined to overturn the Faculty Council decision, but Fawcett was able to convince them not to do so because it would violate Big Ten policy regarding faculty control over athletics and likely get

Ohio State kicked out of the Big Ten. That should have settled the issue, but it didn't.

FALLOUT

In the 1960s Columbus boasted two general-circulation newspapers (the morning *Citizen-Journal* and the *Evening Dispatch*), three commercial television stations (plus Ohio State's station, WOSU), and at least half a dozen radio stations. But the elephant in the room was the *Dispatch* and the media empire that owned it. The Wolfe family of Columbus also owned the local CBS-affiliated television and radio stations. Normally, cross-ownership of TV stations and newspapers in the same town was prohibited by federal law, but the Wolfes' ownership predated the Federal Communications Act and was therefore exempted. In addition the Wolfes owned the area's largest bank, Ohio National, and one of its most successful investment firms, the Ohio Company.[10]

Journalist Neal Peirce, writing in 1972, said the Wolfe family enterprises "may well be the most powerful and ruthless single-city based communications and economic establishment of the United States."[11] The *Dispatch* leaned well to the conservative right. (It had not endorsed a Democrat for president since 1916.) Many of the Ohio State faculty and students distrusted the newspaper and disliked what it stood for. The *Lantern* found it unprofessional and was not shy about saying so. Conversely, state and local elected officials who controlled the university's state appropriations curried favor with the *Dispatch* and its owners.

Where the *Dispatch* stood on the Rose Bowl issue quickly became clear. The newspaper would lose significant reader interest and advertising revenue as a result of the decision to turn down the invitation. In addition to editorializing against the decision, the paper chose to make it an extended news story. *Dispatch* reporters polled every member of the Faculty Council to ask how they voted in the secret ballot. Twenty of the 25 who voted in favor of accepting the invitation disclosed their vote. Only eight of the 28 "no" votes did so. The newspaper printed the names and addresses of those who voted no, or refused to disclose how they voted, in a November 29 story. Many of them began receiving threatening phone calls. Two days later the *Dispatch* ran a story on university-paid out-of-state travel by faculty, including some members of the Faculty Council, accompanied by expressions of outrage by state legislators. Alumni secretary Jack Fullen condemned the *Dispatch* coverage in the February 1962 alumni magazine as "manufactured 'news stories' [that] would have made *Pravda* [the Kremlin's mouthpiece] blush with envy."[12]

Fullen himself remained the prime target of those unhappy with the university's decision. Students hanged him in effigy—giving him the distinction of being the first university official to be so honored in the 1960s (although he would not be the last). Both he and Fawcett received harassing phone calls and death threats.

Woody Hayes, who'd been careful to not criticize the faculty or the administration for the decision, did not hold back when it came to Fullen. He opened his weekly TV show on December 1 by saying, "Only one man [Jack Fullen] has resorted to personal resentment[,] . . . called our players 'professionals,' which they are not . . . [and] used the [alumni] magazine to attack [the football program] endlessly." Hayes accused Fullen of keeping his position by controlling the alumni board and manipulating the distribution of football tickets to alumni.[13]

Hayes called for Fullen to be removed from his job. "I've heard him boast so many times 'they can't fire me because I select the men who keep me in office,'" he said. He also accused Fullen of believing his function was to "needle" the university. He told his viewers to write letters concerning Fullen: "Don't call or harass in any way, just write."[14]

In a statement issued two days later, Fullen accused Hayes of taking his comments about needling the university out of context. Fullen maintained he and the Alumni Association supported Ohio State in a number of ways while also prodding the university to do things such as build student housing and establish a separate research foundation and a development fund.[15]

Some Alumni Association members who'd hoped to go to Pasadena were unhappy with Fullen as well. The Association reported receiving 1,800 letters. Although only half of them were from members, those ran two to one against the decision. But Fullen and the Faculty Council also had their supporters. The *Lantern* praised the council's courage. Some newspapers and columnists outside of Columbus applauded the decision, as did distinguished alumni such as Willard M. Kiplinger, editor and publisher of the highly respected magazine *Changing Times*. Kiplinger wrote in an open letter to the faculty that was published in the

Lantern on January 9: "As you get out of Columbus and Central Ohio, you find this fever lessening with distance, for distance tends to permit better balanced judgment. . . . In the end, when the current shooting has died down, you will be congratulated on your long vision, your wisdom, thoughtfulness and courage."[16]

On January 16 the alumni board met to take up the issue. The directors gave Fullen a vote of confidence, which set off a reaction by other alumni who opposed the decision. They included Dayton businessman John D. Cole, who organized an insurgent slate to run for the four board seats open in the May 1962 election. All four insurgents won in a record turnout, but the Fullen supporters retained a slim majority because the terms of five holdover directors loyal to Fullen would not end until the following May.

Although the opponents of the Rose Bowl trip seemed to carry the day in the short run, no one really came out ahead. To add insult to injury, the University of Minnesota, which had voted with Ohio State to reject the Rose Bowl contract in 1959, decided it wasn't such a bad idea when it was invited after Ohio State declined. The Golden Gophers beat the University of Southern California Trojans 21–3. It would be their first and only Rose Bowl victory.

Lantern sports editor Len Downie, who would go on to be executive editor of the *Washington Post*, hit the nail on the head when he wrote in a November 30 column: "One thing is certain about Ohio State's Rose Bowl controversy—nobody, except for the frustrated football team, will come out smelling like a rose. The Faculty Council, the student body, and the Columbus news media all failed to distinguish themselves."[17]

In October 1962 a new proposed contract between the Big Ten and the reconstituted Athletic Association of Western Universities (formerly the Pacific Coast Conference) came up for a vote before the Faculty Council. Once again the room was filled with reporters. Many of the same people on both sides of the Rose Bowl controversy repeated their same arguments. But others had shifted positions. Richard Armitage, now dean of the graduate school, had opposed the trip the year before. He announced he would support the new contract because it included significant changes that would "eventually bring saneness to, but not kill, intercollegiate athletics in the Big Ten." The changes included new limits on repeat appearances by one team; a requirement of no absences from classes by students for more than one day after the game; and limits on sponsorships and gifts. The council voted to approve the new contract.[18] Ohio State would never again turn down a Rose Bowl invitation.

The fight over control of the Alumni Association took longer to resolve. The anti-Fullen insurgents, having won four seats in the 1962 board election, decided to go for broke and nominated five directors for the 1963 election. They refined their message to say they were not against Fullen, but against his policies. The pro-Fullen slate countered they were not against football, but wanted to make sure athletics did not overshadow academics. Procedures to count the ballots resembled the high drama associated with the Academy Awards. IBM punch cards were used to record votes. They were transported by Brink's truck and validated by a certified public accounting firm. More than 18,000 of the 37,000 Association members voted, even more than in the record turnout the year before. The pro-Fullen slate carried the day, capturing all five contested seats with 49,224 votes, compared to 42,156 for the opposition. Afterward, everyone agreed it was time to move on.[19]

Through it all, Woody Hayes continued to defend his program. At a conference of highway engineers at the Ohio Union in April 1962, Hayes used his platform as keynote speaker to lay out his case before a sympathetic audience. "A kid who comes here to play football is going to be a first class student," he said. He noted that 80 percent of Ohio State football players graduated, compared to 40 percent at other top football schools. He also pointed out that Ohio State ranked only eighth in the Western Conference in scholarship money for players, but first in won-lost percentage. He explained how football revenues built loyalty to the institution and carried a big part of the financial burden of paying for other sports and facilities enjoyed by the entire university.[20] It is likely few in the audience disagreed with him, but the debate over the relationship between big-time athletics, money, and academics would continue to this day.

APATHETIC STUDENTS?

Whether because the Rose Bowl controversy sucked up energy from other causes or the abolition of compulsory ROTC eliminated an issue that had united most students, the new activism of 1960–61 seemed to run out of fuel by the following winter. Student Senate president Phil

Moots and Women's Self Government Association president Mary Kennedy often disagreed, but when they made a joint appearance at the Phi Mu sorority house in January 1962, both warned that lack of participation threatened the relevance of student representation.

Two weeks later a disaffected group of women students threatened to demonstrate against the WSGA slate of officers, arguing it was weak and chosen behind closed doors by the group's board. One student quipped, "I think no one even cares enough about WSGA to demonstrate against it," and indeed, the demonstration failed to materialize.[21] Kennedy, the outgoing president, took the opportunity to criticize apathy in the Student Senate. Only eight senators had attended a demonstration in support of black students at Louisiana's Southern University after all 53 senators voted to support the event, she pointed out. The Freshman Senate added its voice by sending a letter to all presidents of student organizations urging them to back student government.

Student government leaders still tried to make an impact on broader issues. For example, they organized a symposium on the future of the university to explore issues they believed were being ignored by administrators. Student Senate leaders could also claim a victory in the ROTC debate. To the relief of nervous ROTC supporters, 80 percent of incoming freshmen men signed up for voluntary ROTC, allowing the program to thrive while still preserving individual choice.

A record number of students did turn out to elect a new student government at the end of February. Previously, the Student Senate picked its president and various student organizations picked the senate members. However, after a referendum pushed through by activists, students would now vote directly for the president and members, choosing among candidates representing the two campus parties. The Buckeye Political Party (BPP), the more conservative, had been around since 1952. Drawing its core support from fraternity and sorority members, it positioned itself to the center right. At an elaborate convention at a downtown hotel, the BPP chose Jim Gross, a junior in arts and sciences and a member of Phi Delta Phi fraternity, as its candidate. Gross had been active in student government since a freshman and served as chair of the senate educational affairs commission.

The Student Congress Party (SCP) was an upstart, having been formed less than a year earlier and drawing its core support from independents. It positioned itself more to the center left. Niki Schwartz, a first-year law student, carried its standard. Schwartz was the senate's human relations commissioner and had helped lead drives to end housing discrimination, abolish mandatory ROTC, and establish a student defenders' office.

Although the two parties competed fiercely, their platforms were similar. Both proclaimed support for student rights and opposition to in loco parentis. Both wanted to abolish visitation rules and make it easier to change courses. The SCP had the advantage of editorial support from the *Lantern* and an endorsement from the outgoing senate president, but when the votes were counted on February 28, the BPP carried the day. Gross pulled 62 percent of the 7,198 ballots cast. The party also won 32 of 40 senate seats. Niki Schwartz later reflected that students may not have been as ready as he thought for some of the changes he was espousing. For example, some women students told him they didn't want to see curfews abolished because they provided a convenient way to unload a bad date.[22]

The larger problem—and one that would dog student government leaders throughout the decade—was low participation. Even though the election brought out a record number of voters in absolute terms, they represented fewer than 30 percent of those eligible to vote. Even a substantial tuition hike shortly after the election failed to rouse student passion.

On April 6 the university's board of trustees approved a 10 percent tuition increase for in-state students for the coming fall, from $100 per quarter to $110. Out-of-state students faced a larger adjustment, from $225 per quarter to $260. It was the first time tuition had been raised in two years. President Fawcett and Vice President Gordon Carson blamed a parsimonious legislature. Both noted that even after the fee increase, Ohio State's tuition would be the lowest among the five state universities; however, its fees were the highest among the nine public universities in the Big Ten, due to low state support. According to a *Lantern* survey of students, "reactions ranged from annoyance to understanding with most students adopting a 'you can't fight city hall' attitude."[23]

Even the emotional issue of parking failed to generate much reaction. Only two students showed up for what was supposed to be a mass information meeting in April to discuss the administration's new parking plan. "If the students are apathetic now, they will have little cause to complain about possible undesirable consequences in the future," the *Lantern* editorialized with little effect.[24]

Also that year, John Bonner succeeded William Guthrie as executive dean for student relations when Guthrie left over the summer. Bonner—who earned three degrees from Ohio State, culminating with a Ph.D. in speech—had spent nearly his entire adult life at the university. He taught speech for two years before joining the College of Commerce, where he rose to the rank of associate professor. Bonner specialized in real estate, particularly housing, which is why the university, looking to make a major expansion in student housing, chose him for the position.

Bonner and his ever-present pipe would become familiar to students in the 1960s. His knack for saying the wrong thing at the wrong time would often put him at odds with a succession of student activists. In his first year as executive dean, he had to clarify a statement he made about how an alleged communist managed to speak on campus without prior approval. He found himself in a public spat with the *Lantern* over what he told the Council on Student Affairs about limits on its power. And he had to explain that his statement to an international student that "there are boats leaving every day" was meant to be facetious, not a threat.[25]

GOOD TO BE GREEK

Apathy was not a concern for Ohio State's Greek system, which enjoyed a banner year in 1961–62. At the time 45 fraternities and 21 sororities claimed more than 4,000 members. Although they accounted for only about 15 percent of the student body, they exercised great influence on campus life. Jim Gross, president of the Student Senate as of February 1962, was among their members, along with many leaders of major campus organizations.

Greeks also seemed ready to shed their image as privileged rich kids resistant to social change. On September 25 the university announced that all fraternities had removed discrimination clauses from their local constitutions and were in compliance with Ohio State policy. According to Dean Bonner, the university was one of the first eight schools in the country to do so. Phil Moots, Student Senate president at the time, praised the move but said that additional effort was needed to make sure discrimination was eliminated in fact as well as in policy.[26]

The dean of men, Mylin H. Ross, announced in December that the national Inter-Fraternity Council had named Ohio State's fraternity system the best in the country in its large-system category (20 or more chapters) for the fifth time. The designation was based on service to the community, the university, and member fraternities, as well as interfraternity coordination and project activities.

The sororities had good news to share as well. Jane McCormick, assistant dean of women, credited recent improvements in the system of sorority rush for a record yield of 527 new pledges. Among the changes was a new flexible quota system and, for the first time, the use of computers to handle paperwork so that counselors could spend more time with rushees. The sorority system also reported a record number of women from the upper classes, with more than 1,200 active members returning that fall.

SPEAKERS RULE LOCKOUT

In the spring of 1962 the Speakers Rule once again sparked controversy. Shephard Liverant, an associate professor of psychology and adviser to Students for Liberal Action, invited Phillip A. Luce and two other members of a group called the Emergency Civil Liberties Committee to speak on campus, as he was permitted to do under the existing rule. Luce, a former Ohio State student, then reportedly told a New York audience that "two weeks from now we are going to invade the campus at Ohio State. It is time for us to get our guns, man the barricades and mobilize youth for freedom."[27]

When President Fawcett returned from an out-of-town trip on April 24, he was mortified to learn Luce was scheduled to speak on campus the next day. He met with Liverant and asked him to withdraw the invitation. Liverant refused, arguing that he had followed procedure and the Emergency Civil Liberties Committee was not on the official list of subversive groups.

When about 200 students showed up at the law college auditorium the next day to hear Luce, they found the doors locked and access blocked by campus police. Liverant then announced that Luce and the others would speak off campus. That evening, about 150 people gathered in the yard of a rooming house on Chittenden Avenue to hear Luce and his companions. They spent most of their time attacking the House Un-American Activities Committee and the McCarthy-era McCarran Internal Security Act.

Most of the student organizations, the *Lantern,* and Ohio State's chapter of the American Association of University Professors (AAUP) attacked Fawcett's decision to ban Luce. Newly elected Student Senate president Jim Gross also objected. "Although personally I am not in sympathy with Mr. Luce or his views, I believe that the action taken by the university this afternoon was unfortunate," Gross said. "I believe students of this campus are mature individuals, capable of deciding for themselves which views they should hear and which they should accept."[28]

The university establishment, represented by the board of trustees, the Alumni Association, and the Columbus newspapers, supported Fawcett. John Bricker, chair of the trustees, said: "Students who are trying to run the university rather than get an education had better move on. Any professor who is not willing to live by the rules of the university . . . can look for another job."[29]

While students were able to summon only about 250 of their number to a rally three days later, some of the faculty were not ready to give up easily. The AAUP chapter demanded an all-faculty meeting, where it planned to introduce a resolution to overturn Fawcett's decision. Things came to a head at a tense meeting on May 14. Some 1,700 faculty members filled the lower level of Mershon Auditorium, and about 1,100 spectators, mostly students, looked on from the balcony. It was described as the largest faculty meeting ever. It was also the most contentious. Fawcett spoke first for 35 minutes. He explained the Speakers Rule allowed him to disapprove a speaker if the event had no educational value. He concluded by saying his decision was in the best interests of the university. He received a standing ovation from many in the crowd.

Richard H. Bohning, assistant dean of the College of Agriculture and Home Economics, introduced a resolution in support of Fawcett. A motion to table it failed. Those in favor of Fawcett's decision were asked to stand to be counted by impartial tellers, then opponents did the same. The resolution passed easily, 1,036–509.

Foster Reah Dulles, a professor of history and cousin of Central Intelligence Agency director Allen Dulles, opposed the resolution. He followed the vote with a motion asking the faculty to affirm "its full support for the right of free speech on this campus for guest speakers invited by any member of the faculty or by a recognized student organization with the approval of its advisor, free from restraint or intervention by administrative authority." Liverant also spoke in support of Dulles's motion. Citing threatening calls and letters he'd received, Liverant said students lived in an atmosphere of intimidation.

At this point engineering professor Mars Fontana moved to adjourn the meeting. The parliamentarian ruled the motion was not debatable. The motion passed and the meeting adjourned after one hour and 45 minutes without a vote on Dulles's motion.[30]

The controversy continued. Angry faculty opposing Fawcett's action, many from the arts and sciences, were outraged to learn 385 agricultural extension agents and a number of part-time medical practitioners—whom they did not consider to be real faculty and were more likely to support Fawcett's position—had been allowed to vote. They accused the university administration of rigging the vote to assure a favorable outcome. Students who opposed the Speakers Rule were equally disaffected. Even the conservative Women's Self Government Association passed a resolution in opposition to the rule. The Council of Graduate Students went so far as to take out a *Lantern* ad with 509 signatures protesting Fawcett's decision.

Fawcett himself seemed to realize he was in a difficult place, with at least a third of his faculty opposing him, but he was short on ideas. He told reporters at the end of the meeting somewhat ambiguously that "we will feel impelled to find ways to resolve our differences in a manner which will be as satisfactory as possible to all concerned." As for the trustees, they left no doubt about where they stood. At their next regular meeting on May 18 they unanimously approved a resolution "wholeheartedly" supporting Fawcett.[31]

THE UNIVERSITY: COMPETING VISIONS

Despite the Rose Bowl debacle and the Speakers Rule controversy, university officials knew they had to stay focused on a longer-term challenge: the approaching tidal wave of baby boomers reaching college age. The 1961–62 school year started with an enrollment surprise and a harbinger of things to come. Officials had expected 25,000 students on the Columbus campus that fall. Instead, 25,722 showed up, eclipsing the previous record of 25,400 set in 1947. By 1970 enrollment was expected to double.

FAWCETT PLANS

President Fawcett had developed a plan to better prepare the university for the impending surge in enrollment. It included three parts: a master plan to expand the campus to meet facility needs; a review of the academic calendar to better meet instructional needs; and a restructuring of academic units to better align resources. One of Fawcett's first priorities after becoming president in 1956 was to hire John Herrick, a professor of education research at Ohio State, as his executive director of campus planning. Herrick had a reputation as an expert on planning for school districts. He hired a respected Texas architectural and planning firm to help him pull the master plan together. After more than two years of gathering information and talking with stakeholders, they released their preliminary recommendations in late 1961.

The proposed plan called for keeping the Columbus campus unified—that is, with the core disciplines, medical facilities, and agriculture college located in close proximity in one place. The plan also called for clustering academic buildings by discipline, preserving green space, and making the campus more pedestrian friendly, all of which would be accomplished by the end of the decade. Proposals to make the Olentangy River the center of campus and to establish a larger presence west of the river would be less successful.[32]

The specifics of the plan did not generate much opposition. What objections did surface came from faculty who feared the level of expansion reflected in the plan would undercut the quality of academic programs.

Because the master plan was primarily a business decision, it did not require specific faculty approval. Fawcett took the plan to the trustees in February. He used the opportunity to remind the campus community of the realities facing the university over the next decade. "All existing public institutions in Ohio, including Ohio State University, will be taxed to their utmost by substantial enrollment increases beginning almost immediately," he said. "In the face of such facts, The Ohio State University cannot discharge its responsibility to the people of Ohio without making prompt preparations for accommodating more students." The trustees approved the plan unanimously.[33]

Changes in the academic calendar, on the other hand, did require faculty approval. On December 5, 1961, Fawcett used a meeting with 1,000 faculty to float the idea of moving from a quarter system to what was commonly known as a trimester plan. Trimesters involved three 14- or 15-week sessions, compared to four 10-week sessions under the quarter system. Trimesters had been proposed before, but never garnered much support. Fawcett argued that trimesters would increase the university's capacity to handle more students by making better use of facilities year round and also would reduce the time to graduation. Buildings would be used 11 months of the year instead of nine, for example, and students who attended all three trimesters could graduate in three years.[34] The faculty agreed to allow further study of the issue, but it didn't take long for opposition to form. By February a local AAUP panel started raising questions. The *Lantern* editorialized against the idea in April, and in May the usually docile Freshman Senate joined the opposition and the proposal began to lose momentum.

The third element in Fawcett's plan involved the restructuring of academic units. Fawcett had appointed a committee to look at the issue in 1959. It reported its findings in June 1962. The report called for a major reconfiguration of the arts and sciences, establishment of a university college, and changes in how colleges would award degrees. Because it already was late in the academic year, the discussion would carry over to the fall and spark four years of debate.

STUDENT SENATE PLANS

Frustrated by what it saw as a lack of vision on the part of the president and trustees, the Student Senate organized and paid for its own national symposium on "the idea of the university," which drew an overflow crowd of 400 to the auditorium of the Ohio Historical Society on February 15 and 16. The symposium highlighted two challenges that would dog Ohio State through the end of the decade and beyond. The first was the question of what a large public research university was supposed to be. Other than agreeing that they didn't like the restraint on free speech represented by the Speakers Rule, the participants found little common ground on the issue. Nevertheless, the *Lantern* complimented them for drawing attention to the "evident contradiction between the ideal university and contemporary schools."[35]

The second issue involved the role of students in setting the agenda. Throughout his term as Student Senate president, Phil Moots challenged his colleagues to think of student government as more than a service organization. He wanted it to be a force to press the university to "assume a leadership role in our society in promulgating the ethical, moral and democratic traditions of our nation."[36] Moots's successors would initially be wary of taking on this role, but by the end of the decade, students and student leaders alike would be banging on the table, demanding that the university play a more active part in reforming society.

Meanwhile the administration moved ahead with other initiatives that leaders believed would better address growing student demands. The most immediate problem involved students double scheduling courses, then dropping them after the quarter began because they didn't like the class time or the instructor. The registrar cited the case of Fine Arts 494, where 1,500 students signed up for the course and 500 dropped it after the start of the quarter, creating waste in both scheduling rooms and instructors. The problem was expected to become even worse as enrollments grew. Consequently, the registrar proposed a policy limiting drops after classes began to reasons beyond the control of the student, such as clerical error or medical emergency.

Students viewed the change as an intrusion on their rights. A *Lantern* survey of 50 students in November found 37 of them aware of the proposal. All opposed it.[37] Both the Student Senate and the *Lantern* were against it. Jim Gross, chair of the senate educational affairs commission at the time, complained that double scheduling was a reflection of weaknesses in the scheduling procedure or poor instructors—problems that were caused by the university, not the students. In this case, the administration stuck to its guns. After being amended to give colleges some flexibility on exceptions, the policy was approved effective winter quarter 1962.

Other initiatives included restoring the use of large lecture sections and making better use of technology. The economics department announced in September that it would move forward with an experiment to pair large lecture sections taught by faculty with smaller recitation sections taught by graduate students. The technique had been adopted 15 years earlier to deal with the crush of enrollments after World War II, but was dropped after enrollments stabilized.

The major technology initiative involved television courses. At its first meeting of the 1961–62 school year, the board of trustees approved releasing $15,000 to contract with Ohio Bell to provide additional infrastructure for TV instruction for 15,000 students in nine courses. In January the Department of Mathematics reported on its evaluation of TV instruction in one course involving 1,362 students. The department declared success based on an identical distribution of grades between students who took the TV course and a control group of students who did not. However, a *Lantern* reporter observed that both students and instructors were reluctant to say anything negative for fear of retaliation; those who did speak up asked to remain anonymous. They said it was more difficult to see what was written on the blackboard on TV and also harder to understand when an instructor was not physically present in the room.[38]

The university took steps to accommodate demand in two growing fields. The first classes in Chinese were offered beginning in winter quarter as part of an effort to build up the East Asian languages program. And to meet the need for more administrators in primary and secondary schools, a postgraduate program in education and administration was approved. Both programs would thrive in the sixties. On the other hand, the registrar's scheduling system, the classes taught by graduate students, and the impersonality of TV instruction would be sources of growing student discontent.

RESEARCH: DAY OF THE COCKROACHES

At a time when leaders of the world's most advanced nations seemed intent on bringing humanity closer to nuclear war, an unsettling discovery came out of the lab of Frank W. Fisk, an associate professor of entomology. Fisk was studying the digestive systems of cockroaches in an attempt to improve those of humans. He and his students found the humble pests could absorb 40 times more radiation than a human could and still survive because their simpler cell structure was more resistant.[39]

In June 1961 Ohio State opened a million-dollar facility dedicated to the cobalt-60 beam therapy technology developed at the university. This gave University Hospital one of the most advanced radiation treatment programs in the world. Paired with what was already believed to be one of the largest cancer detection programs in the country, it positioned Ohio State to be a leader in researching and treating the disease.

In January university officials accepted a $117,000 nuclear reactor from Lockheed Nuclear Products. The reactor was housed in a facility near Kenny Road on west campus, where safety features included five-foot-thick concrete walls and 6,000 gallons of water for cooling. It was the second reactor in Ohio and would be used by physicists, chemists, and engineers to advance basic research.

SOCIETY: LIVING WITH THE TSAR BOMB

The 1961–62 school year began the way the previous year had ended, with a flurry of Cold War–inspired anxiety. While American and Soviet tank crews glared at each other across the barricades in divided Berlin, the Soviet Union resumed nuclear testing by setting off a series of bombs in the atmosphere. An informal *Lantern* survey of 13 students and faculty at the beginning of October found that a majority thought war of some sort was imminent.

Student organizations took time to educate their members about the issues. Speaking to Kappa Alpha Theta sorority and Beta Theta Pi fraternity as part of a current events program, John Bonner, the new executive dean for student relations, said the most dangerous way for communism to spread within the university was through the faculty: "Any Communist discovered on the faculty of Ohio State will be disposed of forthwith. In the last 10 years there have been only four Communists on this campus. All of these have been dismissed." Bonner praised President John F. Kennedy's stand in support of a noncommunist Berlin, then concluded by saying, "because of personal faith in God and patriotism, we should be able to face the threat of communism calmly, objectively and rationally."[40]

On October 30 the Soviet Union exploded a huge device over Siberia. Known as the Tsar Bomb, the 50-megaton behemoth was the largest nuclear weapon ever detonated. It released 1,400 times the explosive power of the Hiroshima and Nagasaki bombs combined, and produced a fireball seen 620 miles away and a mushroom cloud 40 miles high. This attempt to terrorize the civilized world met with universal condemnation from pro-Western nations and unaligned nations alike. Three months later Kennedy announced the United States would resume atmospheric testing in response.

Federal, state, and university officials moved to reassure nervous citizens. The *Lantern* had already pitched in with a story on state civil defense procedures. In response to the question "Can we survive an atomic war?" the writer confidently observed: "Yes, mankind would not be wiped out. . . . Most people who survive the blast effects of nuclear weapons could save themselves, CD officials say. There is nothing too hard to understand about fallout. It is merely a physical fact of this nuclear age."[41]

Godspeed, John Glenn

In the middle of a winter of terrible weather and high anxiety over nuclear war, Americans yearned for good news. On February 20, 1962—after five years of failure in the race for space—the United States celebrated a major victory as Ohio native John Glenn sped out of earth's atmosphere atop a huge Atlas rocket to become the first American to orbit the planet. At Ohio State and around the world, millions of people interrupted their routines to follow the drama on TV and radio.

A month before the flight, students had showed concern and respect when asked by a *Lantern* reporter how they would feel if they were going up in space. "Scared to death" is how Janet Burnett described it. But sophomore Peggy Jo Leech, who was also a *Lantern* reporter, expressed a powerful sentiment common among the nation's young people: "I imagine if I were a man like John Glenn, I would feel that what I was doing was the greatest service I could give my country."[1]

1. Mary Margaret Griffith, "Glenn's Space Flight Prompts Differing Students Comments," *Lantern,* January 25, 1962, 1.

VISITORS: FROM CHEERING GOLDWATER TO CHANNELING DYLAN

In November 1961 Ohio State hosted one of the hottest speakers on the college lecture circuit. With a best-selling book (*The Conscience of a Conservative*), a clear message, and his trademark black glasses, U.S. senator Barry Goldwater (R-Arizona) was a hit wherever he went. Three thousand people paid 75 cents each to attend a speech at Mershon Auditorium sponsored by the campus Young Republicans.

Conservatism, Goldwater told the crowd, was not a yearning for times long gone, but the belief in making progress based on the proven values of the past. He lambasted the Kennedy administration for allowing the Berlin Wall to be built and for overseeing what he said was the slowest growth of the world's eight leading economies.[42]

His audience loved it. When asked later if he planned to run for president in 1964, Goldwater said all he was interested in was serving the people of Arizona.

Two visitors at year's end captured the contrasts of life in the nuclear age. Young folksinger Joan Baez headed the entertainment for May Week. The highlight of her concert in Mershon Auditorium came when she asked an appreciative audience to join hands and sing "Kumbaya" with her in a celebration of sixties togetherness.

Curtis LeMay—the cigar-chomping, 56-year-old air force chief of staff and Ohio State alumnus—gave the commencement address a month later after making a dramatic entrance from a helicopter that landed south of Ohio Stadium. LeMay—not likely a fan or either Joan Baez or Bob Dylan—ironically seemed to be channeling the latter when he told more than 2,400 graduates and their families: "We are in the midst of an age of technological change that will make the industrial revolution seem dull indeed. . . . Opportunity is not only knocking at the door, it is beating gongs around the house."[43]

CHAPTER 3

IN DREAMS

(1962–63)

Dreams came and went in 1962–63. Activists' dreams of a national student movement were shot down, not by surly Ohio State administrators but by fellow students. Four months later those same students gave campus liberals a victory beyond their wildest dreams. President Novice Fawcett saw his plans for addressing the impending enrollment surge grind to a halt, while researchers jumped at the opportunity to participate in John F. Kennedy's dream to put a man on the moon. An Ohio State dropout achieved his dream of becoming governor. The school year began with the nightmare of nuclear Armageddon, but ended with an inspiring call for peace abroad and justice at home.

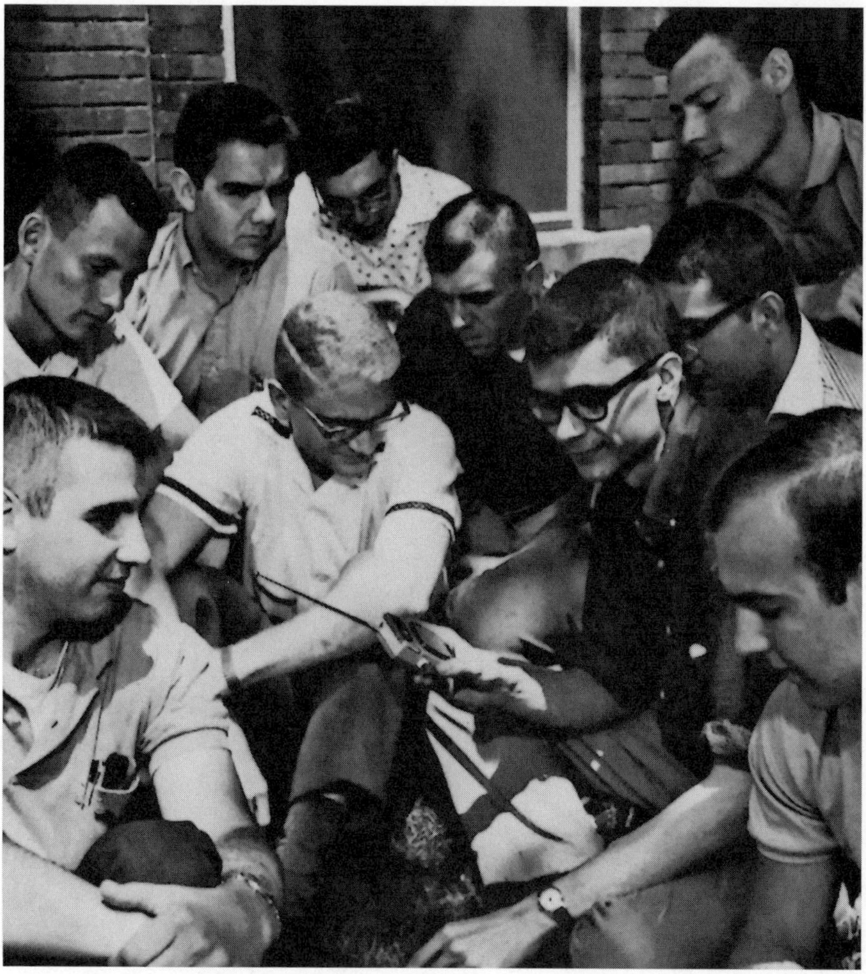

3.1. Students huddle around a transistor radio for the latest news about a space launch from Cape Canaveral. (*Makio*)

STUDENTS: RESTLESS

Ohio State students knew how to follow the rules, or so it seemed. In November 1962 the Office of Student Relations reported that only four students had been dismissed for reasons other than grades during the previous 12 months. Their transgressions included curfew violations, cheating, alcohol use, and criminal behavior. One official boasted, "I think it is amazing that in a school where admission is nonselective, . . . there are not more problems."[1] But beneath the calm surface, students were growing restless with the established order.

THE NSA GOES DOWN

A bizarre combination of Cold War and campus politics turned the National Student Association into a political football as the school year began. That fall the NSA claimed to represent 1.3 million students at 400 colleges and universities across the country. The organization, which had been founded at the University of Wisconsin in 1947, described its objectives as "greater student participation in meaningful issues which face our generation." It also played an important role in the Cold War as a counterweight to communist-inspired youth movements across the globe. Consequently, it benefited from strong bipartisan support from the nation's political establishment.[2]

The NSA's advisory board included such establishment luminaries as T. M. Hesburgh, president of Notre Dame, and Ralph McGill, editor and publisher of the *Atlanta Constitution.* Supporters included leaders from both political parties, not the least of which were President John F. Kennedy and his predecessor, Dwight Eisenhower. Even Ohio State administrators joined the chorus. Christine Y. Conaway, the dean of women, called the NSA the "voice of American students."[3] When the opportunity came for the university to host the group's 1962 annual convention, many saw it as a plum. It would bring an estimated 1,200 visitors to Columbus over 18 days. In November 1961 the Student Senate approved extending the invitation without any serious opposition.

Beginning in 1961 conservatives nationally began to question the NSA's political orientation. They established their own brand of youthful appeal, Young Americans for Freedom. By February 1962 conservatives at Ohio State also were becoming uncomfortable with the NSA's alleged left-wing leanings and undemocratic procedures in support of issues such as an end to nuclear testing and opposition to the House Un-American Activities Committee. When Buckeye Political Party candidate Jim Gross was elected president of the Student Senate in the spring, he was in favor of bringing the NSA convention to Ohio State that summer. However, Gross also called upon the group to adopt a series of reforms or he would not support the university's continued participation.

Gross and his allies achieved some success at the convention, such as limiting the power of the NSA's executive committee, but they did not believe the changes went far enough. Gross came out against the NSA at the first senate meeting in September, calling the organization a "self-proclaimed national union of students concerned not primarily with student government problems but primarily with strictly political issues." He spoke in favor of a resolution providing for a campuswide vote during the Homecoming balloting in October. The resolution passed 18–12 after a long debate.[4]

NSA advocates moved quickly to shore up support. While supporters included predictable liberals such as members of the Young Democrats and Students for Liberal Action, they also included prominent members of the Buckeye Political Party, such as Freshman Senate president Sam McGavran and senate treasurer H. Paul Schwitzgebel. The anti-NSA forces, which included the Young Republicans and the Conservative Club, picked up support from an unexpected source when the usually left-leaning *Lantern* endorsed cutting ties to the NSA in an editorial two days before the election.

A record 8,300 students turned out to vote on October 17. The NSA suffered a decisive defeat, with 4,859 voting to support withdrawal and only 2,207 against. Another 861 voted "insufficient information," even though the debate had raged for months. Ohio State dropped out of the NSA shortly after the election. Other universities left as well, but some chose to stay. When the University of Michigan conducted a referendum five weeks later, students voted by a narrow margin to stay in.

The NSA tilted steadily left as the decade wore on. In February 1967, the left-leaning San Francisco magazine *Ramparts* published the outcome of an investigation that revealed the group had been receiving substantial support ($400,000 annually) from the U.S. Central Intelligence Agency. The money was secretly laundered through private foundations, with the supposed purpose of helping to combat communist-supported youth groups abroad. Only a small group of NSA officials knew about the money. The other employees, supporters, and members who did not felt betrayed. The NSA splintered, and what remained drifted even further left, earning a place on President Richard M. Nixon's list of enemies. In 1972 a group of dissidents in California broke away and started the National Student Lobby, which promised to focus on domestic issues such as the cost of higher education. In August 1978 the two organizations made peace and merged into the United States Student Association, which is still in existence today.[5]

STUDENT POLITICS: HAD ENOUGH?

By the beginning of 1963 liberal activists had suffered two decisive defeats at the ballot box in the preceding 10 months: the Student Congress Party's loss to the Buckeye Political Party in the student government elections the previous February and the National Student Association referendum in October. After some soul-searching, SCP leaders decided to change to a more populist message aimed squarely at Buckeye Political Party/Greek one-party rule. "Our main job is to convince the dormitory residents, town residents and non-BPP [Greek] houses that we best represent their interests," SCP president Gary Warner told the *Lantern* in November.[6]

The SCP decided not to run a candidate for Student Senate president and instead to focus on the senate races under the theme "Had enough of Mickey Mouse student government?" Some SCP activists then announced their support for BPP presidential candidate Paul Schwitzgebel. His opponent would be Donald A. Stuver, who ran as an independent.

The SCP gathered enough money to run two highly effective full-page *Lantern* advertisements aimed at the senate campaigns. The ads featured an annotated copy of the BPP's 1962 platform, highlighting all the things the group had promised but failed to deliver. The broken promises included a more liberalized course-dropping policy, the elimination of unwarranted searches and seizures in residence halls, and an end to discrimination in off-campus housing.

On February 28 the students spoke. Schwitzgebel, the BPP candidate, won easily, 3,925 to 2,239, but the SCP exceeded its wildest dreams, capturing 29 of 40 senate seats, including upsets of a number of BPP incumbents.

The underlying problem of lack of widespread participation remained. Only 6,300 students out of nearly 30,000 voted. A *Lantern* survey of 200 students five days before the election found that 80 percent did not know who their two senators were, nor did they apparently care. Juniors were the most knowledgeable (with an average score of 28 percent correct for all the questions), and freshmen, not surprisingly, were the least informed (8.3 percent average correct score).[7]

Student leaders were able to get some things done before the end of the 1962–63 school year. The Women's Self Government Association gained approval for women over 21 to live in apartments. The Council on Student Affairs approved a student-run publications board to resolve conflicts regarding taste or libel, and the SCP managed to get a resolution regarding antidiscrimination in housing passed in the senate. Nevertheless, low participation would continue to limit the effectiveness of student government throughout the decade.

IS GOD DEAD?

In 1966, amid concerns about falling interest in religion among the nation's young people, a provocative *Time* magazine cover asked the question "Is God dead?" But during the 1962–63 school year religion still played a significant role in the lives of Ohio State students. A survey found that almost 90 percent of them listed a religious preference, well above the national average of 64 percent. According to Milton D. McLean, the university's coordinator of religious affairs, students attended church and participated in religious events more than in any other voluntary campus activity.[8]

As a public university, Ohio State could not directly promote one religious denomination over another, but it did provide opportunities for students to practice their faiths. Many students were involved in activities through more than 24 church-sponsored private organizations. Still, although these groups were highly visible, most students were not members. Only about 1,000 of the 5,100 self-identified Methodists on campus were members of the Wesley Foundation, for example, and only 725 Catholics out of 5,200 were formal members of the Newman Club. William Pietsch of the Westminster Foundation observed that students "have a faith in God, but they question the value of institutional Christianity."[9]

SPEAKERS RULE CHALLENGES CONTINUE

If President Fawcett sought some sort of middle ground after the divisive faculty vote on the Speakers Rule the previous spring, that hope was soon buried. In December the board of trustees unanimously passed a resolution "clarifying" the existing rule. The message: the trustees were in control and were not inclined to compromise. Eric Ogden of the Faculty Council said he had been told that "the board will not accept anything which curtails their authority to allow the president to have the final authority."[10]

Opponents of the rule unsuccessfully sought to mobilize student support. The Student Senate voted 20–9 in November to liberalize the rule, with votes from both political parties. The issue generated numerous *Lantern* editorials and support from the local chapter of the American Association of University Professors, but little from students themselves. A petition drive got about 2,000 signatures but stalled due to a lack of volunteers. A *Lantern* survey done at the same time showed only a low level of knowledge and little commitment.

In January, Fawcett flexed his muscles under the "clarified" rule to turn down a request from Students for Liberal Action to invite Frank Wilkinson, a critic of the House Un-American Activities Committee, to Ohio State. Activists led by former SLA president Niki Schwartz, who was frustrated with campus inaction, filed a lawsuit in federal district court challenging the constitutionality of the rule.

That prompted a quick response from rule supporters. State representative Chalmers Wylie, a Republican whose district included the university, introduced a bill banning speakers on all college campuses in Ohio if they were known to be members of the Communist Party; were known to advocate the overthrow of the Constitution of the United States; had ever pleaded the Fifth Amendment regarding Communist Party membership or subversive acts; or were convicted felons.[11]

Wylie's bill proved to be too much even for the conservative Ohio legislature. The proposed language was watered down to allow university trustees to decide who could speak on campus, and the bill was passed in July.

Meanwhile, the *Lantern* kept up its assault on the rule. In a survey of other campuses, it found that Ohio State and Michigan State were the only Big Ten schools to have banned a speaker in the last year. It also determined that other universities in Ohio, including Ohio University and the University of Cincinnati, did not ban speakers.[12]

The last *Lantern* issue of spring quarter featured a front-page story claiming the Speakers Rule led to an unsatisfactory academic environment and was driving good faculty from the university. The story concluded that eight faculty members in the English department were leaving because "the climate in the university and community is not conducive to academic fulfillment. Better offers from other schools, and dissatisfaction with the prevailing atmosphere, have resulted in their resignations."[13]

When the next issue of the *Lantern* came out at the beginning of summer quarter, Fawcett's vigorous rebuttal was on the front page. The previous *Lantern* story was misleading because only 15 departing faculty members had been interviewed, he said. Statistics showed that faculty resignations were only 1.7 percent (42 out of 2,411), less than in 1959–60 (the last year for which comparable figures were available), when 2.3 percent departed.[14]

The controversy attracted the attention of the *Wall Street Journal,* which sent reporter Lee Berton to Columbus. Berton's piece ran in August and recounted the arguments on both sides of the issue at Ohio State and other campuses. Berton concluded that "what worries many educators is that the repercussions in the political arena may one day breed much broader legal restrictions than the one that Ohio has already adopted."[15] What no one anticipated was that the repercussions would flow from the bottom up. What the rejection of the National Student Association, the Student Congress Party's senate upset, the lawsuit against the university, and the move away from formal religion had in common was a willingness by students to turn away from the established order.

THE UNIVERSITY: A RACE AGAINST TIME

Enrollment ratcheted up another notch in the fall of 1962 to a record 28,160 students on the Columbus campus, an increase of 9.5 percent over the previous fall. Enrollment at the regional campuses grew from 1,843 to 2,340. Ohio State officials knew it was the beginning of pressures that would surge in the fall of 1964, just 24 months away. "The university will face enrollment problems of such magnitude that there is no precedent for their solution," Fawcett warned in his 1962 president's report.[16]

The university had been preparing for this moment since the mid-1950s, but Fawcett's three key initiatives to get ahead of the problem were behind schedule. The effort to streamline the academic calendar through trimesters was dead in the water. The campus master plan had gotten off to a promising start but was now stalled due to lack of funds. Academic restructuring was the third initiative. A faculty committee that Fawcett had appointed in 1959 finally managed to issue its report in June 1962.[17] Since it was late in the academic year, it was necessary to hold off serious discussion until the fall.

The committee, chaired by English professor James Fullington, focused on the dysfunctional structure of Ohio State's liberal arts core, which was scattered by happenstance and history through a number of colleges. Economics and sociology were housed in the College of Commerce, psychology in the College of Education, and biology and botany in the College of Agriculture. In most other top universities these disciplines were consolidated into an arts and sciences college.

Ohio State's College of the Arts and Sciences was already too big, and adding more departments would not work. Instead, the committee recommended four smaller, more nimble colleges clustered around the humanities, physical sciences, life sciences, and social sciences. It also recommended limiting admission in undergraduate degree programs to juniors and seniors only, and requiring all freshmen and sophomores to spend their first two years in a newly established University College. The University College would be geared to undergraduate instruction and helping students prepare to choose a major. This would allow most regular faculty in the colleges to concentrate on teaching upper-level courses and doing research.

This sweeping proposal would eventually require formal approval by the Faculty Council. Fullington estimated that if all went well, the changes could be in place by the fall of 1965, a full year after the first baby boomers arrived. In fact, things would not go well. Deans and faculty both inside and outside the College of the Arts and Sciences were already digging in their heels.

Meanwhile, the university continued to invest in technology as a way to enhance learning. An estimated 17,500 students were enrolled in TV courses in 1962–63, including 2,000 in Zoology 400. The use of technology in the listening center in Derby Hall grew even faster. Twenty-five hundred students a week were using the language labs in the fall of 1961; a year later the figure had doubled. Administrators credited growing faculty support for audiotapes as a teaching tool, especially for foreign languages and music.

In January 1963 the university received a new IBM 7090 computer that was six times faster than its predecessor. While it would be used mainly for research, it had other applications. Vice President Gordon Carson, Ohio State's foremost technology advocate, announced in August that computers would track student grades beginning with the 1963–64 school year. He also pointed with pride at several other innovations, including automated thermostats at the university ice rink, direct-dial phones, an automatic ironing machine at University Hospital, and a new automated food service. "Automation is not replacing people at Ohio State," Carson said. "The university has grown and the work load has become bigger."[18]

Course offerings expanded as well. Eugene Ching of the Division of Linguistics announced in November that Ohio State would offer a major program in Chinese, including 15 courses covering language, literature, philosophy, and linguistics. It would be the only such program in the state. Ching, who had been recruited to Ohio State for this purpose, explained: "If the United States is to be an effective leader of the democratic camp of nations, she must have enough specialists who understand the languages and cultures of the people she deals with." To those who were skeptical about studying a communist country, Ching offered a Chinese proverb: "Know your enemy; know yourself—100 battles; 100 victories."[19]

The following spring the university announced it would delete 90 courses and add 143 for the 1963–64 school year. One of the new courses—Math 590, Introduction to Digital Computing—was sure to be a hit.

WE CHOOSE TO GO TO THE MOON

"We choose to go to the moon and do other things, not because they are easy but because they are hard," John F. Kennedy told a Rice University audience in September 1962. And as the country's space program headed to the moon, Ohio State was right there. Two researchers, Clarence Cole in veterinary medicine and F. A. Hitchcock in medicine, developed the high-altitude pressurized suit Gordon Cooper wore when he orbited the earth in May 1963.

The Aviation Psychology Lab conducted research on developing techniques to train astronauts by observing how students reacted to commands and solved problems on simulated space flights. The Rocket Lab did much of the development work on liquid hydrogen as the fuel that propelled the Atlas and Saturn rockets into space. The Antenna Lab contributed the communications and navigation devices that made space travel possible. But perhaps the most significant contribution came on July 23, 1963, when NASA announced that a former engineering professor at Ohio State, George E. Mueller, would take charge of the Apollo program. His mission: put a man on the moon by the end of the decade and bring him safely home.

While the race for space attracted the most attention, university researchers continued to produce in other areas as well. Ohio State generated $9 million in externally funded research through the Research Foundation in fiscal year 1962, an 18 percent increase over 1961. Alfred B. Garrett, the first Ohio State faculty member to hold the title of vice president for research, predicted a doubling in external research over the next six years.

Money was not the only measure of the impact of Ohio State scientists. That fall Everett Rogers published his first book, *Diffusion of Innovations*. Rogers, an associate professor of rural sociology, had studied 11 different innovations to determine patterns in how long they took to be adopted and the psychological and human factors involved. His work would go through five editions over the next 40 years and is now a classic in the field. It is the second-most cited book in the social sciences.[20]

JIM'S PLACE

Ohio was—and is—a highly competitive swing state in presidential election races, but things were much different in the years between, when turnout fell off and conservative Republicans and some anti-tax Democrats were dominant. As a result, one of the nation's wealthiest states placed near the bottom in tax effort and support of most state services. For example, Ohio ranked 42nd in support of colleges and universities in 1961–62.[21]

In 1958, Republican overreach in supporting an anti-union initiative allowed Democrats to sweep statewide offices and both houses of the General Assembly. Newly elected governor Michael DiSalle pushed through a $300 million tax increase to support better state services. However, two years later the Democrats lost their majorities in the House and Senate. With two years left in a four-year term, DiSalle now found he couldn't get the budget he wanted through the Republican-dominated legislature. What finally passed provided for only a modest increase in operating support for higher education and nothing for building projects.

The November 1962 gubernatorial race turned into a referendum on DiSalle's four years and one of the nastiest campaigns in state history. The Republican challenger, state auditor James A. Rhodes, called DiSalle "Tax Hike Mike" and accused him of costing Ohio 200,000 jobs. Rhodes won in a landslide with a margin of 500,000 votes.

James Allen Rhodes was no stranger to Ohio State. Born in rural Coalton in southeast Ohio, he entered the university in 1932 on a modest basketball scholarship. He left after only one quarter. He told reporters he'd dropped out to earn money to support his mother. (His father, a coal-mine supervisor, had died when he was nine.) Rhodes made an impact in his short time at the university. He rejuvenated the Young Republicans, who'd fallen on hard times after the Roosevelt landslide in 1932. He later opened a combination grill/convenience store called Jim's Place at High Street and 17th Avenue where Depression-era students could get inexpensive food. Rhodes went on to be a popular mayor of Columbus from 1944 to 1952. He successfully ran for state auditor in 1952 and was reelected in 1956 and 1960.[22]

Rhodes spoke in sentence fragments with a rural accent that turned the name of the state into "Ahia" and "push" into "poosh." But those who thought his lack of polish reflected a lack of political acumen found themselves outsmarted.

After the election Ohio State immediately began a campaign for more state dollars in the new governor's budget, which would be introduced in January and take effect July 1, 1963. The campaign was led by the Committee of 88—an effort to contact legislators in all 88 counties that was sponsored by Ohio Staters and the Student Senate. The university administration added its support when President Fawcett used his annual report to the campus at the end of 1962 to make the case. He described Ohio State as "state assisted but not state supported," with state dollars providing only 46 percent of the operating budget. "There is no way possible to handle enrollment increases without a substantial increase in income," Fawcett said, pointing to a projected 50 percent jump in freshman enrollment by 1965. Fawcett went on to tie Ohio State's request to the "jobs and progress" theme Rhodes had offered in his election campaign: "The future economic, cultural, and physical well-being of the people of Ohio is at stake in the decisions now being made relative to the support of higher education in the state."[23]

Before long the aspirations of Ohio State and its sister institutions ran up against the reality of a sluggish economy and a deteriorating state budget picture. On January 15, 1963, the day after his inauguration, Rhodes announced an aggressive austerity program to close what was described as a $50–$60 million budget deficit for the current fiscal year (ending June 30) that had been inherited from his predecessor. Rhodes vowed he would not raise taxes, but instead would cut spending. This included laying off all 3,000 state employees who'd been hired since the previous September. At that time workers at the university were considered state employees, so 188 of them were to be let go, including 75 at University Hospital. The impact on the hospital was so severe, administrators called for a freeze on nonemergency admissions for 48 hours.[24] More cost-cutting initiatives were announced in the following two weeks, including a spending cut of 9.1 percent to most state appropriations.

The extent of Rhodes's austerity drive caught Statehouse observers by surprise and led to charges by Democrats that he had manufactured the crisis for political purposes. At Fawcett's request board secretary John Mount polled the Ohio State trustees to seek their advice. They expressed surprise at the severity of the problem as described by the governor and also doubted that Rhodes had the legal authority to do

3.2. James A. Rhodes is sworn in as governor on January 14, 1963, as his family looks on. From left to right are daughters Sue, Sherri, and Saundra, and wife Helen. Sue and Saundra were students in Ohio State's College of Education at the time. Rhodes would dominate the Statehouse in the 1960s and have a great deal of influence on the university. (*Makio*)

what he was doing. Nevertheless, they counseled it would not be in the university's interest to appear uncooperative in the face of a crisis, and they urged Fawcett to comply with the governor's plan.[25] University administrators followed up with additional austerity measures, including suspension of equipment purchases, a modified travel freeze, limits on the purchase of supplies, and a partial hiring freeze.

In March, Rhodes introduced his long-awaited budget for the two years from July 1, 1963, to June 30, 1965. Declaring his austerity measures a success, he proposed a 16 percent increase in higher education funding for the biennium, along with a balanced budget and no new taxes. Ohio State officials believed the increases were not sufficient in the face of expected enrollment growth. Testifying before the Ohio House, Fawcett argued that aid per pupil would actually decline 11 percent over the biennium because of unfunded increases in enrollment.[26] Fawcett made the same case before the Ohio Senate in May, but in the end it didn't make much difference. The legislature passed the governor's budget pretty much as submitted. That also meant a 13.6 percent hike in tuition, which kept it the highest among the public universities in the Big Ten.

While the increase in tuition and state operating dollars helped pay day-to-day expenses, it wasn't nearly enough to make a dent in the backlog of academic facilities, which needed state capital dollars. As the arrival dates of the huge freshman classes of 1964 and 1965 grew closer, university officials got testier. Speaking to a conference of school supervisors in February, Ronald Thompson, executive dean for special services, referred to the oft-quoted statistic that the number of freshmen at Ohio State would increase 50 percent by 1965. "It would be impossible to obtain the money, make the plans, draw the blueprints, let the contracts and build the necessary facilities in time," Thompson lamented. "The students will come whether we're ready or not, and we must meet these needs as best we can."[27]

The university's efforts had suffered an unexpected blow two months earlier. Officials had been able to make progress in adding housing by floating university bonds backed with room and board fees paid by the student occupants. Construction was proceeding at a furious pace, but on the afternoon of December 3 an explosion rocked the site of the new dormitories on north campus. The blast lifted the roof of one building a hundred feet into the air and was heard more than three miles away. Three pickup trucks parked nearby were crushed under debris. Nine construction workers were injured, three seriously enough to require overnight hospitalization. A crowd of spectators gathered at the scene, hampering recovery efforts.

Damage was estimated at $250,000, but that was the least of the problems. The explosion was caused by a leak in a gas line at the Royer Commons construction site. The commons was scheduled to open in just eight months to feed the 1,200 students who would be living in the new residence halls.

UNWELCOME PARTNERS

As it turned out, Governor Rhodes was willing to support more state dollars for facility construction. But in exchange, Ohio's universities got something they didn't want. In February, Rhodes fulfilled a campaign promise by introducing legislation to establish the Ohio Board of Regents. The board was meant to serve as a coordinating body for the state's many independent colleges and universities that would help them operate more efficiently and better prepare for the expected onslaught of students, now fewer than 18 months away.

This proved to be anathema to Ohio's universities, who feared their autonomy would be reduced. Fawcett testified against the bill, along with a delegation of university presidents, but they soon learned Ohio's new governor was not to be trifled with politically. Rhodes privately told them they had a choice: drop their opposition to the regents bill and get a big slice of a $300 million capital improvement bond issue he was preparing, or oppose him on the issue and take their chances on getting little, if anything, out of the bond issue.

On May 20, 1963, Ohio State came out in favor of the bond proposal and quietly dropped its opposition to the regents bill. The other universities did the same. By the time the legislature ended its session, the governor had his biennial budget with no new taxes, as he had proposed; he had a Board of Regents bill; and he had university support for his bond issue.[28]

While Ohio State faced a dramatic increase in more assertive students, it also now had to deal with a new player at the head of the state political establishment who knew how to get things done. When these forces were in line with what the university wanted to do, it would be smooth sailing. When they were not, it would be a rough road.

SOCIETY: NUCLEAR NIGHTMARE

The Ohio State campus looked particularly lush in the fall of 1962, the result of a three-year beautification program of planting and landscaping. But along with the riot of fall colors, a crisis was unfolding that could plunge the United States and the Soviet Union into a nuclear exchange and unleash a level of destruction unparalleled in the history of humankind.

What became known as the Cuban Missile Crisis began when a U.S. reconnaissance aircraft detected signs of the construction of Soviet missile installations in Cuba. If missiles were allowed to be activated, they could threaten every major population center in the eastern United States and dramatically reorder the balance of power in favor of the Soviet Union.

Rumors about the activity had been building for weeks. On October 22 President Kennedy asked for time on all three television networks that evening to address the nation.

That afternoon at the Ohio Union Conference Theater, Leo B. Lott, an assistant professor of political science, told a near-capacity audience at a previously scheduled talk that one possible course of action would be a naval blockade of Cuba. Another would be an outright invasion—but that would be courting trouble, Lott said, because U.S. forces would be confronting Russian soldiers already on the island.[29]

That evening students, faculty, and staff clustered around their TVs to see what the president had to say. Kennedy explained the nature of the threat and announced a naval quarantine to intercept Soviet ships delivering more missiles to Cuba, just as Lott had predicted. The next day the campus waited along with people across the country and throughout the world to see what the Russians would do. Would they turn their ships around or try to fight their way through?

Because President Fawcett was on a business trip to New York and unavailable for comment, John Mount, his administrative assistant and secretary to his cabinet, spoke for the university. Mount chose his words carefully: "This is a very serious matter, one that all of us should be deeply concerned about. In times like this all of us must have confidence in our national leadership." Faculty members, who usually were prepared to give their opinions on a variety of issues, were quiet. Foster Reah Dulles of the history department told the *Lantern* he could offer no significant statement: "It is a sudden and shocking development. I do not know what to say. I do not want to pretend to be an expert on Cuba when I am not."[30]

Individual students expressed their opinions in a series of anonymous interviews published in the *Lantern* a few days later. One student said she was thinking of going home because she didn't want to die at Ohio State. Another said: "All they would have to do is sink one ship . . . just one . . . and we've all had it." Others were less pessimistic. "This is the first really good, decisive thing Kennedy has done. I'm a Republican, but I respect him for this," said one student. Several women claimed they would enlist if there was a war. There was also the predictable gallows humor. A few students said what many no doubt were thinking: "At least there's no need to study for finals."[31]

On October 24 Fawcett issued a statement to the university community. While his words were designed to reassure people and encourage them to continue about their business, the implications were unsettling. "A study of campus buildings . . . is being used to mark the locations that can be identified for the maximum safety available to us at this point in time. . . . Emergency plans in dormitories and in the health services are in a state of readiness for use if required."[32] "If required" meant in the event of mass casualties from radiation.

In fact, Kennedy administration officials, not wanting to induce panic, were encouraging people to continue activities as normal, even as the crisis intensified. That Friday evening Fred Waring and his Wonderful World of Music performed as scheduled in Mershon Auditorium. And on Saturday—the day the crisis came closest to war when the Soviets shot down a U.S. reconnaissance plane over Cuba, killing the pilot—a crowd of 82,540 gathered at Ohio Stadium to watch the Buckeyes beat Wisconsin 18–14.

On Sunday morning, October 28, Radio Moscow announced that Soviet premier Nikita Khrushchev had ordered his ships to turn around and head home. He also removed his existing missiles in exchange for a public pledge from Kennedy not to invade Cuba and a secret pledge to remove U.S. missiles pointed at the USSR from Turkey. The world heaved a collective sigh of relief. The worst crisis of the Cold War was over.

Fawcett's assurances that Ohio State was prepared for such a crisis turned out to be only partially correct. Information made public shortly afterward revealed that a considerable amount of work remained to be done. For example, while the university did have designated fallout shelters in the basements of 27 buildings, the 12,000 spaces available were not enough to accommodate even half the students, much less faculty and staff and their families. In addition, the shelters weren't stocked with water, food, or other supplies that would be necessary for survival underground for the desired two weeks. As the nation and the campus reflected on Thanksgiving Day that year, they had a lot more to be grateful for than they realized.[33]

YEAR OF THE SYMPOSIUM

Ohio State hosted an unusually large number of symposia during the 1962–63 school year, as experts from throughout the world tried to make sense of the changes sweeping across the landscape. They dealt with topics such as "explosive forces" in Latin America, deinstitutionalization of mental patients, the legal status of Berlin, the Romantic Era, and the future of newspapers.

The most contentious exchange involved academic freedom and came at a February symposium sponsored by the Student Senate on "the student and the university." Fawcett opened the event with a defense of Ohio State's academic reputation before a capacity crowd of 500 at the Ohio Historical Society Auditorium.

Pointing to the establishment of new programs in Slavic languages, Chinese, and geodetic science; the use of new technologies such as closed circuit TV; and the acquisition of a nuclear reactor, Fawcett argued that the university was in a stronger position nationally than at any time in its history. He also took on critics of the Speakers Rule: "The faculty and students of this university do today enjoy great latitude in discussion of controversial issues. Not only do we have from 4,000 to 5,000 off-campus speakers appearing here each year, who incidentally express a wide variety of opinions, we also have an atmosphere of open discussion among our faculty."[34]

Other notable visitors to campus that year included Billy Graham, who addressed a capacity crowd at Mershon in January while another 200,000 watched on television. Graham described the 20th century as an "age of fear," but said he saw hope in young people. When Ohio Staters announced that the popular folksinging trio of Peter, Paul, and Mary would play the same venue in April, all 3,100 seats were sold in 23 hours, a Mershon record. Alumnus and renowned playwright Jerome Lawrence pinch hit as commencement speaker in June when *Washington Post* publisher Phil Graham had to cancel. Lawrence, who co-authored

Inherit the Wind and *Auntie Mame,* told his audience: "Don't diminish or underrate the power of one vote or one angry or disapproving voice. . . . There is no number larger than one, human being."[35]

SUMMER OF DREAMS

With the resolution of the Cuban Missile Crisis behind him and a growing economy ahead, President Kennedy seemed to finally be finding his voice after two and a half years of strife. In a remarkable 15-day stretch in June, Kennedy laid out his vision in three memorable addresses: a peace overture to the Soviets at an American University commencement ceremony; a nationally televised talk on civil rights the next evening; and a rousing defense of a noncommunist West Berlin before 200,000 appreciative citizens of that city.

Two months later, Martin Luther King Jr. delivered what many argue was the most powerful address of the century. Speaking from the steps of the Lincoln Memorial to a crowd of 200,000 people who'd come from across the country to support the civil rights bill stalled in Congress, King told them in his booming voice: "I have a dream that my four little children will one day live in a nation where they will not be judged by the color of their skin but by the content of their character."

Ohio State was on summer break when these speeches were made, but their influence still reverberated among students and faculty. In particular, the growing struggle over equal rights for black citizens would capture the imagination of young people and have an enormous effect on the campus and the country for the remainder of the decade and beyond.

CHAPTER 4

WINDS OF CHANGE

(1963–64)

Students were grinding through their last midterms before the holidays when the assassination of John F. Kennedy in November 1963 shocked the nation. An anxious public found reassurance that things would return to normal, but the forces that would tear the campus and the country apart in the years ahead were already present and picking up momentum. A protest in February by 4,000 students over the arrest of a coed for an unpaid jaywalking ticket attracted the most attention, but less celebrated issues would have a more lasting impact. Students organized a repeal of dress rules, women found a new consciousness, and civil rights activists conducted the university's first sit-in. Issue One provided a funding boost to construct more buildings for a growing student population, but success in teaching undergraduates proved more elusive.

4.1. Students climb on top of High Street buses during the February 1964 jaywalking protest. (*Lantern*)

STUDENTS: SEARCHING FOR JUSTICE

STUDENT HOUSING: UNREST IN THE PROVINCES

Ohio State officials had known for some time that one of their biggest challenges was to find safe, convenient, affordable housing for the growing number of students. Historically, the university had left that up to area landlords, but students and their parents now demanded more. In 1956 the trustees approved an ambitious 10-year plan to expand university-built housing. It would be financed by 30-year bonds to be repaid by housing fees.

In Phase I, six high-rise dormitories with a capacity for 3,000 students opened along 11th Avenue between 1958 and 1963. Phase II consisted of another 5,800 spaces on the north end of campus near Woodruff Avenue. Phase III would be a yet-to-be-determined number of spaces near the Olentangy River. While the south campus high-rises had to be wedged into limited space, the new north campus residential area would be designed from the ground up to fit on cleared land as a more self-contained community.

Five of the north campus dormitories opened in the fall of 1963, providing accommodations for 1,300 students. More would follow. The students loved them. To emphasize the break from the past, the buildings were referred to as "houses," not "halls." The four-person apartment-like spaces had been tested by students living in mock-ups before the plans were finalized. They told the designers they liked the air-conditioning and the semiprivate bathrooms, but women asked for, and received, more space for clothes.[1]

Next, a governing structure needed to be established. Staff from the offices of the dean of men and dean of women worked with students for nearly a year to establish what would be called the North Campus Student Association. Everyone involved seemed to agree the association should reflect the coeducational aspect of an environment where men's and women's living quarters were in close proximity and they shared the same dining facility, Royer Commons. (Despite the explosion the preceding December, the commons not only opened on time but won an award for its design.)

It didn't take long for north campus residents to see themselves as having much in common with the outer provinces of the Roman Empire who suffered under the edicts of Imperial Rome. Fall quarter had barely begun when students objected to the traditional dress code adopted for Royer Commons. Three hundred residents signed a petition protesting the standards developed by their new student association. The association's leaders agreed to put a more relaxed dress code up for a vote by the residents. The revised code would allow sweatshirts at breakfast and lunch and bermuda shorts at lunch only. T-shirts and rubber thongs would continue to be banned at all meals. And male students would still be expected to dress up for Sunday dinner and special occasions. The revised rules were approved overwhelmingly (575–146) in a special referendum. Sixty percent of the eligible students voted, an unusually high participation rate for any kind of campus election.

That caught the attention of the Women's Residence Hall Council, the governing body for the south campus women's dorms. A week later, WRHC announced it would take aim at the rule prohibiting slacks in the south campus dining halls unless the temperature was under 10 degrees at 8 a.m. That in turn caught the attention of the dean of women's office. Associate Dean Ruth H. Weimer responded with a letter emphasizing the importance of what she called three "basic policies" of dining room dress: a clean and neat appearance; skirts for lunch and dinner, except Saturday lunch, when bermudas or slacks were permissible; and hair combed, rather than in pin curls or rollers.[2]

Nevertheless, when they returned to school after Christmas break, WRHC representatives approved a resolution recommending to the dean that their students be allowed to make their own decisions about when to wear slacks to the cafeterias during winter quarter. The *Lantern* editorialized in support the next day: "Women got the right to vote in 1920, but Ohio State dormitory coeds still do not have the right to dress as they please in 1964."[3]

The dean's office didn't like that at all. WRHC officials were told their recommendations had been rejected and, in fact, the dean wanted a rule prohibiting women from wearing slacks in the dining halls except on an "extremely bad day." When asked what constituted an extremely bad day, the group was told it meant when classes were canceled due to bad weather, which was actually more restrictive than the current rule. "This is not an issue of slacks or no slacks," said Rosemary Scurria, a WRHC delegate from Paterson Hall. "It is a question whether the women on this campus have self-government or not."[4]

The dean's office claimed the rules were needed because visitors to campus might see women in slacks in the dining halls and therefore think less of the university. The *Lantern* jumped on that line of reasoning, pointing out that plenty of visitors toured the Ohio Union food facilities, where there was no dress code, and that many "oddly dressed characters . . . frequent[ed the Ohio Union] Tavern."[5]

Even though both groups felt strongly about the issue, neither WRHC nor the Women's Self Government Association (WSGA) was ready to take on the dean's office directly. WRHC had already grudgingly passed a resolution approving the new, stricter policy favored by the dean at its February 17 meeting, rather than what it had proposed earlier. At its meeting nine days later, WSGA passed a resolution that women students should be allowed to use their own discretion as to how to dress. "We want to encourage the use of mature judgment in regard to proper attire," said the group's president, Carol Davis, but she felt it necessary to elaborate on her remarks by saying, somewhat unconvincingly, "This resolution has nothing to do with the controversy between Women's Residence Hall Council and the Dean of Women's Office concerning dress rules."[6]

WOMEN: MOVING TOWARD EMANCIPATION

In addition to student pressure to roll back dress codes, the 1963–64 school year saw the beginning of intensified interest in more equal treatment of women. The proportion of women students at Ohio State was slowly increasing. After a low of 19.8 percent in the wake of the GI Bill rush in 1948, it had grown every year since and reached a high of 33.1 percent that fall. At that rate, the number of women would equal the number of men by the mid-1980s.

By January 1964, 190 women students were living in off-campus apartments as a result of rule changes made the previous year. A *Lantern* reporter wrote that all the women she talked with were happy with their arrangements. They said they didn't stay out any later than they had before, but they enjoyed opportunities such as cooking dinner for their dates. Nevertheless, the dean's office made it clear that living in an apartment was a privilege. If a woman over 21 wanted to move to an apartment, she had to first fill out an application and then be interviewed by the assistant dean of women to confirm her suitability for apartment life and the suitability of the place she wanted to live.[7]

Guest speakers highlighted the challenges facing professional women in what was still very much a man's world. Addressing a group of university women, Marion Stephenson, vice president of administration at NBC Radio, pointed out that only 3.8 percent of business executives were women. That meant women had to "over-prove" themselves if they expected to succeed. "Think like a man, but understand like a woman," Stephenson said.[8]

At the time only 10 percent of medical students at Ohio State were women. A group of physicians and students laid out barriers facing women in the field at a panel sponsored by the local chapter of the American Medical Women's Association. The members pointed out that the pressures involved in earning a medical degree made raising a family at the same time difficult.[9]

The year ended on a positive note when on June 4 the Council on Student Affairs announced it had accepted a WSGA recommendation to liberalize the hated Apartment Rule. All nonfreshman women and freshman women over 21 would be allowed to visit a man's apartment without worrying about getting thrown out of school if not accompanied by a university-approved companion. The new rule would be effective beginning fall quarter 1965.

Still, vestiges of unequal treatment persisted. Joan Leitzel, a newly minted Ph.D. from Indiana University was hired by the math department in 1965 as one of its few women faculty members. Her husband, also a new Ph.D., was hired by the department a few weeks later. Her college dean subsequently told her she was fortunate to be selected because spousal hires were frowned upon. "Research shows smart men tend to not marry smart women," he said, "and we don't want to jeopardize the quality of our faculty."[10]

BLACK STUDENTS: SIT-INS FOR EMANCIPATION

The civil rights movement would have an enormous impact on American society and college campuses in the 1960s. Young people were drawn to the call to reconcile long-standing contradictions between the country's professed beliefs and its treatment of minorities through nonviolent civil disobedience.

The first application of civil disobedience involving Ohio State students occurred in October 1963, just two months after the March on Washington for Jobs and Freedom, the groundbreaking civil rights demonstration. It would fail in the short run, but would open the door to more successful efforts over time.

Both the university and the city of Columbus had a long history of discrimination against black students in on-campus and off-campus housing.[11] During the first week of October a group of Ohio State activists calling themselves Students for Human Rights sent two teams, each with two white students and one black student, to inquire about renting at Northwest Gardens apartments at the corner of North Star and Kinnear Roads west of campus. In both cases the white students were told they could move in as soon as they paid the deposit. The black students were told they would have to fill out an application and wait for their paperwork to be cleared. When one of the white students told the resident manager he was acting as an intermediary for a black student, he was told the black student would receive an eviction notice if any of the other tenants objected.[12]

The rental units in question were owned by Buckeye Property Management. The company's co-owner was Leo Yassenoff, a former Ohio State football player and a prominent community philanthropist and real estate developer who owned the Ohio Stater Inn on High Street, among other properties. The next day pickets showed up at both Northwest Gardens and the Ohio Stater Inn. A spokesperson for Students for Human Rights called on Yassenoff to affirm that Northwest Gardens would no longer discriminate against black tenants. Yassenoff refused to respond. Picketing continued for another 13 days. On October 22 several members of the group staged a sit-in in front of Yassenoff's home. Police were called, and two men, Arthur A. Zebbs, the Columbus leader of CORE (Congress of Racial Equality), and David G. McConnell, an associate professor of optometry, were arrested for trespassing and disturbing the peace, along with seven students.

Three days later Students for Human Rights called off all demonstrations for an unspecified time in the hope of spurring negotiations. It didn't work. Neither did approaching Yassenoff through intermediaries. On November 18 a group of demonstrators conducted a sit-in at the

Buckeye Property Management headquarters to demand a meeting with Yassenoff. Police arrested them.[13]

Eleven protestors, most of them Ohio State students, were ultimately found guilty of trespassing and related charges. The municipal judges handed out stiff sentences that included large fines and time in the city workhouse, but reduced the fines and suspended the jail time if the individuals involved managed to avoid further convictions. At first the demonstrators talked about appealing the decisions or deliberately going to jail instead of paying even a small fine.

That put Ohio State in an interesting situation. It supposedly supported nondiscrimination in housing its students; however, Yassenoff was a prominent member of the community and a supporter of the university. Ohio State officials decided to punt. They announced they would not discipline the students involved, but also would not intervene with the landlord.[14]

The students eventually decided they could not fight city hall on their own. The fines were paid. The group disbanded. In its place arose an organization calling itself SCORE (Student Congress on Racial Equality). Spokesperson Ann Mayer explained why the old group had folded its tent: "Too much organization, perhaps too much ambition, and not enough people."[15] She promised to continue the campaign against Buckeye Property Management, but activists soon found something else on which to focus their energy: the sweeping civil rights bill before Congress.

STUDENT GOVERNMENT: NOT THE NSA AGAIN!

What do you do after you've suffered a shellacking at the ballot box? If you are Ohio State's supporters of the National Student Association, you try again.

Despite the decisive vote to withdraw from the left-leaning NSA the previous October, supporters led by Student Senate president Paul Schwitzgebel argued that the NSA had reformed itself and deserved a second chance. Schwitzgebel's senate colleagues agreed and by an 18–7 vote put the issue of re-joining the NSA on the ballot for November 1963.

Both sides brought in reinforcements. Supporters of the NSA called in national president Greg Gallo. Opponents countered with Indiana

University's conservative organizing whiz, Tom C. Huston (later of Watergate fame).[16] Still, the issue did not energize the student body. Few people showed up for the debates. NSA supporters did manage to pick up the *Lantern*'s endorsement, which they did not have the first time, but when the votes came in, they showed how little influence the newspaper or the Student Senate president had. The referendum failed 3,085 to 1,447, nearly identical to the margin of the previous year. "Most students have no desire to be affiliated with anything larger than themselves," a disappointed Schwitzgebel lamented.[17]

Meanwhile, graduate and professional students had already succeeded in getting administration approval to disaffiliate themselves from the undergraduate-dominated Student Senate. Their group, the Council of Graduate Students, promptly voted to join the NSA.

In the senate elections in March, the more conservative Buckeye Political Party reasserted its control over undergraduate student government. BPP presidential candidate Stan Darling, a member of Sigma Pi fraternity, beat Student Congress Party nominee Jeff Schwartz, the younger brother of Niki Schwartz, 3,651 to 3,046. The BPP also recaptured control of the senate from the SCP by a vote of 25 to 15.

A DARK DAY IN NOVEMBER

The message from United Press International clattered off the *Lantern* teletype machine at 1:45 p.m. on a rainy Friday, November 22: "STAY OFF THIS WIRE . . . STAY OFF THIS WIRE . . . PRESIDENT KENNEDY HAS BEEN WOUNDED SERIOUSLY—PERHAPS FATALLY." Staff members gathered around their transistor radios to wait for further news. Shortly after 2 p.m. the teletype rang 12 times. *Lantern* city editor Jean Heller knew what that meant. "They only use twelve bells for two things," she said, "either when war is declared or when the president dies. When I heard the bells I knew he was dead. I put my head down on the wire machine and cried."[18]

Word spread quickly across campus. Freshman Sharon George heard the announcement over the public address system in the Ohio Union. "There was kind of a gasp," she said.[19] Professor John C. Rule walked into his History of the French Revolution class at 2 o'clock. Most of the students had already heard something, and they waited nervously to

4.2. Students' faces reflect the events of November 22, 1963. (*Lantern*)

learn what he had to add. "We were supposed to discuss the execution of Louis XVI today," Rule said. "But there is something far more important for you to think about, something within yourselves. The President of the United States has been shot. . . . Nothing is ever solved this way. . . . Louis' death did not solve anything. . . . You are dismissed."[20]

Many other faculty members let their classes out early that afternoon. Mabel Freeman, a sophomore at the time, later recalled that a distraught department secretary went from classroom to classroom to deliver the news. Freshman Shirley Smith told the *Lantern* that when she and her friends in Baker Hall got the news, "it was terrible—all down the halls there were sobs and girls screaming and crying."[21]

Campus bars, usually crowded by late Friday afternoon, reported a 50 percent drop in business. Those who did show up sat quietly and watched the TV coverage. Staff members trekked into the *Lantern* newsroom all afternoon offering to help. Phone lines were tied up, but the paper managed to get an extra edition out by 5 p.m. By then flags were at half-staff across campus, and according to one report, "people walked along the street as if in a daze."[22]

As the day came to a close, university officials faced a number of decisions about what to do: cancel, postpone, or carry on? Sixty thousand tickets had been sold for the next day's football game against Michigan in Ann Arbor, including 12,200 in Columbus. President Novice Fawcett talked by phone with Michigan president Harlan Hatcher Friday evening. Both decided it would be best to go ahead. At 7:15 a.m. Saturday, the last of three excursion trains left from Union Station headed north for Ann Arbor. When the train arrived south of Toledo two hours later, the passengers were told the game had been called off and would be played the following Saturday. Michigan governor George Romney had intervened, telling both Michigan and Michigan State that their games that day should be canceled out of respect for the late president.[23]

After waiting two hours in Toledo for a new crew, the train began the slog back to Columbus. *Lantern* reporter Thomas Buckingham was on board. "No one really cared, it seemed," he wrote. "Word that the trip was over was met with silence and a few half-hearted protests."[24]

After the murder of suspected assassin Lee Harvey Oswald by Jack Ruby on live TV on Sunday, the dazed nation faced a day of mourning on Monday, November 25. Classes and other events were canceled, and all government offices and most businesses were closed. The *Lantern* produced a 12-page issue that tried to put the events in perspective. It included an interview with two faculty experts in political science, Harvey C. Mansfield and Myron Q. Hale. The two foresaw few changes in national policy, but Hale predicted (incorrectly, it turned out) a year of "standing, waiting, watching" during which the late president's programs "will all take an immediate setback if not a total loss."[25]

President Fawcett presided over a memorial service in front of the Administration Building at noon, the same time as Kennedy's funeral in Washington. For the most part faculty, staff, and students stayed home and watched the events unfold on TV. Some, including Student Senate president Stan Darling and two fraternity brothers, drove all day to be in Washington on Monday for the funeral.[26]

The following Saturday the rescheduled football game was played in Ann Arbor. Ohio State won 14–10 before a record low turnout of 36,424. "We all played for the sake of self-respect, but I don't believe anybody's heart was 100 percent into it," former Ohio State player and Greg Lashutka recalled in 2014.[27]

As students headed home for the Thanksgiving holiday, a *Lantern* editorial seemed to capture the prevailing mood—a deep sense of unease about the havoc caused by what appeared to be a lone gunman with a

$12 rifle and unclear motives. Yet the *Lantern* also pointed out how, despite the circumstances, power had been transferred peacefully and a legitimate elected government remained in control: "We can be thankful that this nation is so constituted that it cannot fall into anarchy. Under our constitution the President cannot be killed, only the man holding the office."[28]

A few days later the paper reported that several groups of students from Ohio State had joined an estimated 45,000 others who waited in line up to eight hours to visit the late president's grave on Sunday, December 1. Senior Jim Zavocky explained: "It was the least we could do."[29]

JUSTICE FOR JAYWALKERS

One day at the end of fall quarter, sophomore Marjorie Cocoziello and a friend walked across High Street between 14th and 15th Avenues outside the crosswalk. A Columbus police officer spotted them and issued a ticket for jaywalking.

As in many cities, it was illegal to cross a street anywhere other than in a marked crosswalk. However, enforcement in Columbus was particularly aggressive. According to John Moore of the police department: "The law might save only one life a month, but that makes it worthwhile."[30]

Cocoziello later said the police officer who ticketed her told her he had a daughter her age and was sympathetic, so he suggested that the women split the $5 fine (about $38 in 2015 dollars). She said she planned to pay, but forgot about the incident in the end-of-quarter rush.

Two months later, on February 10, a Columbus police officer showed up at Cocoziello's sorority house to arrest her for failure to pay the ticket. At first, she and her sorority sisters thought it was a joke. It wasn't. She was taken downtown in a paddy wagon.

At police headquarters Cocoziello and her friends learned she could either pay the fine or post bail and come back later to appear in court. They called the father of one of the group, who was an attorney in Chicago. He advised them to post bail and appear before a judge.

Things went downhill from there. What Cocoziello and her friends apparently did not understand was that under standard Columbus police procedure, she would be booked and processed while bail was being posted. Normally, this took only about 10 minutes. This time it didn't. While her friends worked on finding the money to post the $13 bail (the $5 fine plus $8 in court costs), Cocoziello was searched, left in a darkened cell, and ignored when she asked to make a phone call.

Meanwhile, her friends were having trouble coming up with the bail. They were 13 cents short when a sympathetic police officer gave them the difference. Cocoziello was released into their custody, physically well but emotionally shaken. "I don't know what will happen now, I'm a nervous wreck," she told *Lantern* reporter Jean Heller the next day.

In court that same day, the entire room, including Judge Alan Schwarzwalder, broke into laughter when the bailiff read the charge against Cocoziello. She pleaded no contest, as she had been advised. Upon hearing her story, the judge told her, "After all you've been through, I'm only going to charge you a penny." He then suspended her sentence.[31] The case was closed legally, but the controversy was just beginning.

The next morning, February 12, the *Lantern* published Heller's interview with Cocoziello from the day before. Heller, who went on to become a prize-winning reporter, did a masterful job of putting the reader in Cocoziello's shoes. The newspaper devoted its front page to the story, including a banner headline that read "Coed in Jail 1½ Hours; Crime? Jaywalking." "People, Place Frighten Her," said a subhead.[32]

RED ROVER, RED ROVER

At about 4:30 that afternoon students started jaywalking in twos and threes near the intersection of High Street and 15th Avenue. "Red Rover, Red Rover, you kids cross on over," they shouted to each other, and "We'll win! We can't be beat! Where we want, we'll cross the street." The crowd quickly swelled to 500. Police scrambled to reroute traffic. A few minutes later the WCOL Radio Newsmobile arrived, welcomed by loud cheering. By 5:30 all traffic had stopped and frustrated motorists were honking their horns.

The Columbus media would later blame the *Lantern* for inciting the event with its front-page coverage. The *Lantern* countered that nothing had really happened until WCOL broadcast a report at 3:55 p.m. that a demonstration was "brewing." A High Street record store then blared the WCOL newscasts out to the street via its public address system.

When the TV stations arrived at 5:45, the *Lantern* reported, the camera crews urged students to shake their fists and yell, and they gleefully complied.[33]

By 6 p.m. traffic, including 20 city buses, was backed up for six blocks. The crowd grew to between 4,000 and 5,000 and, as is typical, included a small core of activists and a larger, more amorphous number of spectators and fence-sitters. Some students jumped onto the roofs of the buses, which in those days ran off electrical wires overhead, and pulled down the connectors, further immobilizing them. Not everyone approved. One Student Senate member lamented, "I think it's too bad we don't get this excited about civil rights." Another group of students helped two elderly ladies navigate the traffic jam. But more typical responses came from the coed who declared, "I'm watching for kicks," and the one who said, "I think it's funny. I've never seen [a demonstration] before."

Sometime after 6, parts of the crowd decided to head downtown to police headquarters. Before they reached First Avenue, their numbers had dwindled to 200. At the station they sang songs and chanted, "We want the chief! We want the chief!" When Student Senate president Paul Schwitzgebel emerged from the building and encouraged the crowd to go home, he was roundly booed. Police chief George Scholer then came out and told the crowd, "You've gathered people who are not from Ohio State and who are damaging property. The crowds are giving Ohio State a bad name."

"Why did you put her in jail?" someone yelled back. The crowd finally left after Scholer said he would meet with a delegation of students the next day. The group headed back up High Street sometime after 7 p.m., picking up others along the way and growing to about 500. They banged on cars, stopped buses, and chanted as they marched.

Back at High and 15th some of those who had stayed behind had started a bonfire to stay warm. A second one was lit about 9:50, but people soon started drifting away. By the time a fire truck showed up at 11, almost everyone had gone home.

The seven hours of activity incurred more than $1,000 in damages and $10,000 in police overtime. Protesters smashed the windows of one car and dented its roof when the driver brushed against a young woman trying to move out of traffic. Long's Bookstore lost three tables and a bookstand worth $200 to the bonfire. Physical damage to city buses was minimal, but hundreds of riders were inconvenienced. Six students were arrested on charges ranging from traffic violations to assaulting a police officer.[34]

AFTERMATH

The university moved quickly to contain the damage. The following day John Bonner, the executive dean for student relations, said that student rioters would face disciplinary action in addition to any legal action from city. The *Lantern* ran a front-page editorial condemning the violence, but also putting blame on the "irresponsible" radio commentary. That evening the Student Senate unanimously passed a resolution apologizing to the city. However, the senate also made it clear it was not apologizing for the demonstration itself. In the same resolution it called on Schwitzgebel to recommend measures "to prevent violations of five students' due process in Columbus." For his part, Schwitzgebel expressed "disappointment" in the *Lantern* coverage.[35]

George Scholer, the police chief, released the results of his own investigation the same day. While they corroborated the *Lantern* story in some ways, they also highlighted significant differences. For example, Scholer reported Cocoziello had not been strip-searched. Instead, she was instructed to remove her shoes and unbutton her blouse so the matron could make sure she hadn't hidden anything—which was standard practice. In fact, a careful reading of Jean Heller's interview made it clear that Cocoziello did not claim she was strip-searched. A subheadline in the story read "Stripped and Searched," which many readers misinterpreted.

Scholer confirmed Cocoziello's cell was dark when she entered, not by design but because the light bulb had burned out. It was subsequently replaced. The chief also confirmed Cocoziello was not permitted initially to make a phone call to her father, a construction official in New Jersey, because it was long distance and needed the approval of a supervisor. She was eventually allowed to make the call. He also maintained she was in the cell for only 20 minutes, not an hour and a half.[36]

The *Lantern* published nearly 30 letters regarding the incident. A few of them lamented the lack of student interest in other causes, such as civil rights, but most supported the actions of the Columbus police and blamed the *Lantern* for blowing things out of proportion. Both the

Dispatch and the *Citizen-Journal* accused the paper of "tabloid" journalism and "inflammatory" coverage.[37]

Even the Alumni Association weighed in. Secretary and alumni magazine editor Jack Fullen, a former *Lantern* editor, defended the newspaper against the attacks, particularly those from the *Dispatch*. The March issue of the magazine featured a comparison of *Dispatch* coverage of the Rose Bowl protests a little more than two years earlier—a cause the *Dispatch* supported—with its coverage of the jaywalking protest. The *Dispatch* referred to the Rose Bowl protests as "orderly . . . demonstration[s]," while it referred to the jaywalking protest as a "riot."[38] The *Lantern* advisers feared President Fawcett would use this as an excuse to censor the newspaper. The anxiety increased when Fawcett asked Dean Bonner to investigate the matter, because Bonner had clashed regularly with the *Lantern* in the past.

On February 22 municipal judge Tom Moody ruled on the cases of the four students charged with non-traffic-related offenses ranging from disorderly conduct to assaulting a police officer. Moody found three of them guilty but handed down the relatively mild sentence of having to write an essay on a topic selected by him. The fourth student voluntarily agreed to submit an essay. Two students would be tried later in traffic court for failure to obey an officer's command.

The university was much less forgiving. The two students convicted of resisting arrest were suspended, and five others were placed on probation. Bonner detailed this (but did not name the students) in a report to Fawcett on March 4. He also recommended the university send a letter to all parents along with winter quarter grades, reminding them of the consequences facing students engaging in riotous activities. What Bonner did not do was blame the *Lantern*. His report concluded the demonstration was a product of "a series of events and could not be attributed to any one specific incident," and went on to praise the professionalism of the *Lantern* staff. Bonner found WCOL's arrival on the scene was prompted by a phone call from a student in Park Hall who had nothing to do with the demonstration but was hoping for a reward the station paid for news tips. (He didn't get one.)[39]

Like the Rose Bowl demonstrations, all this activity didn't accomplish much more than embarrassing those involved. The police looked heavy-handed, the *Lantern* inflammatory, the *Dispatch* hypocritical, and the students spoiled. Information reported by the *Citizen-Journal* shortly after the event put the issue in context. For all of 1963, Columbus police issued 239 jaywalking tickets in the university area, out of 1,776 citywide. Ninety-one percent of the tickets were paid on time, compared to 79 percent citywide.[40] Why the police felt they had to make an extreme example of Marjorie Cocoziello was never explained.

THE UNIVERSITY: WE LOVE ISSUE ONE

After spending the first six months of his term successfully imposing an austerity program on state agencies, Governor James Rhodes shifted gears to generating support for an ambitious state-funded construction plan. The proposal called for extending the cigarette tax of one cent per pack, due to expire in 1965, for another 10 years to fund construction bonds. Because the state would have to take on new debt, voter approval was required.

In a rare display of unity, the Ohio State family rallied to support the measure dubbed Issue One. President Fawcett told the *Lantern* that voters' approval of the financing plan would mean "we now have assurance help is on the way" in terms of building the facilities needed to accommodate the approaching tidal wave of students. The university's expected share of the bond proceeds would meet about two-thirds of its capital needs for the next six years. The remainder would be met by federal dollars and university funds.[41]

The Alumni Association provided support in the form of volunteers and money. The *Lantern,* the Faculty Council, and the Student Senate formally endorsed Issue One. Students sent 4,000 postcards to parents urging them to vote for the measure. Thomas F. Patton, chair of the board of trustees and president of Republic Steel in Cleveland, chaired the Citizens for Ohio's Future campaign. On November 5, 1963, voters responded. Issue One passed by more than 300,000 votes out of 1.8 million cast.

It didn't take long for state officials to turn on the spigot. Just three weeks later the Board of Regents announced plans for how the money would be distributed. Ohio State's share would be $70 million, almost half the total for all of higher education. The General Assembly approved the enabling legislation on December 5, including $8 million more for the regional campuses than the university had requested. The regents released the first round of funds on January 13, and on February 20 Ohio State's trustees approved going out for contracts on 10 projects—record speed for the often slow-turning wheels of the university and state bureaucracies.

Even more good news came from Washington in December when Congress passed a measure for $1.2 billion in federal construction assistance to colleges and universities. The bill had originally been proposed by President Kennedy and now moved forward with bipartisan support, including from Kennedy's successor, Lyndon B. Johnson. Ohio State could expect about $35 million for science, engineering, and medical facilities, in addition to the Issue One money.

INSTRUCTION: FRESHMEN DO NOT LOVE MATH BY TELEVISION

While the university scrambled to find ways to accommodate even more students, those already on campus were becoming increasingly vocal about their unhappiness with the instruction they were receiving. The Freshman Senate came out in January with a critical report on first-year instruction. The report reflected the results of 3,000 questionnaires distributed to freshmen during the first two weeks of fall quarter 1963. Respondents were asked to rate 126 courses as good, adequate, or poor. About 20 percent of the questionnaires were returned.

"Poor" was the most common response (1,040), followed by "adequate" (989) and "good" (617). Critics could argue the results were not representative, since presumably those who were unhappy were more likely to respond, but the magnitude of the negative responses still was unsettling. Two course sequences—Math by Television and Education 400, 401, and 408—tallied more poor ratings than good and adequate combined. Freshman Senate educational chair Timothy P. O'Reilly, whose committee tabulated the survey, pointed out two sets of complaints that permeated the responses: definite distaste for TV courses and concern about instructors who were not properly trained or motivated.[42]

A series of *Lantern* interviews with instructors who taught freshman courses elicited some sympathy for the students, but the instructors also said too many students came to Ohio State poorly prepared to do college-level work. Some lacked curiosity, they said, and others were too timid or disengaged to ask questions.[43] Comments made by one production supervisor for instructional television earlier that fall blamed the students: "College students are used to being entertained by TV. Most of them don't want to listen when it is instructional."[44]

The Freshmen Senate pushed the issue even further at its February 12 meeting by passing a resolution calling on the administration to "investigate possible solutions to the mounting problems concerning the quality of the graduate assistants," who did much of the freshman instruction. The best graduate students were siphoned off as assistants for prestigious research projects, senate members said, and the ones who remained were inadequately prepared for instructional duties.[45]

With a third of incoming freshmen requiring remedial math, John Mount, now vice president for educational services, told the Freshman Senate that some form of selective admissions would be necessary in the future. But Richard Armitage, dean of the graduate school, put the blame squarely on the university. He told a faculty meeting in March that Ohio State and other large American universities had lost the "art of teaching." "In our struggle to maintain a competitive quality of our graduate programs, we have recruited and promoted our faculty almost solely on the basis of published research," Armitage said. He acknowledged that many faculty and graduate students were good teachers. "But the fact remains that much good teaching goes unrewarded, that in some departments all 400-level freshman courses are taught by inexperienced and largely unsupervised graduate students, and that no one seems to be doing much to remedy this situation."[46]

In May the Faculty Council received a long-awaited report on improving instruction. The "Blueprint for Action" reflected the work of the Council on Instruction, a committee of the Faculty Council. It called for a review of service courses (those taught by one college for majors in another college) and greater separation between graduate and undergraduate instruction, and it made a strong recommendation to improve departmental training programs for inexperienced instructors.[47]

Speaking to an alumni group two weeks later, Fawcett said he favored a plan to create a two-year general college mainly for freshmen. Promising freshmen would be admitted to the main campus, he said, but others would be diverted to a new campus west of the Olentangy River. The campus could house up to 10,000 students, Fawcett predicted, and would allow the university to address the increasing "deluge of humanity that could conceivably swallow us in a sea of mediocrity."[48]

WE LOVE MORE COMMITTEES

How to reconcile all these proposals? Fawcett announced in June that he would appoint a special committee to review his proposal for a general college. He sent the Freshman Senate requests and the Blueprint for Action Committee recommendations to Fred Heimberger, chair of the Council on Instruction. As vice president for instruction and chair of faculties, Heimberger was Ohio State's highest ranking administrator after the president. And with 36 years at the university as a student, faculty member, and administrator, he certainly understood how the place worked. But he was now at the mandatory retirement age of 65. Fawcett, who'd inherited Heimberger from President Howard Bevis, thought he was an obstructionist and was not inclined to ask for a waiver, so Heimberger retired in June.[49] His successors would have to pick up the ball, but continued turnover in leadership positions would hamper the university's ability to make changes when they were needed most.

In what would turn out to be a controversial decision, another faculty committee recommended to Dean Donald Cottrell that the school run by the College of Education be phased out. University School, located in Ramseyer Hall, was established in 1932 as a center for research and experimentation in elementary and secondary education. All the teaching was done by Ohio State faculty, and many of the students were children of faculty and staff. The faculty committee majority believed research could be done more effectively in the city schools and the community. Ten members voted for the recommendation, and four opposed it. The controversy would continue until the school closed in 1968.[50]

RESEARCH: GLOBAL REACH

In just four years, from 1960 to 1964, the dollar amount of contract research at Ohio State had doubled, with the federal government providing 80 percent of the funding. The remainder came from private industry and foundations.

The impact of research grew, too, particularly in India, the world's second-most populous country. When the land grant colleges were established in the United States in the 1870s, their research was expected not only to create knowledge but to disseminate it in ways that benefited society. Experts from extension services flooded the country like missionaries, spreading the gospel of research-based seed selection, fertilization, irrigation, and crop rotation and helping American farmers become the most productive in the world.[51]

Beginning in the mid-1950s the Eisenhower administration joined with the Indian government to enlist America's top agricultural scientists in the war against hunger in India. U.S. policymakers were worried that if the country's fledgling democracy failed while an increasingly belligerent communist China seemed to be on the march, it would destabilize all of Asia.

Ohio State and the Universities of Missouri, Illinois, Kansas, and Tennessee agreed to work together to apply modern agricultural techniques developed in the United States. Ohio State signed its first contract in 1957 and took responsibility for three states in the northwest corner of India. The university contributed an average of at least 20 to 30 full-time faculty a year over an 11-year period. The effort paid off spectacularly. By the beginning of the 1970s India had moved from being plagued by near famine to what one historian called "sensational success" in self-sufficiency in food grains.[52]

Ohio State researchers made their mark elsewhere as well. In September 1963 sociologists Enrico L. Quarantelli and Russell R. Dynes won a five-year federal grant to travel all over the world in an effort to better understand how to manage disasters. Thus Ohio State's Disaster Research Center was born—the only group of its kind in the country at the time.

The Institute for Polar Studies, founded in 1960, sent its 30 to 35 faculty and staff to the North and South Poles numerous times during the following decade to do pioneering work in mapping and environmental studies.

While success in research advanced institutional and national goals, it also complicated Ohio State's traditional teaching mission. Experienced faculty members were being sent out of the classrooms and away from campus at a time when finding qualified instructors to address growing enrollments was already difficult. In the long run students would benefit from the knowledge the faculty members would gain, but in the short run it meant bigger classes and less experienced instructors.

RISE OF THE MEGAVERSITY

Officials at Ohio State and other large universities clearly believed size was now the key to greatness. Clark Kerr, president of the University of California system, was among them. Kerr coined the term "megaversity" to describe institutions such as Berkeley and Ohio State that captured most of the federal research dollars, taught large numbers of students, and made enormous positive contributions to society as a whole. Kerr acknowledged that undergraduate teaching suffered as a result. "There seems to be a 'point of no return' after which research, consulting, graduate instruction become so absorbing that faculty efforts can no longer be concentrated on undergraduate instruction as they once were," he wrote. "How to escape the cruel paradox that a superior faculty results in an inferior concern for undergraduate teaching is one of our more pressing problems."[53]

Kerr probably understood the megaversity better than anyone, but even he couldn't control it. His response to student protests at Berkeley in 1964 would eventually cost him his job.

SOCIETY: LET US CONTINUE

On November 27, 1963, President Lyndon Johnson sought to rally the country after the shock of the Kennedy assassination. His nationally televised "Let Us Continue" speech to a joint session of Congress reassured Americans that a peaceful transition had occurred; but the forces of change that had been gathering before the assassination would continue to press on as well.

VOICES FOR CHANGE

Over a 60-day period in the winter of 1963–64, three of the most influential voices calling for change spoke at Ohio State. Between them, they would help define a new role for women, a new way to look at moral choice, and a new meaning of racial equality. And a short time thereafter, one of the newest and most strident voices *against* change would have his say as well.

Betty Friedan, whose best-seller *The Feminine Mystique* is regarded by many as the manifesto of the women's movement, appeared on campus on December 3. Speaking to a packed house in the Ohio Historical Society Auditorium, she challenged the conventional wisdom that a woman's place was in the home. "Women have long been thought to be stupid, mindless, little housewife drudges who are only capable of cooking and keeping the sink clean," she told her audience. "When [women] find their own self-identity, then, and only then will they be able to make adult commitments to members of the opposite sex."[54]

When the Student Senate chose "the new moral challenge" as the theme for its winter symposium, Paul Tillich emerged as the favored choice for keynote speaker. The professor of religion at the University of Chicago used a mix of faith and rational thinking to address the issue of whether morality was unchanging or relative. Critics on the left chastised Tillich for trying to have it both ways. Critics on the right accused him of wandering from traditional values. The majority in the middle, who saw themselves as both faithful Christians and rational citizens, loved his teachings.

It was no surprise that on January 29 Mershon Auditorium was packed with people interested in what Tillich had to say. Students gobbled up 1,375 free tickets courtesy of the Student Senate, but nearly 2,000 other people, including many faculty and staff, paid their way in. Tillich did not disappoint. There are no moral absolutes, he told his audience, even in treasured pronouncements such as the Ten Commandments. Instead, he argued for a more forgiving society where "justice means the acknowledging of every person as a person and not as a thing."[55]

Bayard Rustin, a confidant of Martin Luther King Jr. who had organized the March on Washington the previous August, also spoke at the symposium. Rustin challenged his predominantly white audience to think differently about race relations: "In the past, the question has been swept under the rug, but today it can no longer be swept away. . . . Unless it is answered, no further political progress is possible." He added: "If anyone thinks I am pleading for proper education of the Negro alone, he is mistaken. The Negro will not be educated until everyone is educated."[56]

Not everyone who spoke on campus that winter advocated change. A year earlier George C. Wallace had commenced his term as governor of the highly segregated state of Alabama by declaring "segregation now, segregation tomorrow, segregation forever." He quickly became a folk

Meet the Beatles

On the evening of February 9, 1964, four young British musicians captured the largest television audience ever—76 million people—as they performed on the *Ed Sullivan Show.* As popular as the Beatles were, no one realized that a fundamental change in American pop culture was taking place—a release of pent-up energy that society would find impossible to control or even understand.

College students, who viewed themselves as above adolescent crazes, were a tough sell initially. The *Lantern* dismissed the Beatles as "this year's fad" in a February 12 editorial. By summer the paper had changed its tune. After the Beatles produced 13 hit singles, three albums, and a popular movie (*A Hard Day's Night*), even students took notice. "The long lines in front of university-area theaters reflect [the group's] attraction for college students as well as the teenager," the *Lantern* conceded in an August editorial.[1]

1. "Revenge," *Lantern,* August 20, 1964, 4.

hero to segregationists by verbally confronting Kennedy administration officials trying to enforce federal court orders protecting the rights of Alabama's black minority. Now he was capitalizing on his celebrity to test the waters for a presidential run.

Some wondered whether the university should offer Wallace a forum, but Bob Strapp, chair of the Student Senate's human relations commission, expressed the majority sentiment: "[The commission] disagrees with both the spirit and the letter of Gov. Wallace's public statements concerning racial segregation, . . . [but the governor] has a democratic right to a forum in which he can present his views."[57]

Wallace spoke on campus on February 13. A small number of supporters and a large number of the curious filled Mershon Auditorium to capacity. The crowd "alternately applauded and hissed" as Wallace delivered his standard stump speech. He got his loudest applause when he said, "A central government is a servant of a nation, not its master," but a majority of the students and faculty expressed their disagreement when Wallace attacked the civil rights bill pending in Congress. "The most vicious feature [of the bill] is that which threatens the use of our private property," Wallace argued. "There can be no human rights in a country in which there are no property rights."[58]

TOWN VERSUS GOWN

While the Ohio State campus entertained the voices of change, many doubted the willingness of the greater community to do so. Speaking at a "town and gown" symposium at the Faculty Club in February, economics professor Paul Craig described it this way: the community's interest in a public university is that of an owner who believes the university's responsibility is to protect and promulgate the values of the community. But Craig pointed out that the university, particularly a research university, sees itself as a source of new knowledge, new ideas, objective scholarship, and the freedom to challenge conventional wisdom. "In extreme cases, I think a community tries to kid itself that it can have innovation and discovery and change in general but [can] subdue those specific cases of it that are, at the moment, annoying," Craig said.[59]

The tensions defined by these conflicting roles flared up with particular intensity in Columbus during the 1963–64 school year. It began in October when local activists pressured the city schools to remove from library reading lists books they described as "filthy, blasphemous, revolutionary or anti-white." The offending books included J. D. Salinger's *Catcher in the Rye,* George Orwell's *1984,* and Harper Lee's *To Kill a Mockingbird.*[60] Ohio State was not directly affected, but many students, faculty, and administrators had close ties to the public schools and rallied to the district's defense.

A week later the city's vice squad announced it would be visiting bookstores to tell owners that Henry Miller's *Tropic of Capricorn* was considered obscene and should be removed from their shelves. In addition, Columbus City Council passed an ordinance prohibiting the purchase of goods from communist countries, which made it difficult for Ohio State to build up its Slavic and Chinese language programs.

This was too much for a growing number of faculty and students who believed provincialism was holding the university back. In an editorial at the height of the controversy, the *Lantern* speculated on what was preventing Columbus from being a great intellectual and cultural center such as Athens, Greece. It listed the city's plusses: intellectual energy, vigorous cultural life, rich human and natural resources—much of which it attributed to the university. Then it listed the things that supposedly cast the city in a negative light, including book banning and the unquestioning small-town mentality of the media.[61]

In January a group of 60 faculty members calling themselves the Committee for the Study of Alternatives purchased a full-page *Lantern* ad accusing Columbus and its media of being "smug" for censoring books and ignoring the legitimate needs of its black citizens.[62]

The book-banning activities ultimately failed. The school board successfully resisted the call for a ban; a new mayor reined in the vice squad; and a municipal judge declared the city ordinance banning the sale of communist books and other items invalid. Nevertheless, the divide in values between the campus and the community would widen as the decade wore on.

Ideally, the mayor could help bridge the divide. For most of the 1960s that was M. E. "Jack" Sensenbrenner. He had already served as mayor for six years in the more placid 1950s before losing a reelection bid in 1959. But in 1963 he came back, winning by 5,000 votes.

Like many successful politicians Jack Sensenbrenner espoused a collection of seemingly inconsistent positions. The Circleville native, who once sold Fuller brushes door to door, was a pro-growth Democrat but also a strong social conservative. Vocally anti-communist, deeply religious, and highly patriotic, he wore a rhinestone-studded flag lapel pin and brought an evangelical zeal to his work that he called "spizzerinctum."[63]

The new mayor faced growing frustration over poor city services in the campus area when he assumed office in January 1964. Shortcomings in trash removal, lighting, and sidewalk and street repair dominated the city's conversation with the university community. Sensenbrenner would also face challenges from another quarter. Between 1950 and 1960 Columbus's African American population grew by 25,000, or 64 percent. Between 1960 and 1970 it grew another 30 percent. By 1970 the black population was 18.5 percent of the electorate.[64]

In his first two terms Sensenbrenner had enjoyed strong support from African Americans, but a new generation of leaders was less inclined to follow his lead. One was Arthur Zebbs of CORE, who before 7,000 supporters at a January 1964 civil rights rally called Columbus a prejudiced city. Zebbs criticized city leaders, including Sensenbrenner, for not doing enough to end de facto segregation in housing, schools, and employment.[65] More often than not, black activists in the city worked independently of campus activists (and in some cases they were at cross purposes), but when the two forces coalesced, as they would in 1970–71, not even spizzerinctum could save the day.

EYES ON THE PRIZE

While civil rights activists in Columbus skirmished with the city power structure, the heavy hitters in Washington, D.C., were lining up for the most significant civil rights vote in almost 100 years. John F. Kennedy's bill, introduced the preceding June, had been widely regarded as dead on arrival. Now, after Kennedy's assassination, the bill began to pick up momentum. Lyndon Johnson, a southerner, seized the moment to call for its passage in honor of the slain president.

Campus organizers decided to schedule a rally on the Oval on May 18. But they had to get permission from the administration, which seemed wary of the idea. First, the president's cabinet told them the rally could not be held before 5 p.m. because it would disturb classes. The organizers agreed to hold the rally after 5. Austin E. Ritchie, dean of special services, told them they could not use a microphone because that presumably would disturb those who remained in classes after 5. The organizers agreed to not use a microphone. University police chief Joe Webb told them they would need three plainclothes officers and two uniformed officers to provide security, and they would have to pay $50 for them. They came up with the money.[66]

With the location lined up, the sponsors turned to student organizations for backing. By May 11, a week before the rally, they were able to announce support from 29 campus groups, including the YMCA, YWCA, and many religious organizations. Some other major organizations had cold feet. The Freshman Senate took up the issue at its meeting on May 12. After what the *Lantern* described as a "scalding debate" of more than an hour, the body voted on a carefully worded resolution that supported students attending the rally, but not the rally itself, nor the civil rights bill. Even that watered-down resolution was able to pass only after the Freshman Senate president Tom Sawyer cast the deciding vote to break a 24–24 tie. The Student Senate had an equally contentious debate two days later. After a two-hour filibuster by the rally's opponents, a majority was able to agree on language that "urge[d] all students to attend the rally." A subsequent resolution to allow the Senate's name to be listed in support of the rally failed, 17–19.[67]

The rally went forward without incident and was a modest success. About a thousand students and other members of the university

4.3. Black and white students join together to mail postcards to Senator Frank Lausche in support of the Civil Rights Act after a rally on the Oval in May. (*Makio*)

community showed up on a warm spring day—a fairly large crowd as political issues went. After the speakers addressed those assembled, folksinger Chuck White led them in a few choruses of the civil rights anthem "We Shall Overcome." They then marched to a nearby mailbox and deposited several hundred postcards addressed to Ohio's senior U.S. senator, Frank Lausche, who was still on the fence regarding the bill.[68]

On June 10 the U.S. Senate, in an unprecedented move, voted to cut off debate on the civil rights bill, thus assuring its passage. The letters and postcards to Senator Lausche must have had some effect. He joined fellow Ohio senator Stephen Young and others in voting 71–29 to move the bill forward. Less than a month later, on July 2, Lyndon Johnson signed the Civil Rights Act into law. The sweeping legislation, thought impossible just a year earlier, prohibited discrimination in public accommodations, public facilities, public education, and employment. Many years of struggle still lay ahead, but the face of the country had changed. There was no turning back.

Woody's World

Not everyone who supported the goals of the civil rights movement also supported the means to the end. Woody Hayes was one such person. Hayes saw himself as more than a football coach. He was a teacher who showed how traditional values not only led to success on the gridiron, but translated to society as a whole. In the spring of 1964 he used the occasion of a talk at Ohio State's Newman Center to expound. Referring to the recent murder of Kitty Genovese, who was killed in the courtyard of her New York City apartment building while dozens of her neighbors reportedly stood by and did nothing, Hayes said, "I'll bet there wasn't a single athlete in that apartment house." The implication was that had there been, that person certainly would have done something to help Genovese.

Hayes then talked about demonstrations, of which he clearly disapproved. Hayes was a pioneer in judging black athletes by their talent and desire, rather than their skin color. What he did not support was any kind of civil disobedience or other protest, regardless of cause. "Football players never take part in demonstrations," Hayes said. "The guy who starts demonstrations is the little guy with the briefcase who never got any attention and still has to prove his masculinity. Football players don't have to prove theirs."[1] Regardless of what was happening elsewhere, in Woody's world traditional values endured.

1. Carole Edwards, "Woody Praises Athletes for Victories over Books," *Lantern,* May 19, 1964, 1.

ALL NECESSARY MEASURES

President Johnson went on national television on August 4 to say he would ask Congress for authority to use "all necessary measures" to protect U.S. forces operating in or near Vietnam. The precipitating events were described as two unprovoked attacks on U.S. warships in international waters. Three days later, Congress approved the Tonkin Gulf Resolution with only two dissenting votes. The country was well on its way to war with North Vietnam.

Like the rest of the nation, Ohio State supported the president. Soviet expert Louis Nemzer concluded Johnson "had no choice" but to retaliate. Curry N. Vaughan of Army ROTC and Joseph W. Beadles Jr. of Navy ROTC both said they supported the decision.[69] The *Lantern* added its approval. What no one besides the most direct participants knew was that the supposed attacks were not unprovoked, and in fact the second attack on August 4 may not have occurred at all. That would become known later.

By the end of the summer of 1964, most of the elements that would make the second half of the 1960s so volatile were in place. The passage of the Civil Rights Act signified a new but even more contentious chapter in the struggle for equality. The arrival of the Beatles marked a massive shift toward the new youth culture. The Tonkin Gulf Resolution paved the way for escalation of the war in Vietnam. Key authority figures—President Johnson, Governor Rhodes, and Mayor Sensenbrenner—had taken their place on the stage and settled in for the long haul. In a few months the first legions of baby boomers would be headed toward the nation's colleges, including 8,000 destined for Ohio State. Before long it would be clear they were marching to a beat of their own.

CHAPTER 5

BOOMER INVASION

(1964–65)

The baby boomers arrived en masse as predicted, and Ohio State managed to survive the onslaught. The university also leveraged the passage of Issue One into a building boom and warily welcomed the Ohio Board of Regents as a major player in its decisions. U.S. president Lyndon Johnson dominated the national discourse as his policies began to drive the course of events for the remainder of the decade.

5.1. President Novice Fawcett welcomes the largest entering class to date at Freshman Convocation, September 1964. (*Lantern*)

STUDENTS: SHIFTING FOCUS

THE BOOMERS HAVE LANDED

On September 23, 1964, Ohio State officials met head-on the challenge they'd spent years getting ready for: the first of the tidal wave of baby boomers arrived on campus for move-in day. In a logistical feat reminiscent of the Normandy landings 20 years earlier, the university managed to get several thousand freshmen settled into their living quarters by the end of the day. Several days of Welcome Week activities came next, followed by the first day of classes.

Four years of planning seemed to have paid off. The dorm construction boom meant the new students had a place to live. The opening of Bradford Commons on south campus and Raney Commons on north campus the year before meant they had somewhere to eat. And the cafeterias could easily be converted to study halls in the evenings and on weekends to supplement the crowded libraries.

Enrollment on main campus soared to a record 33,384, and the university hired 200 more instructors to meet the anticipated course demand. After some 300 last-minute room changes and the addition of chemistry labs on Saturday mornings, schedulers found enough classroom space. Where 5,500 student drivers would park, in addition to 4,200 faculty and staff vehicles, remained a problem, but everyone managed to adjust. Meanwhile, High Street bars, merchants, and pizzerias enjoyed a business boom from thousands of new customers.[1]

WOMEN AND SAFETY

While the boomers settled in, students continued to push against in loco parentis and the stereotyping of women, with some signs of success. In May 1965 the associate dean of women reversed her office's previous position and agreed to let south campus women wear slacks to lunch every day during winter quarter except Sunday. The liberalized rule would take effect spring quarter 1966.

The *Lantern* began to reflect changing attitudes toward professional women. In January it ran a series on Ohio State women in research that celebrated the achievements of anthropologist Erika Bourguignon, nutritionist Virginia Vivian, and physiological chemist Gertrude Orth. On February 12 an unusual pre–Valentine's Day editorial headlined "Sugar to Spice" celebrated the "rapidly spreading breed of female noted for talent, ambitions, independence and personality."[2]

Campus safety, especially for female students, emerged as a major issue. The Women's Self Government Association got the ball rolling with a major educational campaign to kick off fall quarter. President Kay McDaniels explained: "Due to the increased number of evening classes, more women are returning to their residences after dark. We are especially concerned for girls who must walk to the bus stop and to off-campus rooming houses and sororities." McDaniels said the off-campus area was poorly lighted, with ample places for potential attackers and exhibitionists to hide. WSGA asked faculty members who had women in their evening classes to make sure they had an escort home. The group also suggested that women travel in groups of two or more after dark, and asked Greek houses and rooming houses to turn on outside lights after dark.[3]

Then as now, statistics showed the campus itself was a relatively safe place. Of the 99 districts for which the Columbus police kept detailed records, campus ranked 95; in other words, it was the fifth-safest district in the city. However, the neighborhoods east and south of campus, where many students lived, were not so safe. The blocks bounded by King Avenue on the north, Fourth Avenue on the south, High Street on the east, and Olentangy River Road on the west were the city's 12th worst area. Neighborhoods near 11th and Chittenden Avenues and King Avenue and Perry Street were not far behind. Poor lighting in these areas had been an issue for some time.[4]

The Student Senate and WSGA joined forces for a petition drive to get the campus area moved up on the city's priority list for lighting. The goal was 5,000 signatures. By spring 8,845 signatures were turned in to Columbus City Council. The city agreed to expedite 66 new or brighter lights for the area between Woodruff and Maynard Avenues and High Street and the state fairgrounds east of campus.[5] It was a start, but the university area would continue to be plagued with soaring crime rates for the rest of the decade.

GREEKS ON THE DEFENSIVE

Fraternities and sororities enjoyed widespread support across campus for most of Ohio State's history, even though most students were not members of a Greek letter society. Critics were few and not very influential. That began to change when people both inside and outside the Greek system began to question some of its basic tenets.

At the end of fall quarter the *Lantern* ran a story on racial integration within fraternities and sororities. Reporter Tom Seslar found that of the 64 social fraternities and sororities recognized by the university, five were almost all black and 55 of the remainder were all white and had never had a black member. Most of the black students interviewed said they would not attempt to pledge a white fraternity or sorority because they knew they wouldn't be accepted. Many white members privately agreed, some blaming informal pressure from their national organizations.

Seslar asked John Bonner, executive dean for student relations, about Ohio State's position. Officially, the university had maintained a policy of nondiscrimination in housing since 1960. "It is unthinkable for a university to force integration," Bonner said. "We have fought long and hard to abolish all discriminatory clauses from the constitutions of student organizations here. If we now were to force a group to accept a person because of his race, his religion, the color of his skin, or because his name is John, we would destroy all that we have fought for."

Patricia L. Duren, a member of black sorority Delta Sigma Theta, also did not see forced integration as a solution. But she framed the issue differently: "We have accepted white girls into our Negro sorority. I hope that someday Negro girls will be accepted by the white sororities here, but integration of the white fraternities and sororities should be based upon a genuine desire for brotherhood rather than upon integration for the sake of integration."[6]

Response from the white fraternities and sororities was quick and negative. *Lantern* city editor John Huddy wrote a column several days later defending his reporter and explaining the paper's position. He said he had received a flood of calls and letters, most of them hostile. Many asked what business it was of the *Lantern*'s in the first place.

Huddy acknowledged the positive role played by the Greek chapters in campus life, but he also argued that the university's formal recognition of them made them semi-public. If the Greek system failed to act, he wrote, "it paints a self-portrait as an inert, outmoded mammoth in an age in which a major social revolution is taking place."[7]

Two *Lantern* reporters did an update on the state of the Greek system at the end of spring quarter. They pointed out that over the last 10 years, undergraduate enrollment had grown five times faster than fraternity and sorority membership. They also found that younger students tended to view the Greek system as outdated and not relevant to their needs. "In order to survive, the Greek system must be like the church," former fraternity president Jon Richardson said. "It must absorb changes rather than buck them."[8] The Greek system would survive the sixties, but a difficult road lay ahead.

THE *SUNDIAL* ON THE OFFENSIVE

By 1965 the *Sundial,* Ohio State's student-run humor magazine, had been around for 54 years. It boasted prominent alumni, including humorist James Thurber, cartoonist Milton Caniff, and Broadway columnist Earl Wilson. It billed itself as the "world's funniest college magazine" but did not have the cachet such a distinguished group of alumni would suggest. That began to change after Bob Stine joined the staff in the fall of 1961 and took over as editor the following spring. "Jovial Bob" revamped the magazine into what one observer described as "sarcasm, satire and sex."[9] The *Sundial* was at its best when poking fun at those in power. The *Lantern,* which it referred to as the "Slantern" and the "Latrine," was one of its favorite targets. The *Dispatch,* the Greek system, WSGA, Ohio State athletics, and of course the university administration were also subject to ridicule. In the first half of 1965 Stine took the *Sundial* to new heights with two campaigns that fused biting satire with brilliant marketing. The magazine began selling a line of sweatshirts with the phrase "The Big Farm: Ohia State" stenciled on the front along with two haystacks. They were available in three colors for only three dollars.

Stine also announced he would run as a write-in candidate for Student Senate president. Stine's critics pointed out that because he was graduating in the spring, he would not be able to serve, even if elected. It didn't matter, he countered: "During the past year, the students at

5.2. *Sundial* editor "Jovial Bob" Stine's 1965 write-in campaign for Student Senate president featured staffers walking the Oval in clown suits. (*Makio*)

Ohio State have come to expect absolutely nothing from Senate. Since I'm graduating this spring and won't be around next year, I feel I'm in a better position than the other candidates to give the students absolutely nothing." Stine proceeded to send staffers dressed as clowns onto the Oval with signs bearing slogans such as "Return dignity to student government—elect a clown."[10] *Sundial* sales that quarter shot up to a record 8,000, and the magazine won its first and only award as one of the top college humor magazines in the country.

Both traditional parties nominated fairly traditional candidates for senate president. The Buckeye Political Party chose Tom Workman, a junior who was a member of Young Americans for Freedom and had helped lead the fight against the National Student Association several years earlier. The Student Congress Party selected Alan Ross, a junior who'd been active in the senate. Both candidates did choose untraditional running mates. Workman teamed with Eileen Roach, making her the first woman to run since the position was directly elected by the student body as a whole. Ross tried to appeal to the growing number of dorm residents by running with Vic Frost, who lived in Park Hall and was secretary of the Men's Residence Halls Association. Frost was the first dorm-elected officer to run for campuswide elected office.

Stine's campaign generated 1,163 votes, a substantial amount for a write-in candidate but not enough for him to win. The Workman-Roach team captured 4,175 votes, compared to 3,328 for Ross-Frost. The BPP kept control of the Senate 22–17 (with one independent). Stine went on to achieve international fame as the author of young adult novels, including the popular "Goosebumps" series. The *Sundial* fell on hard times and was out of business by 1968.

THE UNIVERSITY: A NEW PARTNER

While students pressured university administrators from below, the state of Ohio introduced a new management partner for them from above. As described in chapter 3, state universities had a change of heart when Governor James Rhodes told them they could support his bill to establish a board of regents and be part of a $300 million bond issue, or fight him over the bill and get no capital funds. They all opted for the funds. The enabling legislation sailed through the legislature, and the Ohio Board of Regents officially began its work on September 20, 1963. Three months later the regents announced the start of a comprehensive review of Ohio's colleges and universities, with the goal of developing a statewide master plan.

The next step was to name a chancellor. In March 1964 Rhodes announced his choice: John D. Millett, the longtime president of Miami

University. Millett had come to Ohio from Columbia University, where he established a reputation as an expert on higher education financing. He was the only university president to not initially oppose the regents legislation.[11]

While Ohio State had been preparing for the influx of baby boomers for more than four years, Millett had six months. And while he was responsible for all of the state's colleges and universities, Ohio State was the elephant in the room. Millett had been critical in the past of Ohio State's behavior toward its sister institutions, but both Millett and President Novice Fawcett recognized they needed to hang together to address the enrollment onslaught, or find themselves hanging separately.

"The Master Plan for Public Higher Education in Ohio" was released in April 1965. The first person to receive the draft was Rhodes, who seemed to sign on. "We want to be number one," he told reporters. "We can only do this through research . . . through higher education."[12] The next step was a series of hearings across the state.

The report reflected the work of the Academy for Educational Development, a nonprofit think tank, assisted by the staff of the Board of Regents and several advisory committees that included Ohio State officials. It presented statistics that showed Ohio as an underachiever in the race for brainpower. For example, it lagged behind other large states in the proportion of young people in college and in the share of federal research dollars captured.[13]

The plan identified Ohio State as the state's primary center for graduate education and research and made the following recommendation: "The Ohio State University should consider graduate education at the doctoral level its most important educational purpose and should give increased attention to this part of its educational operation. An expansion of graduate enrollment and improved quality in graduate study should be major goals of the university at this time."

The report envisioned a major change in the composition of the student body to reflect upper-level work. Freshmen and sophomores would decline from 50 percent of all students to 30 percent, while juniors, seniors, and graduate and professional students would increase to 70 percent.

Enrollment at the Columbus campus would be limited to 40,000 under the plan, which also called for more access for students through urban universities and two-year campuses. Ohio State would be responsible for running a branch campus for Franklin County.

If university officials thought the limits on enrollment would allow them to move to selective admissions, they were wrong. Even though he supported enrollment limits and improved quality, Millett told an Ohio State symposium in July that "the only defensible policy for our universities is open access."[14]

The report also called for the Board of Regents to have the authority to coordinate programs across campuses and for state support to be distributed via a formula that recognized the differences in the cost of instruction between various disciplines. For example, the proposed allocation for freshmen and sophomores was $250 per student per year, while the amount for a doctoral student was $5,000 per year. Obviously, Ohio State stood to benefit as it increased graduate enrollment.[15]

But making plans and funding them were two different things. Joe Walsh, a writer for *Science,* had penned a feature on the changing environment in Ohio for the magazine's July 31, 1964, issue. Walsh complimented Ohio's political leaders for finally acknowledging the connection between universities and economic growth. He also praised the Board of Regents for making Ohio's colleges and universities act more like a system, but wondered how, under the governor's pledge of no new taxes, the state would have enough money to accommodate growing undergraduate enrollments and improve and expand graduate education and research at the same time.[16]

Over the short run, money did not appear to be a problem. A strong economy helped lift state tax revenues as 1965 began, making the austerity of two years earlier a distant memory. Rhodes celebrated in his State of the State address on February 15. "Ohio has moved from the shadow of bankruptcy to a new place in the sun," he told the General Assembly, and higher education would benefit. "We have developed and are building on the boldest and most imaginative blueprint for brainpower in the nation." Rhodes promised that the passage of another bond issue he proposed for the May ballot would mean "every county of 80,000 or more population in Ohio will have state-supported or assisted higher education facilities by 1967."[17] Already established universities such as Ohio State would also get their share of largesse. Powered by the new funding formula that recognized the higher cost of educating graduate and professional students, Ohio State stood to receive annual increases averaging nearly 9 percent a year for the coming biennium. Fawcett said the increase would allow the university to raise faculty salaries

7.5 percent in July and hire 115 new faculty to accommodate growing enrollments.

A BANNER YEAR FOR RESEARCH

The quantity and impact of sponsored research at Ohio State continued to rise. In October 1964 Alfred Garrett, vice president for research, reported that research spending grew 14 percent in 1963–64. He expected similar increases in 1964–65. He also said Ohio State had moved into the top 15 universities in the country in terms of funded research and was "still growing."[18]

The nation's goal of putting a man on the moon before the end of the decade was approaching. Ohio State researchers continued to play a critical role as Project Apollo picked up momentum:

- In February 1965 four Ohio State student volunteers emerged from a 9 1/2-by-27-foot chamber at Dayton's Wright-Patterson Air Force Base after six weeks in isolation. For three of those weeks they subsisted solely on a liquid diet being tested for use by astronauts on long voyages. Their verdict? They agreed the food was adequate but not very good.[19]
- Charles H. Shultz, assistant professor of geology, used radar equipment from Ohio State's Antenna Lab as part of a NASA-funded project to map the surface of moon. The information would be used to pick a lunar landing site.
- Finding a way to prevent communications blackouts during a space capsule's reentry into the earth's atmosphere was the charge given to the Aerodynamics Lab. Director John D. Lee said the university's "shock tube," one of only six in the country, would be used to help find a solution by simulating reentry.
- To be sure rocket and space capsules did not fail under the stress of rapid acceleration, NASA adopted a nondestructive testing protocol originally identified at Ohio State. Robert C. McMaster, a professor of welding engineering, developed the process called X-ray image enlargement. It was used to test the Gemini-Titan rocket sent into space in August 1965.

- In March 1965 Ohio State became the home of the Refractories Institute, which it captured from the Mellon Institute in Pittsburgh. The center was the only laboratory in the United States equipped to run a complete line of tests on refractories, which are compounds made of ceramics and other materials designed to withstand the heat and pressure found at high speeds, such as during space travel.

The university also explored the promise of improving health. Ohio State became only the third site in the United States to have a skin bank to help treat severe burn victims. Ronald Berggren, director of plastic surgery, explained the process involved taking skin from cadavers and sterilizing and freezing it until it was needed.

Howard Sirak, a pioneering surgeon in the College of Medicine, and Walter Starkey, professor of mechanical engineering, combined efforts to perfect artificial heart valves, which were now being tested after 10 years in development. Arthur James, associate professor of surgery and director of the Columbus Cancer Clinic, worked on using new compounds to kill cancer cells without harming healthy ones. "This drug therapy is not a cure for cancer, but it is a step in the right direction," James said.[20]

Ohio State matched a federal grant to build a laboratory that was the only complete set of facilities in the United States outside the government for the study of environmental health problems.

The university also inaugurated the most modern and complete behavioral sciences laboratory in the country. Nestled under the stands in Ohio Stadium, it featured rooms with one-way mirrors and electronic devices that enabled researchers to observe and record the behavior of individuals and small groups in a variety of settings.

At the Ohio Engineering Conference on April 7, Governor Rhodes announced plans to build the world's "greatest and largest" highway research and development center. Rhodes said the site would cover about three square miles and be located within a 30-minute drive of Columbus. The state would build it, but it would be run by the College of Engineering. Although the governor was often prone to exaggeration, in this case his enthusiasm was justified. Ohio State's leadership in highway research and the state's strong presence in automobile manufacturing made this an ideal match.

In July agricultural engineering instructor Kenneth A. Harkness and W. E. Stuckey of the Cooperative Extension Service announced a significant advance in road safety. Under a grant from the Automobile Safety Foundation, they had developed a system of highly visible symbols to identify slow-moving farm vehicles. Their reflective orange triangles would eventually be adopted around the world as the standard warning of road hazards.

INSTRUCTION: CALLS FOR REFORM

While the university was well positioned as Ohio's research and graduate education center, it continued to struggle with its role as the state's largest undergraduate teaching institution. Administrators could take some satisfaction in having addressed the immediate housing needs of the new crop of students; what remained unanswered was whether they would learn anything and from whom, as increasing numbers put pressure on an already overloaded system.

For example, an attempt to streamline the university course bulletins landed with a thud. Complaints about the unwieldiness of the 22 often conflicting bulletins issued by individual colleges and schools resulted in a consolidated catalog for the 1964–65 school year. The new document weighed three pounds. Critics immediately dubbed it a "telephone book" and a "704-page mistake." James O'Brian, head of the distribution effort, defended the work: "When the budget and size of the university is considered, we've come up with an outstanding publication."[21]

In March the registrar reported that only 36 percent of freshmen who enrolled at Ohio State eventually graduated. The rest either flunked out or withdrew voluntarily. Even though the university claimed to be recruiting better students, the number of dismissals was up slightly from the previous fall. In the College of Commerce, 9.7 percent of students failed to make it even through the first quarter.[22]

The announcement of the prestigious Woodrow Wilson Fellowships in April prompted soul-searching about teaching and learning at the university. The fellowships were awarded by the foundation of the same name and were designed to attract top undergraduates into college teaching. Tiny Oberlin College in northern Ohio (enrollment 3,000) received 22 awards. Ohio State (with more than 25,000 undergraduates) garnered only two. Richard Armitage, dean of the graduate school and regional chair of the Woodrow Wilson Foundation, pointed to Ohio State's lack of selective admissions, lack of a strong honors program, and lack of commitment to intellectual accomplishment (read Speakers Rule) as the culprits. But perhaps most telling, Armitage revealed a perception among Woodrow Wilson judges that many Ohio State students tended to think in terms of specific courses and "not fundamental principles, or exciting new directions."[23]

The Freshman Senate added fuel to the fire when it released the results of a review of Arts Survey 401 in May. The course was required of all first-quarter freshmen in the College of Arts and Sciences in order to help them navigate the college's requirements and take advantage of opportunities. The course met four times a quarter amid a bundle of contradictions that seemed to reflect a cavalier approach to teaching freshmen. The class was required, but no one took attendance. Students received a grade, but it didn't count because the course was not for credit.

Ruann Ernst, chair of the senate's educational affairs commission, reported that of the 1,166 questionnaires distributed to students during fall and winter quarters, 528 were returned. They showed how much students disliked the course: 33 percent said they received no real benefit, and only 40 percent said they attended all four sessions. Many students said they were bored with the material, much of which was a rehash of what was in the university bulletin.[24]

At a general faculty meeting in February, John Weaver, vice president for instruction and dean of faculties, lamented the lack of senior faculty in the classroom and called on the university to do more to improve teaching for both undergraduates and graduates. Students and faculty were generally supportive. Freshmen interviewed for a *Lantern* follow-up complained they rarely if ever had classes with instructors other than graduate assistants. The *Lantern* ran an editorial praising Weaver's speech. The paper cited university statistics that showed the dollar volume of research grants to Ohio State had tripled since 1958, as well as evidence gathered by the American Association of University Professors that teaching loads were down from 12 hours a week a decade ago to only six to nine hours a week currently. The blame, the editors said, lay with the post-Sputnik emphasis on research.[25]

Faculty were supportive, but pointed to some of the obstacles. History chair Harold Grimm predicted: "It will be years before we see any significant results. University enrollment, both undergraduate and graduate, is increasing so rapidly that it is hard to keep pace with it." He also emphasized the nearly prohibitive cost of doing so at the current levels of tuition and state support.[26]

Weaver soon appointed a faculty committee to identify measures of excellence in teaching. Probably sensing the difficulty of the task, he did not give the committee a specific deadline.

THE BIRTH OF UNIVERSITY COLLEGE

The challenge of accommodating additional enrollment pressures under the regents' guidelines spurred nontraditional thinking from the university. Prospective freshmen were encouraged to consider enrolling in one of the branches, or entering summer quarter. In both cases they could look forward to smaller classes and more emphasis on counseling services. The university also announced that entrance requirements for out-of-state students would be toughened. Nonresidents would need to be in the top quartile of their high school class instead of the top third, effective the coming fall.

The major initiative would be the two-year college that President Fawcett had proposed the previous May. He envisioned it as a home for students seeking education beyond high school, mostly commuters from central Ohio. It would have its own faculty and facilities, most likely across the Olentangy River on west campus. Eventual enrollment could be as much as 10,000 students.

In December 1964 Fawcett appeared before the Faculty Council to enlist its support for what he said was "the best answer we have been able to find" for the problem of exploding enrollments. He assured the group the proposal had the full support of the Board of Regents. "It will help meet both the quantity and quality problems of education beyond the high school level," he said. He asked the council to approve the creation of a faculty committee to help structure the curriculum and address other academic policies. The council did so, and by January the committee was hard at work.[27]

The new University College, also called the General College, would not be ready to accept students for two to three years. Meanwhile, administrators had to figure out what to do with the 2,000 students who had applied for admittance to the Columbus campus the next fall, but under the regents' guidelines would not be funded by the state if they were admitted. Fawcett went to the board of trustees in March with a proposal for a temporary Columbus branch of Ohio State. Classes would be taught in the evenings by additional faculty hired for that purpose. Students would pay the same tuition—$125 a quarter—as their counterparts on main campus. The rationale was that state support was less for the students. Fawcett told the trustees the policies were "intended as an interim solution to demands growing out of the tidal wave of students now seeking enrollment. . . . They will operate until we have full operation of our two-year general college, still in the planning stage." The proposal was approved unanimously.[28]

While the University College and branch proposals did not generate organized opposition, dissent did surface. Alumni secretary Jack Fullen was the most vocal. In the July 1965 alumni magazine, Fullen used the release of a report on disturbances at the University of California at Berkeley the previous fall to draw some lessons for Ohio State. While acknowledging the differences between the two campuses, Fullen made this comparison regarding what he called Public Enemy No. 1: "SIZE—BIGNESS—UNWIELDINESS—although Berkeley itself is limited to 27,000 [enrollment]. . . . Ohio State's enrollment will reach 42,000 this fall and in the biennium will be increased by the 10,000 in that proposed department euphemistically called the General College, but already alluded to by campus wiseacres as 'Knucklehead U,' alias 'The Monster.'" Fullen argued that University College would be like "a tapeworm" sucking resources from the rest of the university. "Why not a Community or Junior college of its own for Franklin County's academic risks, giving The Ohio State University a fighting chance to stay big AND good rather than just good-and-big."[29]

Vice President John Mount later recalled that Fawcett and Chancellor John Millett did explore a model similar to Cleveland's successful Cuyahoga Community College, but decided Franklin County voters would not support a property tax levy to fund it. Edward Q. Moulton, who at the time was an associate dean responsible for academic unit budgets, recalled the driving force behind the decision to keep the two-year college under Ohio State was the desire to control the additional tuition and state support that would flow from increased enrollments.[30]

TOWER MANIA

The year 1965 marked the biggest building boom in Ohio State history up to that time. Officials announced $80 million in campus expansion and improvement projects for the next four years, compared to $57 million for the entire preceding decade.[31] The projects included five new academic buildings, a plan to replace aging University Hall, completion of the north campus housing complex, a Center for Tomorrow, and a major expansion of the Medical Center.

Buildings were going up so fast, the university decided to hold its first mass groundbreaking ceremony. On June 30 a shovel-friendly Governor Rhodes joined Fawcett and a small entourage who moved from site to site to break ground for the five academic buildings: material sciences, chemistry, engineering, and pharmacy on main campus and an aeronautical and astronautical research facility at Don Scott Field, about seven miles north of campus. Construction was scheduled to be completed by February 1967. Funds came from the state's 1963 bond issue.

But the biggest project and most radical new design would be two 24-story residence towers, the largest construction projects ever undertaken by Ohio State and reportedly the largest of their kind in the country. They also would be the most controversial. In November 1964 Gordon Carson, vice president for business and finance, announced plans to build the two towers—at $7.5 million each—along the east bank of the Olentangy River south of Ohio Stadium. At 250 feet high, the towers would be the tallest buildings on campus by a long shot, and the second highest on the Columbus skyline after the Lincoln-LeVeque Tower. They would house 3,840 students in hexagon-shaped suites. Each suite would have 16 students in four four-person bedrooms, along with a central lounge and a bathroom. There would be six suites on a floor, along with a separate suite for an upperclassman resident adviser. Each tower would have 22 floors of living space plus dining facilities, meeting rooms, and a main desk on the lobby floor. The buildings would be air-conditioned throughout, and each would be served by six high-speed elevators.[32]

Carson stressed the efficiency of the towers' design. "They are more economical in terms of space and in terms of cost," he said, and "the design allows considerably more space per student than present dorms."

Fawcett officially broke ground for the project on March 29, 1965, with the goal of opening the towers to students for fall quarter 1966.

Carson said the plans for the buildings were "thoroughly investigated" by the dean of men and dean of women's offices. While it is true that a group of students lived in a mock-up of a suite and seemed to like it, what Carson failed to mention was that many of his colleagues, including those in student relations, strongly opposed his plan.[33] He went ahead anyway.

Fawcett agreed with the critics. "I'm not proud of . . . the tower dormitories," he recalled later. "[Carson] and I disagreed many times in the course of construction of those dormitories." Fawcett took the unusual step of sending Carson a letter that said: "As I have indicated previously and largely in conformity with the Master Plan, we began by thinking about three 14 story dormitories. I later found that we had addressed ourselves to the construction of two 18 story dormitories. It was not until later when the buildings were well along in design that I discovered we were going to 24 stories."[34]

This letter was sent in June 1968, more than three years after ground was broken on the project but just two weeks after a fatal fire in one of the towers. It's hard to know if Fawcett was reminding Carson who was in charge or if he was trying to insulate himself from criticism.

Although Carson had a reputation for seeing things his own way, the university found this approach attractive for financial reasons. Administrators were worried about keeping up with demand and also about the high cost of housing. (Ohio State's costs were the highest among the six public universities in the state.) At the time the towers were approved, the university had almost finished the north campus complex at a cost of about $4,200 per bed. The proposed budget for the two towers was $3,900 per bed, or 7 percent less, even before adjusting for inflation. So the project offered the opportunity to provide more beds, more quickly and more cheaply, without having to tie up a lot of additional land.[35] In his zeal for the economics, Carson was not interested in listening to concerns about the impact of stacking so many students in such a concentrated space. As more details came out, criticism would grow and, like University College, the towers would become a symbol of a university more interested in warehousing students than in teaching them.

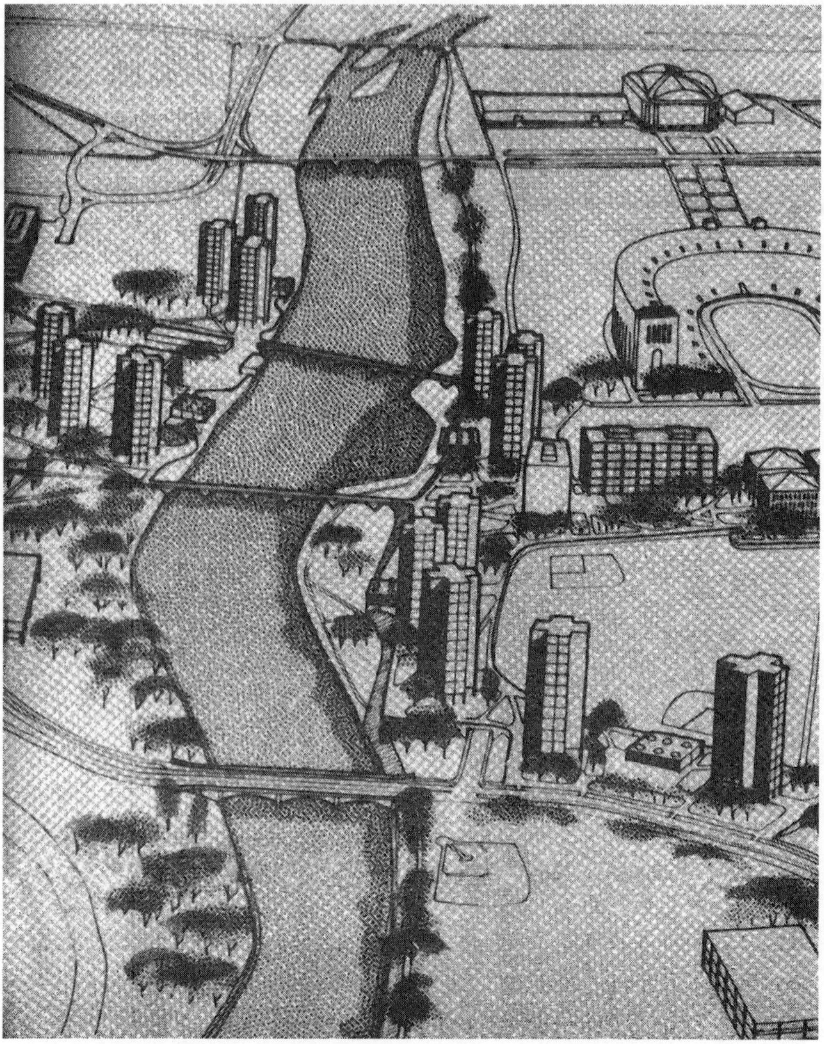

5.3. Artist's rendering of the Olentangy River corridor as envisioned in the master plan. Only two 24-story residential towers were built. (*Lantern*)

SOCIETY: ALL THE WAY WITH LBJ

The personality and aspirations of Lyndon Baines Johnson dominated the nation's political discourse in 1964 and 1965. Ascending to the presidency as a result of a tragedy, Johnson worked tirelessly to win the affection and support of the American people in his own right. Initially, he succeeded. Nowhere would that be more evident than in the 1964 presidential contest against Arizona senator Barry Goldwater.

The campaign did not bring any major candidates to campus, but they did come to Columbus. When Goldwater spoke at Veterans Memorial on September 30, four busloads of Ohio State students were among the crowd estimated at anywhere between 10,000 and 60,000. Goldwater promised his followers a clear break from business as usual. "Johnson has so much power and wants so much more that the Democrats don't know whether to vote for him or plug him in," Goldwater said, to the crowd's delight.[36]

Johnson had visited campus in 1960 as a vice presidential candidate, but four years later he decided to appear presidential and left much of his campaigning to surrogates. His running mate, Minnesota senator Hubert Humphrey, addressed a crowd estimated at 5,000 from the steps of City Hall on October 6. "I can't tell you how happy I am to be in Ohio in a year when Ohio State doesn't play Minnesota," he quipped.[37]

A mock election held on campus in October signaled big problems for Goldwater: Johnson won handily, 6,095 to 3,255. Results were similar throughout the Big Ten, in sharp contrast to 1960, when Richard Nixon captured 64 percent of the vote. On November 3, the country voted for real. The Ohio Union provided seven TV screens and four faculty members to interpret results. Not much interpretation was necessary. Buoyed by a robust economy, public respect for his leadership in the difficult period after John F. Kennedy's assassination, and a series of intemperate statements by Goldwater that struck many voters as extreme, Johnson scored a victory of epic proportions. He carried 44 states and won the popular vote 61 percent to 37 percent. He won Ohio by a million votes and carried usually Republican Franklin County by 23,000 votes.

Six days later the *Lantern* published an eight-page postelection edition. Most of the experts interviewed expected Johnson to use his election mandate to aggressively advance his legislative agenda. Another group speculated that moderates would try to regain control of the Republican Party. But some faculty experts saw roadblocks ahead. Myron Hale of the political science department, for one, pointed out that deep splits existed between the segregationist and integrationist wings of the Democratic Party, "and this election isn't going to heal them over."[38]

In his January 4 State of the Union address a triumphant Johnson called for a sweeping roster of government programs to bring his vision of the Great Society to all Americans. For the next six months he behaved like a man possessed: wheeling and dealing, threatening and promising—whatever it took to get his legislation passed. He knew his window was narrow, so he moved ahead forcefully. At the end of August the *Lantern* published an appraisal of Johnson's first eight months as president on his own. The consensus among Ohio State experts was that he would become one of our greatest presidents, comparable in many ways to his hero, Franklin Delano Roosevelt. But where Roosevelt had almost four terms to make his reputation, Johnson's window had already started to close.

ESCALATION IN VIETNAM

On March 2 the U.S. Air Force began Operation Rolling Thunder, the systematic bombing of targets in North Vietnam. Six days later the first U.S. combat troops splashed ashore on the beach at Da Nang. March also marked the birth of the term "credibility gap," coined by journalists who believed the Johnson administration was not leveling with the American public about its intentions in Vietnam. Activity against the war escalated as well. Students for a Democratic Society (SDS) organized the first Vietnam teach-in at the University of Michigan in late March. On April 17 SDS and other groups brought an estimated 10,000 to 20,000 people to Washington for the first mass antiwar protest.

The first reported protest involving Ohio State students occurred on a chilly Saturday in February. Twenty or so students, mostly members of Students for Liberal Action, joined about 20 others to march in downtown Columbus. They identified themselves as the Columbus Citizens Committee for Peace in Vietnam. They were protesting the U.S. bombing by passing out form letters opposing the escalation of the war to passersby to send to Johnson. They were met by seven counterprotestors, one of whom carried a sign reading "SLA Seems to Mean 'Soviet Lovers Association.'" None of the counterdemonstrators were identified as Ohio State students. Both groups went about their business for more than two hours without incident.[39]

Meanwhile, speakers on both sides of the issue started to appear regularly on campus. On March 28 the Fellowship for Social Justice at First Universalist Church sponsored a debate featuring associate history professor Clayton Roberts and dentistry professor Duncan McConnell. Roberts argued that the Vietnam War was a civil war and the United States should stay out. McConnell contended the country needed to make a stand in Vietnam against communism.

The ROTC department invited faculty historian Foster Reah Dulles to speak to 200 cadets and their guests on April 1 as part of a series on the United States in world affairs. "To get involved in a war in Asia would be the wrong war at the wrong time," Dulles told his listeners. Three weeks later, the same group heard from Major General H. G. Sparrow of the U.S. Army, who said the nation was "doing the right thing" in Vietnam. The *Lantern* chimed in the next day with an editorial supporting Sparrow's position.[40]

Pierre Rocheron, secretary and public affairs officer for the French embassy in Washington, came to campus on May 17 at the invitation of Phi Alpha Theta, the national history honorary. Speaking from the perspective of France's own failure in Vietnam after nine years of warfare against the Viet Minh, Rocheron said the United States was fighting a war that it could not win by military force.

Students in Harold Harding's spring quarter Speech 402 class spent five days role-playing various U.S. officials involved in the Vietnam decision-making, including Johnson, General Maxwell Taylor, Secretary of State Dean Rusk, and Senator Everett Dirksen. They surprised Harding when they concluded war with China was inevitable. "We have no alternative but to escalate the war in Vietnam, and if we do this we will soon be at war with Red China," said junior Philip Becker, who played Johnson in the simulation.[41]

Although the war with China was hypothetical, rising draft calls were not. College students retained their deferments, but the increased need for manpower in Vietnam meant deferments would be harder to get. The Franklin County office of the Selective Service announced in August that draft calls were likely to double from 123 a month to nearly 250 by October. Students were warned they needed to be enrolled full time and remain in good standing academically to retain their deferments. Those who dropped out for a quarter to work, or for any other reason, were likely to be drafted.[42]

ESCALATING RACIAL TENSIONS

Despite passage of the Civil Rights Act in 1964, racial tensions intensified in the spring and summer of 1965. In March state and local police in Selma, Alabama, set upon peaceful marchers with clubs, tear gas, fire hoses, bullwhips, and rubber tubing wrapped in barbed wire in what would become known as Bloody Sunday. The brutality of the attack sparked outrage across the country that helped galvanize support for the Voting Rights Act, which became law in August. But it also energized black militants who advocated a more confrontational approach to white America.

Just days after the passage of the Voting Rights Act, the worst race riots the country had ever seen erupted in the poor, black Los Angeles neighborhood of Watts. The five-day confrontation, which began with white police officers arresting a black man, left 34 people dead, 1,000 injured, and nearly 4,000 arrested, and resulted in $35 million in property damage. Some 14,000 police and National Guardsmen eventually restored order, but race relations in the nation's second-largest city were in shambles. Black residents expressed impatience with a lack of jobs and mistreatment by white police. White residents grew impatient with what they saw as irresponsibility on the part of black citizens.

After the Watts riot the *Lantern* queried local civil rights leaders about what might be in store. A survey conducted earlier in the year in Columbus and 67 other cities had shown that unemployment among nonwhite workers and the percentage of nonwhite families living in poverty in Columbus were at or above the rates for the five cities that had seen inner-city riots during the last 12 months. "Until this [unemployment] problem is taken care of there will always be demonstrations and riots," warned Arthur Zebbs, local director of CORE (Congress of Racial Equality).[43]

The senior black leadership in Columbus and elsewhere, which was church-based and nonviolent, now found itself challenged by younger and more militant voices who were less inclined to reject violence. This in turn scared white voters even more, some of whom would turn to the more extreme voices calling for law and order. One of those voices belonged to Alabama governor George Wallace, who had stunned the political establishment in both parties with his strong showing among white voters in northern states, including Wisconsin and Indiana, during the 1964 primaries.

Despite the passage of civil rights legislation and Lyndon Johnson's overwhelming victory in the fall, the politics of resentment and confrontation were beginning to coalesce, with the worst yet to come.

CHAPTER 6

THE END OF THE SPEAKERS RULE

(1965)

Ohio State's first wave of baby boomers arrived in force in the fall of 1964; but over the following spring and summer it would be an unlikely coalition of nonboomers who engineered the year's most newsworthy event. They would topple one of the most visible bulwarks of the old order on campus—the Speakers Rule.

6.1. Dennis Knepley, a leader of the Free Speech Front and Students for Liberal Action, addresses a rally in front of the Main Library in spring 1965. (University Archives)

STUDENTS: BERKELEY COMES TO OHIO STATE

BERKELEY BOILS OVER

While the 1964–65 school year started peacefully at Ohio State, it was anything but peaceful at the University of California's Berkeley campus. There, a confrontation between student demonstrators and the university administration over free speech had consequences that would reach across the country and especially affect Columbus.[1]

The controversy began when Berkeley administrators decided to end a long-standing practice of allowing student political activists to set up recruiting tables in front of the campus's main gate on Telegraph Avenue. It escalated into a confrontation on December 2 when a group of about 1,500 students calling themselves the Free Speech Movement (FSM) staged a sit-in at the central administration building. They threatened to stay put until their demands to reinstate the policy were met.

At about 3 o'clock the next morning Berkeley chancellor Edward W. Strong read a statement to the protestors telling them they could get up and leave without having any action taken against them, but if they didn't go on their own, they would be arrested. Few left. Seven hundred state highway patrolmen and local police then moved in to clear the building in the largest mass arrest in California history to that time. The protestors, some of whom were veterans of sit-ins in the south, responded by going limp, meaning it took two officers to haul them out. While the officers were careful at first, they became more impatient as time went on. Some of those arrested had their heads banged as they were dragged down steps or were otherwise handled roughly. The process dragged on for 12 hours, allowing plenty of time for curious spectators to gather.

Up to that point the FSM seemed to have support from most of the students and faculty for its goals of free speech, but it drew less sympathy for disobedience as a tactic. However, the sight of uniformed police officers manhandling unarmed students made the administration look heavy-handed. Many faculty members objected to police on campus in the first place, especially those who were refugees from Nazi-occupied Europe. Now the opinions of the uncommitted on campus began to swing in favor of the FSM.

On December 8 the faculty voted 824–115 in support of the protestors' position. A student strike followed, led in part by disaffected graduate teaching assistants. This put additional pressure on the administration and the state's political leaders to find a solution. By the time classes started again in January, authorities had acceded to the protestors' demands. The tables returned to Telegraph Avenue. Chancellor Strong was fired and replaced with someone more sympathetic to student needs.

The students at Berkeley had challenged the existing order and won. Print and electronic media across the country carried the story of the protest, including the now famous speech by FSM leader Mario Savio in which he exhorted: "Put your bodies upon the gears and upon the wheels, upon the levers, upon all the apparatus, and you've got to make it stop. And you've got to indicate to the people who run it, to the people who own it, that unless you're free, the machine will be prevented from working at all."[2]

Whether because of the Berkeley situation or not, Ohio State officials approved a February 1965 speaking engagement by Russ Nixon, the controversial general manager of the left-wing *National Guardian*. The request came from Students for Liberal Action, a recognized campus organization. Nixon had been accused by some of being a communist and was under a contempt of Congress citation for repeatedly refusing to appear before the House Un-American Activities Committee. Speakers Rule opponents speculated about whether the approval meant the administration was loosening up.[3]

Then, at the April 13 meeting of the Faculty Council, engineering professor Mars Fontana made a surprise announcement. Fontana was chair of the Faculty Advisory Committee, which had been working on possible revisions to the Speakers Rule since May 1962 without coming up with an agreement on anything the board of trustees would accept. Fontana said he'd been contacted by President Novice Fawcett on behalf of the board. The trustees invited Fontana to their July meeting to discuss possible changes in the rule. "This means the trustees are ready and willing to talk," Fontana told his colleagues.[4]

RISE OF THE FREE SPEECH FRONT

Dennis Knepley, a sophomore honors student who was vice president of Students for Liberal Action, believed the university was still moving too slowly to make the necessary changes. Early in April he and several other SLA members agreed to form a new organization, the Free Speech Front (FSF), and to use the Berkeley tactics of direct action to get the administration moving. Knepley saw Fontana's April 13 announcement as a possible ploy to delay action until after students had left for the summer.[5]

Knepley also contacted student Robert Lonzo, a 23-year-old air force veteran. Lonzo was planning his own rally to protest a decision not to offer tenure to Charles J. Brauner, a popular associate professor of education. Knepley and Lonzo decided to combine forces and called for a rally on April 14. Battle lines were now being drawn—not between those for or against the Speakers Rule, but among the proponents of various protest tactics.

A crowd of about 2,000 activists and onlookers gathered on the Oval for the rally. Knepley announced that the FSF was establishing a three-week deadline for the abolishment of the Speakers Rule, implying a disruption of the ROTC Corps Day review on May 6 if the demands were not met. The aggressive stance did not meet with immediate support from other opponents of the rule. Even Students for Liberal Action was noncommittal.[6]

Knepley and Lonzo were subsequently joined by senior Jeff Schwartz, from the Columbus suburb of Bexley. Schwartz was the younger brother of Niki Schwartz, the Student Congress Party leader of three years earlier. He had previously coordinated a rally in support of the Civil Rights Act, then spent the summer in rural Louisiana helping black citizens register to vote. His experience taught him the importance of focus and discipline in nonviolent protest. "We knew Ohio was not California," Schwartz recalled later. "We were determined to make the Speakers Rule the issue, not our conduct."[7]

A little more than a week later the FSF held a second rally on the Oval. This time Students for Liberal Action was on board, as the assembled crowd applauded enthusiastically for "direct action." The FSF followed up on April 25 when a group of students estimated at 300 conducted an orderly sit-in on the second floor of the Administration Building. FSF leaders told those participating to dress to make a favorable impression (coats and ties for the men and dresses for the women). The university responded cautiously. No uniformed police were visible. No threats

6.2. Students stage a sit-in at the Administration Building to protest the Speakers Rule. Protest leaders encouraged students to be well dressed and to clean up after themselves. (University Archives)

were made. After three hours the protestors cleaned up after themselves and left, but they promised to return if no progress was made.[8]

On April 28 they were back. This time about 150 demonstrators stayed past the building's usual closing time of 5 p.m. University officials locked the doors, but let people leave. Women students departed before midnight so they did not violate curfew. Officials at first refused to allow food to be brought in, but later reversed themselves. Those who spent the night read, slept, talked among themselves, and sang folk songs. The university made no moves against them.

The students stayed on after the building opened the next morning but made no effort to disrupt operations. At noon they cleaned up and left of their own accord. There was no property damage and no arrests. An FSF spokesperson said the group would wait a week to see how the university would respond. The university did nothing.[9]

The FSF held another rally on the Oval on May 3 to announce it would not disrupt Corps Day on May 6, but instead would conduct a teach-in against the Speakers Rule the same day. The teach-in—which included folksinger Phil Ochs, who had attended Ohio State but dropped out several years earlier—attracted about 800 people. Jeff Schwartz explained the FSF's next steps. First, the group and its faculty allies would picket the board of trustees meeting scheduled for the following week. In addition, they would bring Marxist scholar Herbert Aptheker to campus later in the month to test the Speakers Rule. The announcement provoked an enthusiastic ovation from the crowd.[10]

From the FSF's perspective Aptheker was the ideal person to test the Speakers Rule. He once described himself as a "leading spokesman for the Communist Party in the United States." But Aptheker was also a respected scholar who had earned a Ph.D. in history from Columbia University and had written several books and articles on the history of black people in America. He had already spoken at a number of universities, including Yale, the University of Washington, the University of California at Berkeley, Howard University, and most recently, the University of Kansas. He'd also served honorably in the army in World War II, rising from private to major.[11]

University officials were not impressed. They turned down the request for Aptheker to speak on campus. FSF leaders were told that if they brought him to campus anyway, they would be disciplined. Instead, he spoke at an off-campus location to a group of about 450. Aptheker called for nothing more subversive than speeding up racial integration. "Why must this be slow?" he asked. "Is three centuries such dizzying speed?"[12]

The FSF tried to keep the pressure on the trustees, who met on May 13. About 80 faculty members picketed behind the building where the meeting was held, while 120 students picketed the front. Inside, Fawcett told the trustees he was committed to a "rational and satisfactory" resolution to the Speakers Rule issue and would bring forth a proposal in July from the Faculty Advisory Committee. Newly elected chair Alan B. Loop seemed to strike a conciliatory note: "We look forward to an excellent discussion with the Faculty Advisory Committee in July and we share the hope expressed by so many that from these processes will come an effective solution."[13] Some Speakers Rule opponents feared this was part of a delaying tactic hatched by the administration and the board to stall until most students and faculty were gone for the summer.

The same day faculty members opposed to the Speakers Rule released a letter signed by 428 of their colleagues calling for an emergency board meeting to change the rule.[14]

The FSF did its part to keep the issue alive by bringing Aptheker back to campus. Would the group's leaders defy the administration and risk expulsion? A standing-room-only crowd of about 900 packed the auditorium in University Hall for Aptheker's appearance on May 21. Graduate student Sanford Weinberg began by reading excerpts from Aptheker's writings in a book checked out of Ohio State's library, while Aptheker sat silently offstage. The original plan called for him to be seated onstage, but a credible death threat prompted a change in tactics. Nevertheless, this early form of guerrilla theatre accomplished its objective of dramatizing the absurdity of a rule that prohibited an author from reading his own words. Jeff Schwartz told the crowd it was a "rehearsal for what is to come," then led a "funeral march" for free speech across campus.[15]

Three days later the FSF announced Aptheker would not return to campus for a third time that spring, amid reports of disagreement within the group between the leadership and a faction that wanted to take a more confrontational stand. At a tense meeting that night the more moderate side managed to carry the day, at least for a time.[16] On May 28 the Faculty Advisory Committee released its version of a liberalized rule, which would presumably form the basis for the discussion at the July board of trustees meeting. Both the *Lantern* and Students for Liberal Action supported the proposal, as did a number of other student organizations.[17] The campus moderates looked forward to what they hoped would be a successful resolution to the long controversy.

THE UNIVERSITY: LAST STAND OF THE OLD GUARD

The nine members of Ohio State's board of trustees in July 1965 represented a cross section of the power elite who dominated state government and business at mid-decade. The board included no women, no nonwhite members, and no one younger than 57.[18] Three members had been appointed by Democratic governor Mike DiSalle (1959–63) and

6.3. Ohio State trustees, 1965. Exclusively male, white, financially successful, and in their late 50s or older, they were not sympathetic to critics of the existing order. (*Makio*)

six by his successor, Republican James Rhodes. While the board sought to minimize partisan politics during Novice Fawcett's tenure, the emotions surrounding the Speakers Rule would put everyone's patience and goodwill to the test.

DiSalle's appointments included Alan Loop, a 57-year-old Toledo attorney who served as chair; Jacob E. Davis, 59, of Cincinnati, president and chief executive officer of the Kroger Company; and Stanley C. Allyn, 73, of Dayton, chair of the National Cash Register Company. Loop and Davis were Ohio State graduates.

One of Rhodes's first acts upon taking office in January 1963 was to reappoint former Ohio governor and U.S. senator John W. Bricker to the board. Conservative, opinionated, and connected, Bricker represented the old guard Republican establishment that had run the state for most of the middle of the 20th century.[19] Bricker had earned an undergraduate degree in 1916 and a law degree in 1920, both from Ohio State. He rose through the ranks of the Republican Party and was elected governor in 1938. His brand of fiscal conservatism and opposition to Franklin Roosevelt's New Deal played well with Ohio voters, who reelected him for two more two-year terms. Bricker was Thomas

Dewey's vice presidential running mate in 1944 and helped Dewey carry Ohio, even though he lost nationally. He ran for the U.S. Senate in 1946, won, and was reelected six years later. In 1948 Governor Frank Lausche appointed him to Ohio State's board of trustees.

In 1958 Bricker backed an unpopular initiative by Republicans to limit union shops in Ohio and went down in defeat along with almost all of the state's Republican officeholders. When his second term on the university's board expired in 1962, Rhodes appointed him to a third seven-year term ending in 1969.

Obsessed with the influence of communism at Ohio State, Bricker twice asked the FBI to investigate faculty members he thought were communists, so they could be dismissed. The FBI declined.[20]

Bricker never did accept the changes sweeping the country in the 1960s. Writing in 1970 on the occasion of the university's centennial, he fired a shot at all the people he considered subversives: "We cannot yet determine the damage done to Ohio State as an educational institution or to the State of Ohio and its people by the radical and agitating professors and by troublemaking outsiders and insiders among the students."[21]

Like Bricker, Carlton S. Dargusch was a longtime member of the board, having served since 1938. While Bricker was the voice of the old guard, General Dargusch, as he preferred to be called, was the man behind the scenes, the guy who knew how to get things done. An independent lobbyist, Dargusch had clients that included the powerful Ohio Manufacturers' Association and the Ohio Council of Retail Merchants. One Statehouse reporter recalled how he was such a familiar presence lurking around the governor's office, his colleagues nicknamed him the "Gray Eminence" for his shadowy but powerful role.[22] While on the Ohio State board Dargusch helped develop the university's first retirement plan for faculty and staff, as well as the plans to expand student housing and the Medical Center.

Unfortunately for Dargusch, he violated the first rule of a true insider, which is to not attract unfavorable publicity on ethical issues. In late 1964 allegations surfaced that he misused a corporate trust fund for personal use while acting as general counsel and director of a local coal company. In an unusual move the Ohio Supreme Court voted to suspend his law license for a minimum of two years. Dargusch resigned under a cloud from Ohio State's board in October 1965, but before that he would play an important role in supporting Bricker in the Speakers Rule fight.[23]

In 1963 Rhodes and his legislative allies passed language to expand the number of trustees on university boards from seven to nine as part of the bill creating the Ohio Board of Regents. This gave Rhodes two more appointees that year, in addition to normal turnover. The first appointee was John G. Ketterer, a 64-year-old attorney from North Canton who had earned a bachelor's degree in 1923 and a law degree in 1925, both from Ohio State. The second was Frederick E. Jones, 59, of Columbus, chair of Buckeye Union Insurance Company and Ohio State Life. Mervin B. France, 63, of Cleveland joined the board in 1964 to fill an existing vacancy. France was the chief executive officer of Society National Bank.

In May 1965 Rhodes nominated Springfield, Ohio, native James W. Shocknessy, 58, to fill another vacancy. A graduate of Notre Dame and Harvard Law School, Shocknessy began practicing in Columbus in 1939. He was not confirmed by the Ohio Senate until after the July board meeting.

Despite being a collection of strong personalities, the trustees had managed to avoid a public split among themselves or with Fawcett during his first nine years as president. That was about to change.

Over the previous month the May 28 proposal by the Faculty Advisory Committee had continued to pick up support across campus. There still were some advocates for the existing rule, but they were becoming increasingly isolated. The Ohio American Legion sent a letter to Fawcett in favor of the rule. A group calling itself Citizens for Law and Order paid for a *Lantern* ad. The *Columbus Dispatch* had reiterated its hostility in a May 23 editorial. According to the *Dispatch*: "The controversy at Ohio State, in which an arrogant minority seeks to impose its will on the less volatile majority of the student body and even upon the university administration, suggests strongly subversion directed from outside."[24]

In fact the growing body of evidence suggested just the opposite. A referendum conducted in conjunction with the May Queen balloting in the spring showed that 80 percent of the 3,760 students who voted supported an abolished or modified Speakers Rule. A more scientific poll of the faculty revealed that 1,088 of the 1,496 who responded wanted the rule changed. The survey had a return rate of 58 percent.[25]

Both the administration and student activists had shown restraint in avoiding the conflicts and mass arrests that had created political backlash at Berkeley. Fawcett knew some board members were uncomfortable with a rule change, but he believed the time had come to address the issue.

A SPLIT IN THE RANKS

At the July 8 board meeting, Fawcett began the discussion by saying he thought communist political doctrine was "abhorrent," but "this university must be no less free than others to test ideas that flow from the frontiers of thought despite the fact that at times an idea may be highly controversial and even repulsive to our keener insights." He went on to say he was opposed to the existing Speakers Rule because it conflicted with federal and state laws that granted equal freedom even to those considered subversives and had brought negative publicity to the university, disrupted the orderly pursuit of education, and given unwarranted publicity to controversial speakers.[26]

Next, John Bricker read a statement that he said reflected his views and perhaps those of other board members: "Communists, Nazis and Fascists, and members of other subversive organizations and their supporters, have no right to speak at a tax-supported state university, for they are not free men, and hence, are incapable of the objectivity which must attach to all speakers at a state university. . . . So far as I am concerned, there will be no Communists, Nazis, Fascists, or other subversives, or their supporters, teaching or speaking at Ohio State while I am on the board, if I can prevent it."

No other board member had anything to say. After the proposed rule was read and the motion made to approve it, the members were polled in order of their seniority:

LOOP: "Yes."
ALLYN: "Yes."
DAVIS: "Yes."

All three had been appointed by former governor Mike DiSalle. Next came Governor Rhodes's appointees.

Bricker: "No."
Dargusch: "No."
Ketterer: "No."
Jones: "No."
France: "No."

The motion failed. The meeting was over. The entire conversation had taken seven minutes. Stunned officials were not sure what to say, so they reacted cautiously. Fawcett said he was "disappointed" but promised to keep the issue alive.[27] Mars Fontana, chair of the committee that had reworked the rule, told the *Lantern,* "I'm disappointed. . . . I spent a lot of time on the proposal." Others were less inhibited. Political science professor David Spitz predicted that a "good number" of faculty would leave. The *Lantern* called the vote an "academic repudiation" and said it "invited trouble in the fall." The president of the Council of Graduate Students said he was "appalled." Jeff Schwartz of the Free Speech Front, who had watched the meeting from the audience, said he was "outraged" and promised "massive demonstrations" in the fall. Campus conservatives joined in the criticism, although they differed with the FSF on tactics. Student Senate president Tom Workman called for collaborating with the administration to change the trustees' minds. In an informal *Lantern* survey of 25 students, graduate student Scott Utley called the decision "incredibly stupid."[28]

Criticism came from off campus as well. Newspapers in Cleveland, Toledo, Dayton, and Akron attacked the decision. (The *Columbus Dispatch* and *Cincinnati Enquirer* supported it.) U.S. senator Stephen M. Young, the Democrat who had defeated Bricker in 1958, accused the trustees of being stuck in the "Age of McKinley."[29]

Fawcett now had to navigate tricky political waters. Ironically, the board's action solidified his standing with the faculty, students, and alumni. The local chapter of the American Association of University Professors, which had sparred with Fawcett in the past, sent a letter of support. The board of the Alumni Association, which up to this point had remained neutral, was so upset it voted unanimously to support Fawcett. Even the university's student orientation leaders felt compelled to speak up. Members of this group of young men and women—a cross between the Eagle Scouts and the National Honor Society—were selected from hundreds of applicants because of their good grades, good citizenship, and positive attitudes. They seldom dabbled in campus politics, but in this case nine of them signed a letter to the board supporting Fawcett's position, saying in part: "Denying these groups the right to express themselves is only the first step to the suppression of all controversial doctrines, and there is hardly a popularly accepted tenet of twentieth century democracy that was not at one time generally considered to be controversial."[30]

Key figures in the community also chimed in. Charles Lazarus, chief executive officer of the Lazarus department stores, sent a letter of support, as did Bill Guthrie, chief executive officer of Buckeye Federal, and Supreme Court justice and former Republican governor C. William O'Neill. Even *Dispatch* publisher Preston Wolfe sent Fawcett a letter, and the newspaper subsequently refrained from criticizing the president's actions.[31]

Although members of the university community clearly disliked the existing Speakers Rule, they didn't agree about the best way to change it. A *Lantern* straw poll found both students and faculty about evenly divided on the value of more demonstrations versus further negotiations. (The Berkeley campus had been similarly divided until moderates shifted their stance against the administration when the police were called in. Chancellor Strong lost his job when the powers that be threw him under the bus.)

Fawcett knew he had one more chance before classes resumed in the fall. The next board meeting was scheduled for September 14. He had roughly two months to come up with some way to turn the situation around.

FINESSING A SOLUTION

The trustees held their September meeting at Ohio State's agricultural campus in Wooster. Rumors had circulated that something was up regarding the Speakers Rule, but no one in a position to know was talking for the record. As the lengthy meeting appeared to be drawing to a close, Alan Loop introduced a revised version of the rule. The board's newest member, James Shocknessy, who'd since been confirmed by the Ohio Senate, asked for a clarification of any changes from the July 8 version.[32]

Loop explained the revised proposal would still allow recognized student organizations to invite guest speakers to campus solely upon approval from their faculty advisers, but two new requirements had been added. Certain additional procedures had to be followed with speakers whose appearancc was "attended by extreme emotional feeling," and university facilities could not be reserved for "meetings or other purposes for student organizations not qualified under university rules."

Shocknessy said he would have preferred that all members of the board be present, but he would vote his convictions. (Ketterer was absent on business, and Jones was out of the country. Both had voted against changing the rule in July.)

Bricker reiterated his position: "I am opposed to communism or any other enemy of orderly government. I would like for Ohio State to stand out as an institution that favors civil obedience and respect for the law."

Fawcett pointed out that the two changes were "designed to emphasize the need for orderly procedure in events for which the university makes some provision. Personally, I believe this recommendation is in the long range, best interest of the university."

As the roll was called the three most senior members (Loop, Allyn, and Davis) voted yes, as they had in July. The next three (Bricker, Dargusch, and France) voted no, as they had previously. Eyes turned to Shocknessy.

Although Shocknessy had been appointed by Rhodes, he was a lifelong Democrat. And although a Democrat, he was aligned with the more conservative Lausche wing of the party. As the respected head of the Ohio Turnpike Commission, he had developed a reputation for speaking his mind. When asked about the Speakers Rule at the time of his appointment, Shocknessy had replied, "I haven't an opinion on the Speakers Rule and I have no comment."[33] Now, if he voted no or decided to abstain, the motion would fail.

The board secretary called, "Mr. Shocknessy?"

Shocknessy looked out from behind his oversized black-framed glasses. "Yes."

The meeting adjourned. Reporters rushed to call in their stories, speculating that a deal had been made in advance because a preprinted statement from the university was available immediately after the vote. Next came the questions of how the campus would respond and whether the vote would stand or be reversed when the absent board members returned. Over the next several days it became clear it would stand. Officials quietly confirmed that the board had agreed not to reopen the issue.[34]

The response from faculty and students on campus (classes had not yet started) was generally positive, although some remained wary. An FSF spokesperson told reporters: "We must realize that a rule in itself doesn't establish free speech on campus or anywhere—it is in the application of the rule."[35] But most seemed willing to give Fawcett the benefit of the doubt, at least for now. One faculty member expressed what was likely the most common reaction when he said, "There may be some strained and unpleasant incidents as we work this out—and there may be a cloud over the university for a while—but it is no longer a pall."[36]

SOCIETY: AN ODD ALLIANCE

The Speakers Rule controversy marked one of the defining moments of the demise of the old order during Ohio State's passage into the 1960s. As such, it provides an opportunity to peek behind the curtain of the intersection of academics and politics during that period.

After the blow-up in 1962 over the lockout of Phillip Luce of the Emergency Civil Liberties Committee, Fawcett knew that even though he had won that vote, he had a festering problem on his hands. Although not publicly known at the time, in the summer of 1963 Fawcett went so far as to submit a more liberal Speakers Rule to the board of trustees, but when he found it lacked support, he didn't push it.[37]

By early 1965 he was ready to try again. Three things had changed to make the attempt less risky. First, tensions between the United States and the Soviet Union had lessened significantly since the 1962 Cuban Missile Crisis, making concern over subversion less acute. Second, the recent free speech demonstrations at Berkeley had sent a clear message about what could happen if administrators found themselves on the wrong side of the issue. Third, in September 1964 Fawcett had agreed to remain at Ohio State after being courted by the American Automobile Association to become the group's executive vice president. He had even told his family he was taking them to Washington, but was talked into staying in a long private meeting with the board.[38] This experience with his trustees may have made Fawcett more comfortable pushing them in a direction they previously hadn't been willing to go.

It's less clear where the lawsuit regarding the Speakers Rule that students filed against Ohio State in early 1963 fits into the equation. In September 1964, the federal judge in the case finally ruled in favor of the university. The plaintiffs appealed, and a hearing was scheduled for October 1965. Although some activists believed their appeal prompted the university to act, evidence suggests Fawcett had already decided to either weaken or abolish the rule.[39]

Whether it was out of principle, expediency, or a combination of both, Fawcett made some sort of resolution of the Speakers Rule issue a priority for calendar year 1965. The next question was why the usually conservative Fawcett proceeded to a vote in July when he didn't have the full backing of his board. Fawcett later blamed the FSF demonstrations for causing board members who otherwise would have switched their votes to yes to change their minds, but there is no evidence to support this. In a private letter to Ohio Supreme Court chief justice C. William O'Neill written just two weeks after the July board meeting, Fawcett admitted he knew he didn't have the votes going in, but felt he had to move ahead anyway: "We had no alternative if we are to keep this place hanging together."[40] Nevertheless, administrators believed they could flip a vote or two and get the problem resolved.[41] They would now find a very powerful ally.

STRANGE BEDFELLOWS

Governor Rhodes and President Fawcett were not close, but their interests now started to converge. James Rhodes was not the kind of person to pick fights he didn't need. In fact, he'd not yet commented publicly on the Speakers Rule controversy. John Millett, head of the Board of Regents and a Rhodes confidant, recalled that the governor was becoming concerned about what was going on at Ohio State as early as May, when the actions of the Free Speech Front started to generate news. According to Statehouse reporter Abe Zaidan of the *Akron Beacon Journal*, "Rhodes couldn't have cared less one way or the other whether

[Herbert] Aptheker spoke on campus. His ideologies don't run that deep. His only interest was to keep the boat from rocking." The boat was beginning to rock a lot. Not only was statewide press coverage intense, but ambitious Democrats such as Representative Carl Stokes (D-Cleveland) were making the Speakers Rule an issue. Rhodes apparently did not want the controversy to detract from his jobs agenda just a year before his reelection campaign.[42]

Fawcett did not later recall talking to Rhodes directly about it, and there is no reason to think otherwise, but shortly after the July dust-up the governor's operatives let Ohio State officials know they disagreed with the trustees' actions and wanted to see the issue taken care of. Rhodes's appointment of Shocknessy was the first step. Although Shocknessy was publicly noncommittal, university officials knew he was a likely yes vote.[43] Then trustee Frederick Jones, also a close friend and financial supporter of the governor, announced he would be in Europe in September and could not attend the board meeting. With Shocknessy in and Jones out, Fawcett was only one vote short.

Although John Ketterer was opposed to weakening the Speakers Rule, he told Fawcett he was concerned about the impact of the board's action on Fawcett's presidency.[44] The problem was, Ketterer's law firm represented Timken Steel, and the Timkens were archconservative anticommunists. The family also was close to Rhodes. A few days before the September meeting, Ketterer announced he could not be there because of pressing business, even though he had never missed a board meeting before.[45]

The passing of the Speakers Rule proposal was a victory for almost all concerned. Unlike with the eruptions over the Rose Bowl and a jaywalking ticket, a nagging issue was addressed without making everyone look bad in the process. The self-restraint shown by both the FSF and the university administration proved to be critical in resolving the drama. The students and other critics of the rule got the changes they were hoping for. Administrators managed to look like they were still in charge while remaining reasonable and maintaining order. No one on the board needed to make an embarrassing vote switch. The governor's office got what it wanted, with no fingerprints. The process could have served as a model for peaceful change in a complex institution, but in the supercharged days to come, that was not to be.

REQUIEM

The Speakers Rule had been changed in words at the September board meeting, but would it change in practice? That was the question on campus as classes resumed. Toby Emmer, a spokesperson for the Free Speech Front, reflected the concerns of many. Emmer said the changes were "very important," but she expressed misgivings about the remaining limitations, particularly Section 3, the "extreme emotional feeling" clause, which represented a loophole that could undermine the intent of the changes.[46]

The answers would come when Students for Liberal Action invited Herbert Aptheker back to campus. The Faculty Advisory Committee, designated under the revised rule to oversee the process, quickly granted approval. But the approval came under Section 3, which meant a faculty member chosen by the committee would moderate and another faculty member chosen by the committee would present an opposing point of view. Dennis Knepley, now president of SLA, accused the committee of "raping SLA and free speech" by invoking Section 3.[47]

Nearly 400 people filled Hughes Hall Auditorium the evening of October 18 and another 100 listened from the lobby as Knepley introduced Aptheker as "a leading spokesman for the Communist Party." Aptheker didn't hold back, describing what he called the "degeneration of society and the ethical decay in the United States," which he blamed on capitalism. He cited as evidence an increase in child beating, civil disobedience, and incidents where hecklers had urged suicidal persons to act. He praised the socialist revolution that would make possible a "human social order" while its alternatives "increasingly require inhuman societies."

When Paul Craig, chair of the Department of Economics and the designated opposition speaker, was offered the opportunity to address the audience, about 30 people, many of them members of SLA, walked out in protest against Section 3. Craig said that although he disagreed with much of what Aptheker said, he would not make a formal rebuttal. He pointed out that crime and abuse are not limited to capitalistic societies, that "they exist in socialist states; they have existed in other societies." He encouraged the members of the audience to compare Aptheker's arguments to their own experience, then complimented them on their attentiveness.

Craig received a strong round of applause from most of the audience. Aptheker thanked the audience as well and also received applause. An effigy of Aptheker had been hanged from a tree on the Oval that morning, but was quickly taken down by university employees. There were no other incidents.[48]

In November SLA invited Frank Wilkinson, who'd been banned from campus in 1962, to speak. Wilkinson was approved, this time without Section 3 being invoked, which prompted Knepley to declare "the end of the free speech controversy at Ohio State." In addressing a reported 250 people, Wilkinson accused the House Un-American Activities Committee of violating the Bill of Rights and acting as a defender of segregation by conducting "witch hunts" against innocent people in the civil rights movement.[49]

The third person on the list of previously banned speakers, Phillip Luce, returned to campus in the spring. It was Fawcett's decision to ban Luce in 1962 that had set off the controversy that resulted in the faculty vote and the lawsuit. It was a radically different Luce who spoke to students on May 12. He had renounced his ties to the Communist Party and was now a leading conservative spokesperson. Luce told his listeners they should not join communist organizations in order to bring about social, economic, or political progress. Instead, "a whole lot can be done within the freedom provided by this country."[50]

Dennis Knepley's declaration about the end of the Speakers Rule turned out to be correct. University administrators would never again deny a speaker on political grounds, nor would they invoke Section 3.

CHAPTER 7

SOARING

(1965–66)

Both enrollment and sponsored research continued their upward spiral in the mid-1960s. The campus building boom continued. The resolution of the Speakers Rule controversy and the adoption of the Board of Regents master plan removed major sources of contention and uncertainty. But beneath the surface, both students and faculty were becoming restless—students because change wasn't coming fast enough, and faculty because change was coming too fast. The country was prospering, but growing violence at home and abroad began to threaten domestic tranquility.

7.1. The river towers under construction in May 1966 were part of the largest building boom in Ohio State history. (*Lantern*)

STUDENTS: NEW COALITIONS

DUELING REFERENDUMS

With the Speakers Rule controversy winding down, the question became, what would the Free Speech Front do next? At its second meeting of the quarter, on October 11, the group decided to go for broke and voted 74–0 to support a referendum to abolish the Student Senate. Jeff Schwartz originally proposed the idea of replacing the senate with a student union. "There is no student government because they are not governing anything or anyone," he said. Senate president Tom Workman denounced the proposal as an "act of revenge" by the people who had lost the previous election.[1]

To get on the ballot the proposal needed 1,000 signatures, or 4 percent of the student body. Next, 55 percent of those voting would have to vote yes for it to pass. The FSF, now calling itself the Free Student Federation, announced on January 20 that it had the requisite number of signatures. The Student Senate approved a referendum vote for March 2, while the FSF and the senate leadership agreed to four debates in the days leading up to the vote.

Meanwhile, the campus's two political parties, the Buckeye Political Party and the Student Congress Party, needed to decide what they wanted to do regarding the senate elections scheduled for the same day. The BPP decided to oppose the referendum and run a full slate of candidates. It selected two juniors, Tim Neustadt and Doug Smith, as its presidential and vice presidential ticket at the annual party convention on February 5. The BPP also nominated a full slate of 40 senate candidates.

The Student Congress Party surprised everyone when it decided at its February 14 meeting not to run any candidates. Instead, members agreed to devote their efforts to backing the FSF referendum. Since the direct election of the Student Senate president and senators had been instituted in 1962, the SCP had lost three races for president to the BPP (it did not run a candidate one year). It captured the majority of senate seats only once in four years. SCP spokesperson Allen Pack explained the party was backing the referendum, not the FSF, which the SCP accused of advocating a "negative approach." Two days later all eight SCP senators walked out of a senate meeting, saying they would not be back. "Student government on the Ohio State campus is dying," the *Lantern* observed in a critical editorial.[2]

Buckeye Political Party leaders worried the FSF referendum might get enough votes from disgusted voters to pass. At the February 21 debate the party dropped a bombshell that changed the nature of the campaign. Neustadt, the presidential candidate, announced he would introduce a competing referendum to establish a convention to rewrite the constitution of the Student Senate. This was clearly an effort to go after the people who were unhappy with the senate but thought the Free Speech Federation was too radical.[3]

FSF supporters immediately cried foul, claiming this was an attempt by the BPP to confuse voters. The rhetoric escalated rapidly. The BPP charged that passage of the FSF referendum would end May Week and Homecoming because funding would be frozen when the source (the Student Senate) was abolished. The FSF said this was a scare tactic—pointing out that the referendum included language to authorize the Traditions Board to continue to operate—and accused the BPP of deliberate misinformation. A subsequent debate at the Ohio Union got so heated, one student rushed to the information desk and warned, "You'd better get an adult in there. Things are getting pretty tense."[4]

John Bonner, executive dean for student relations, interjected himself into the fray by telling the *Lantern* he agreed that passage of the FSF referendum would cut off funding for May Week and Homecoming. He also offered his opinion that parts of the BPP referendum delegating authority to a constitutional convention were not feasible.[5]

On March 1, the day before the election, the *Lantern* came out with an editorial supporting the FSF referendum and opposing the BPP version. That morning 4,500 *Lanterns* disappeared from loading docks at dorms and Greek houses across campus. Supporters of both referendums denied any culpability, and student leaders deplored the act. Campus police were called in to investigate, but didn't turn up anything. The Student Congress Party announced it would post guards around delivery sites the next morning.[6]

A record 10,500 students turned out to vote on March 2. They supported the BPP referendum 5,941 to 4,152 and voted down the FSF referendum 5,738 to 4,814. A breakdown by senate district revealed a lot about who voted and why. The districts populated with Greek houses and commuters supported the BPP referendum. The districts with men's dorms and apartments and rooming houses supported the FSF referendum. The surprise came in District 20, the south campus women's dorms. A swing district, it had gone narrowly for the SCP in the presidential elections the previous spring. But this time the BPP referendum passed 527–167 and the FSF referendum failed 191–514. Apparently these students, mostly freshmen and sophomore women, found the FSF proposal just too radical.[7]

THE CONVENTION AND THE OLD GUARD

Thanks to the Student Congress Party's decision not to run anyone, the Buckeye Political Party had total control of the Student Senate for the first time in its history. It also had a commitment to call a constitutional convention, something else that had never been done and that could totally restructure the senate.

The referendum provided for the election of a 45-member convention to write a new constitution. Ten members were to be elected at large and the remainder selected from four living areas: south dorms, north dorms, Greek houses, and rooming houses and other off-campus residences.

One hundred students filed for the 45 positions. On election day, April 25, only about 2,000 voters turned out. They chose an eclectic combination of political insiders and outsiders, liberals and conservatives. Dennis Knepley, president of Students for Liberal Action and a founder of the Free Student Federation, led the candidates with 1,062 votes, but six of the remaining nine at-large delegates chosen were members or former members of the existing senate.

The constitutional convention met for the first time in late April and immediately demonstrated it would go its own way. Delegates passed a resolution declaring the independence of the senate, then voted by acclamation to name junior Alan Melamed the convention chair. Melamed was an at-large delegate but an active SCP member and former senator with close ties to the FSF. All this occurred under the auspices of the Student Senate, which had sponsored the referendum. The people who had opposed the BPP referendum were skeptical of new senate president Tim Neustadt's commitment, but were pleasantly surprised when he followed through by promising to work with the FSF and others to reform student government.[8]

In many ways Neustadt fit the profile of Student Senate presidents in the first half of the 1960s—he had graduated from an affluent high school in Shaker Heights, was a member of the Buckeye Political Party, and was affiliated with a fraternity—but he turned out to be something different. His father was a salesman, and Neustadt had had to work to support himself since he was 14. His fraternity, Zeta Beta Tau, was not usually associated with campus politics. He majored in the classics, not business or political science. In the end he would serve as a transitional figure between the old conservative order and the more change-oriented activists that followed.

Neustadt's conciliatory stance did not go down well with his political base. Things blew open on May 18 when six of the BPP's vice presidents resigned en masse. One of them, Bill Geiger, accused Neustadt of yielding to "a radical fringe group like the Free Student Federation by adopting their proposals and attitudes."[9] The six vice presidents issued a statement the next day reaffirming their support for in loco parentis for students under 21.

Neustadt responded by calling the senate structure "archaic" and accusing the six of obstructionism. "You are not just answering to a fraternity but to the whole student body," he told them. "If you don't want to get on board get off now."[10] Bill Stern, Neustadt's hand-picked party chair, then called an emergency meeting of the BPP membership. Only 25 people showed up, but they were enough to replace all six vice presidents with younger and more supportive members. "We can't tolerate people afraid to take stands on controversial issues," Stern told them. "This party will no longer tolerate conservatism."[11] In a stunning reversal of fortune, in less than seven weeks the BPP had gone from a 14-year tradition as the ruling campus party to lying in shambles.

Despite the contentious election campaign, the delegates to the constitution convention found they had a lot in common. They agreed on five committee chairs who reflected diverse opinions, including two with BPP ties, two with SCP ties, and one with close ties to the FSF. The convention continued to meet weekly for the remainder of spring quarter. Before long, discussions coalesced around three issues: ending the veto power of the dean of students over actions of the Council on Student Affairs; placing students on key faculty committees, such as the Council on Instruction; and developing a student bill of rights.

At first the administration was not sure how to respond. On the Council on Student Affairs issue Dean Bonner tried to have it both ways. He told the *Lantern* he seldom used his veto power anyway, so he had no problem giving it up. Then he added it was not his to give up, but rather a decision of the Faculty Council. When it came to students on key faculty committees Bonner said he was all for it, but the reaction from other administrators and faculty was negative. Albert J. Kuhn, chair of the English department, spoke for many of his colleagues when he said that students should not make policy that involves instruction.[12]

The convention also tried to broaden its base of support. It approved a voting seat to Neustadt, the Student Senate president. It awarded a nonvoting seat to the president of the Council of Graduate Students. Undergraduates had not attempted to work with graduate students since the two governments were split in 1962, but common ground on issues such as students serving on committees offered an opportunity for mutual support. However, the delegates turned down a request for a voting seat from the Women's Self Government Association, which they believed was an interest group not aligned with the convention's goals.

With the agenda now set, the constitutional convention chairs would use the summer to draft the planks for the new student government so that real deliberations could begin when school started in the fall.

MORE NEW VOICES

While the BPP fractured internally, another bedrock of the system held together—barely. WSGA faced strong pressures both internally and externally. On February 23 the organization voted to slightly liberalize women's hours. The WSGA board approved a recommendation to the dean of women to extend curfews by one hour a night four nights a week, from 11 p.m. to midnight, and to give all sophomore, junior, and senior women the right to stay out until 2 a.m. on Friday and Saturday nights. A proposal to abolish hours for all senior women was voted down. The dean of women approved the proposed changes a month later, which was fast by university standards.

But not fast enough for many of WSGA's younger members. Eight undergraduate women, led by freshman Donna Goodman and junior Judy Winkler, announced they would initiate a petition drive calling for no restrictions on hours for sophomore, junior, and senior women and for abolishing the hated Apartment Rule, which placed restrictions on women students visiting men's apartments. They wanted to get 2,500 signatures, which would represent about a quarter of the 10,000 women on campus. "The overbearing controls and restrictions imposed on the woman student stifles maximum development of responsibility and maturity," the petition read. "The university recognizes the right of the male student to govern his own hours. It must now recognize this right for the female student also." The effort quickly picked up support from the Free Student Federation, the Freshman Senate, the new South Campus Student Association, and the *Lantern.*[13] Even the BPP-dominated Student Senate endorsed the proposal "in concept."

On May 18 Goodman and Winkler presented their petition to the WSGA board along with 2,361 signatures. After a brief debate over the advisability of moving so quickly, the petition was referred to the standards commission for further study. Goodman and Winkler were livid. They had tried to work through the system. The system had not responded. They followed up by resigning from WSGA. Winkler elaborated to the *Lantern*: "Ideally, being a member provides representation. Realistically, it provides nothing." That prompted Christine Conaway, the dean of women, to remind the pair that resigning from WSGA did not mean they could resign from WSGA rules.[14]

The *Lantern,* among others, was quick to jump on the action (or inaction). In an editorial titled "The Ponderous Pace of Self Government," it attacked WSGA's position on the issue and reminded readers it had taken the organization nearly three years just to allow women to wear slacks to lunch.[15] The battle for the hearts and minds of Ohio State women students was beginning, and WSGA was on the wrong side.

Younger members challenged the old guard at the Buckeye Political Party as well. When the six vice presidents resigned en masse in May, Neustadt and Stern replaced them with freshmen and sophomores ready to move up in the ranks. One of them, Lloyd Siegel, would be elected president of the Undergraduate Student Government (the renamed Student Senate) the following year, but not as the BPP standard-bearer.[16]

Residence hall students expressed themselves in new ways. Since the fall of 1960 the number of "dormies," as they called themselves, had doubled, and they were now starting to play a more active role in campus policy. In January south campus students voted to merge the Men's

Residence Halls Association and the Women's Residence Hall Council into the South Campus Student Association to help them speak with one voice. The SCSA quickly asserted itself. In April it challenged the university's decision to search student rooms between quarters. It also voted to support allowing women to wear slacks at all meals. In May it came out in support of the Goodman-Winkler petition.

PUNTING ON DISCRIMINATION

While activists succeeded in repealing the Speakers Rule and in realigning student government, another group of students took on the problem of discrimination in housing. Twenty students identifying themselves as the Ohio State chapter of the National Association for the Advancement of Colored People tried unsuccessfully to get the university to more aggressively enforce its nondiscrimination policy. A survey of area landlords conducted the previous spring by the University Area Fair Housing Commission had revealed that only 26 percent of the rooming houses registered with the dean of men's office said they were open to renting to black students. Another 26 percent were undecided, and a whopping 42 percent flat-out refused, even though university policy required them to do so.

The group's spokesperson, graduate student Nancy Silver, chastised Ohio State administrators for not enforcing their own rules. Lowell A. Wrigley and Barbara P. Quilling, the assistant deans responsible for off-campus housing, denied the charge. Quilling said she had received no complaints since she took the job three months earlier. Silver countered that no complaints had been lodged because black students knew it was futile; instead, they went on to the places they knew would accept them. She also said her group had identified specific examples they would share in a follow-up meeting with the dean of men's staff.[17]

That meeting with Dean Mylin H. Ross in December was inconclusive. Of the four cases presented by the students, none was sent on to the housing review board. Wrigley explained one landlord was deleted from the list of university-approved housing when he confirmed he would not rent to black students; one was dropped because he didn't have the minimum number of beds; and a third was dropped because the landlord couldn't be reached by phone and the property had a "for sale" sign in the front yard. No action was taken on a fourth because the landlord denied she had talked to anyone from the NAACP.

To add insult to injury, Ross also announced the university would no longer maintain a list of apartments available to students. The list was intended to help married couples, he explained, but was being misused by single men. "Also we feel guilty about listing places we can't inspect," he said. Silver accused the dean's office of abdicating responsibility and sought support elsewhere on campus to reverse the ruling on apartments. Support was not forthcoming. Even the *Lantern,* which had usually been a leader in calling for an end to housing discrimination, dismissed the effort, reasoning that apartments were not the university's business.[18]

The Columbus NAACP also tried to get the university to agree to pursue affirmative action in future construction projects after six members lay down in front of delivery trucks at the river towers construction sites in May. They protested there were no black plumbers, electricians, sheet metal workers, or ironworkers among the dozens of workers on the site. The NAACP subsequently announced an agreement, but it was vague and did not apply to current construction.[19]

President Novice Fawcett seemed above it all. He told the national convention of Kappa Kappa Gamma in June that the prolonged battle against discrimination by fraternities and sororities "has been won for the most part," and that current college and university students were "more tolerant and less discriminatory toward the so-called minority groups."[20] In fact, Ohio State could take some pride in being among the first universities to have fraternities and sororities remove discriminatory clauses, but significant issues remained. When faced with a choice between offering more opportunities for black students and confronting the existing white establishment, the university proceeded with extreme caution or not at all.

THE *LANTERN* PSEUDO-CONTROVERSY

Winter quarter featured a controversy over who controlled the *Lantern*'s editorial policy. At a January press conference, Free Student Federation spokesperson Robert Hoerger announced that after a week of talking to *Lantern* faculty and staff, the group had concluded the university

New Traditions

While some old traditions passed, new ones were born. On October 9, 1965, the Ohio State Marching Band performed a new arrangement of a popular rock anthem by the Dayton-area band the McCoys before nearly 84,000 rain-soaked football fans in Ohio Stadium. The crowd didn't show much reaction to John Tatgenhorst's version of "Hang On Sloopy." But the next week, as the Buckeyes were losing to Michigan State in East Lansing, Ohio State fans started chanting "Sloopy, Sloopy, Sloopy!" The band obliged, to the delight of the crowd. The response grew with each game that season.[1]

The university chose Brutus Buckeye as its official mascot that November after a campuswide naming contest. Winner Kerry Reed said he chose "Brutus" because it meant "heavy." He received a $50 gift certificate and Buckeye immortality.[2]

1. Eric Lyttle, "The Real Story of 'Hang On Sloopy,'" *Columbus Monthly,* September 2003, 40–41.

2. "'Brutus the Buckeye' Is Name of Ohio State Mascot," *Lantern,* November 22, 1965, 6.

administration viewed the newspaper as a public relations tool and used "personal pressure and fiscal threats" to censor its content or shape its policies.[21]

Fawcett denied any attempt to censor the *Lantern,* but said students had complained to him about biased coverage. Three days later it became clear who they were. Fourteen students calling themselves SATA (Students Asking for Truthful Answers) announced they would conduct their own investigation into the *Lantern*'s editorial policies. The group's spokesperson, Thomas G. Sawyer, said they had met with Fawcett to let him know what they were doing, but they were dedicated to objectivity.[22]

The founding members of SATA represented a who's who of the Buckeye Political Party. They included varsity football co-captain Greg Lashutka (who would later become mayor of Columbus), as well as the presidents of WSGA, Inter-Fraternity Council, Women's Pan Hellenic, Ohio Union Activities, and three current or former presidents of the Freshman Senate, including Sawyer. Tom Workman, the outgoing president of the Student Senate, spoke for many in the group when he used his farewell address in March to blame student government's lack of credibility on what he called the *Lantern*'s negative coverage. SATA announced that a report would be out in February.

By May the still-unfinished report had become a running joke. "SATA, Where Are You?" the *Lantern* taunted in an editorial.[23] On May 31 the Freshman Senate, which had passed a resolution endorsing SATA in January, debated a second resolution undoing the first. Freshman Senate president Bruce Core, a founding member of SATA, spoke against the repeal resolution but it passed anyway. SATA never did release its promised report, and by the time classes resumed in the fall, the question of who controlled the *Lantern* was a dead issue, symbolizing how much the influence of campus conservatives had declined.

COMMUNICATIONS AND THE PRESIDENT

As the school year moved to a close, President Fawcett had two face-to-face meetings with student leaders focused on communications. The first, held in April, involved what the administration liked to call "responsible student leaders" (as opposed to protesters), such as the elected representatives of living units, college councils, and so on. The meeting came about at the request of former SCP vice presidential candidate Vic Frost, who suggested Fawcett meet with a cross section of student leaders in an unfiltered conversation. Fawcett quickly agreed, but John Bonner, who followed up, let Frost know in no uncertain terms that he, Bonner, would set the agenda. Frost was not even invited to the meeting, in which Fawcett and nine of his cabinet members focused on how students could have more influence on university decisions.[24]

A month later Fawcett met with a delegation from the Free Student Federation for the first time. The FSF had originally proposed a mass meeting on the Oval, which Fawcett declined, fearing it could turn into a media circus. He agreed instead to meet with three representatives in his office. The ground rules reflected continuing distrust. Fawcett insisted that questions be submitted in advance and that no tape recorders be used; nor could the *Lantern* be present, under the argument it would limit the free exchange of ideas.

The FSF submitted 37 questions as requested, some of which revealed distrust on its part as well. For example, one question asked: "Are university administrators authorized to tape-record conversations with students without informing them?" Fawcett answered that there were no tape recorders or microphones in his office that he knew of, which was odd, given that as president he should have known if there were. He also said he was advised there were no such devices in other administrative offices.

Despite low expectations going in, the meeting did not turn into a shouting match. FSF chair Robert Queisser described it as "constructive, friendly, open and honest." Fawcett also spoke positively. "I am not enough of an idealist to think we are going to solve our communications problems with this meeting," he said, but he called the gathering "useful and stimulating." The most substantive discussion involved what FSF leaders believed was a lack of communication from the administration. They used the example of Ohio University president Vernon Alden, who regularly had open meetings with students to discuss problems. According to a *Lantern* account published after the meeting, Fawcett's answer resembled those he had previously given to similar questions. He said he spent as much time as possible with students and probably more than any president at a comparable university. He said his job usually kept him busy 10 hours a day, seven days a week. The university was a complex place, he said, and he was physically limited in the amount of communicating he could do.[25]

While Fawcett could continue to legitimately claim he would meet with any student group that asked, he saw no need to initiate such meetings himself. Fairly or not, students saw this as either hostility or indifference, a disconnect that would fester as tensions rose during the remainder of the decade. Speaking years later for Ohio State's Oral History Project, *Cleveland Plain Dealer* reporter David Hopcraft, who had covered Fawcett for the *Lantern,* said the president's relations with students became "increasingly hostile" as students became more assertive. "It just shocked me how formal he was," Hopcraft said. "That's who he was. And he was certainly not equipped for the generation of students that he found himself with."[26]

As for student activists, even though the FSF lost its bid to abolish the Student Senate outright, it had dramatically changed the nature of the campus discussion. The political balance in the student body had clearly moved leftward. By the end of spring quarter 1966, the Speakers Rule had been overturned, in loco parentis was teetering, and the ruling conservative political order had fractured.

THE UNIVERSITY: PLANS AND MORE PLANS

John Mount, recently named vice president for educational services, made a presentation to the trustees at their November meeting about how much Ohio State had changed since Fawcett arrived in the fall of 1956. Mount painted a picture of progress, comparing the overall enrollment growth of 80 percent during that period with certain subcategories of students. For example, the number of undergraduates grew 56 percent and new freshmen grew only 14 percent on the Columbus campus. At the same time graduate student enrollment increased 119 percent, reflecting a more serious academic atmosphere. Summer enrollment grew 116 percent, reflecting a more efficient use of facilities. In addition, admissions to branch campuses (including the new Columbus branch) had increased to more than 5,000. This allowed the university to raise the academic profile of the incoming freshman class at main campus. In 1956 only 43 percent of new freshmen were in the top third of their high school class; by the fall of 1965, 73 percent were.[27]

THE BENEFITS OF FEDERAL LARGESSE

In July the trustees approved receipt of a record amount of research and training grants: $6.7 million, more than twice the previous one-month record set in December 1962. Ohio State was ranked 13th nationally in research volume in 1965 and fourth in the Big Ten, behind Michigan, Illinois, and Wisconsin. Space and defense spending continued to lead, but federally funded research in other areas grew as well.[28]

For example, in February 1965 the U.S. Department of Education approved Ohio State's proposal to become the nation's leader in research in vocational education. The multidisciplinary Center for Research and Leadership Development in Vocational Education was founded to address one of the main goals of the Economic Opportunity Act of 1964 (the War on Poverty): to help young people who needed skills—not necessarily a college degree—to land a job. The faculty included experts in education, agriculture, and the behavioral sciences. The original grant amounted to $610,000, but in October 1966 the center leveraged that into a five-year, $10 million grant, the largest received by the university to date.[29]

The federal government also provided funding for the Center for Water Resources as part of the Water Quality Act of 1965. The center had been established by the university in 1959 and included faculty and other experts from chemical and civil engineering, zoology, and geology. The 1965 law designated Ohio State's program as the center for the entire state. Director George P. Hanna said researchers would focus on the environmental impact of acid water runoff from coal mines in southeast Ohio and the increasing pollution of Lake Erie.

Other education and human services grants from the federal government that year funded projects that evaluated antipoverty programs in Columbus schools, increased the number of dentistry and medical students in order to relieve shortages, and established a graduate program in information sciences.

All the activity reflected the belief that there wasn't a problem too big or too small to be solved by federal funding and the application of the best minds in the country's universities. The social sciences were even called on to improve the effectiveness of the U.S. effort in Vietnam. James C. Naylor, associate professor of psychology, headed a project funded by the Department of Defense that conducted interviews with about 450 Green Berets after they returned from Vietnam. The purpose was to determine the psychological impact of various weapons on both the Viet Cong and civilians, presumably to increase casualties among the enemy and decrease collateral destruction to civilians.[30]

FAWCETT PLANS—MOVING AHEAD

The plan President Fawcett proposed in 1962 for dealing with soaring enrollments had three parts: expanding facilities, amending the academic calendar, and restructuring academic programs. The passage of Issue One in 1963 provided the financial support to move the facilities plan forward on a crash basis. As fall quarter 1965 began, 80 major construction projects worth $178 million were in either design or construction. They included 10 projects scheduled to be finished over the next 12 to 18 months, which would complete the first phase of the plan.

The proposed amendment to the academic calendar—a conversion from quarters to trimesters—failed due to opposition from the faculty. Instead, a faculty committee developed a system to equalize all quarters at 11 weeks. The new system took effect in the fall of 1964 and passed with flying colors.[31]

Academic restructuring took longer. The original plan prepared in 1962 ran into fierce opposition from the deans and other interests, so university officials developed a revised plan to include a two-year general college and a less sweeping reconfiguration of the College of the Arts and Sciences.

Ohio State's two-year Columbus branch finally admitted its first students in the fall of 1964. Richard H. Zimmerman was appointed dean in October 1965. He presented a proposal two months later that would establish a permanent general college west of the Olentangy River to serve freshmen and sophomores. In a 137-page report his committee described the types of students who would be taught there. Top students would still begin their work on main campus. Others, such as those who had not chosen a major or who wanted a two-year degree, would remain at what would be called University College.[32]

After allowing for several months of discussion, the proposal came back to the Faculty Council for a formal vote in May. Some members criticized the concept. Paul Craig, chair of the Department of Economics, said the college across the river would become an academic "scrap heap." Physics professor Philip Jastram argued there had not been enough time to fully evaluate the proposal. However, the Faculty Council gave the go-ahead, and two days later the board of trustees unanimously approved the new University College.[33]

University College would begin operations in fall quarter 1967. The Columbus branch was designed to handle the overflow of students in the interim. In June, Edward Rhine, assistant director of admissions, declared the branch a success because it allowed the university to accommodate 1,300 additional freshmen within existing facilities by offering evening classes. Most of the students were late applicants to Ohio State from Columbus-area high schools. Branch director James Bell reported that both the faculty and students involved were satisfied with the arrangement.[34]

Reconfiguring the College of the Arts and Sciences constituted the remaining portion of the academic restructuring plan. After the hostile reception to the initial report in 1962, the administration pulled back to a less ambitious plan but still sought to decentralize the college decision-making in order to overcome what one dean called "paraplegia" in the administration of the arts and sciences. The first step was to create a free-standing college in the rapidly growing field of biological sciences. The Council on Instruction recommended that the existing departments of entomology, zoology, botany and plant pathology, and agricultural biochemistry be moved from the College of Agriculture and Home Economics to form the core of the new College of Biological Sciences.[35]

The proposal came to the Faculty Council for approval in February and sparked a heated debate some compared to the Rose Bowl dispute in 1961. Agriculture dean Roy Kottman objected to moving entomology and botany and plant pathology out of his college, but was voted down in a show of hands. The motion to approve the college passed on a voice vote and was sent on to the trustees, who approved it in March to be effective July 1.[36] It was Ohio State's first new college in 50 years.

The university also took steps to reconfigure colleges and add programs. The Faculty Council approved the creation of the new School of Allied Medical Services as part of the College of Medicine. The school was designed to meet the growing demand for medical dietitians, illustrators, and technicians, as well as physical and occupational therapists. The College of Education reorganized itself into four divisions. Five graduate-level programs were added, including master's degrees in architecture, fine arts, and music. A Ph.D. program was added in linguistics, as well as master's and Ph.D. programs in the fast-growing field of nuclear engineering.

THE BOARD OF REGENTS MASTER PLAN

The Ohio Board of Regents did not exist when most of these plans were developed in the early 1960s. But by 1965–66 the regents were making their presence felt. By and large their goal of making Ohio State the premiere graduate and research center in the state aligned with where the university wanted to go. It was also Ohio's largest undergraduate teaching institution and one of the largest in the world. The problem was, what to do with all those undergraduates?

Differences in approaching the issue surfaced in public for the first time in November when the regents floated the idea of capping enrollment at the Columbus campus at 35,000 because, according to Chancellor John Millett, it was becoming too congested.[37] Ohio State officials were horrified. Their elaborate planning process was built around an enrollment of 40,000 students on the central campus. Losing the tuition and state support of 5,000 students would precipitate a financial crisis. The regents backed off somewhat and—after a series of confusing statements, clarifications, and restatements about who would be admitted—capped enrollment for new first-quarter freshmen only.[38]

The regents released the final version of their master plan in June. For Ohio State, it turned out to be a mixed bag. The plan recognized the university's role as Ohio's center of research and graduate studies, but otherwise emphasized increasing enrollments. It put priority on expanding enrollment in the state's urban areas, including Columbus, and on establishing a college within 30 miles of every Ohioan. It also called for increased enrollment in Ohio State's medical and dental schools and for continuing open enrollment at all campuses for undergraduates.[39] This ambitious agenda would soon find itself up against the reality of a nonambitious resource base in terms of state operating support.

PLANS TO IMPROVE INSTRUCTION

While the university and the Board of Regents untangled their policy differences, a special committee worked on a preliminary report on improving instruction. The Committee on Teaching had been appointed the year before by John Weaver, vice president for instruction, and was chaired by economics professor Meno Lovenstein. The committee's report, which came out in April, covered a number of areas but made specific recommendations regarding four items:

1. Given Ohio State's research mission, it was understood many introductory undergraduate courses were taught by graduate teaching assistants; therefore, the university needed to invest in making those teaching assistants better teachers.
2. The university and the faculty needed to make better use of new facilities and equipment to improve teaching.
3. The university needed to support innovative teaching methods already underway in various colleges, including the honors programs in the College of the Arts and Sciences.

4. Teaching was so bound up in course content that the current review of undergraduate course content needed to be sped up, particularly for the lower-division courses.[40]

The university moved quickly on many of the suggestions, but less so on others. In July, for example, it announced a pilot summer program to improve the skills of selected graduate students who would be teaching freshman English, mathematics, chemistry, and accounting. It allocated $30,000 in general funds for the purpose, but covered only 26 of the 1,300 graduate teaching assistants. The Committee on Teaching also submitted a grant request to the Ford Foundation for $1.2 million over five years to expand training for graduate teaching assistants even further. The application noted that teaching literature, which graduate students in English were reasonably well trained for, was "radically different" from teaching freshman composition. The request was turned down, and an opportunity was missed for Ohio State to take a leadership position in improving undergraduate instruction.[41]

In August, the university announced it was expanding its use of technology through the enormously popular remote listening centers program, which was already the world's largest. The listening centers allowed students to practice with foreign language tapes at their own pace. A total of 114 stations would be added to various locations on campus, including the new river towers. Another 50 remote stations would be available for a rental charge of $15 a month to off-campus living units, such as fraternities, sororities, and scholarship houses.

The College of the Arts and Sciences announced a program beginning in the fall to create a "small-college atmosphere" for 200 to 300 freshmen who would be matched up to share living quarters and some classes. "We believe this program will help reduce the cultural shock and sense of anonymity which many new students experience upon coming to a big university," explained Associate Dean John W. Gustad. He said one student who had already been accepted to a private eastern college changed her mind and chose Ohio State when she was invited to participate in the program.[42]

Not everything went as smoothly. Jackson W. Riddle, associate dean of faculties in charge of the course revisions that the Committee on Teaching wanted sped up, announced in May that, in fact, the process would be slowed down. The revisions intended to take place in the fall of

Cheating Scandal

As college enrollments soared in the 1960s, so did concerns about cheating. A scandal at the Air Force Academy in 1965 fueled media interest in the subject. How widespread the practice was at colleges across the country was a topic of much speculation, but little hard evidence was found. Nevertheless, Ohio State was not immune. The story of the largest cheating scandal in the university's history broke in July 1966 when 39 students were disciplined for cheating in a freshman math course. All were given failing grades. Ten who had circulated stolen tests were dismissed outright, and 16 others were suspended for six to nine months. The remainder, except two, were put on probation. All but eight of the students were freshmen, and many had not been doing well in the class. University officials said the incident was an exception and that widespread cheating was rare. However, some students countered that claim and said most people simply didn't get caught.[1]

1. Joseph D. Keefer, "Three Ohio State Officials Say Cheating Is Isolated," *Lantern,* July 15, 1966, 1.

1966 would be delayed a year. Riddle blamed the delay on administrative overload in key departments caused by conflicting priorities related to the reorganization of the College of Education and the creation of University College and the College of Biological Sciences.[43]

The students tried to do their part to improve teaching, also with mixed results. The Student Senate announced a pilot program for student-conducted course evaluations in the College of Commerce. With the support of Dean James R. McCoy, the senate's education committee distributed 4,500 questionnaires. Students were asked to evaluate textbooks, outside readings, tests, and lectures. More than 1,000 questionnaires were returned. While the survey did provide useful information, many courses had too few responses to be valid.[44]

The 1965–66 school year also saw unplanned losses of key personnel involved in instruction. Vice President Weaver announced in January that he was leaving to become president of the University of Missouri. Economics professor Meno Lovenstein, whom Weaver had appointed to chair the Committee on Teaching, said in May that he would be joining the faculty at Ohio University. Three weeks later the highly regarded head of the arts and sciences honors program, Associate Dean William Boyd, announced he would be taking over as vice chancellor for student affairs at the University of California at Berkeley.

THE FACULTY PUSHES BACK

The multiple structural changes confronting Ohio State in the midsixties suggested half a dozen freight trains speeding down a track, presumably toward the same destination. The prospect was particularly unsettling for faculty who just wanted to be left alone to teach and do research in the ways they felt most comfortable. By the middle of the school year, some of them began to rebel.

It began with a controversy over who would succeed George Kienzle as director of the School of Journalism. Kienzle had passed away unexpectedly from cancer in March 1965. The following February, a faculty search committee chaired by the school's acting director, Paul Barton, voted 12–2 to recommend Barton for the position.

Arts and sciences dean J. Osborn Fuller did not find this acceptable and announced he would organize a new search committee with himself as chair. He explained he wanted an outside candidate in order to broaden the school's focus, as recommended by an independent review panel. Members of the panel had agreed the school was doing an excellent job of training aspiring news reporters, editors, magazine writers, and public relations practitioners, but said it was not living up to its potential as part of a comprehensive research university responsible for creating new knowledge. They recommended the school expand and improve its graduate programs and research output.[45]

That did not sit well with the faculty, who felt threatened by the change in emphasis. They accused the administration of trying to take over the school in order to gain control of the *Lantern* and turn it into a house organ. The *Lantern* staff rallied in support of the faculty, and the war was on. *Lantern* supporters feared the administration was retaliating for the newspaper's history of criticizing its decisions. The reporting on the president's house controversy the previous fall quarter was just the latest example.

At that time the president's house was located on 12th Avenue, across from the south campus women's dorms. The 40-year-old house was regarded as too small and out of date. A proposed new residence would be built on west campus on North Star Road at a cost of $300,000 in privately raised funds. After the trustees approved a plan in December 1965 to hire an architect, the *Lantern* led the charge against it, calling the proposed residence a "mansion" and a "blatant excess."[46] The subsequent public outrage across the state forced President Fawcett to withdraw the request.

Fears of censorship of the *Lantern* increased when the person Fawcett chose to succeed Kienzle, William E. Hall, director of the journalism program at the University of Nebraska, made inflammatory remarks in a *Lantern* interview on April 14. Hall said Ohio State's program ranked "quite low." He also told the dissenting faculty to shape up or ship out: "If the nine protesting faculty members are as sincere in their principles as news stories indicate, there is no alternative but for them to resign, and as quickly as possible, to permit us to begin our rebuilding program."[47]

That statement provoked a barrage of criticism across campus. Again the *Lantern* staff rallied around the faculty. The faculty in the Department of History voted their support as well. The Free Student Federation denounced both the appointment and censorship of the *Lantern.* An anti-Hall rally on the Oval drew 300. Three campus groups announced independent investigations into the affair. But as spring quarter wore on, the controversy seemed to lose steam. Hall tempered his earlier comments and pledged to protect the independence of the *Lantern.* His colleagues at Nebraska spoke up in his defense. The reports from the independent investigations criticized the administration for its handling of the situation but found no evidence of censorship.[48]

As the journalism controversy died down, the conflict over the faculty's role in running the institution heated up. Richard A. Popham, an associate professor of botany and plant pathology, was the outgoing president of the respected Ohio Academy of Science. He used the occasion of his farewell address to the academy in April to read a 28-page statement blasting Ohio State's leaders—both the faculty and the administration. Citing the decision to create the College of Biological Sciences, he said: "Far-reaching decisions on matters that affect the academic quality of the university are too frequently made by administrators on the spur of the moment and without sufficient facts or expert counsel when both are readily available." He went on to criticize the Faculty Council, which he saw as a "rubber stamp" for the administration.[49]

Popham's faculty colleagues on the nine-member Council on Instruction issued a joint statement disputing his account. They identified what they said were 15 factual errors in his presentation, including his assertion that the proposal to create the College of Biological Sciences had been sprung on the faculty without prior warning. Council members said the proposal had been under discussion since 1960, and they challenged Popham's conclusions as "gross misunderstandings and misconceptions."[50]

While Popham may have been on the fringe, others who expressed similar concerns were not. Myron Q. Hale, associate professor of political science, announced in February that he would chair a special committee of the local chapter of the American Association of University Professors to look at faculty governance at Ohio State. Hale referred to a set of principles the AAUP had adopted in 1962 that said in part: "Faculty should have primary responsibility for determining education policies of the institution."[51]

The end of the school year brought a number of departures of prominent faculty in addition to Weaver, Lovenstein, and Boyd. That wasn't new; faculty came and went all the time. What was new was an increasing propensity to bash the university while leaving it. A year earlier Eric Solomon, who had left the English department after six years for San Francisco State, decided to write about his experiences at Ohio State. His article was published in November 1965 in the *Atlantic Monthly* under the title "Free Speech at Ohio State." Solomon directed most of his exasperation at the Speakers Rule, which was not changed until after he left, and at the local power structure that supported it. He described Columbus as "one of the three most reactionary cities in the United States"—too small to be cosmopolitan, like Chicago or Los Angeles, but too big to be dominated by a university, like Bloomington or Urbana. Some of his Ohio State colleagues, while sympathetic, disputed the accuracy of many of his charges.[52]

One person Novice Fawcett was happy to see leave announced his impending departure in June. Alumni Association secretary Jack Fullen said he would retire in a year, effective July 1, 1967, after 38 years with the university. A persistent gadfly who used the Association's magazine to criticize decisions he disagreed with, Fullen remained true to form even on his way out the door. He told the *Lantern* Ohio State was pursuing quantity at the expense of quality. Citing the new University College as an example, he said, "We are building across the river a $15 million institution for 10,000 day-school commuters to satisfy Franklin County when we are supposed to be THE state university now." He argued that if the university took "half that much money, time and thought and developed an honors college for OSU, we'd be balancing quality with quantity."[53]

At their July 14 meeting the trustees approved Fawcett's nominee to replace John Weaver as vice president for instruction. John Corbally, Fawcett's administrative chief, assumed the new title of vice president for academic affairs and provost, which reflected his broader responsibilities as the university's No. 2 administrator. Corbally received his Ph.D. in education from the University of California at Berkeley and came to Ohio State as an assistant professor in 1955. He was one of the few senior administrators in the 1960s who had the trust of both Fawcett and the board of trustees, and who also managed to maintain good relations with faculty and student leaders. But even Corbally would find it difficult to unite such a divided campus.

SOCIETY: EVE OF DESTRUCTION

"The eastern world, it is explodin'. Violence flarin', bullets loadin'. You're old enough to kill, but not for votin'. You don't believe in war, but what's the gun you're totin'?"[54]

So began the prophetic "Eve of Destruction." Featuring 19-year-old P. F. Sloan's biting lyrics and former New Christy Minstrel Barry McGuire's snarly vocals, it became one of the landmark protest songs of the 1960s. Although its cynical tone appealed to younger listeners, others saw it as over the top. After all, in the fall of 1965 the country was prosperous. Washington was working to make a Great Society better for all Americans, and that nasty war in Vietnam would be finished as soon as U.S. troops took over. But all this would start to change during the 1965–66 school year, when violence internationally, nationally, and even locally began to intrude on the Ohio State campus.[55]

THE GREAT VIETNAM DEBATE

As the war in Vietnam escalated, groups on campus sought to educate anyone who bothered to listen about what was going on in that troubled country. Speeches, debates, and forums featuring concerned citizens and experts from within and outside the university proliferated, sparking a rich debate that reflected what America was thinking on the onset of its most divisive conflict since the Civil War. Nationally prominent speakers on both sides of the discussion came to campus, including U.S. Army chief of staff Harold Johnson and his boss, Earle Wheeler, chair of the Joint Chiefs of Staff. Both Johnson and Wheeler supported President Lyndon B. Johnson and his administration's case for involvement in Vietnam. NBC news anchor and war critic David Brinkley spoke, as did a fellow critic, Democratic senator Ernest Gruening. University experts also had their say. Faculty members contributed multiple essays, pro and con, to the *Lantern* opinion page. The Committee for the Study of Alternatives ran ads questioning the war. Sigma Chi fraternity sponsored a debate. More than 700 people attended a forum sponsored by Students for Liberal Action.[56]

Servicemen returning from Vietnam were beginning to show up in campus discussions. This early group consisted of career officers who'd served as advisers. Navy lieutenant Charles R. Fike, who was interviewed by the *Lantern,* advised South Vietnamese riverine forces in the Mekong Delta before coming to Ohio State as a Navy ROTC supply instructor. Captain Thomas D. Ginex, an assistant professor in Army ROTC, spoke to the university's 4-H club about his experiences as an adviser to the South Vietnamese Rangers. Both men strongly supported the U.S. efforts in the war.[57]

CHOOSING SIDES

While some wanted to learn more about Vietnam and others didn't care, a small group of students believed they knew all they needed to and were ready to act on their beliefs. The first recorded antiwar demonstration on campus proper took place on October 13, 1965. Two students, sophomore John Perera and grad student Bernard Richards, showed up on the back steps of the Ohio Union with signs reading "Learn war no more" and "Military training denies human values." The *Lantern* described the responses from passersby as ranging from "agreement to argument, laughter and jeering."[58]

The newspaper editorialized that the protest would have no effect because the draft was clearly needed: "Therefore, the end-the-draft protest has the same defect as most other pacifist demonstrations: The goals for which they demonstrate may be desirable, but realities place them far beyond reach."[59] Of course, neither the *Lantern* nor the protestors could foresee that within 36 months of that day, the end of the draft would indeed be within reach.

John Perera turned out to be the point person for antiwar and antidraft activity throughout the mid-1960s. A 31-year-old sociology major from Cleveland, Perera was a Quaker and had spent two years of alternative service as a peace worker in Central America when he became a conscientious objector in the early 1950s. Perera was undaunted by *Lantern* editorials or the taunts of other students. He showed up as an army of one for the Veterans Day taps ceremony in front of the Administration Building on November 11. He stood silently by, sporting a "Stop the war in Vietnam" button and a sign that read "Stand for peace, without arms, war and veterans. Fight the causes of war." Not everyone thought the solemn taps ceremony was an appropriate place for a protest. "It is a disappointment to see you," a passerby scolded him.[60]

By the end of the school year it was clear the antiwar movement, such as it was, could count only half a dozen to three dozen core supporters and was not growing beyond that. The weight of student opinion in 1965–66 would instead be with supporters of the war. Senior Stephen Foley read about a "support the troops" blood drive conducted by a fraternity at the University of Illinois. He decided he would do one better at Ohio State and enlisted his roommates, seniors Richard Stoudt and Neils Christiansen, president of Ohio Union Activities, to assist. With enthusiastic support from student relations dean John Bonner, himself a veteran, and various groups across campus, they organized the Save Our Soldiers All-Campus Blood Drive for a two-day period ending on Veterans Day.

Even though local Red Cross officials explained the blood collected at the drive would not necessarily end up in Vietnam, that did not seem to dampen enthusiasm. The Red Cross scrambled to find extra nurses, cots, and bloodmobiles to meet the demand. Students filled the Ohio

Union ballrooms as they waited in line for as long as an hour to be processed. They donated 1,297 pints, exceeding the goal by 97 pints. In addition, 250 more students signed cards pledging to donate later. The Red Cross official in charge of the blood program in central Ohio said it was the largest drive he had ever seen.[61] Donors were also invited to sign a scroll in support of the troops, creating a document 140 feet long and weighing 30 pounds. Executive Jet Aviation of Columbus flew the scroll to Washington free of charge via one of its corporate aircraft. From there, it was to be delivered to Vietnam commander William Westmoreland by military transport.

Other students launched a "You have our support" petition campaign with a goal of 50,000 signatures. "We are circulating this petition to prove that OSU doesn't contain only a bunch of bearded radicals, and to prove that the students and responsible citizens support the President's policies in Vietnam," said spokesperson Alan Fisher. Columbus mayor M. E. Sensenbrenner proudly signed the petition. "We've got boys dying over there so that students here can go to school," he said.[62] Other students collected books and miscellaneous goods to support the troops throughout the year. Ohio State even sent its ultimate morale booster. Football coach Woody Hayes left for a 17-day trip to Vietnam on July 4. He would return three more times.

LEWIS B. HERSHEY WANTS YOU

In the 1960s the Selective Service System, also known as the draft, was the law of the land, particularly for the army, which could not fill its ranks with volunteers alone. Between the end of 1964 and the end of 1966 the number of American soldiers serving in Vietnam soared from 23,000 to 389,000. Pentagon planners had always expected to augment a relatively small standing army with trained reserves if a rapid buildup was needed. However, Lyndon Johnson did not want to activate the reserves because he believed it would call more attention to the size of the Vietnam buildup and undermine public support for his highest priority, the Great Society. Consequently, he chose the more indirect method of increasing the number of draftees.

Under the policy in effect at the time, college students in good standing were deferred from the draft as long as they were in school. Known

First Blood

Through most of 1964 and 1965 the Vietnam War was a far-off abstraction. But as the war intensified, its impact became more tangible. The first Ohio State graduate to die in Vietnam was 29-year-old air force captain William J. Barthelmas Jr. of Circleville. Barthelmas, a 1958 graduate, was killed on July 27, 1965, when his fighter-bomber was shot down after an attack against a missile base in North Vietnam.

At Ohio State Barthelmas had served in the Student Senate and chaired the Military Ball. He was single and was survived by two sisters, one an Ohio State graduate and the other a student at the university.

By the time the war in Vietnam ended in 1975, at least 48 Ohio State alumni had died there. That compares to the 691 alumni who died in World War II and the 21 who perished in the Korean conflict.[1]

1. "Taps," *OSU Monthly,* February 1966, 20; "Alumni Who Lost Their Lives in Vietnam," in Francis P. Weisenburger, *History of the Ohio State University: The Fawcett Years, 1956–1972* (Columbus: Ohio State University Press, 1975), appendix VIII, 275–77.

as the II-S exemption, it meant that by the time these students graduated they might be old enough to avoid military service altogether. But as draft calls rose through 1965 and 1966, anxiety on college campuses rose proportionally. At Ohio State, where a third of the freshmen were expected to flunk out or drop out each year and thus become draft bait, it was a very real threat. For the remainder there was the nagging uncertainty that deferments could suddenly become harder to get, or be abolished entirely.

Front-page stories about the draft began to appear regularly in the *Lantern* as 1966 began, with provocative headlines such as "College Students: Next Draft Target?" This particular story was prompted by a statement from Selective Service director Lewis B. Hershey that if manpower needs continued to increase, he would look to the nation's colleges and universities to help fill the gap, similar to what had happened during the Korean War. Students judged to be in the lowest quartile academically would be particularly at risk.[63]

In March the Selective Service announced all college students would have to take a standardized examination as part of their request for a deferment. At Ohio State more than 1,800 students filed into Page Hall on May 14 to take the test. Students later told university officials they thought the 150 multiple-choice questions were "pretty easy." As for the thousands who hadn't signed up, the university told them they would have three more chances to take the test over the next two months. Almost all complied.[64]

DRUGS, SEX, AND PERVERSION

The 1960s are often thought of as a time when society became more tolerant of behaviors once considered deviant or immoral. At mid-decade, however, the old rules were still in play. Abortion was illegal in Ohio, as in most states. It was also dangerous and expensive. A rare public glimpse into the problem occurred in November when an Ohio State student ended up in a Columbus hospital with complications following an illegal abortion. She agreed to be a witness in prosecuting the others involved. Authorities were able to protect the identity of the student, but other aspects of the case became public when a grand jury in adjacent Licking County approved indictments that included a male Ohio State student who had accepted $500 from the woman to arrange the procedure.[65]

Later that month university police denied they were cracking down on homosexuals after local newspaper reports. Ohio State officials did admit to six arrests over the previous three months for homosexual soliciting on campus, but said that two or three such arrests a month was routine.[66]

Access to birth control information was another case in which the old standards were not ready to give way. In April 1965 the conservative Ohio General Assembly repealed the state's Civil War–era Comstock Law, which forbade distribution of such information. This led some to call for more widespread dissemination of birth control information on campus. Dean Bonner made it clear in a February 1966 *Lantern* interview that the university had no intention of changing its policy, which limited contraception advice and distribution through the Student Health Service to married students or engaged couples within two months of marriage.

Nancy Clatworthy, who taught Sociology 520, disagreed. The class dealing with marriage and the family was probably Ohio State's most popular elective course in the midsixties. Even though six or seven sections were offered each quarter, they always closed out early because demand was so high. "Every student should have a chance to take this course and the course ought to be expanded," Clatworthy said. "Students really should have [birth control] information in high school, and even in grade school. I think the upper and middle class people are actually more naive than those of the lower classes."[67]

Regardless of Ohio State policy, students' views on sex were changing. In a March 1964 conference on selfhood and sex sponsored by the campus YMCA and YWCA, Donald Clapp, an associate minister at nearby St. Stephen's Episcopal Church, put it this way: "There is a shift in the codes that govern moral behavior. Today 65 plus percent of college men and women between the ages of 18 and 25 have had, are having, or will have premarital intercourse according to recent research." The old double standard was in transition, he said, and "today people say that 'most men do, and nice girls don't—unless they're in love.'"[68]

The biggest story of the year involved drugs. When Columbus police arrested 20 people over four days in January, the *Dispatch* featured what it called the discovery of a campus-area drug ring on the front page every day for a week. The key player in making the case was a *Dispatch* crime reporter and former *Lantern* reporter. John Huddy spent six weeks working undercover with the police, then wrote about his experiences after the arrests were made. "Marijuana flowed as abundantly as soft drinks in the High Street campus hangouts," Huddy wrote.[69]

Although marijuana was the only drug found, it was still a serious offense. Under Ohio law at the time, possession carried a sentence of two to 15 years, consumption 10 to 20, and sales 20 to 40. A young woman arrested in the sweep committed suicide. Huddy received death threats. And university officials worried about the reputation of the campus as a drug haven.[70]

As the details emerged, it turned out only four of the 20 people arrested were current students, and the case against eight of the defendants was dismissed due to lack of evidence. The *Lantern* used the opportunity to attack the *Dispatch* coverage. It also printed an interview with Herman Beck, head of the Columbus vice squad, who defended

Ohio State students: "If the whole city were as well behaved, we would have practically no police problem."[71]

SUMMER OF FEAR

The summer of 1966 saw a rising tide of violence. The escalating conflict in Vietnam was thousands of miles away, but closer to home, crime rates soared.

In Chicago, unemployed handyman Richard Speck, carrying only a knife, broke into an apartment the evening of July 13 and over the next several hours brutally terrorized and murdered eight student nurses. Speck was captured three days later after a massive manhunt. Although eventually convicted and sentenced to 400 to 1,200 years in prison, he left behind fear among women living on their own. Christine Conaway, Ohio State's dean of women, called the murders "shocking" and encouraged women not to live alone and to travel only in groups.[72]

Long-simmering tensions between the predominantly black residents of the Hough and Glenville neighborhoods in Cleveland and the predominantly white city police force exploded into six days of rioting and arson in July. Thirty-eight U.S. cities were touched by racial unrest that summer. The *Lantern* speculated that the rise of black power advocates reflected a growing sense in the black community that the nonviolent approach of Martin Luther King Jr. and his followers had failed.[73]

In August an ex-marine named Charles Whitman took a small arsenal to the observation deck of a tower at the University of Texas at Austin and started picking off passersby below. Whitman left 14 dead at the site and wounded dozens of others. The *Lantern* ran a photograph of what a sniper's view of the Ohio State campus might look like from the top of the William Oxley Thompson Library. That prompted a letter from junior William H. Hurley, who complained: "Now some mentally deranged person knows where to set up his arsenal and how much ground he can cover."[74]

CHAPTER 8

THE BEAT GOES ON

(1966–67)

Since the jaywalking protest in 1964, Ohio State had taken on a number of controversial issues and resolved many of them without dissent turning into disorder. This trend held steady in 1966–67. Students continued to work through the system to reform their governing structure and rid themselves of in loco parentis. The faculty and administration squabbled over what it meant to be a great university, but succeeded in crafting the most sweeping academic reorganization in 50 years. Although 1967 became the year of the counterculture in the national conscience, many at Ohio State were not yet ready to jettison middle-class values and embrace alternative lifestyles.

8.1. By 1967, Ohio State's ROTC program had become the largest in the country and a target for protestors. (*Makio*)

STUDENTS: CALM BEFORE THE STORM

MOMENTUM FOR REFORM

After a surprisingly productive spring quarter, those students hoping to reform their government looked forward to picking up where they had left off when classes resumed in the fall. Instead, they received a lesson in why it is difficult for students, who are transient by nature, to mount a sustained drive toward reform. The Student Senate found itself with 27 vacancies out of 40 seats. Five senators failed to qualify because of low grades; 22 had moved out of their districts. The constitutional convention lost 14 of its original 45 delegates for the same reasons. The senate, the constitutional convention, and the Women's Self Government Association all had problems generating a quorum. Even the Free Student Federation stalled when it failed to file a routine report and temporarily lost university recognition.[1]

But throughout the fall a small but determined group continued working on the reform of student government at the committee level. The first results began to surface by mid-January. The convention filled its vacancies and adopted an attendance requirement for delegates, and members agreed to extra sessions to get the work done. By early March the delegates were ready to vote on the first set of recommendations. The new structure called for a student bill of rights; greater student participation on policy-making committees; a Council of Governments chaired by the president of the new Undergraduate Student Government in order to better coordinate the many student organizations; and a Student Assembly with only 25 members that would act as the legislative arm of the Undergraduate Student Government.

Convention chair Alan Melamed hailed the "potentially powerful new government" but cautioned it would be meaningless without strong support from students.[2] The first hurdle would be how the Student Senate responded. Key student organizations slowly lined up behind the bill of rights, and when it came up for consideration on April 6, the senate voted unanimously to endorse it.

The next step was an all-campus referendum scheduled for April 12. Melamed called for a turnout of between 8,000 and 14,000 students to validate the convention's work. A total of 7,866 voted—fewer than the preferred amount, most likely because of the complexity of the issue and the lack of controversy surrounding it. But those who did vote sent a clear message, with 7,509, or 95 percent, voting in favor.[3]

With the Student Senate's two traditional parties officially dead, who would take their place in the elections scheduled for May? On March 4 a group of students who had worked on the constitutional convention applied for recognition as the University Party. They announced their first priority would be to get the referendum passed.

On April 16, four days after the referendum vote, the party announced its candidates for president and vice president of the Undergraduate Student Government. Sophomore Lloyd Siegel and junior Reginald Jackson pledged to focus on undergraduate education. Siegel, an honors student, had served as a delegate to the constitutional convention and chair of the structure committee. Jackson also had been a convention delegate. Both had been members of the wing of the Buckeye Political Party supportive of Student Senate president Tim Neustadt.

In a lofty statement, the two talked not about dorm food or Homecoming skits but the quality of undergraduate education: "Our campaign has a single aim: to bring about a government that will work with the faculty and administration to enrich the quality of the undergraduate education and ensure that all students are treated as full citizens, enjoying all the freedoms that citizenship in this country implies. . . . While [the university] has made a policy of admitting more and more students, it has made little effort to strengthen the instruction these students are receiving. The classes are too large; the professors too far away."[4]

Siegel and Jackson's opponents would be senior Charles E. Hunter and sophomore Michael Heyman. Hunter had been *Lantern* editor the previous fall and had taken the paper in a much more leftward direction, editorializing against the Vietnam War more than a dozen times in 10 weeks and endorsing Robert Kennedy for president, even though Kennedy would not declare for another 10 months. Hunter explained his campaign as a departure from business as usual in two ways. First, he had no prior experience in student government, which he saw as a plus. Second, he wanted the government to get more involved in national issues that affected students, such as opposing the Vietnam War. Hunter and Heyman would campaign under the banner of the Campus Peace Democratic Party.[5]

Students went to the polls on May 2, and the turnout again was disappointing. Only 6,400 of 28,000 undergraduates bothered to vote. Those who did expressed a clear choice. The Siegel-Jackson ticket outpolled Hunter-Heyman 4,806 to 907. Siegel was the first non-fraternity candidate to become president of an undergraduate student government body since direct election of the presidents began in 1962. The University Party carried all but one of 25 seats in the new Student Assembly.

First on the agenda was completing the reform of student government. The elections settled the issues that students themselves could decide, such as the structure of the new Student Assembly. However, the fate of three critical recommendations from the constitutional convention still needed to be resolved. The student bill of rights, student representation on faculty committees, and the structure of the Council on Student Affairs required review by the council itself and the Faculty Council. The newly elected leaders put these items high on the agenda for fall quarter 1967.

THE BEGINNING OF THE END OF IN LOCO PARENTIS

While some students worked on the new government, others continued to bang away at in loco parentis. Annoying dress rules were the first target. In 1963–64 the Women's Residence Hall Council lost a test of wills with the dean of women's office over allowing students to wear slacks to the cafeterias on cold days. Things would be different this time. The South Campus Student Association, the successor to the Women's Residence Hall Council and the Men's Residence Halls Association, was barely seven months old when it sponsored a referendum on dress rules. Students would have a straight up or down vote, and both the dean of men and the dean of women pledged the administration would abide by the outcome.

On November 15 a record turnout of 3,731 south campus residents—52 percent of those eligible to vote—cast ballots in their cafeteria lines. They voted almost three to one in favor of total repeal. The North Campus Student Association conducted its own referendum on December 7. Turnout there was slightly less (48.5 percent) and the vote somewhat less lopsided in favor of repeal (982–715), but the result was the same.

The repeal took effect immediately. Women were no longer required to wear dresses and skirts to dinner, nor were they prohibited from wearing shorts, slacks, or sweatshirts at any time. Men no longer had to wear dress coats and slacks to Sunday dinner. The administration kept its word, although women's dean Christine Conaway disapproved. "It is really unfortunate that they don't want to have any standards about their appearance," Conaway said after the vote.[6]

Activists now started chipping away on the next bulwark of in loco parentis: restrictions on women's hours. The previous year, Conaway had approved a recommendation by the Women's Self Government Association to eliminate hours for seniors and women over 21 on weekends. These changes, which she labeled "an experiment," took effect with the start of classes in September. Initial reports from living units revealed no problems regarding enforcement or abuse.[7]

At its February 1 meeting WSGA voted on a proposal to expand unlimited hours for junior women. Representatives from the sororities objected, saying the added freedom would distract the juniors who held many of the leadership positions in sorority chapters. In previous years this would have been enough to stop the process. Instead, WSGA delegates voted to move ahead. Conaway approved the proposal a week later, saying she had "great confidence in the maturity and responsibility" of the upper-class women. The new rules would take effect in the fall. As a safety valve, individual units (dorms, rooming houses, and sororities) could opt out. Few would.[8]

Ohio State now joined the six other Big Ten schools that had no restricted hours for at least some junior and senior women.[9] It was the only one to not require some sort of parental approval. Clearly, the days of restricted women's hours were numbered. WSGA had evolved into more of a force for change than a means of protecting the status quo. Junior Penny Maza, the group's vice president and the newly elected chair of its powerful (and sometimes hated) standards commission, told the *Lantern*: "If it were up to me there would be no hours for anyone, including freshmen." She promised to work through the system to bring about further changes.[10]

The elimination of curfews for junior and senior women highlighted other inconsistencies with in loco parentis, including the despised Apartment Rule, something critics were quick to point out. "Women want to go to apartments without being pushed into signing out falsely," said senior Rebecca Rowe, president of West Baker Hall. "They want to leave emergency numbers where they can be reached, but they can't because they would be admitting to breaking the Apartment Rule."[11]

It is important to recognize that the pressure on in loco parentis was coming not from radicals, but from established student leaders with deep Ohio roots. For example, Rowe was from the small town of Greenfield, Ohio. Maza hailed from Toledo.

Rowe found a supportive audience when she presented a proposal to her colleagues at WSGA. It called for a modification of the Apartment Rule so that women with extended hours could visit apartments after 2 a.m. Ruth Weimer, associate dean of women, told students she had received letters and calls from concerned parents who feared the university was condoning women's spending nights in men's apartments.[12] The proposal passed WSGA unanimously, anyway. It was approved by the Council on Student Affairs on February 1.

Next, activists pressed for giving more women the flexibility to live in an apartment if they chose to do so. WSGA passed a resolution allowing all senior women, not just those over 21, to live in apartments effective fall quarter 1967. The dean of women's office approved the change over Christmas break.

In loco parentis took another blow in February when two of its traditional supporters announced they were leaving the university. Conaway and Mylin Ross, dean of men, announced they would retire the coming summer. Conaway had been with the university 29 years and had been dean since 1944. Ross had been with the university 19 years and had been dean since 1952. Their top assistants, Ruth Weimer and Milton Overholt, would succeed them. Neither Weimer nor Overholt were inclined to disrupt the status quo; for example, both opposed eliminating hours for all women. "Brand me as an old fuddy-duddy if you want," said Overholt, "but if my daughter were in college and the object of some misdeed, I'd want to know that someone there was aware of it before she was missing 24 or 48 hours."[13]

Dean Bonner announced in May that Weimer and Overholt would not assume the titles of dean of women and dean of men. Instead, they would report to him as associate deans of student relations. Weimer would be responsible for student programming and organizations for both men and women. Overholt would be responsible for housing, both on and off campus, for men and women. The reorganization, Bonner said, "will establish a completely coeducational program of student relations." With that commitment, it would be harder and harder to justify separate policies for women and men. And without separate rules, it would be increasingly difficult to maintain in loco parentis.[14]

LINES, LINES, AND MORE LINES

Both enrollment and prices continued to soar in 1966–67, which meant students would have to pay more for less. Resident undergraduate tuition rose 20 percent for fall quarter, from $125 per quarter to $150. The first increase in two years was blamed on what administrators described as a combination of rising instructional costs and inadequate state support. This was followed in March by the announcement of a hike in the student activity fee (which included football tickets) from $12 to $14 annually. It was the first increase since 1956. In May the university announced that room and board fees for campus housing would increase in the fall of 1967 for the first time in 10 years. The average charge for living in a residence hall would jump $26 per quarter, to $293.[15]

Ohio State was not alone in raising fees, officials pointed out. Inflation in 1966 was the highest in 10 years. The university still had the lowest room and board rates in the Big Ten. And lack of state support was the major culprit behind the tuition increases. But whatever tolerance administrators may have gotten from students on that front was offset by growing frustration over long lines for necessary services. Parking was one such problem, but it mainly affected commuter students; most of the others didn't have cars. Telephone service in the residence halls, which university officials admitted was overloaded a third of the time, was another, but only students who lived in the dorms were inconvenienced.

Scheduling, on the other hand, affected everyone. And it became a bigger and bigger problem as enrollment grew. A three-by-seven-inch piece of thin cardboard called a schedule card was supposed to unlock the system. The card was a variation of the IBM punch card, which had been around since 1928. Its 12 rows and eight columns produced 96 combinations that could be sorted by mechanical card readers to tally all kinds of information. The cards, which usually came with the warning "do not fold, spindle, or mutilate," became a symbol of the growing depersonalization of the American university. During the 1964 free speech controversy at Berkeley, students coined a phrase: "I am a human being, so do not fold, spindle, or mutilate."[16]

Students at Ohio State filled out the front of the card by hand when they registered for each quarter. They would list the courses they wanted from the catalog, then put in the times they preferred from the offerings in the quarterly bulletin. More than 40,000 of these cards involving more than 160,000 course requests would have to be initially processed by hand in the registrar's scheduling office, a mammoth undertaking. When a course filled up or was otherwise unavailable, someone in the scheduling office would make the change by hand in red ink and the card would be returned to the student. Every student's worst nightmare was a returned schedule card covered with red ink.[17]

Even so, this part of the scheduling system worked reasonably well most of the time. But when students wanted to change a course or time for any reason—and each quarter about a third of them did—things deteriorated quickly. Most people who needed to make changes had to do so after the schedule cards were returned late in the current quarter and before the start of the next quarter. The system would soon overload, leaving students in line for hours, or in limbo for days. The *Lantern* once referred to the ordeal as "comparable to the voyage of Homer's Ulysses."[18]

At the beginning of winter quarter 1967, the *Lantern* sent a photographer along with freshman Wanda Ingmire as she tried to resuscitate her schedule after being closed out of three courses. It took her four hours to reschedule just one of the courses. And Ingmire was lucky. She'd planned ahead and made an appointment to see her academic counselor in the College of the Arts and Sciences, or she would have waited in a long line there as well. The college had eight advisers for 10,000 students. That was enough to handle normal traffic, but not the heavy loads in the fifth week of each quarter when schedules were due and the first week of the next quarter when people tried to make changes.[19]

University officials claimed relief was on the way. A new IBM computer was powerful enough to run a student information system that was supposed to be up and running the next year. It promised one-stop shopping and an end to multiple cards and forms, but savvy students were wary. They had heard the happy talk regarding a new computerized system for delivering grades for fall quarter 1966. The system, which promised quicker delivery and a running total of each student's

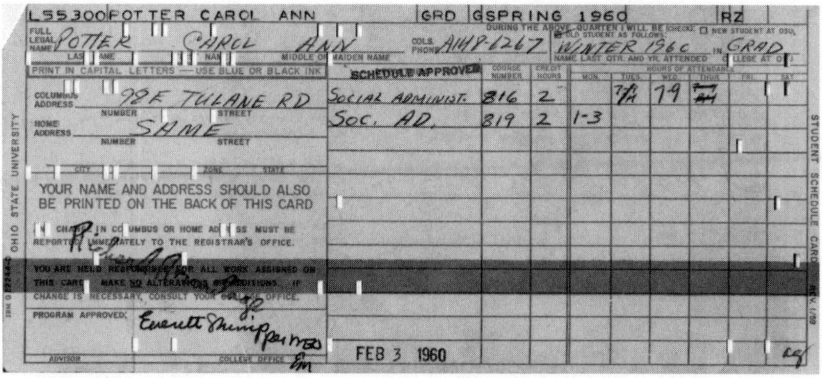

8.2. Do not fold, spindle, or mutilate: IBM cards were used for scheduling classes in the 1960s. (University Archives)

all-important cumulative grade point average, debuted in December and seemed to be working well. But when it came time to send out winter quarter 1967 grades, a programming error resulted in 4,875 students getting their grades later than they would have under the old system.[20]

TOWERS A-GO-GO

Morrill Tower, one of the two new high-rise residence halls along the Olentangy River, opened at the beginning of fall quarter 1966. Space was available for only 916 students at first because strikes and material shortages had delayed construction. Morrill Tower was named after U.S. congressman Justin Morrill, sponsor of the 1862 legislation establishing land grant universities. Its twin, Lincoln Tower, was named after Abraham Lincoln, the president who signed the Morrill Act into law. The towers—the tallest buildings on campus and reportedly the tallest residence halls in the country—quickly attracted attention.

Student reaction was initially mixed, but more positive than negative. A *Lantern* reporter spent two weeks talking with residents soon after Morrill Tower opened. Some complained about porthole-sized windows, thin walls, and mud from the continuing construction activity. However, many liked the suite configuration and the coed living arrangement.[21]

Roberta Katherine Jones, a graduate student in student personnel, did her master's thesis on the tower's first year and found much the same result. She administered a questionnaire to a random sample of 400 residents during spring quarter 1967, after they had been living in Morrill for more than six months. A near majority (44.9 percent) said they found living there "enjoyable." Another 42.5 percent said they were "satisfied." Only 7.2 percent found the towers "unpleasant." What students enjoyed most was the coeducational aspect. Although men and women lived on separate floors, they mixed in the lobby and in the cafeterias.[22]

University officials set up a press event to mark the completion of both towers in August 1967. Two hundred newspeople attended an open house highlighting the use of technology in the dorms, including a heating and cooling system housed on the 24th floor of each building that was powered by natural gas. President Novice Fawcett said the towers provided 40 percent more capacity in campus housing—4,000 new beds—addressing what he unartfully described as the "steadily increasing hordes of students."[23]

The *Lantern* was not impressed. In a caustic editorial titled "Beauty and the Beasts," it critiqued the architecture of all Ohio State residence halls constructed since the end of World War II, saving a special blast for the towers, which it described as "colorless, formless, dull beige." Creative critics across campus rushed to give the two buildings derogatory nicknames: silos, grain elevators, prisons, spaceships, salt shakers, Polynesian gods, phallic symbols, Carson's Folly (after the vice president for business and finance), and, for Morrill Tower, Immoral Tower.[24]

The critics drew attention away from a larger issue. The river towers, like all residence halls at Ohio State, were built without state support. Instead, they were financed with self-liquidating 30-year bonds. The bonds would be paid off with room and board charges to the residents. In order to sell the bonds at a favorable rate to investors such as banks and insurance companies, the university needed to assure them they would be paid off on schedule. This was done through the so-called Dorm Rule, a board-approved requirement that ensured a continuing income stream by mandating that freshmen and sophomores live in university residence halls.

Up to this point the rule was in the books but went unenforced because of a housing shortage. But when both Lincoln and Morrill Towers would be open at full capacity in the fall of 1967, the number of beds on campus would increase at a time when enrollment was beginning to level off. Skeptical students therefore feared the Dorm Rule would be enforced. This upset students who didn't want to live in dorms and those who did. Those who didn't cited a variety of reasons: residence halls were too noisy, too expensive, and had too many rules. Those who did feared being stuck with roommates, suitemates, or neighbors who didn't want to be there.

The Free Student Federation sensed this was an emerging issue and succeeded in adding the right to live where one chooses to the student bill of rights. Although it was unlikely to get administration approval, this at least set a marker. The FSF told students to write DORM (Disapprove of Residence Mandate) in the comment box when they voted for the new constitution in April 1967. Almost 47 percent (3,654 out of 7,832) did so. The problem was, administrators had put themselves in a box. After the rush to build the towers, they now had to pay for them. They would try to ameliorate the problem by closing obsolete facilities such as Neil and Oxley Halls and by inviting town students to live in university housing, but it wasn't enough to offset the excess capacity. No matter how unfairly, Lincoln and Morrill would now stand as a symbol of a university more concerned with money than the welfare of its students.[25]

ROTC BECOMES A TARGET

At the end of the 1966–67 school year Ohio State's reserve officer training program was at the summit of the ROTC world. Eighty-three percent of eligible students signed up for a two-year introductory program that had been voluntary since 1961. The number committing to an advanced course, which meant two years of active duty as officers, also increased. The largest program in the country also was one of the most respected. ROTC instructors carried faculty rank and collaborated with other faculty members, even those who opposed the war in Vietnam, to give cadets a broader view of the world. And so far the escalation of the war seemed to spur ROTC participation, rather than discourage it.[26]

But in the world of politics and protest symbolism was everything; and to some, military uniforms on campus represented what was wrong with American policy in Southeast Asia. On most large campuses, the local chapter of Students for a Democratic Society formed the nucleus of the antiwar movement. Ohio State at the time lacked an active chapter of SDS. Instead, a loose coalition of individuals calling themselves the Ohio State Committee to End the War in Vietnam provided most of the opposition energy. Although they tried hard, they did not enjoy much success in stirring the mass of students. A November teach-in had little impact. A march to the Statehouse the next day drew almost as many counterprotestors as marchers.[27]

The group did manage to gain university recognition as a student organization in January. That presumably made it easier to schedule and publicize events, but it didn't seem to help. The one bright spot was the growing support from area religious leaders, who saw the war as a moral issue. At the end of January, 40 central Ohio clergy joined 2,000 other ministers, priests, rabbis, and laypeople from 45 states in Washington, D.C., to protest the war. In February Ohio State antiwar activists and clergy sponsored their own symbolic fast for peace and a silent vigil, but only about a hundred people showed up.[28]

The beginning of 1967 also marked the first appearance on campus of Vietnam veterans who spoke out against the war. Steve Borstein, a junior who had served with the First Air Cavalry Division, told a Park Hall audience of 135 that the U.S. strategy to run up kill ratios was not winning over the Vietnamese people. But for the most part the number of antiwar veterans was small, and they tended to keep to themselves.[29]

After failing to gain much attention over the course of a frustrating winter and early spring, the Committee to End the War in Vietnam decided to try something else. The 75 active members voted to make a statement using the May Week Corps Day ceremonies as their platform. A silent vigil was proposed, but after extensive debate, the majority decided to take things a step further. They would interrupt the proceedings to sing an antiwar song, then leave.[30]

On May 4, after all 6,300 ROTC cadets had assumed their places in front of the reviewing stand at the east end of the Oval, a group of about a hundred protestors led by one carrying an American flag marched in from the direction of the Main Library at the west end. They chanted "peace now, peace now" while ringing cowbells and carrying signs. Some passed out Tootsie Rolls to the assembled cadets. While some in the crowd of 1,500 spectators applauded, others yelled, "Look at the weirdos" and "Beardies go home."

The small parade stopped at the reviewing stand and sang three choruses of "we ain't gonna study war no more" while President Fawcett

The Chief Inquisitor

Charles R. Gambs Jr., associate dean of student relations, maintained a relatively low profile until student disturbances became more confrontational in the second half of the 1960s. Gambs held a law degree from Ohio State and had served in the FBI as a special agent for eight years before joining the university staff in 1958. His FBI background was well known among students, and those summoned to his office viewed the experience with great anxiety. Some students, particularly activists on the left, saw him as the equivalent of the chief inquisitor of the Spanish Inquisition. His fellow administrators saw Gambs as a straight shooter who performed well in a difficult job.[1]

Gambs elaborated on his role in an October 1966 *Lantern* interview in which he responded to a charge by a member of the judicial subcommittee of the constitutional convention that he was handling disciplinary cases without appropriate due process. Gambs said his job was not to conduct a trial but to make a recommendation to John Bonner, the executive dean for student relations, about the nature of the alleged offense(s). Bonner would then decide on the next steps. If the alleged misconduct could result in a permanent mark on the student's record, such as recorded probation, suspension, or dismissal, then the case would be referred to the individual's college judicial body. If unrecorded probation was involved, the case would be referred to the dean of men or dean of women.

In all cases, the buck stopped with Bonner, who, Gambs maintained, was the decider on all recommendations for disciplinary actions by the colleges and the deans. The system was fair and efficient, Gambs concluded.[2] His critics disagreed. When it came time to sort out discipline in the wake of the 1970 disturbances, Gambs's role would be a major sticking point between the university and student activists and civil libertarians, but administrators continued to support him.[3]

1. John Mount (August 6, 2013) and Roger Meyer interviews with author.
2. "Dean Disclaims Student Charges," *Lantern,* October 28, 1966, 1.
3. Louis Heldman, "Gambs to Remain as Discipline Officer," *Lantern,* December 3, 1970, 1.

looked on impassively. They then turned around and headed back toward the library. A spectator ran out from the crowd, spit at them, and disappeared. Another threw a soft drink in a paper cup. In 10 minutes it was over and the ceremony continued as planned.[31]

The Corps Day ceremonies had attracted demonstrators before, including in the early 1960s, but this marked the first time the event had been interrupted, if only briefly. The *Lantern* called it a "harmless spectacle." The administration was not so sure. Charles R. Gambs Jr., associate dean of student relations, likened the protest to disrupting an instructional lab. Gambs reportedly interviewed five or 10 of the participants over the next week; however, the university never released the results of his inquiries.[32] Administrators took no further action against the protestors, either because they didn't want to provoke an issue or because they believed they lacked sufficient grounds, or both. But in August a spokesperson for the Committee to End the War in Vietnam told the *Lantern* the group had reassessed its tactics, and although members would continue to adhere to nonviolence, they would be much more militant when classes resumed in the fall.[33]

THE UNIVERSITY: SQUABBLING OVER GREATNESS

Another 6,200 freshmen started at Ohio State's Columbus campus in the fall of 1966. Research continued to grow, while the university struggled with what to do about undergraduate education. The faculty struggled with accelerated change. And administrators struggled to keep up with state officials. But the big story of the year didn't directly involve any of these. Instead, it reflected struggles with the question of what is a great university and what would it take to become great. Some saw greatness as size. Others saw it as something else. The debate would dominate academic discourse during the school year and provide a look at how various players viewed the university and each other in the middle of the decade.

RANKINGS RANCOR

In the spring of 1966 the prestigious American Council on Education, the umbrella organization for all colleges and universities in the United States, released the results of a study it called the "most comprehensive ever undertaken" of the quality of graduate education. The heart of the study consisted of responses to questionnaires mailed in 1964 to nearly

5,400 faculty, including department chairs, at 106 of the largest doctorate-granting universities in the country. Respondents were asked to rate only departments in their field of expertise. Twenty-nine departments ranging from anthropology to zoology were included. The study generated 4,008 usable responses, a return rate of 75 percent.[34]

The results, published in a 131-page book, were troubling to people who cared about Ohio State's academic reputation. Although the study did not rank institutions, cumulative totals of departmental rankings placed the university in the mid-20s rather than in the top 20, where it had been a decade earlier. Even more troubling was a pattern of decline. Of the 11 Ohio State departments ranked in the top 15 in a 1957 study, only one had moved up. The other 10 had moved down.

The faculty group calling itself the Committee for the Study of Alternatives responded with a provocative *Lantern* ad in the fall of 1966. The group had formed after the 1962 Speakers Rule controversy to counteract what it believed was biased reporting in the Columbus media, particularly the *Dispatch*. Its ad began:

> **What counts at Ohio State?**
> Ohio State has a distinguished ROTC program.
> Ohio State is distinguished in intercollegiate athletics.
> Ohio State has a distinguished fraternity-sorority system.
> Ohio State is distinguished in the numbers of its students and buildings.
>
> **But Ohio State is not distinguished as an academic institution. It is not distinguished as a center of learning.**

The ad cited figures from the American Council on Education report and other sources that showed how Ohio State compared unfavorably to highly rated public universities such as the University of California at Berkeley and Michigan, Wisconsin, and Illinois. It concluded with a plea for the university to stop congratulating itself and "confront the real question—whether Ohio State is to remain outstanding only as a military and recreational facility or to become a major center of teaching and research."[35]

The *Lantern* jumped in and took Fawcett to task for the emphasis in his most recent newsletter on growth in enrollment and dollars.

"President Fawcett ought to stop making claims about the wonderful world of Ohio State so that members of this university can begin to realize the academic weaknesses here and correct them," the editors argued in the January 6 issue.[36] Before the end of the year, the paper would publish seven more editorials generally supporting the position of the Committee for the Study of Alternatives.

Administrators responded aggressively. Fawcett pointed out that the study addressed only 29 of Ohio State's 100 academic departments. Provost John Corbally called attention to the university's centers of excellence, such as the Center for Textual Studies, the Disaster Research Center, and the Institute for Polar Studies, all of which had achieved international recognition but were not included in the American Council on Education ranking because they were cutting-edge interdisciplinary programs rather than traditional academic departments.[37]

Dean John Bonner presumably was trying to be helpful when he told Delta Upsilon fraternity that Ohio State was "one of the 20 great universities of the world." Part of the evidence he cited was Ohio State's rank as sixth in the number of doctoral degrees granted. His remarks found their way into the *Lantern,* where they had the effect of pouring gasoline on a fire. David Spitz, a professor of political science and frequent critic of the administration, wrote a letter to the *Lantern* in which he presented a list of the world's leading universities and invited Bonner to specify which 11 of them he would remove so that Ohio State could be in the top 20. The *Lantern* editorialized that Bonner's obsession with big numbers was an example of what was holding the university back.[38]

Some players used the controversy to criticize others. The *Cleveland Plain Dealer* questioned Fawcett's leadership. The *Citizen-Journal* attacked the Committee for the Study of Alternatives for running down the university. Richard Mall, the Alumni Association's new director, called the university's critics short-sighted.[39]

The committee showed no interest in backing down. On January 27 members placed a second ad, this time in the form of an open letter to Governor James Rhodes. They complained about "failures of judgment and imagination" on the part of the administration and the board of trustees on matters such as prolonging the Speakers Rule controversy and trying to graft a community college (University College) onto a university that was supposed to emphasize excellence in research and graduate study.[40]

On April 7 the committee issued a third ad listing 17 recommendations to improve the university.[41] Some of the recommendations, such as improving the honors program and graduate teaching capability, had broad support and were already being implemented. Some, such as selective admissions, were desirable but politically unfeasible. Others reflected a not-too-subtle attack on Ohio State's leaders. For example, one recommendation called for the creation of a vice president for public affairs to better articulate the university's message. For faculty to endorse the addition of another expensive senior administrator was extremely unusual and had to be interpreted as a slap at Fawcett's communications skills as well as those of university relations director Frederick Stecker.

While there appeared to be a large amount of disagreement between faculty and administrators as to Ohio State's academic standing, students seemed to have a good idea of where things stood. In May the *Lantern* asked 20 students at random to rate the university as poor, mediocre, good, or great. It was obviously not a representative sample, but the distribution of responses was nonetheless telling. One student said the university was great, and one said it was poor. Four answered mediocre. Fourteen, or 70 percent, said the university was good.[42]

With the Speakers Rule clash settled, most of the needed facilities open or under construction, and the Board of Regents master plan completed, this would have been an ideal time for interested parties to take stock and discuss what Ohio State should do to better itself during the next five to 10 years. Instead, factions inside and outside the university saw it as an opportunity to settle old scores.

RESTRUCTURING ARTS AND SCIENCES

While the debate over Ohio State's standing may not have produced much in the way of tangible action, the debate over the future of the College of the Arts and Sciences did. University officials, particularly Provost John Corbally, believed the structure of the college had become too big and unwieldy and was getting in the way of serving the students and maximizing the talents of the faculty. In December the Council on Academic Affairs (formerly the Council on Instruction) unveiled its recommendations for breaking up the college into four ideally more nimble and cohesive administrative units: biological sciences (which had already been approved), social and behavioral sciences, physical sciences, and humanities. All arts and sciences faculty would reside in academic departments in one of the four colleges, but some services, such as academic counseling, would be centralized under the Arts and Sciences Federation. The federation would be chaired by one of the four college deans on a rotating basis. In this way the proponents hoped to gain the benefits of decentralization while maintaining some degree of central coordination.[43]

Corbally called the proposal a framework for discussion and asked faculty, chairs, and other stakeholders for input. He hoped to bring it to a vote in the spring.

Input was quick in coming. Arts and sciences dean J. Osborn Fuller, along with many of his faculty and department chairs, called for strengthening the existing college rather than breaking it up. At a special meeting called by the faculty on January 17, those attending voted unanimously to oppose the measure, although they accounted for only 124 of the college's 616 faculty.[44]

Corbally responded several weeks later in an address to the Ohio State chapter of the American Association of University Professors in which he characterized the tradition of the arts and sciences at the university as less than stellar. "The tradition exists in the minds of many, but not in reality," Corbally said. He challenged his colleagues: "I want to worry people who are concerned with the preservation of the *status quo,* because some of our *status* is not worthy of preservation." He described the university as a "conservative community . . . with a deep suspicion of change and a fear of establishing precedents for future change."[45]

The decentralization proposal picked up support from the Council of Graduate Students and the *Lantern.* In an unusually thoughtful editorial, the newspaper noted that while 75 percent of fine arts majors were not interested in teaching, their program was still housed in the College of Education. It also pointed to a separation of related social sciences, with political science in the College of the Arts and Sciences but sociology in the College of Commerce. Courses with similar subject matter, such as sociology and psychology, had duplicative material, while undergraduates lacked a uniform liberal arts background. The *Lantern* concluded that although reorganizing the arts and sciences was

The Free University

Students and faculty unhappy with the direction Ohio State was taking came up with their own alternative with the debut of the Free University in October 1966.

The Free University had no administrative connection with Ohio State. It charged no tuition. Its students earned no credit for completing its courses. So why do it?

"The Free University differs from Ohio State by seeking new approaches to learning," explained a spokesperson, senior Michael Andes. "It is challenging Ohio State's bigness, impersonality and expensiveness."[1]

Half a dozen Ohio State faculty volunteered to teach without compensation. Organizers claimed 200 students enrolled. The courses included Psychology of Black Power, Societal Structure in the Cold Society, and Creative Photography. The Free University lasted at least through the early 1970s, and although its impact was small in terms of numbers, it symbolized a growing disenchantment with the "megaversity" Ohio State had become.

1. "Free University Operates without OSU Recognition," *Lantern,* March 31, 1967, 7.

not a panacea, it would remove major barriers to better instruction of undergraduates.[46]

When the proposal came to the Faculty Council for a vote in April, opposition from faculty in the arts and sciences remained strong. After two hours of debate that left everyone exhausted, the vote was postponed. The issue came up again on May 9, and after a three-hour debate, the council approved the recommendation 39–8. The most significant change from the original proposal was the addition of a dean of undergraduate studies.

Because of the complexity of the move, details still needed to be worked out. The proposal would not go to the board of trustees for approval until October 1967 and would not be effective until the fall of 1968.[47] But after 50 years with no changes, the university now had created five colleges (the four in arts and sciences plus University College) in a little more than two years, affecting one-third of the undergraduate students and 60 percent of the faculty. Ohio State was clearly taking itself in a new direction.

RESTRUCTURING THE FACULTY COUNCIL

In addition to restructuring the arts and sciences, the Faculty Council took on the contentious issue of restructuring itself. The question of who should have voting rights on the council had festered since the Speakers Rule vote in a faculty meeting in the spring of 1962. Many of the regular faculty who opposed the Speakers Rule remained convinced Fawcett had rigged the outcome by bringing in agricultural extension agents and part-time medical instructors to pack the vote.

The Ohio State chapter of the American Association of University Professors initiated a proposal to eliminate Faculty Council voting rights for extension agents, clinical faculty, and administrators on the grounds they were not real faculty. Marvin Fox, professor of philosophy and head of the local AAUP chapter, said the move would assure that the Faculty Council operated as a "genuine faculty group." Roy Kottman, dean of the College of Agriculture and Home Economics, led the opposition to the proposal. "The subject matter of instruction doesn't make a man more or less of a faculty member," he said.

The Faculty Council appointed its own ad hoc committee to develop a compromise plan. The proposal, reported in late February, would remove about half the administrators, such as deans and vice presidents, from the council and provide that faculty outnumber administrators at least three to one. Faculty membership would be limited to those who spent at least 75 percent of their time on the Columbus campus, thus eliminating some but not all extension agents and adjunct faculty. The ad hoc committee also recommended reapportioning the number of voting members to more accurately reflect the distribution of faculty across colleges, something that hadn't been done since 1938. In the end the compromise proposal carried the day. Supporter Paul Craig, chair of the economics department, summarized the thinking of the majority when he said that sometimes it was better to let a solution "just evolve, rather than trying to make people sign oaths in blood."[48]

RESEARCH: STILL SOARING

Despite such potentially distracting controversies, researchers continued to grow the size and impact of Ohio State's portfolio. In the fall of 1966 the university and the state of Ohio announced a $25 million partnership supported by Governor Rhodes to make Ohio State the nation's leader in transportation research. The project became official on November 11, when the board of trustees approved the first purchases of what would eventually grow to 5,000 acres of land near Marysville, 30 miles northwest of Columbus. When completed, the Transportation Research Center would include at least 70 miles of roadways for testing vehicles, signals, design configurations, and human responses. It would be the largest independent facility of its kind in the world.

The TRC was meant to capitalize on Ohio State's already strong leadership in transportation research, which included engineering faculty Thomas H. Rockwell (who studied electronic safety devices), Robert L. Cosgriff (steering controls), and Robert C. McMaster (nondestructive testing). Faculty members were already generating more than $3 million annually in sponsored research contracts from the Ohio Department of Highways, the U.S. Bureau of Public Roads, the National Academy of Science, and other industry leaders.[49] The TRC would turn out to be a highly successful venture, critical to attracting a significant investment in Ohio in future years by Japan's Honda Motor Company.

In another area, economics professor Herbert S. Parnes won the largest grant ever awarded by the Department of Labor for a market research project. The National Longitudinal Survey of Work Experience was designed to track the same set of people over five years to see what factors influenced their employment and participation in the work force. It was the first time individuals would be followed over time instead of through one-shot random sample surveys. The longitudinal survey provided a treasure trove of data to help shape policy decisions. The Labor Department considered the work so valuable, it is still being conducted at Ohio State by the Center for Human Resources Research.

At an open house in January 1967 to celebrate its 25th anniversary, the Antenna Lab, now renamed the ElectroScience Lab, featured the work of Ohio State physician and cancer research fellow John Minton, who discussed his pioneering work using lasers to treat cancer. Charles Csuri, a professor of art, announced that he and computer programmer James Shafer were working on something no one had really explored before: using computers to produce art. Csuri would come to be regarded as the father of modern-day computer graphics.

Ohio State also finally showed signs of trying to tie its research mission more closely to undergraduate instruction. Fawcett made that the topic of a panel discussion before 600 students at a scholarship recognition banquet in February. Four undergraduates talked about their studies in widely different areas: West African economic unification; the impact of Project Hope in Peru; the use of lasers in cancer treatment; and French symbolist poetry.

INSTRUCTION: STILL SEARCHING

The work of the Committee on Teaching, which had gotten off to a promising start in 1965, came to a premature end when its two major backers, Vice President John Weaver and economics professor Meno Lovenstein, moved on at the end of the 1965–66 school year. In early February 1967 Lovenstein sent a letter to Weaver's successor, John Corbally, recommending the committee's final report not be issued. He argued the committee had already said what it wanted to say in its preliminary statement of April 26, 1966. Lovenstein also said he believed the pending reorganization of the arts and sciences would consume whatever energy people had for the immediate future.[50]

Corbally followed Lovenstein's recommendation; meanwhile, a number of academic initiatives that were already underway continued. For example, the "small college" program to match up students in living quarters and classes admitted its first group of 165 freshmen in the fall. The students responded positively, and program director John Gustad trumpeted the effort to "humanize" student life. C. Grey Austin, associate dean of arts and sciences, took William Boyd's place as head of the honors program, which had grown to 301 freshmen. Administrators talked of expanding the program university-wide.[51] Richard Zimmerman, dean of the new University College, announced in May that all new freshmen who had not declared a major—about 10 percent of the total—would now have the college as their point of entry beginning in the fall of 1967. And the process to restructure and also renumber courses was approved and implemented for fall quarter 1967.

The university continued to be overwhelmed by numbers and budget problems. Fall enrollment at the Columbus campus shot up by more than 1,500 students to 36,640. While state appropriations also increased, they didn't grow as fast. Ohio State now had the highest tuition of any land grant school in the country and a student-faculty ratio of 20 to 1, which was 25 percent higher than the Big Ten average.[52] The university found that while Governor Rhodes was a great ally in building buildings, he was not so helpful in addressing operating needs.

RUNNING WITH RHODES

The school year began with James Rhodes heading into the final stretch of his reelection effort. He campaigned on a record that he said demonstrated strong jobs growth, eliminated a huge state deficit, and promised to bring the benefits of a college degree to within 30 miles of every citizen. And he had done it all without raising taxes. Rhodes's Democratic opponent, state senator Frazier Reams Jr. of Toledo, focused on failing public services throughout Ohio due to what he called Rhodes's "penny-pinching." Reams linked unpopular tuition increases to a lack of state support for higher education. He argued businesses would not bring jobs to Ohio without a progressive education climate, and predicted that if Rhodes's policies continued, incomes in the state would decline relative to the rest of the country.[53]

Governor Rhodes and Ohio's largest university had a complex but mutually beneficial relationship. Ohio State depended on Rhodes and the legislature for funding. Rhodes's appointees made up the board of trustees that determined the university's policies, and his Board of Regents oversaw the state system for all of higher education. Rhodes cultivated a reputation as a job creator, and Ohio State created jobs. The governor saw himself a builder, and Ohio State loved to build. The governor knew the university well, and university officials had known him since his time as a popular mayor of Columbus and as state auditor.

There were touchy issues. The university needed more money. The governor had money, but not a lot, and had pledged not to raise taxes to get more. Rhodes and Novice Fawcett had a businesslike relationship and were not particularly close.[54] They both came from small towns, but the similarities ended there. Fawcett was cautious and reserved. Rhodes was outgoing, folksy, almost frenetic at times. Fawcett held two degrees. Rhodes had spent only a quarter at Ohio State before leaving.

And there were those left-wing professors and students, a small but vocal faction whose members weren't shy about expressing their dislike for the governor's policies and his allies. A *Lantern* survey before the election showed that students were split in Rhodes's favor. However, results differed greatly by type of student. Reams enjoyed strong support among education majors and graduate students. Rhodes had a solid lead among arts and sciences students and a huge lead among students in agriculture, commerce, and engineering.[55] Ohio's voters made their choice clear on November 8. Rhodes won a lopsided victory by more than 700,000 votes, 65 percent to 35 percent. He carried with him Republicans in all the statewide offices and kept Republicans in firm control of the Ohio General Assembly. The next question was, what would Rhodes do with this mandate in his second term?

In his State of the State address in late February, an energized Rhodes called education his No. 1 priority. He bragged that more than a hundred campus building projects statewide had been completed or were under way and promised even more if voters would approve his Ohio Bond Commission proposal. He also pledged to "bring the finest academic brains in America to Ohio." Higher education advocates lauded the governor's emphasis on education, but skeptics noted the frustrating lack of details.[56]

Before long it became clear what those details were: more of the same, except more. The governor's budget proposal for the biennium beginning July 1 called for only a modest increase in state support for operating funds such as faculty salaries, counselors, and utilities, well below the request of his own Board of Regents. It was a different story when it came to building. The proposed Ohio Bond Commission would be the linchpin of Rhodes's second four years. He called it the "most important concept the Ohio General Assembly has ever submitted to the voters." It provided for amending the state's constitution to allow the legislature to approve issuing debt without a vote of the people. Ohio's constitutional provision had been in effect since 1851, after the state nearly went bankrupt issuing debt to build canals. Rhodes argued the limitation was out of date and inhibited long-term planning. Under his proposal the General Assembly could authorize debt on its own, and it would be administered by a five-member board appointed by the governor for nine-year terms.[57]

In classic Rhodes fashion, the governor lined up support from likely beneficiaries such as construction and design firms, banks, unions, local officials, and university presidents. Novice Fawcett was among those to step forward in support. At an April press conference sponsored by the Board of Regents, he described the Ohio Bond Commission as "the only foreseeable means to provide long-range capital improvements for Ohio State."[58] Organized opposition, if it could be called that, came from what was left of the Ohio Democratic Party, and even Democrats were divided. One of their rising stars, Representative Carl Stokes, supported the issue because of what it promised for inner-city Cleveland.

Fawcett and his staff went to work securing endorsements from student organizations. What they thought would be a slam dunk turned out to be anything but. The first resistance came when the Student Senate (the new Student Assembly hadn't been elected yet) voted 13–8 to oppose the issue after hearing a pitch from Robert Esmond, assistant director of university relations. Alan Melamed led the opposition, arguing that the debt financing would divert state general funds money away from operating funds for higher education. Melamed was part of a group of student leaders who had asked to meet with Rhodes about the operating budget back in January. Rhodes had turned them down.[59] A week after the senate vote the South Campus Student Association voted to table a motion to support the Bond Commission. The North Campus Student Association followed suit. The Council of Graduate Students voted to oppose it outright.

Fawcett doubled down on his efforts in support of the issue. In a letter to all faculty, friends, and alumni in late April, he explained that because prior bond issues were winding down, the Bond Commission proposal was "the only hope which Ohio State has at present for meeting some of its building needs." He also made the somewhat specious argument that passage of the proposal would help the university get more operating funds from the legislature by showing public support for higher education.[60] Fawcett's plea apparently was enough to sway the often truculent *Lantern* into an endorsement. Most of Ohio's newspapers also fell into line with the formidable coalition supporting the plan.

On election day, May 2, voters crushed the Ohio Bond Commission by a two-to-one margin in what the *Lantern* described as a "stunning political upset."[61] It turned out Ohio State student leaders were more in alignment with the voters than the supposed professionals. Postmortems showed that voters found the Bond Commission too complicated, and they did not want to give up that much power of the purse to politicians, even one as popular as James Rhodes.

Fawcett saw nothing but dire consequences, saying that projects including the University Hall replacement and the new pharmacy and journalism buildings were now in jeopardy. He warned that projected enrollment of 42,000 in 1970 would have to be cut back to 36,000 because of lack of space.[62] In fact, none of his predictions came to pass. Voters passed a more limited bond issue in 1968 that allowed the projects to continue as planned. Instead, the more lasting impact was on the psyche of the governor himself. In a period of just six months Ohio voters had gone from giving him his greatest victory to handing him his soundest defeat.

Publicly, Rhodes's response was short and simple. He would "abide by the will of the people." Privately, the defeat sapped much of his energy and self-confidence, confidants said later. He'd campaigned tirelessly for the issue. Now, one of his aides said, all he wanted to do was "head for the weeds."[63] Rhodes would eventually bounce back, but any hope for bold new initiatives regarding Ohio's support of higher education was gone for the remainder of the decade. If Ohio State aspired to greatness, it was on its own even more than before.

SOCIETY: RISE OF THE COUNTERCULTURE

TUNE IN, TURN ON, DROP OUT

The counterculture registered on the national consciousness with the Human Be-In at San Francisco's Golden Gate Park in January 1967. The Gathering of the Tribes, as it was also called, brought together 100,000 young people to listen to rock music, indulge in drugs if they chose, and be themselves, free of the usual constraints of society. It was there that former Harvard instructor Timothy Leary encouraged people to "tune in, turn on, and drop out." Five months later the nation's first outdoor music festival in nearby Monterey cemented the San Francisco Bay area as the epicenter of the counterculture revolution.

Similar to the Beatles phenomenon, the hippie subculture took a while to catch on in straitlaced Columbus. In fact, the initial response was downright hostile. In March, Larry's Bar on High Street, long known as a mecca for campus nonconformists, decided that some people were unwelcome. Owner Larry Paoletti developed a list of patrons who were not to be admitted because they had been involved in fistfights or were known to be underage. That produced protests, even picketing, from some customers, but Paoletti stood his ground.[64] Several months later Charbert's restaurant, also known as Dirty Charbert's for its unconventional clientele, decided it was time to clean up its reputation by banning people with long hair. "Teenage hippies are now excluded," co-owner Robert Gordon said. "They don't go swimming, they don't play ball, they don't work, they don't study, they just come to Charbert's and freak-out . . . taking up space and buying nothing."[65]

A major clash came over the recreational use of drugs. Hippie culture maintained people should have the freedom to blow their minds as long as they didn't harm anyone else. Columbus law enforcement did not see it that way. The city's vice squad reported eight arrests, including two Ohio State students, after raids on three campus-area apartments in February. Two of the arrests were for illegal possession of marijuana, and six were for possession of "suspicious" capsules.

Five more individuals, including an Ohio State student, were arrested in May for possession of marijuana. One man was arrested for illegal sale of LSD. Three days later an angry neighbor called city police about a party on East 14th Avenue. While police were breaking up the gathering, a phone in the house rang. An officer picked it up, and the caller, without asking to whom he was speaking, invited him to a pot party a block away. The police promptly accepted the invitation and busted seven students on charges ranging from illegal possession of drugs to resisting arrest. One student was detained after being spotted running naked down the street.[66]

The counterculture was making itself felt in other ways as well. The university area's first head shop, Trade Winds, opened its doors in early 1967. The store featured water pipes, beads and incense, and other artifacts that were legal but associated with the drug culture. Underground films—shot by amateur artists and often designed to be viewed while under the influence of hallucinogens—were shown at the World Theater on High Street every Friday at midnight. *Lantern* movie critic Bruce

Vilanch, who went on to a successful career as a writer and actor in Hollywood, was not impressed. "The films were, without question, the most insipid celluloid droppings ever to splatter against a screen," he wrote of one night's offerings.[67] But the World kept showing them, and eventually supplemented them with psychedelic light shows.

The *Lantern*, which had been slow to pick up on the popularity of the Beatles, also initially misread the influence of the counterculture. In an editorial in May senior Carole L. Siemon blamed its proponents' habit of "dropping out" for undercutting the "American ideal of an active, interested populace."[68] While the counterculture was clearly associated with drug use, Siemon's column overlooked the broader implications of a growing tendency among the young to question what they saw as the materialistic culture of the postwar era. That same month the university registrar released the results of questionnaires filled out by the previous fall's entering class. Only 5 percent of the students said they came to college to enable themselves to earn more money. Another 51 percent indicated an interest in learning "saleable skills," which was also a traditional outlook. But a significant minority of 40 percent emphasized developing their "minds and intellects."[69] These students tended to cluster in the arts and sciences and education and would provide much of the energy behind the protests that would shape the closing years of the decade.

MISPLACED PRIORITIES

The priorities of Columbus police in protecting students and others in the university area continued to be an issue. A brutal murder just three weeks after classes started in the fall put the campus on edge. Sometime during the night of October 16 or the following morning, Robert Spike was bludgeoned to death in the United Christian Center on East 15th Avenue, just a block from campus. Spike, a professor of theology at the University of Chicago and an outspoken civil rights advocate, had come to Columbus to help dedicate the new center. The motive was unknown, and the perpetrator was never found.[70]

In August a Columbus officer made a decision that to students symbolized police insensitivity to the people they were supposed to protect. Student Larry M. Soine was walking a date home along High Street between Chittenden and 11th Avenues at 2:30 on a Saturday morning. Soine said that when he stepped off the curb to get a better look at something on the sidewalk, a policeman in a passing patrol car stopped and arrested him for jaywalking.

Soine had to go downtown to be booked, leaving the question of what to do with his date. The arresting officer told her she should walk home, which was about four blocks away. The woman was walking down 11th Avenue toward Hunter Avenue when a man leaped out of the bushes and tried to grab her. She screamed and pushed back. The man yelled epithets and made obscene gestures before exposing himself to her. The woman managed to break free and ran to a friend's apartment to call police. Meanwhile, Soine was released after posting bail. The attacker wasn't identified or found.

A police spokesperson later explained that officers were reluctant to give rides to unescorted women for fear of being accused of molesting them.[71] The *Lantern* took the police to task in an editorial, pointing out that the department's official position was to discourage women from walking alone at night. The *Lantern* asked if the police were more worried about themselves or the people they were sworn to protect. While acknowledging that the officer was not legally required to transport Soine's date four blocks, the editorial argued that common sense would have dictated otherwise.[72]

Because the incident occurred at the end of summer quarter, it did not trigger a strong reaction among the student body. But when the majority of students returned to campus shortly afterward, the story made the rounds by word of mouth and assumed the characteristics of an urban legend, further undermining student trust in law enforcement officers.

CAMPUS VISITORS

The war in Vietnam still had a great deal of support from the campus community in 1966. Army staff sergeant and former Green Beret Barry Sadler was part of the halftime show at the football game against Michigan on November 19. Sadler had released a song called "The Ballad of the Green Berets," which became a No. 1 hit across the country. According to the *Lantern,* Sadler—accompanied by the Marching Band in the formation of two giant berets, plus the Navy ROTC glee club, the Army ROTC singing group, and the Men's Glee Club—"brought spectators to their feet" in a tribute to army officer and recent Medal of Honor winner Charles Q. Williams.[73]

University organizations continued to bring prominent opponents and supporters of the war to campus to educate anyone who would listen. The opponents included U.S. senator Wayne Morse, a Democrat from Oregon, and University of Chicago history professor Hans Morgenthau. The supporters included House minority leader Gerald R. Ford (R-Michigan) and *Newsweek* international editor Arnaud De Borchgrave. But it was Arizona senator Barry Goldwater who showed that even after his stinging defeat in the presidential election two years earlier, he could still draw a crowd. Goldwater was the only political figure that year to fill Mershon Auditorium when he spoke on March 7. He told his listeners he strongly supported the objectives of the Vietnam War. He said the United States was winning in three of the four war zones, and the only thing holding back chances for an American victory was the timidity of Lyndon Johnson's administration.[74]

SUMMER OF LOVE

The school year ended with a national celebration of the Summer of Love that brought a horde of young people, many of them runaways, to the Haight-Ashbury section of San Francisco. But all the talk of peace, love, and flower power played out against a backdrop of escalating violence. In Vietnam a large buildup of American troops gave commanders the resources they wanted to fight all along the South Vietnamese border. Body counts of enemy soldiers rose. But heavier fighting also meant more U.S. soldiers wounded and killed and more casualties among innocent civilians. Public uneasiness with the war continued to grow.

For six days in June, Arabs and Israelis fought across the Sinai desert before settling into an uneasy truce. At home, summer brought another spasm of racial violence. Detroit exploded into mayhem so widespread, federal troops had to be called in. It was the country's worst unrest since the New York draft riots during the Civil War a century earlier.

New voices arose who claimed to have the answers to domestic violence and disorder. Californians elected Ronald Reagan governor on his promise to crack down on campus radicals. Reagan then fired University of California president Clark Kerr for being too lenient. His action met with overwhelming public support.

A little more than a hundred years earlier, future president Abraham Lincoln had warned that a house divided against itself could not stand. By the end of the summer of 1967, the United States was deeply divided, and the worst was yet to come.

CHAPTER 9

DOWN THE RABBIT HOLE

(1967–68)

After a period of relative peace, the Ohio State campus descended into a spiral of angry rhetoric, confrontation, and repression. Students engaged in a physical confrontation with Columbus police, tried to disrupt military recruiters, and temporarily took over the Administration Building. University leaders and law enforcement responded forcefully. The tumultuous year ended with a tragic fire that took the lives of two students, while society itself seemed to come off its hinges as war abroad and violence at home split the country apart.

9.1. Ohio Highway Patrol officers guard the Administration Building, spring 1968. (*Makio*)

STUDENTS: SEETHING

At the beginning of the 1967–68 school year it looked like a left-centered coalition of moderates was in the driver's seat. Student government leaders focused on pushing through reforms that had been started the year before. They would find institutionalizing reform was a lot harder than starting it. First up was getting university approval for the new student bill of rights, which had already been approved by students in a campus-wide referendum the previous spring.

The Council on Student Affairs (CSA) finally granted a go-ahead in October, but only after changing some critical provisions, particularly regarding the right of students to choose where they lived and the right of women to equal treatment with men. The newly elected Student Assembly voted unanimously to oppose the changes. That put the ball in the lap of the Faculty Council, which would be the next level of review. Frustrated students were told to expect the process to take a year.[1]

Undergraduate Student Government president Lloyd Siegel went to work quietly behind the scenes with the faculty committee charged with reviewing both the original referendum and the changes made by the CSA. To everyone's surprise the committee completed its work in just seven weeks. It resolved the conflict by splitting the difference in most cases. For example, the committee supported giving students the right to live where they chose, but required additional language recognizing the university's need to meet financial commitments related to paying off residence hall bonds. Some student rights advocates, notably Maurice Solkov, a Free Student Federation member who led the effort to create the bill of rights, called the compromise a sellout.[2] But Siegel and former constitutional convention chair Alan Melamed said they had won most of what they wanted and should build on that. In the end the pragmatists carried the day. The Faculty Council approved the committee's recommendations in December, and the board of trustees approved the necessary rule changes four months later.[3]

Meanwhile, the University Party continued to control the restructured Undergraduate Student Government. Siegel chose not to run for reelection in the spring, but the party's ticket of Jay Shaffer and Crofford Macklin, both juniors, won the presidential election over two opponents.

The party also captured 19 of 22 assembly seats. Nearly 7,750 students voted, 1,300 more than the year before.

The assault on in loco parentis continued. The Women's Self Government Association won administrative approval to get rid of a rule that prohibited women students from staying overnight in a local hotel or motel without parental permission. The CSA approved jettisoning the rule that required chaperones at off-campus events; the officers of the sponsoring organizations now assumed responsibility for the behavior of their members.

However, an effort to grant extended hours to sophomores hit a roadblock. Even though the proposal passed the WSGA board unanimously, Ruth Weimer, the associate dean of student relations, turned it down because of concerns regarding compliance with the existing rules. She pointed to an increase in infractions from 53 to 133 during the last year, and called on students to do a better job of gaining compliance from juniors and seniors before adding sophomores. That prompted student Susan Harrington to observe: "Giving us extended hours won't make us immoral. We already have our set beliefs and we won't change them because we can stay out longer."[4]

The biggest issue of the year turned out to be alcohol. The campus had been dry since the days of Prohibition. In January the Council of Fraternity Presidents proposed to the CSA that residents of fraternity houses be allowed to consume low-alcohol (3.2 percent) beer on the premises if their individual chapters elected to allow it. A proposal for dorm residents followed shortly thereafter. The north, south, and newly created west campus residence halls associations combined forces to put a referendum on the ballot in February. It passed by a lopsided two-to-one majority.

The Council on Student Affairs raised concerns about enforcement, particularly regarding students who were under the legal drinking age of 18 (about 10 percent of the total). Ohio State would be the only public university in the state to allow drinking on campus, and one of only three in the Big Ten. In the end, the CSA recommended approval to the board of trustees. When the trustees took up the topic at their July meeting, they unanimously turned down the fraternity and residence hall proposals, based at least in part on President Novice Fawcett's concern about the impact on students who didn't want a living environment where alcohol was freely available. The trustees did approve alcohol in the Faculty Club after 5 p.m. and in the Ohio Union.[5]

Although the system seemed to be blocking as much as it was enabling, students remained relatively calm. Instead, pent-up anger was focused on issues traditionally outside the system: the conduct of Columbus police, protests over the Vietnam War, the treatment of minority students, and at year's end, a tragic fire.

THE "MORBID AMUSEMENT" OF D PLATOON

More than three years of relative calm, free from student confrontations with police, ended after nonteaching employees voted on October 4 to walk off their jobs in a dispute with the university. Sixteen hundred maids, janitors, and food service and laundry workers represented by Local 138 of the American Federation of State, County, and Municipal Employees had been negotiating with Ohio State for nearly six months over a package of wage and benefit increases. The university said granting what the union asked for would cost $5.5 million. The money wasn't in the budget, administrators said, so the cost would be passed on to students to the tune of an average increase of $80 per year in tuition and an additional $60 per year in room and board fees for those living in dormitories.[6]

Union pickets showed up at the corner of High Street and 15th Avenue promptly at midnight that evening. Within 15 minutes about 30 students had gathered as well. Some of them heckled the pickets, and some cheered them. Others amused themselves by rolling a trash can back and forth across the street. The racket attracted students from nearby fraternity houses and from the south campus men's dorms, as well as assorted street people. (Because it was a weeknight, most of the women were already locked in.) Before long the crowd had grown to around 700. A column of police cars drove slowly through the intersection at about 12:30 in an attempt to disperse the crowd. Instead, trash cans were rolled into the street and set on fire. Some onlookers threw aerosol cans and fireworks into the blaze. Motorcyclists who roared through the flames drew cheers from the onlookers.[7]

Columbus safety director Frederick J. Simon appeared and announced via a bullhorn that the police were on their way. He was greeted with boos and catcalls. Shortly after he left, a line of about 60 officers outfitted in riot helmets and black leather jackets marched up High Street brandishing 18-inch nightsticks. It was D Platoon, a special unit of the police.[8] The officers methodically moved to clear the street. Most of the spectators scattered, but not until after one policeman was hit by a rock. Two students broke the windows at Hill's Tailoring on High Street and were arrested for malicious destruction. Fourteen others were arrested on charges ranging from disorderly conduct to resisting arrest and disregard of a lawful order. Of the 16 arrested, eight were Ohio State students. Once the crowd was dispersed, the fire department extinguished the trash can fires.

Simon said afterward that the crowd offered little resistance to D Platoon. "Just a few of the animals kept acting up," he said. "You can quote me on that, too. They aren't people when they act like this, they're nothing but animals."[9]

D Platoon deployed again Thursday evening, October 5, and arrested 13 people, including six students, in a crowd of about 600. On Friday evening D Platoon was replaced by regular uniformed officers and only four persons were arrested, none of them students.[10] D Platoon's actions over the first two nights generated numerous complaints about excessive force. *Citizen-Journal* reporter Robert MacVicar described how he was grabbed by three officers and jammed into a headlock so tight it broke his glasses, just because he didn't produce his press identification card fast enough. A *Lantern* reporter saw officers holding a man down on the hood of a patrol wagon and beating him with clubs. A TV crew filmed an individual being repeatedly hit and maced while being loaded into a paddy wagon.[11]

Columbus police tried to mend fences with the media in a contentious press conference on October 9. Several reporters complained that officers told them "I don't care who you are" when they tried to show their press credentials, even though the credentials had been issued by the police. Reporters also said they could not identify the officers involved because D Platoon members wore no badges or other identification as a matter of policy. Police officials maintained this was necessary to protect the officers from becoming targets for snipers and refused to change the policy. Police chief Robert Baus did apologize to the media and promised to do a better job of educating his officers about protocols. But both Baus and Simon, the safety director, dismissed suggestions that it would have been better to let the crowd alone until it wore itself out. "It just wasn't that kind of crowd," Simon responded. "We tried to make D Platoon's arrival as flamboyant as possible so the students would be afraid to tangle with them and so we could use as little real force as possible."[12]

Meanwhile, as the strike by the service workers continued, supervisors and student employees kept the cafeteria lines open with ready-to-eat food (which students joked was better than the regular offerings). The strike ended six days after it began when the union and the university agreed on a package that included paid hospitalization and life insurance, a discount on meals, and a more formal grievance procedure. Union members did not get a wage increase or free parking. Instead, the university committed to a wage study (which later did support a pay raise). The concessions would be funded by reallocating money from existing equipment budgets. Workers returned to their jobs the next day.[13]

Still, major issues remained. Some faculty and students took the administration to task for threatening disciplinary action against students who supported the strike. But the biggest casualty was the already strained relationship between students and the Columbus police. Groups including the Undergraduate Student Government, the Council of Graduate Students, the local chapter of the American Association of University Professors (AAUP), and Students for Liberal Action announced investigations into allegations of excessive use of force. Columbus mayor M. E. Sensenbrenner pledged to "get rid of any police officer that we [the city] can associate with any acts of brutality." He added: "I'll back my police one thousand percent as long as they're right . . . and those people [the High Street crowd] had no business out there." No disciplinary actions were ever announced.[14]

Several months later an AAUP committee issued a report on the incident. After analyzing news film and interviewing 25 witnesses, the committee concluded: "The testimony strongly suggests that the crowd, had it not been provided with the morbid amusement furnished by the presence and antics of 'D' Platoon, would have dispersed earlier and probably not have returned in such great numbers on Thursday and Friday." The committee said it could document at least two incidents of excessive force on the first night and three more on the second night. The report found that while most members of D Platoon conducted themselves appropriately, some "exhibited animosity to college students far out of proportion to the necessities of the situation." At least one student subsequently won a civil suit against the police for excessive force.[15]

Why the Columbus police shifted tactics in this case has never been fully explained. During the 1961 Rose Bowl protests and the 1964 jaywalking protest, police were content to cordon off the area and let the exuberance wear itself out. Perhaps by this time police officials were seeing rising lawlessness elsewhere and decided to nip things in the bud. Perhaps, with municipal elections just one month away, Mayor Sensenbrenner wanted to make a strong statement for law and order. Regardless of intent, many students now saw D Platoon officers as some sort of stormtroopers whose appearance in the streets invited confrontation.[16]

FRUSTRATED WAR PROTESTORS

By the fall of 1967 public support for the Vietnam War was eroding rapidly. A Gallup Poll in October showed that for the first time, twice as many Americans opposed President Lyndon Johnson's handling of the war than approved it. In November, six members of the sociology faculty at Ohio State joined 1,300 of their colleagues nationwide to send Johnson a letter that warned of the adverse consequences on American society of the continuation of the war. The *Lantern* described the war as having "dubious validity." Rumors swirled throughout fall quarter about an end to graduate student draft deferments. Antiwar protests drew huge crowds on other campuses, but at Ohio State frustrated activists still were unable to engage many students. Organizers had decided over the summer to try something different when classes resumed in the fall. They would focus not on ROTC but on another symbol of military presence on campus: armed services recruiters.

On the last day of classes in December, about 60 protestors confronted a handful of navy recruiters who had set up a table in the Ohio Union. The demonstrators first asked the recruiters to leave. When they refused, the demonstrators sat down in front of the table but did not attempt to prevent anyone from approaching the recruiters. A crowd of about 150 gathered around the protestors, at times heckling them. University officials looked on but took no action, although police were on call nearby. After four hours the protestors left.[17]

The demonstration earned a blast from Mayor Sensenbrenner. "[Ohio State] is one of the greatest universities in the United States," he said. "If these demonstrators don't like it here, they should get out." Instead, it was the air force that decided to get out, at least temporarily. In January a recruiter told the *Lantern* he'd canceled a visit because "my job is to get people, not create incidents."[18]

Demonstrators next focused on marine corps recruiters for three days in January. On the first day 50 demonstrators and half a dozen faculty members gathered for an orderly protest at the Main Library. The participants left open an aisle for students who wanted to approach the recruiters. The protestors returned the next day without any faculty. Twelve demonstrators occupied what had been the aisle the day before, but did not interfere with people who threaded their way through to see the recruiters.[19]

On day three 50 protestors showed up at a marine recruiting table at Denney Hall, again without faculty supporters present. A crowd of spectators gathered, some heckling the protestors. A male student trying to walk through the crowd kicked one of the female protestors sitting on the floor. It was not immediately clear whether it was intentional or accidental. The male protestors seated next to her rose to their feet, fists clenched. A clash was preempted when the recruiters intervened, playing the role of fight preventers at a peace demonstration. The protestors left without further incident shortly thereafter.[20]

Things finally came to a head several days later, on January 31. A group of about 25 protesters entered Hamilton Hall, where Paul S. Metzger, an assistant professor and a commander in the naval reserve, was offering a counseling session for medical students on fulfilling their two-year military obligation after graduation. The demonstrators were met by Richard L. Meiling, dean of the College of Medicine, who asked them to leave. They refused. Charles Gambs, associate dean of student relations, told them, "You're blocking academic activities here." David Travers, a graduate student in philosophy and leader of the group, objected: "How are we disrupting things? We're students here."

Marion Curry of the university police cited the definition of trespassing in the Ohio Revised Code and again asked the group to leave. About half did. Next, several three-man teams consisting of Ohio State police, Columbus police, and Ohio Highway Patrol officers, who been waiting in an adjacent room, came in. One team escorted Travers to a waiting bus. The other protestors also were escorted out. In all, 13 protestors were taken downtown for booking. They were released on $20 bond four hours later.[21]

The arrests, which clearly had been prepared for in advance, triggered criticism on and off campus. Benson Wolman, chair of the central Ohio chapter of the American Civil Liberties Union, provided two attorneys to defend those arrested on the grounds that their constitutional right to assembly had been violated. Meanwhile, the university announced it had changed its policy on military recruiting. Acting on a resolution originally proposed by Undergraduate Student Government president Lloyd Siegel as a compromise, all recruiters—including those from the military, the Peace Corps, and other government agencies—would be treated the same as those from private companies; that is, they could recruit in college offices, but could no longer use the library or the Ohio Union.[22]

The demonstrators returned in early February with a new tactic. About a dozen of them staged a "mill-in" to protest navy recruiters in the lobby of Hitchcock Hall. This involved standing around the recruiting tables conversing with the recruiters and reading literature while blocking others from doing so. After the protestors refused to leave, teams of police moved in and put 11 of them on a bus to be taken downtown. All were charged with trespassing and released a short time later on $20 bond.[23]

Twenty-four protestors were now facing charges. The remainder switched for the time being to less confrontational tactics. Their next target was recruiters from Dow Chemical, the company that produced napalm, the jellied gasoline used extensively in Vietnam. An anti-Dow demonstration at the University of Wisconsin four months earlier had resulted in a battle between students and police that left more than 60 injured and the campus in turmoil. On February 12 about 80 people marched from Denney Hall, where the recruiters had set up a table, to the Oval and back. Six of them carried a small coffin containing charred toy babies representing Vietnamese children burned by napalm. The protest lasted about 40 minutes and ended without incident. Few students bothered to pay attention, the *Lantern* reported. Three days later a dozen students staged a counterdemonstration, sitting for three hours next to a table that had been set up in the lobby of Morrill Tower by the Committee to End the War in Vietnam. The counterprotestors carried a

9.2. Students marched across campus in February 1968 to protest a visit by Dow Chemical recruiters. Note the Lyndon B. Johnson mask in the lower left corner and the burned doll on top of the coffin. (*Makio*)

sign that read "The only good communist is a dead one. Kill for peace." They were largely ignored as well.[24]

War opponents now turned their energy to organizing support for the 24 arrested students. Five faculty members wrote a letter to President Fawcett asking him to withdraw the charges in order to "protect our students and reassert the dignity of the academic enterprise." Nearly 190 of their colleagues signed the letter.[25] When Fawcett met with representatives of the group, he refused to drop the charges but did agree to appoint a faculty committee to review the incidents and recommend policies going forward. Two weeks later students presented Fawcett with a petition containing 1,112 signatures calling for the university to drop the charges. Fawcett referred the petition to the committee he had just appointed.[26]

Spring was traditionally a good time for student activists to generate larger crowds, but while they gave it their best shot, they came up short. Organizers claimed a rally for student rights in April would draw a thousand students to the Oval. Worried officials closed the Administration Building to visitors as a precaution, and Governor James

Rhodes ordered 900 National Guardsmen to stand by at the state fairgrounds, two miles away. A large crowd of curiosity seekers showed up, attracted by rumors that something big might happen. When it didn't, they drifted away.[27]

Ohio State activists planned a teach-in and strike on the Oval on April 26 in conjunction with a national antiwar event organized by Students for a Democratic Society. Between 300 and 2,000 protestors were expected to show up. Only 150 did. The most telling moment came when senior Phil Kalban grabbed the microphone and asked how many students supported the demonstration by black students that was going on in the Administration Building at the same time. According to the *Lantern,* about a dozen raised their hands. Then Kalban asked how many in the crowd were there just because they were curious about what was going on. Almost everyone else raised a hand. Rally over.[28]

April and May also brought news on the legal front. Verdicts were handed down for the 24 students who had been arrested at Hamilton Hall and Hitchcock Hall. Most of them were found guilty of trespassing and sentenced to court costs of $30 to $50, plus 15 days in the county workhouse, with 12 days suspended. Supporters were surprised at the inclusion of workhouse time. In previous cases jail or workhouse time had been suspended for nonviolent offenders. Thomas Moody and Robert M. Duncan, two of the judges who handled the bulk of the 24 cases, were known as moderates, but moderation no longer seemed to apply.[29]

Even Corps Day turned out to be anticlimactic. The university had already decided to move the program from the Oval to the athletics fields near University Hospital because, administrators said, it had grown and needed more space.[30] That wasn't enough to prevent protests, nor were protests enough to stop Corps Day, but a rainstorm put an end to both.

The final demonstration of the year occurred in May, when about a hundred protestors showed up at a navy information table at Hitchcock Hall to rally against what the *Lantern* described as "alleged university intimidation of demonstrators." The protestors were careful to leave access to the table. No uniformed police were visible. Comic relief was provided by two of the protestors' dogs who couldn't decide whether they'd rather be inside the building or out. *Lantern* reporter Roger Myers found additional humor in the activities of photographers attracted to the scene. He wrote: "City and *Lantern* newsmen were taking pictures of demonstrators, the Navy team and students who talked to the team. A University plainclothes policeman was taking pictures of newsmen and demonstrators. And some of the demonstrators were taking pictures of newsmen, plainclothes policemen, university officials and everyone else in sight. . . . Everyone was either posing for someone else or trying to avoid being photographed."[31]

After two hours the demonstrators cleaned up after themselves and left. And so ended a frustrating year for campus activists opposed to the Vietnam War. Despite political turmoil, mounting casualty lists, the potential loss of draft deferments for hundreds of Ohio State students, and the examples set by antiwar protestors at other universities, the only thing the activists seemed to be successful at was getting themselves sent to the county workhouse. Even the *Lantern,* which by this point opposed the Vietnam War, had condemned their attempts to disrupt recruiters as "crude" and "silly."[32]

In the spring of 1968 antiwar students turned in increasing numbers to a more traditional form of insurgency, the ballot box. At the same time other students chose to explore the tactics of civil disobedience.

FRUSTRATED BLACK STUDENTS

A census taken by Ohio State to comply with the 1964 Civil Rights Act estimated that in the fall of 1967 nonwhite students comprised only 2.5 percent of U.S.-born undergraduates and 4.8 percent of graduate and professional students at the university. At the same time, nonwhite residents comprised 8.1 percent of Ohio's total population.[33]

Except for attempts by students to get Ohio State to do something about housing discrimination and the efforts of the Columbus NAACP to get university contractors to hire more African Americans, there was little organized activity on campus in the midsixties to promote opportunities for black students. Many black students seethed in isolation and fear on the predominantly white campus.[34] Nevertheless, the alumni magazine prematurely declared: "Ohio State, unlike some campuses throughout the nation, has been relatively free of racial overtones throughout the years."[35]

Galvanized by a conversation with black activist Dick Gregory, who visited Ohio State in January, a group of 60 students calling themselves the Black Student Union met with John Bonner, the executive dean for student relations, on February 1 to present eight demands for immediate action by university officials. The demands included an increase in African American faculty and administrators; more aggressive enforcement of the university's antidiscrimination policy in off-campus housing; and better recognition of the contributions of African Americans to the country's and the university's history.[36]

The students stressed they used the term "demands" because they believed these were steps the university should have taken on its own a long time ago. Senior John Evans, a spokesperson for the group, said: "If the administration had communication with the black students, it would have anticipated our needs as it does for other groups on campus."[37]

Bonner met with the group for about 90 minutes and promised to "forcefully" take the list to his administrative colleagues. At a meeting a month later, eight senior university officials, including Provost John Corbally, explored the next steps with the students.

But the assassination of Martin Luther King Jr. in Memphis on April 4 upset everything. Many black people who were already impatient with the slow pace of change since the passage of the 1964 and 1965 civil rights legislation saw the assassination as the symbolic end to King's gospel of nonviolence. The growing militancy of some black leaders made many white people more paranoid. The rhetoric on both sides of the racial divide escalated. At a rally in honor of King, one unidentified black man reportedly told the crowd: "The time for people to pick up a gun is now."[38]

In this contentious atmosphere, a white campus bus driver got in an argument with four black women students over what he said was loud and obscene language. He asked the women to leave the bus. When they refused, he stopped the bus, called police, and had them removed. The next day, after a group of about 40 black students went to campus police headquarters to file a complaint, they said they were treated rudely by the officers there.[39]

The same group of students then requested a meeting with Gordon Carson, vice president for business and finance, to whom both the campus bus service and police reported. Carson thought he'd be meeting with five or six students, but at 9 a.m. on Friday, April 26, a group of about 40 black students entered his office in the Administration Building and told him they would stay until an apology was issued and the bus driver and police officers involved were fired. Carson refused, saying he

9.3. Dean John Bonner meets with members of the Black Student Union, February 1968. (University Archives)

needed to conduct an investigation. The students told Carson he could not leave his office or make any outgoing phone calls. About noon, a group of white students gathered on the second floor of the building in a sympathy protest.[40]

At around 1:45 some of the black students began wiring the building's doors shut with coat hangers and telephone wires. Employees, other than those in Carson's office, were invited to leave via an open bathroom window on the first floor. Someone had turned off the ventilation system, and both the temperature and tempers began to rise. The students used abusive and obscene language, Carson later said. They made him stand for long periods of time and refused to let him go to the restroom for six hours. He also maintained they did about $1,000 worth of damage. At the state fairgrounds, 50 Ohio Highway Patrol officers stood by. About 40 Columbus policemen also were on alert.

Sometime after 3 p.m. a delegation of black students approached Provost Corbally, who was still in the building, and asked if he would intervene as a mediator. President Fawcett was in Cleveland on business, so Corbally was the ranking university official present, although he stayed in touch with Fawcett by phone. Corbally knew time was running out. First, he called the highway patrol and told it to hold off. He knew the students needed a face-saving way to extract themselves from the situation they had created. "A number of [them realized the lock-in] was a mistake on their part," he said later.[41]

Corbally then talked to Carson about crafting some sort of joint statement. Carson, unhappy about being held in his office for six hours, was reluctant but finally relented. After about an hour of negotiations and with the help of some local black community leaders, Corbally, Carson, and the students agreed to a statement. It consisted mainly of platitudes about the need to improve conditions for black students at Ohio State, but didn't promise anything beyond what the university had already agreed to do, including conducting an impartial investigation into the bus incident. The black students left the building at about 5:30. The takeover had ended, but the controversy had not.

Columbus Dispatch reporters called members of the board of trustees at home over the weekend for their reaction. Instead of declining to comment or deferring to the board chair or Fawcett, some trustees felt compelled to offer their opinions. James Shocknessy said the agreement ending the lock-in was "reached under coercion" and not "entitled to respect." John Bricker and Don M. Hilliker both said they thought the lock-in amounted to trespassing. William C. Safford, the newest trustee, said, "We're going to have to come around to the point of some law and order although some people might not like it."[42]

The *Dispatch* doubled down on Tuesday, April 30, with a story headlined "OSU 'Kidnap' Victims Said to Fear for Lives." The story, which quoted unnamed police sources, said Carson was "pale and shaken," that he was "roughed up" when he tried to use his phone, and that the black students had "knives and gasoline bombs."[43] A subsequent university investigation found evidence of abusive language and minor property damage, but no evidence of weapons or physical violence.[44]

The trustees called a special meeting that same day to discuss the matter further. The real showdown came beforehand at a private dinner at the Scioto Country Club, where some of the trustees unloaded on the administration for "giving in" to the protestors. Corbally, who accompanied Fawcett to the dinner, later recalled that trustees complained they were embarrassed when they were accosted by colleagues in the community with questions such as "What the hell is going on?" and "Who's running the university?"

Corbally finally lost his temper when one trustee was particularly critical of Fawcett. "If there is to be criticism it should be addressed to me," he interjected. He later remembered saying that "if it was their view that I could not handle this kind of event, then I would quickly and quietly go and do something else."

"Now, John, just calm down," Senator Bricker responded. "No one is going anywhere because of this event. We just don't want it to become a habit."[45]

By the time the trustees convened for their public meeting later that evening, unity had been restored, at least on the surface. The meeting was limited to press only, because of the fear of more demonstrations. The building where the meeting took place was protected by a cordon of 50 highway patrol officers with nightsticks. As acting chair Bricker made a statement expressing support for the administration's handling of the lock-in. He said the trustees supported an investigation into the incident by university officials and possible disciplinary action against those involved.[46]

That was not enough to end the controversy. The *Dispatch* ran a story on May 3 saying alumni and elected officials believed Ohio State was "too soft" on protesters. State senator Gordon Sherer (R-Cincinnati) called for a special legislative session to take action against what he termed "criminal insurrection" at the university. Congressman Sam Devine (R-Columbus) claimed the black students violated the civil rights of university administrators. Congressman William H. Ayres (R-Akron), ranking minority member of the House Education Committee, called for an investigation of events at Ohio State and at Columbia, where between 800 and 1,000 students protesting Vietnam War–related research had recently taken over five administration buildings. (After the university forcefully removed the protestors, the backlash from faculty and students against the administration and police forced Columbia to close down for the rest of the school year.)[47]

At Ohio State, protestors calling for the reform of the university's relations with black students had their supporters. Jay Shaffer, the newly elected president of the Undergraduate Student Government, called the lock-in an "excellent and significant victory." Many campus organizations, while not endorsing the lock-in, did support the changes called for in the Black Student Union's list of demands. Even the Council of Fraternity Presidents announced its support.[48]

The university did manage to move forward with a number of changes agreed to before the lock-in. James B. Boyer, a doctoral candidate in education, was introduced in May as Ohio State's first black academic counselor, with additional counselors to be hired down the road. Also in May the university announced the creation of a civil rights information center in Orton Hall. A previously scheduled exhibition in the Ohio Union celebrated black history.

William E. Conley, a 1960 graduate of Ohio State, joined the administration in July as minority affairs coordinator in the Office of Student Affairs. That same month the new College of Social and Behavioral Sciences announced it would offer at least five new courses featuring the contributions of African Americans to American culture, and the College of Humanities said it would develop a course in black history.[49]

These initiatives were overshadowed by the way the university disciplined the black students involved in the April 26 lock-in. On May 3 Fawcett appointed a committee to recommend possible action. The following week the Franklin County prosecutor announced a grand jury probe into the lock-in. At the end of May the grand jury issued secret indictments on 12 criminal counts against 34 students. They included charges such as unlawful detention, kidnapping, making menacing threats, blackmail, and conspiring to abduct. It is not clear whether Ohio State asked the prosecutor for these charges or he issued them on his own, although Corbally attributed the action to Carson.[50] In either case the black community and other supporters of the students were outraged at the severity of the charges—kidnapping was a felony under Ohio law—considering that no weapons had been involved and the incident had been settled peacefully. The NAACP provided legal counsel to the students being charged. The Black Student Union announced it was suing 13 university officials and trustees in federal district court for violation of civil rights. The disciplinary committee appointed by Fawcett recommended that no university action be taken until the charges initiated by the county prosecutor were resolved. Instead, Fawcett announced on July 10 that eight black students had been dismissed for their role in the lock-in.[51]

At the board of trustees meeting the next day, the administration brought forward a new Disruption Rule that had been developed by the Faculty Council at Fawcett's request. The rule said that students could not individually or collectively disrupt any building or function. Violation would be penalized by suspension for no less than a year and could result in prosecution by nonuniversity sources. A special disciplinary committee could dismiss students immediately with a preliminary hearing while a full hearing process was completed. Fawcett and Corbally both maintained the new rules were necessary in light of threats from white students to repeat the tactics used during the lock-in.[52]

At the same meeting the university announced that John Mount would become vice president for student affairs and John Bonner would succeed Mount as vice president for educational services. Although some student leaders distrusted Bonner and others thought he was out of touch, they feared that Mount, who also would continue as secretary of the board of trustees, would take an even harder line.[53]

University administrators had succeeded, at least temporarily, in dissuading other students from employing tactics similar to the lock-in, but they did so at the expense of their relationship with black students and the black community. Of the remaining 26 black students who participated in the lock-in but were not disciplined by the university, five dropped out and 10 flunked out at the end of spring quarter. It was clear that unless the university and the black community could find ways to increase success for black students, simply admitting more of them would produce failure and frustration.[54]

TRAGEDY IN LINCOLN TOWER

With the opening of Lincoln and Morrill Towers at full capacity in the fall of 1967, Ohio State officials achieved something they had been working toward for nearly a decade: safe, convenient university-run housing for any student who wanted it. The problem was, the presumed beneficiaries did not share the enthusiasm. The newly expanded residence hall system showed 2,500 vacancies (out of 10,000 spaces) at the start of classes that fall. Some 1,300 of them were in the towers. Enrollment limits applied by the Board of Regents and the growing student preference for apartment living combined to leave the university holding the bag with a big investment and fewer customers to help pay it off.[55]

Frequent criticism of the towers from a variety of critics, particularly faculty, didn't help. Wayland W. Bowser, an associate professor of architecture, told the *Lantern* they were a "terrible mistake." He said the occupants would be "packed into a room with more human beings than most cities will tolerate in slum real estate." David Templeton, an assistant professor of art, said the towers embodied an "incredible lack of human and esthetic consideration."[56]

Even guests felt compelled to offer their opinions. Sim Van der Ryn, an associate professor of architecture at Berkeley who spoke on campus in November, said: "You get a clear picture of what Ohio State stands for from the dormitories which house 2,000 people and a campus dominated by a football stadium." On the other hand, Peter Janssen, education editor at *Newsweek,* spent two nights in Lincoln Tower while researching a story on large universities. Janssen said he liked the design of the suites as well as the coed aspects of life in the towers.[57]

The real flash point for students was not the architecture of the buildings but the method used to secure the bonds to build them. The despised Dorm Rule required all freshmen and sophomores to live in university residence halls unless they were married, living with parents, or could prove financial hardship. Virtually all student government organizations opposed the rule. Up to this point the university had not needed to enforce it, but the large number of vacancies created a problem. When it was announced in April that the rule would be enforced for sophomore men beginning in the fall of 1968, the outcry was predictable. Compounding the aggravation in the eyes of some was the exemption granted to fraternities, many of which were suffering financially.[58]

The timing could not have been worse. Three weeks after the announcement, the trustees approved an increase in room and board fees for fall quarter 1968. A week after that the residence and dining office announced that maid service would be cut back for cost reasons. Now students would be required to pay more to get less to live in university housing where many of them didn't want to be in the first place. Then, after a small fire in Morrill Tower on May 12, residents circulated a petition protesting alleged hazardous conditions in both towers.[59]

In the early morning hours of May 22 another fire broke out in the 1140 suite of Lincoln Tower. Columbus firefighters rushed to the scene within minutes, but by the time the residents were evacuated and the fire was put out, freshman Pamela Sue Patterson was dead. Sixteen other students were hospitalized, and one of them, freshman Retta D. Foster, later died. That evening Fawcett and Carson went to Lincoln Tower to meet with 600 angry, frightened residents. They tried to assure the students the towers were safe. They announced they were launching an immediate investigation and said they would place 10 special-duty Columbus police officers in each tower, effective immediately, to serve as fire guards. And the university would allow anyone who wanted to move out of the towers to do so.[60]

Reassuring words were not enough. Students and their parents questioned the buildings' controversial design. Rumors spread about flammable furniture, inaccessible escape routes, fire doors that opened the wrong way, and fire equipment that didn't work. The *Lantern* added to the anxiety with a provocative editorial the next morning that blasted the "incredibly unsafe conditions" in the towers. "Chronic deficiencies of the buildings render them virtually uninhabitable. . . . The very design and construction of the buildings appears to be an enormous blunder on the part of the university," the editors wrote.[61]

That same day students circulated a petition signed by 1,350 residents calling for improvements in fire safety. A silent vigil was held in the rain for the victims. About a hundred students marched to the Administration Building with a list of demands for improvements. The West Campus Student Association passed a resolution that evening that

9.4. Pamela Sue Patterson was one of two students who died in the Lincoln Tower fire that brought a tragic end to the tumultuous spring of 1968. (*Lantern*)

censured Carson for his "contemptible attitude toward student rights." Students in residence halls on north and south campus raised questions about their safety as well.[62] By the end of the next week three separate entities were conducting investigations: the city fire department, the Ohio fire marshal, and experts hired by the university.

As more information emerged, anxiety began to decrease. On May 28 the fire marshal announced the blaze had been deliberately set. In an odd way, that calmed people: at least the fire hadn't been started by a careless match or some sort of spontaneous combustion. As one Lincoln Tower resident put it: "It had to be arson because it's very hard to burn anything in those suites at all. Even a cigarette won't burn it. It will just melt the upholstery." But it also meant an arsonist was on the loose.[63]

Immediately after the fire the university had hired civil engineering professor Richard W. Bletzacker, head of Ohio State's highly regarded Building Research Laboratory, to conduct an independent investigation. In his preliminary report, issued on May 29, Bletzacker concluded there were no shortcomings in the towers' design, although he recommended better evacuation procedures.[64] Freshman Dave Work, president of the Lincoln Tower Student Council, challenged the rumors about design flaws and defended Carson in a guest column in the *Lantern*. Work wrote: "[Carson] came to [Lincoln Tower] to answer, in person, as fully as he was able, any questions that students might ask even though he too was suffering from smoke inhalation. . . . Each time that Lincoln Tower Council came to see him this past year with a proposal that would truly benefit the students, he did not make a little note and promise vaguely that he would see about it tomorrow. He picked up the telephone then and there and started action immediately. This is the man that you are asking to resign. It would serve you right if he did."[65]

At a packed press conference on May 29, the assistant state fire marshal announced that freshman Harriet Frances Leeb, a resident of Lincoln Tower, had been charged with arson in connection with the fire. She was immediately sent to a psychiatric hospital in Cleveland for evaluation.[66]

Six weeks later the National Fire Prevention Association released a report that was similar to Bletzacker's in that it concluded the towers were "completely fire resistant." The organization also called for better fire training for students and staff, noting that the two women who died probably would have survived if they'd closed their bedroom doors and stayed inside, rather than trying to crawl through the fire in the lounge.[67]

At the same time the university announced that even though the towers had sufficient fireproofing, they would be retrofitted with sprinkler systems in each suite's central lounge as an added layer of protection. The systems were expected to be installed and working before students returned in the fall. The 1140 suite in Lincoln would remain closed for further examination.[68] This seemed to officially close the books on the immediate controversy surrounding the fire. Leeb's case would drag through the legal system for three years before she was judged not guilty by reason of insanity and released in 1971.[69]

The river towers would enjoy a clean safety record after that, but issues remained. *Dispatch* reporter David Lore captured the mood of many students when, after interviewing some of them in the wake of the fire, he wrote: "To many dormitory students, the great walkways, the soaring slate walls and the postage stamp windows of the river towers have come to symbolize the detested impersonality of the 37,000 student OSU campus."[70]

THE UNIVERSITY: TRIANGULATING

Ohio State administrators spent a good part of the 1967–68 school year maneuvering among angry factions of students, faculty, staff, alumni, parents, and trustees. The year began with a call for reform from an unlikely source.

THE MEGAVERSITY RECONSIDERED

Clark Kerr, the well-known former president of the highly regarded University of California system, came to Columbus in November to speak at a conference. Kerr had been dismissed earlier that year by Governor Ronald Reagan for failing to keep his unruly faculty and students under control. Five years earlier Kerr had trumpeted the unlimited potential of "megaversities" such as Berkeley and Ohio State. Now, somewhat chastened and more introspective, he saw the future differently.

At a press conference in Morrill Tower, Kerr called on the megaversities to reform. They needed to take an active role in making the general education curriculum more personalized for their students, he said. They needed to be more engaged in helping their surrounding communities. And, most important, they needed to decentralize decision-making away from the central bureaucracy and closer to the faculty and students. Kerr cited Ohio State's "small college" program as a good example of this practice.[71]

The university did embark on several initiatives designed to make itself more student friendly. The freshman honors program expanded to enroll 600 students. The effort to decentralize the arts and sciences moved toward implementation. The Faculty Council approved a student-initiated proposal to allow students to take up to 15 credit hours on a pass-fail basis for courses such as ROTC and physical education.

But with every step forward the university seemed to stumble backward. Enrollment at the Columbus campus in the fall of 1967 rose to 38,834, including 6,940 freshmen—600 more than expected. This put additional strain on the resources of departments that taught a lot of freshmen, such as English and mathematics. Those departments now had to scramble to find slots in already overcrowded classrooms. Then the new and highly anticipated computerized scheduling system fell behind schedule. The startup was delayed by a quarter, then for at least a year. Registrar Dean O. Clark blamed the delay on private employers who lured away his computer programmers with the promise of more money, as well as on the additional workload created by academic reorganization. Clark admitted that his remaining staff was disappointed and "everyone was kind of embarrassed" at the delay.[72] Meanwhile, it was full speed ahead for the new University College, which was expected to improve the experience of first-year students but would end up as a symbol of their isolation.

University College began as a way of taking enrollment pressure off the Columbus campus by giving central Ohio a de facto community college. By the spring of 1968 it had morphed into something different. The Faculty Council voted in February to require almost all undergraduates to spend their first two years there, effective summer quarter 1969. The council also made the college a free-standing unit independent of the College of the Arts and Sciences. Although the move came at the initiative of the faculty, the administration supported it.

Provost John Corbally said the move would help freshmen—many of whom were not sure of their majors—make better course and career decisions. "Students often have to transfer from one college to another in their freshman and sophomore year because they made the wrong choice of colleges while in high school. The present system causes the students unnecessary emotional trauma and causes the university excessive paperwork because of all the transfers," Corbally said. "The students end up taking a number of courses that eventually won't count in their final program."[73]

In a university that loved to debate every issue, the only dissenter of record, other than retired Alumni Association secretary Jack Fullen, was Gideon Frankel, an associate professor of chemistry. Frankel raised a number of issues in a piece for the *Lantern*. He argued that shipping freshmen and sophomores to west campus for their instruction isolated them from upper-level students and most faculty, as well as from the Main Library and the benefits of a large comprehensive research university. Departments such as chemistry that had a broad teaching and research mission would have to split their resources in order to, among other things, shuttle faculty and graduate students back and forth. It was a waste of time and effort, he said.[74] But University College went ahead as planned.

AN EMOTIONAL TIME

Even the classroom was not immune to the passions of the day. History 670 and 671 covered American foreign policy from the founding of the republic to the present. Word of mouth from students who'd taken the courses previously was so favorable, both spring quarter sections filled immediately, closing out many students. Some of those who had been shut out attended anyway, standing in the back of the room just to listen in. The instructor for both sections was David E. Green, a first-year assistant professor with a Ph.D. from Cornell who challenged and engaged his students in ways that made them want to learn more.

On the morning of Friday, April 5, the day after Martin Luther King was assassinated in Memphis, Green walked into his 11 a.m. class and told the students that in light of what had happened he didn't feel it was right to conduct business as usual. Instead, he would talk about the importance of nonviolence. Since this wasn't to be a formal lesson, Green said, anyone who wanted to leave could. No one did. Green went on to say Americans had to make a choice either to commit to nonviolence or to allow black citizens to buy guns to defend themselves. He produced two envelopes—one labeled "nonviolence," the other "standard American solution"—and said that he chose nonviolence. He held up his draft card, touched a lighter to it and let it burst into flames, then dropped it on the floor before stepping on it to extinguish the flames. After depositing the charred card in the "nonviolence" envelope, he passed both envelopes to his students, inviting them to put their own draft cards in one or donations to help black students buy guns in the other. (Most students did neither and simply passed the envelopes along.) Green then left the room and went out to a rally on the Oval, where he repeated what he had said in class. He returned to Denney Hall for his noon class and made the same presentation.[75]

It didn't take long for word to get out about what had happened. The following Monday the *Lantern* carried a story about the incident on its front page. University officials announced they would conduct an investigation. The FBI also got involved, because burning a draft card was a violation of federal law. Instead of letting things blow over, Green continued to speak out. At an April 30 event sponsored by Tau Kappa Epsilon fraternity, Green accused a photographer of trying to intimidate members of the audience by taking pictures of them. Before the photographer could respond, he was assaulted by someone in the audience. The photographer turned out to be a reporter from a local television station. President Fawcett appointed a faculty committee to investigate possible misconduct, as required in university rules.[76]

The committee concluded Green showed "a serious lack of judgment" in burning his draft card and soliciting money for guns in his classes on April 5. It also found he showed "poor judgment" by contributing to the atmosphere that resulted in the attack on the TV reporter. The committee acknowledged that it was an emotional time and that while Green was inexperienced, he had established himself as an excellent teacher and researcher. They recommended he be placed on probation, in addition to the probation he was already serving as a first-year nontenured faculty member.[77]

Fawcett presented a summary of the findings to the board of trustees at its July meeting. But instead of probation, Fawcett recommended Green be let go a year from that time, as provided for in the Faculty Misconduct Rule. The trustees wouldn't hear of a delay. A *Lantern* reporter noted they were visibly unhappy as Fawcett outlined his position. Insurance executive Frederick Jones spoke first. "We are shocked by the committee's recommendations," he said. "I won't even dignify [Green's] name with a title." After saying it was important to "keep faith with the citizens of Ohio," Jones moved that Green be immediately discharged, which the trustees were authorized to do under faculty rules. The motion passed unanimously. Green was fired on the spot.[78]

The liberal community on campus was appalled. This seemed to be a step back to the red-baiting days of the Speakers Rule. Informal *Lantern* polls of both faculty and students found mixed reactions. Few agreed with what Green had done, but the respondents were split roughly down the middle about the propriety of the trustees' action. Even the students in Green's classes were divided. Some supported him, arguing his actions were symbolic and were meant to make them think, rather than an attempt to encourage insurrection. Others believed violating federal law in a classroom environment went too far. Perhaps the most troubling aspect of the *Lantern* faculty poll was the reluctance of even tenured faculty to commit themselves. The most common response was "no comment," probably a reflection of lingering paranoia or concerns about how colleagues might react.[79]

Most of the people outside the university who sent letters to Fawcett and other officials praised the decision to fire Green. Correspondence from inside the institution was more varied. Green's home department voted 18–1 to support the more lenient recommendations of the faculty committee. Senior Steve Breyfogle identified himself as a prototypical member of the "establishment"—a member of Theta Chi fraternity and a cadet in advanced Army ROTC, which meant he would most likely find himself in Vietnam within a year. Breyfogle had been in History 670 when Green burned his draft card. He wrote to Fawcett: "[Green] is the possessor of a brilliant and incisive intellect, and his lectures bespeak extensive preparation and reveal a clear and profound insight. . . . Certainly I learned to open my mind and to think in his class as I never had before. And isn't learning to think things through (and not mere memorization) the purpose of a college education?"[80]

In addition to losing his job, Green was convicted in August 1969 of burning his draft card and sentenced to three years of probation and a fine of $1,500. He returned to Cornell as an instructor and eventually landed a teaching job at the University of Saskatchewan. In April 1973, five years after the incident, the American Association of University Professors voted to censure Ohio State for its actions in the case, saying the university had given neither "adequate consideration" to the evidence nor sufficient notice of termination. This gave Ohio State the dubious distinction of being the only Big Ten school to be censured twice. (The first time occurred in 1956 over the firing of a physics professor, allegedly for political reasons.) The 1973 censure was lifted in 1980.[81]

The trustees had managed to assert themselves and draw a line regarding the consequences of unacceptable behavior by faculty, but in doing so, they undercut the credibility of the administration, chilled dissent, and deprived students of a teacher who inspired them.

RESEARCH: SHIFTING TIDES

Sponsored research at Ohio State continued to grow in 1967–68, up another 8 percent in 1967 alone. Activities continued the recent emphasis on relevance and community impact that Clark Kerr called for.

In November the university announced that 14 faculty members had been serving as an informal brain trust for officials in Columbus city government. The group included experts from economics, education, geography, political science, sociology, and social work and was believed to be the first of its kind in the country. Another task force worked with the Columbus public schools to help them cope with the challenges of racial balance and community support. On the other side of campus, physicians and administrators at University Hospital launched an effort with the Ohio National Guard and the Ohio Highway Patrol to speed the treatment of traffic accident victims. Using a surplus army helicopter called a Medicopter, they experimented with evacuations linked to the hospital emergency room. The project would become the model for a system of medical evacuation helicopters nationwide, saving thousands of lives.

Despite these good deeds, the golden age was coming to an end. Alfred Garrett, vice president for research, warned in January that spending for Vietnam was squeezing other parts of the federal budget, including future funding for sponsored research. Richard Armitage, dean of the graduate school, said in April that the end of graduate deferments would limit manpower for research projects. In May the Committee for the Study of Alternatives, which was generally supportive of research, came out against defense-related research. In a paid *Lantern* ad the group characterized such activity as counterrevolutionary, secretive, and immoral.[82] Activists had protested war-related research on other campuses, but not at Ohio State. Now a respected group of faculty had raised the issue. Discussions about funding priorities and war-related research would grow in intensity, with ramifications felt for a decade.

WHO'S IN CHARGE?

The end of the contentious 1967–68 school year prompted reflection from various members of the Ohio State community. Alumni director Richard Mall felt compelled to reassure constituents who were worked up over what they saw as the disintegration of authority at the university. "Despite some alarmist reaction, the university has not been suffocated in an atmosphere of strife, division and insecurity," he wrote in the July issue of the alumni magazine. "The business of the institution has continued: classes have been held, examinations have been given on schedule, laboratories and libraries have been in full use, and most activities have proceeded in normal fashion."[83]

Lantern columnist Jeffrey Tannenbaum approached the same theme from a different angle. In April he wrote: "The fallacy of 'Student Power' at Ohio State is that the students aren't really interested. . . . Ohio State students—let's face it—are: c-o-n-s-e-r-v-a-t-i-v-e, particularly when compared with the students who steal national newspaper headlines. . . . Even among the habitual radicals, there is general anti-administrative sentiment but no agreement on specific goals. The protest leaders spend as much time badmouthing each other as they spend cussing the dean's office. . . . While a great number are willing to use normal channels to seek change, most Ohio State students reject radical methods."[84]

Compared to the recent past the university appeared to be in a state of turmoil, with weekly demonstrations and a growing number of arrests. But the number of hard-core activists was small compared to the campus's enormous size, and the mischief was minor compared to what was going on elsewhere. One question remained unanswered, however: if the underlying sources of divisiveness—the Vietnam War, racism, and dehumanization—continued to roil, would Ohio State also see a major escalation in unrest?

At the end of July two of the university's most prominent researchers, sociology professors Russell Dynes and Enrico Quarantelli, co-directors of the Disaster Research Center, sent a letter to Executive Dean John Bonner attempting to address this question. They shared the perspective from their studies of civil disturbances, including those in Watts, Cincinnati, and Detroit. In recent field work with black communities throughout Ohio, they found growing anger directed at Ohio State from a wide spectrum of black leaders—even the more moderate elements—because of the treatment of African American students. In particular, leaders saw a selective application of discipline that was more severe for black students than for white students, specifically in the case of the April 26 lock-in.

Dynes and Quarantelli also warned of what they saw as the increased potential for an emerging coalition of the disaffected—including white antiwar activists, black power activists, and others—with "tremendous power . . . to disrupt existing institutions." They acknowledged barriers to the development of such a coalition in the short run, but urged the university to adopt a more conciliatory approach so as not to allow such a coalition to build momentum.[85]

There is no record of the university's response to the letter, perhaps because of the transition in leadership between Bonner and John Mount (although Fawcett, Corbally, and Mount all received copies). However, it is unlikely administrators were in any mood to be conciliatory at this point, and it is even more unlikely the trustees would have allowed them to be. In the toxic atmosphere of mid-1968, the time for conciliation had passed.

SOCIETY: COMING APART

In September 1960 Lyndon B. Johnson, the Democratic candidate for vice president, stood on the steps of the Ohio Historical Society on High Street and urged college students to vote. He reminded them that the decisions their president would make would affect their lives directly. Now, in 1968, after a dramatic shift in the nation's mood, President Johnson found himself vilified on college campuses throughout the country. Students, including many at Ohio State, would help fuel the effort that in the first 90 days of the year would result in his announcement that he would not seek reelection. At the root of the drama were continuing divisions over the war in Vietnam and the war over the meaning of justice at home.

UNCLE SAM WANTS JOE COLLEGE

The specter of the military draft lurked on the edges of campus life during the entire span of the Vietnam War, but prior to 1968 the reality was more speculative than personal. As long as a student stayed in school, he could keep his coveted II-S deferment and not have to worry. All that changed in the middle of the 1967–68 school year, and suddenly hundreds of Ohio State students who had been planning the next steps of their lives sheltered from having to participate in the conflict faced a harsher reality.

It began with the amendments to the Selective Service Act that were passed by Congress in the summer of 1967. The legislation was designed to close loopholes in the law and make the draft fairer, while still meeting the military's manpower needs in wartime. One of the loopholes was the open-ended nature of student deferments. An enterprising student could continue on to graduate or professional school after earning his undergraduate degree and at 24 or 25 be too old to be drafted when finished. The legislation attempted to end this practice by limiting the life of a student deferment to four years or by age 24, whichever came first. What was not immediately clear was how this would affect college students who had already begun their academic programs. After six months of angst on campuses across the country, the Johnson administration issued final guidelines in February 1968. They provided that any student who started in graduate school before September 1967 would continue to have virtually unlimited deferments as before. Those students who started after September 1967 would not. That meant most first-year graduate students, and seniors graduating any time in 1968, would no longer be eligible.[86]

At that time only the army and the marines relied on the draft. Those draftees tended to end up in the slots hardest to fill with volunteers, particularly the dirty and dangerous jobs such as light weapons infantryman. With eight weeks of basic training, eight weeks of advance training, and one month of leave, it was conceivable Joe College could be carrying a rifle in Vietnam in less than six months. By that time the war's casualties had risen to more than 560 killed, wounded, and missing each week.

The process of determining who ended up doing the fighting was not well understood but was generally believed to be arbitrary and unfair. Statistics compiled after the war showed a relatively low probability of a person being exposed to enemy fire in a combat unit for a significant length of time; but fear is a powerful motivator, and fear of being part of that minority added to the anxiety.[87]

Campus reaction to the legislation varied. Some students believed it was fair for everyone to be subject to service. Others thought it was grossly unfair. Still others complained the system produced too much uncertainty and thought a draft lottery would be better. Overall, about 3,500 to 4,000 Ohio State students were directly affected. They included about 2,500 men who were graduating seniors and 1,000 to 1,500 first-year graduate students. Of them, 400 to 500 had voluntarily enrolled in ROTC advanced programs and knew they would go into active duty as soon as they graduated.[88] Others faced difficult choices. Should they take a chance on the draft and end up in Vietnam as a rifleman? Should they enlist and have some control over their service lives, but at the expense of delaying career plans for three or four years instead of two? Should they try to avoid service altogether with a documented medical or mental condition? Should they be a conscientious objector, go to Canada, or just disappear?

All the options carried their own risks and trade-offs. Worse yet, some of the most popular options were quickly disappearing. Army ROTC reported a flood of applications for its two-year program. Reserve and National Guard units, who were rarely sent to Vietnam, had so many applicants it took political connections to get in. Services were now limiting enlistments to the combat arms. Local draft boards were limiting conscientious objector status to people who could show evidence of a lifelong religious affiliation. A cottage industry of draft advice arose. The *Lantern* ran such features regularly. Military recruiters were glad to expound about enlistment options. For those who didn't want to serve in the military, 15 campus ministries offered draft counseling.[89]

The vast majority of Ohio State students were not ready to demonstrate against the war at that point, but that doesn't mean they were apathetic. In the *Lantern*'s annual spring survey 78 percent of readers listed Vietnam War news as their most important topic, eclipsing even the perennial favorite, the "Peanuts" cartoon strip.[90] When the university offered Vietnam History and Politics as an elective in the spring of 1968, it was described as the first credit course of its kind in the country. More than 300 students enrolled.[91] Students also began to see the war touch themselves and their friends more directly. Richard M. Vasko, a third-year student in agricultural economics, had a student deferment but decided Vietnam was worth fighting for. He enlisted in the army in January 1967. By November he was in Vietnam serving with the Fourth Infantry Division. By the following February he was dead from enemy gunfire.[92]

Twenty-three-year-old Brian Krill wrote to Ohio State's dean of women on behalf of his squad, which was serving with the First Cavalry Division in the central highlands of Vietnam. He asked for letters because, as he put it, "contact with the civilized world is rare." Dean Christine Conaway forwarded Krill's letter to the *Lantern,* which published it on June 27. A number of students answered him, including senior Deborah Emm. Krill wrote back to the *Lantern* three weeks later to express his appreciation for so many letters he couldn't answer them all, but he did individually answer Emm's letter. He said that his squad was "horribly outnumbered" and wondered if he and his comrades would make it out alive. Emm's second letter to him was returned a few weeks later with the notation "PFC Brian Krill—Verified Deceased, killed in action." Krill died on July 21, 1968.[93] Emm would go on to counsel people with post-traumatic stress disorders.

Ohio State students responded in different ways to how the world was changing around them in 1968. Clearly the war was beginning to encroach more and more on people's daily lives and plans for the future. Would that be enough to shake passive students out of their apathy? One test would be the upcoming presidential campaign.

DUMP JOHNSON

Dumping Lyndon Johnson and his hated war was the top priority of Democratic antiwar activists at the end of 1967. The first stirrings of anti-LBJ activity at Ohio State came on November 29 and didn't even involve a declared candidate. Ira Gaffin, a graduate student in political science, announced the formation of Ohioans for Kennedy. The group's goal, Gaffin explained, was to coax Robert Kennedy, brother of the slain president and a U.S. senator from New York, to challenge Johnson for the nomination. Kennedy repeatedly denied any interest in doing so, but Gaffin and other Kennedy supporters on campus would not be deterred.[94]

The next day dissident Democrats finally got their wish for someone to run against Johnson, but it wasn't Bobby Kennedy. Instead, Eugene McCarthy, a little-known Minnesota senator, threw his hat into the ring. He based his campaign on promises to break sharply with the Johnson administration and get out of Vietnam. Political pundits gave him no chance against a sitting president who had the power of the incumbency and knew how to use it.

What the pundits overlooked was that in the turbulent year of 1968, incumbency could also be an albatross.[95] On January 30 communist forces in Vietnam launched a major countrywide offensive. The intense fighting filled the news for six weeks. U.S. and South Vietnamese troops finally claimed victory, but to a war-weary public it was clear the enemy was still full of fight.

The voters had their say in the first presidential primary in New Hampshire on March 12. McCarthy captured 40 percent of the vote against a sitting president when experts had predicted half that number. The upset was enough to motivate the reluctant Bobby Kennedy, who officially announced on March 16. McCarthy's supporters immediately accused Kennedy of opportunism, foreshadowing a split in the antiwar forces that would prove hard to heal.

Kennedy's entry into the race seemed to energize everyone. More than 350 students jammed into a Denney Hall classroom on March 28 to kick off the campaign on campus. Political science instructor John Champlin told the students that Kennedy could win, but without him it would be a choice between Johnson and likely Republican nominee Richard Nixon, which was no choice at all.[96] The Ohio State Committee for McCarthy kicked off three days later. Operating out of an office at High Street and Norwich Avenue, spokesperson and history professor R. Clayton Roberts told supporters Kennedy had filed too late to be on the Ohio primary ballot, so if they wanted to stop the war McCarthy was their only choice.[97]

On March 31 Johnson stunned the nation when he announced he would not run for reelection. Cynics at first thought it was some sort of typical Johnson manipulation to engineer a draft, but it soon became clear the president had thrown in the towel. The antiwar insurgents had toppled a sitting president. Now both Kennedy and McCarthy had a real chance to capture the nomination, win the election, and end the war. With the Ohio primary only six weeks away, enthusiasm soared.

Five hundred people attended a McCarthy rally on the Oval on April 4. They claimed to have a thousand volunteers ready to canvass every household in the 12th Congressional District, which included the university area. Ohioans for Kennedy opened its Columbus office that same day. On campus, Students for Kennedy already had 400 members, many of whom were being bussed to Indiana to help in the primary there.

All campaigning came to a halt later that day with the news that Martin Luther King Jr. had been assassinated in Memphis. Students moved to appropriately honor King by holding a memorial service on the Oval the next day. The student government announced that May Week proceeds would go to a scholarship in King's name. President Fawcett said all daytime classes on April 9 would be canceled in recognition of King's funeral.[98]

Memorial services alone could not overcome the country's growing racial divide. Black militancy, already on the rise, gained more credibility with the revelation that a white man had pulled the trigger. Militants argued the killing meant the end of King's dream of integration and nonviolence. Riots broke out in a hundred cities.

On April 27, to no one's surprise, Vice President Hubert Humphrey announced he was running for president. In 1968 the Democratic and Republican political apparatus controlled the nominating process, so open primaries were much less common than they are now. Most of the 2,600 delegates were controlled by party regulars (usually elected officials such as governors, mayors, and legislators), and most of them were loyal to Johnson and now Humphrey. In Ohio, only 10 of the state's 115 delegates would be determined at the May primary. As a result Ohio did not receive a lot of personal visits from the candidates, but it did receive attention from surrogates. The Kennedy and McCarthy campaigns held back-to-back events at the end of April. The Kennedy campaign paired former assistant secretary of state Roger Hilsman with former astronaut and local hero John Glenn for an Oval rally on April 24 that attracted about 500 enthusiasts. The McCarthy campaign one-upped them the following day when it produced movie star Paul Newman, a graduate of nearby Kenyon College. Newman filled all 3,000 seats in Mershon Auditorium, although there were likely as many curiosity seekers as McCarthy supporters.[99]

At the Ohio primary on May 7, McCarthy supporters won only three of the 10 contested delegate seats and did not even carry the 12th District. The remaining seats went to Ohio senator Stephen Young, who was running as a favorite son. Kennedy and McCarthy spent most of their time and effort in the states with open primaries. Now it all came down to the vote-rich and wide-open California primary on June 4. When the results came in that evening, Kennedy had achieved a narrow but significant victory. Shortly after midnight he thanked his supporters in a boisterous rally at the Ambassador Hotel in Los Angeles and headed out through the kitchen, where assassin Sirhan Sirhan was waiting with a gun. Kennedy died the following day, June 6, and with him the hopes of so many.

The assassination occurred during finals week at Ohio State, and the *Lantern* was on hiatus. When the paper resumed publication on June 18, its eulogy spoke for many who had supported Kennedy's candidacy and even some who didn't: "Shocked by the murder and stunned at having had their ideals shattered by a bullet, youth now is uncertain where to turn. McCarthy seems unlikely to win, and none of the other candidates

Choice '68

One of the running controversies of the 1960s was the degree to which activists and protestors spoke for anyone other than themselves. Through an initiative called Choice '68, *Time* magazine and Univac computers teamed up with student governments across the country to poll students on 1,450 campuses. The students were given the opportunity to vote via computerized secret ballot for their choice for president. About a million students voted on April 24, or about a quarter of those eligible. The results were collected nationally and released in mid-May. Among Ohio State students Eugene McCarthy led the polling with 31 percent, Robert Kennedy placed second with 22 percent, and Richard Nixon came in third with 18 percent.

Respondents were also asked how they wanted the next president to approach the Vietnam War. Ohio State students clearly were dissatisfied with the current policy, with only 6 percent voting for its continuation. Eighteen percent wanted out immediately. The same percent wanted to escalate the war further, but 50 percent favored a gradual withdrawal.

The Ohio State findings closely reflected the national results regarding both candidate preferences and war policy.[1] They also showed that students at Ohio State were more middle of the road than conservative or radical, but they reflected an increasing dissatisfaction with the existing order.

1. "Primaries," *Time,* May 10, 1968, 28; "McCarthy Wins Choice '68 Mock Presidential Primary," *Lantern,* May 15, 1968, 1.

personify youthful ideals as Kennedy did. The campaign now appears useless to many students. . . . The loss of Sen. Kennedy was the nation's loss, but it was especially a loss for youth."[100]

The campaigns listlessly drifted to convention time. The Republicans nominated Richard Nixon in an orderly gathering in Miami Beach. Democrats met in Chicago at the end of August. Antiwar forces chafed under the tight controls of party regulars inside the convention hall, and demonstrators and bystanders outside felt the wrath of the Chicago police. Ubiquitous TV cameras captured the chaos, while 79 million viewers looked on in disbelief. Hubert Humphrey got the nomination he coveted so badly, but left Chicago with a party divided and dispirited and Nixon far ahead in the polls. Many thought Humphrey's campaign was over before it even started.

ANGRY VOICES

The assassination of Martin Luther King Jr. sparked a surge in violence and angry rhetoric in American race relations. Ohio State had arranged for a series of African American speakers for the 1967–68 school year; even before the assassination their tone showed how polarized race relations had become. Comedian and social commentator Dick Gregory came to campus in January to kick off a symposium sponsored by the Student Assembly and the South Campus Student Association. The *Lantern* described Gregory's talk as "at times impassioned, at times violent, and frequently comical." Gregory blamed the American system for furthering racial hatred and violence. "We don't hate you as white folks, we hate your system," he told the packed house at Mershon Auditorium. "That's not war, that's revolt, and you don't stop revolt with numbers." The mostly white audience gave him a standing ovation.[101]

Ralph Bunche, undersecretary of the United Nations and winner of the Nobel Peace Prize for his work in brokering an Arab-Israeli ceasefire in 1949, wasn't quite so blunt but struck a similar theme when he spoke in March to an audience of 300 in the College of Law auditorium. "Unless we can strike the fatal blow to racism in the United States," he said, "we will face as an alternative racial strife to such a degree that the great cities of this country will no longer be livable."[102]

Henry Austin—a spokesperson for Deacons for Defense and Justice, a Louisiana black militant separatist group—told an Ohio Union audience in April that King's assassination destroyed the "buffer zone" between black and white citizens. He warned that angry black people would start burning small businesses that summer, and that the following year, "Ford and the big ones will go up."[103]

Also that spring Walter Cronkite, the CBS evening news anchor who later was dubbed "the most trusted man in America," spoke at commencement. Cronkite's reports from Vietnam in February calling for an honorable withdrawal in the face of an endless stalemate had helped convince Johnson that he had lost Middle America. Cronkite spoke on June 7, the day after Robert Kennedy died. In a more understated way, he delivered the same message Dick Gregory and Ralph Bunche had. "The ferment abroad today in the land borders on anarchy, and there are frightened calls for law and order," he told the graduates. "But as surely as a boiling kettle will not stop generating steam just because a lid is clamped on it, our ferment cannot be suppressed by tanks and guns. . . . May I suggest that to preserve what we have we must lead, or at least join, the revolution against that which is evil in our society. Let our new gentry—the gentry of the educated and the wise—become radicals and seek bold new solutions to our problems."[104]

CHAPTER 10

COME TOGETHER

(1968–69)

After the bruising confrontations of 1968, students, faculty, and administrators wondered what additional conflicts the new school year would bring. Instead, they found a welcome hiatus from the convulsions of the year before. It seemed, at least for a while, to harken back to a time when everyone played by the rules, people pulled together, and the home team could actually win the big one.

10.1. Columbus mayor M. E. Sensenbrenner and students cheer the Buckeyes at the 1969 Rose Bowl. (*Makio*)

STUDENTS: THOSE WERE THE DAYS

A song that lamented the loss of idealism—"Those Were the Days," performed by 18-year-old Welsh folksinger Mary Hopkin—struck a chord among the nation's young people as school started in the fall. Signs that the good old protest days of the 1960s were coming to an end were obvious to Ohio State's 7,200 freshmen. In his first meeting with the class on September 23, President Novice Fawcett warned that the university "is not an arena for political action, nor a fortress from which one may defy constitutional government." Fawcett had a tough new set of antidisruption rules passed by the board of trustees in July to back him up. The rules prohibited indoor demonstrations of any kind. Outdoor rallies, marches, and pickets were allowed, but only as long as they didn't block building entrances.[1]

A committee on student rights and responsibilities that Fawcett had appointed the previous February released its final report in September. It struck many of the same themes, but tried to draw a clearer distinction between demonstrations, which were acceptable, and disruptions, which were not. The report also called upon the university to be more responsive to student concerns.[2] The outside world, however, was in no mood to tolerate what it considered the coddling of dissenters. As fall quarter progressed, the campus found something uplifting that the whole embattled university family could rally around, at least for a time.

WE'RE NO. 1

Traditions fell like dominoes in the 1960s. In the fall of 1967 it looked like even Ohio State's vaunted football program was at risk. Woody Hayes's teams had not been good enough to qualify for postseason play since the Rose Bowl debacle of 1961. The Athletic Ticket Office reported student ticket sales for the season had fallen to a 10-year low. In 1957, 88 percent of eligible students bought tickets. By 1967 only 55 percent did so. "Football dominance on campus is over," the *Lantern* declared in an October 12 editorial. "Times are changing. Students just don't have the time to become enthusiastic about football."[3] After a particularly ignominious 41–6 defeat at the hands of the Purdue Boilermakers, rumors spread of a player rebellion against Hayes's outdated approach to the game.[4]

Reports of the demise of Buckeye football turned out to be premature. Hayes managed to rally his troops to finish the Big Ten season 5–2, including a 24–14 win over Michigan. As he touted the strength of his recruiting class for the next year, fans began to speculate about a possible Rose Bowl at the end of the rainbow.

The 1967 class, already dubbed the Super Sophomores (freshmen were not allowed to play at that time), included the likes of quarterback Rex Kern, defensive backs Mike Sensibaugh and Jack Tatum, and middle guard Jim Stillwagon. They won their first two games of the 1968 season against nonconference opponents by a combined score of 56–20. Nevertheless, critics expected them to be humbled when mighty Purdue came to town on October 12.

The No. 1–ranked Boilermakers roared into Columbus sporting an offensive juggernaut averaging an incredible 41 points a game. But the Super Sophomores shut them down 13–0 before a record crowd of 84,834. It was the first time Purdue had been shut out in 28 games. Four thousand fans celebrated afterward at High and 15th in what was described as a "giant-sized party." Columbus police took a much more restrained posture than during the labor strike the year before. Cruisers escorted about 350 students who marched downtown and back. There were no arrests, and no property damage was reported.[5]

Ohio State went on to win the next five games, running its record to 8–0 and its poll ranking to No. 2. The university already had a Rose Bowl contract, and this time no one was going to say no. All that stood in the way of a trip to Pasadena was the University of Michigan, whose Wolverines boasted an 8–1 record and a No. 4 ranking in the polls. More than 60 media outlets crammed into Ohio Stadium's press box and onto the sidelines on November 23 to cover a game that was also broadcast overseas via Armed Forces Radio. For the third time that season, a record-breaking crowd filled the Horseshoe.

The fired-up Buckeyes rolled over Michigan 50–14, and delirious fans began celebrating immediately. The steel goalposts came down for the first time in 10 years and were carried downtown by a boisterous crowd. It was one of several marches that evening, including a procession of 6,000 students led by the Marching Band. As one *Lantern* reporter described it, "Thousands of Ohio State students threw a nine-hour party on High Street, from the campus to downtown Columbus." City police again remained low key. They escorted marchers. They cordoned off High Street from 11th to Lane as a party zone and ignored open containers. Many students expressed their appreciation by bedecking officers with roses. D Platoon was nowhere to be seen.[6]

By midnight things got a little ragged. Police had to arrest 12 students. A cold drizzle helped break up the party by about 1:30 a.m. It left in its wake a significant amount of property damage. Some 200 traffic signs and parking meters had been pulled up and carried down High Street, and at least 50 windows in cars and businesses were broken. The emergency room at University Hospital reported treating 50 people for injuries, mainly cuts and bruises. The official cost was put at between $9,000 and $14,000. Police "didn't expect [the celebration] to be of this magnitude," one officer confessed.[7]

Business owners in the campus area complained to city officials about the lack of police protection. Other critics, including 15 students and faculty in the philosophy department, wrote the *Lantern* chastising Columbus police and university officials for a double standard regarding demonstrations for athletic events as opposed to political causes. City officials brushed off the criticism, drawing a distinction between what they called the "rioting" of October 1967, which resulted in less than $1,000 in damage, and the "frolicking" of November 1968. The latter was "accidental rather than deliberate," one official said.[8]

As cleanup began on Sunday morning, the campus was already looking ahead to the Rose Bowl on January 1. Ohio State's opponent in Pasadena was the No. 2–ranked University of Southern California, which featured a high-powered offense led by running back and Heisman Trophy winner O. J. Simpson. It marked the first time two unbeaten teams met in the nation's premiere postseason contest. The crowd of 105,000 included at least 15,000 Ohio State fans, among them 5,000 students who paid $4.50 each (about $28 in 2015 prices) for tickets. Numerous luminaries attended as well, including president-elect Richard M. Nixon and his wife, Pat. Millions more watched the broadcast in color on NBC.[9]

It hardly mattered that the Trojans scored first. The Super Sophomores forced five USC turnovers, including two by Simpson. Ohio State triumphed 27–16. Woody Hayes was named Coach of the Year and then headed off for another Vietnam tour to share highlights of the game with the troops.

Football madness let people take their minds off war, assassinations, and riots. It helped keep the Ohio State campus relatively calm throughout the fall and into the New Year. But even the power of a winning football team couldn't change the underlying dynamics of a society deeply divided against itself.

BLACK IS BEAUTIFUL

Ohio State produced a blizzard of initiatives throughout the 1968–69 school year that administrators believed would improve conditions for black students at the university and black people in the community. A second black academic counselor, Myrtle L. Smith, joined James Boyer in University College, while Boyer developed a tutoring program called Students into Scholars that was designed to help at-risk students master study skills. The university hired its first black administrator when army veteran Madison Scott was selected to lead the new Office of Employee Relations. Academic departments introduced seven courses on African American issues, including black history, the economics of the ghetto, and black America and white racism. Provost John Corbally appointed a committee to help him find ways to recruit more black faculty. The university celebrated Black History Week with an exhibit in the Ohio Union and brought aspiring black artists to campus, including Earl L. Scarborough, the man credited with popularizing the phrase "Black is beautiful." The law school, medical school, and graduate school announced programs to add more black students to their ranks. The university reached out to the black community to provide summer recreation for inner-city youths, job training for adolescents, and construction jobs for adults.[10]

Governor James Rhodes lent a hand when he appointed the first African American to Ohio State's board of trustees in 82 years. Jack Gibbs, the principal of Columbus East High School, earned degrees from Ohio State in 1954 and 1957 and played three years for Woody Hayes as a fullback.

And after 10 years of delays and excuses, the university finally moved to more forcefully address discrimination in off-campus housing.

It began with a report prepared by a group of law students and faculty released in November 1968. The group had sent students to ask about several hundred rental units in 41 properties in the two weeks before school started. A black student would inquire about a unit first, then a white student would ask about the same unit at least half an hour later. For 214 of the 411 rental units, both black and white students were told there were no vacancies. In 129 of the remaining cases, the landlord or rental office told the black student the unit was either unavailable (although the white student was told it was available) or would cost more than the white student was told.[11]

Student government leaders made the report a high priority that spring, with activities including a peaceful fast on the Oval in April and a call for university action. In May President Fawcett brought a proposal to the trustees that would forbid university students to rent from landlords who discriminated and provided the enforcement mechanisms to go with it. University officials had worked with the Ohio attorney general to make sure an appeals process was included in the proposal so it could withstand legal challenges. Gibbs made the motion to approve. The proposal passed unanimously.[12]

While such actions were admirable, the fate of the 34 students facing felony charges from the takeover of the Administration Building in April 1968 still poisoned the atmosphere. In November visiting judge Thomas Mitchell threw out most of the charges due to a lack of evidence. Prosecutor C. Howard Johnson refiled the other charges (illegal detention and conspiracy among them) on the grounds the dismissals were technical in nature. This sparked calls from the campus community for the university administration to influence the prosecutor to drop the remaining charges. Virtually all student organizations as well as the Faculty Council lined up in support. Students and others collected more than $1,000 for a legal defense fund. In May the popular singing group Sly and the Family Stone made an appeal from the stage while performing at Veterans Memorial Auditorium downtown. But the administration remained officially silent.[13]

More than a year of legal and political wrangling finally came to an end in July. In a plea-bargained settlement brokered by Mitchell, reportedly with behind-the-scenes support from Governor Rhodes and the Ohio State Bar Association, charges against six students were dismissed entirely. Six other students pleaded guilty to trespassing only. Ten students pleaded guilty to trespassing and making menacing threats. The cases of two students who were out of town were referred to a different court and eventually dropped. Jail time in all cases was suspended. Fines for trespassing cases were limited to $10 each, and fines in the menacing threats cases were limited to $250 each. In addition, the defendants signed a "statement of regret" for their treatment of Vice President Gordon Carson and his staff. They were also put on probation for two years and required to pay court costs.[14]

While the decision removed an immediate flash point, hard feelings remained. The inability of the prosecution to make the felony charges stick underscored in the minds of students and others the vindictiveness of the charges in the first place.

The campus settled back into its summer doldrums, but racial issues were far from resolved. Columbus civic leaders had just congratulated themselves for having escaped the race rioting that had plagued other cities when on July 21 a white store owner shot a black man on the predominantly black near east side. Widespread rioting and arson went on for three days. Order was restored with the help of 1,500 Ohio National Guardsmen, but not before a white man was killed by a sniper. Nearly 250 people, mostly black, were arrested, and a portion of a three-square-mile area was burned to the ground. Although the east side of Columbus was seven miles from the Ohio State campus, the conflicts that erupted there reflected tensions that existed across the city.[15]

SDS GO HOME

Students for a Democratic Society attracted the more radical activists on many college campuses during the 1960s. Up to the last years of the decade, Ohio State was not among them. SDS began at the University of Michigan in Ann Arbor in 1960. It did not have a national presence until 1962, when it held its first convention and adopted a policy document called the Port Huron Statement. The 30,000-word manifesto, drafted by Tom Hayden, a former editor of the *Michigan Daily* student newspaper, called for a major restructuring of American society to achieve "participatory democracy."[16]

Nationally, SDS devoted a lot of energy to the civil rights movement, but as the Vietnam War escalated the members spent more and more time opposing it and the American imperialism they said it represented. By 1968 SDS was identified on many campuses with militant attacks on ROTC, military recruiters, and war-related research. Members provided the leadership and core support for the takeover at Columbia University in the spring of 1968 that resulted in more than 700 arrests and the resignation of the university's president.

The SDS chapter at Ohio State gained official recognition as a student organization in April 1968. It claimed at the time to have 50 members, 13 of whom were also members of the national SDS.[17] They spent most of fall and winter quarters trying to spark interest through guerrilla theatre, where live drama was used to make a political statement. In one instance in October, they marched across campus with a pig and a black coffin to protest the choices in the 1968 presidential election. About 50 SDS supporters participated, and they managed to draw about 250 spectators, many of whom laughed at or heckled them. The campus group also arranged for a bus to take students to Washington, D.C., to be part of the national protest against the inauguration of Richard Nixon on January 20, 1969. But both the national rally and Ohio State student participation fell short of expectations.

In January the *Lantern* did a series on the Ohio State chapter. Reporter Roger Myers had attended SDS meetings, and his account gave insight into the organization's membership and operations.[18] Myers wrote that SDS prided itself on the high degree of autonomy it gave its chapters and its emphasis on participatory democracy instead of top-down leadership. Engineering student Thomas L. Reardon was the official chair, but the agenda was set by an eight-member coordinating committee. Most of the heavy lifting came from 10 workshops or committees, each led by unofficial chairs who rotated periodically to prevent a "leadership cult." The workshops included topics such as community organizing, dormitory organizing, draft information, and women's liberation.

In practice, the organization struggled to get things done. Myers reported few people actually spoke up at SDS meetings, and often it was the same people. Others who spoke up but disagreed with accepted dogma frequently were accused of being FBI informants, administration plants, or closet right-wingers. Myers said that in some cases only half the people who attended the meetings actually voted on key issues.

SDS seemed to recognize it had a problem with following through. After a self-proclaimed "hard look at itself" in February, the group announced a pared-down set of priorities for the remainder of the school year. It would focus on internal education and guerrilla theatre. SDS also tried to broaden its base by supporting issues important to African American activists, such as dropping the charges against the 34 students involved in the April 1968 lock-in. However, black leaders both nationally and locally remained wary of SDS involvement.[19]

SDS made its big move on May 8 against Corps Day, the annual ROTC awards ceremony.[20] Heavy rains forced the ceremony indoors to Mershon Auditorium, which gave the administration the opportunity to keep the ROTC cadets in and the protestors out. The result was a test of wills outside the building. The crowd of about 500 included equal numbers of pro- and anti-ROTC demonstrators. According to news reports, the first scuffling began when a female demonstrator grabbed an "SDS go home" sign from pro-ROTC demonstrators. Five male counterdemonstrators grabbed it back. By this time all the uniformed ROTC cadets were in the building behind locked doors, protected by 30 Ohio Highway Patrolmen in riot gear.

Outside, the two groups of protestors shouted at each other. Someone with a bullhorn directed the anti-ROTC protestors to the east side of Mershon facing High Street, but the pro-ROTC demonstrators got there first and placed themselves between the anti forces and the doors. Several firecrackers and at least one smoke bomb went off, dispersing the crowd temporarily. When both groups reformed, one of the counterprotestors set fire to a North Vietnamese flag, which sparked a round of egg throwing and epithets. Someone burned an American flag, prompting more shouting and scuffling.

A dozen or so members of the Green Ribbon Commission—a volunteer group of about 200 faculty who served as neutral buffers in such situations—inserted themselves between the two factions. "Students are fairly reluctant to smash a faculty member in the mouth," quipped philosophy professor and commission chair Paul Olscamp later.[21] Apparently eggs were a different matter. Olscamp's suit and those of other faculty members were splattered with them. Police arrested one demonstrator who had managed to sneak into Mershon Auditorium and tried to interrupt the proceedings, but there were no other arrests or injuries.

By the time the ceremony was over, both groups of protestors had migrated to the Oval and cadets reported no trouble leaving the building.

10.2. Pro- and anti-ROTC demonstrators trade punches outside Mershon Auditorium during the May awards ceremony. (*Lantern*)

No one claimed credit for organizing the demonstration, although it was clearly an SDS-instigated event. Young Americans for Freedom and freshman and sophomore ROTC cadets (who were not part of the ceremony due to space limitations) both claimed credit for organizing the counterdemonstration. The administration credited the Green Ribbon Commission for helping keep the peace, and the commission complimented the administration for exercising restraint by not calling in additional police. Later that month the Student Assembly conducted a poll asking students what they thought the future of ROTC on campus should be. Of the 625 students who responded, only 5 percent favored the SDS position of banning ROTC altogether. But 75 percent thought the required alternative courses for students not enrolling in ROTC should be removed.[22]

As the school year came to a close, the only thing SDS seemed to have done well was galvanize opposition against itself from across the political spectrum. The Young Americans for Freedom chapter organized a statewide leadership meeting in July to advance a program to counter SDS. It included possible legal action and public information under the banner of protecting free speech. The plan was drafted by left-wing radical turned right-wing radical Phillip Luce. Luce was the former Ohio

State student who sparked the 1962 Speakers Rule controversy when he was banned from campus as a supposed subversive.[23]

The more or less center-left *Lantern* editorial page took a swipe at SDS in May, saying the organization was alienating more students than it was converting. Even members of the political left were not impressed. Earlier that year R. Clayton Roberts, the history professor who had chaired Eugene McCarthy's campus campaign and who was a long-time and vocal opponent of the Vietnam War, said: "I share every single goal of the SDS, but I cannot accept the appeal to the revolution of rhetoric, slogans and obscenities."[24]

SDS found itself with organizational issues nationally as well. At its fractious convention in Chicago in June, the organization split into factions and subfactions. The Ohio State delegates reportedly cast their approximately 30 votes in support of the more militant Weathermen, who were particularly strong in Ohio and Michigan.[25]

SDS in general, and the Weathermen in particular, did attract the attention of law enforcement. The Cincinnati office of the FBI had been tracking SDS and other suspected campus subversives at Ohio State through an elaborate network of informers since as early as 1965.[26] Columbus police established their own intelligence unit after the spring 1968 protests on campus. A team of five to six officers worked undercover to monitor campus radicals such as SDS and the Young Socialist Alliance that were suspected of advocating violence to further their goals.[27]

Law enforcement had legitimate reasons to be concerned. In April 1969, for example, university officials received a tip from a reliable source that an East Coast Black Panther leader was coming to Ohio State in three days and "bringing several bombs with him." This particular threat never materialized, but between September 1969 and May 1970 various radical groups were responsible for at least one bombing a day across the country. Legitimate fear of what radicals might do preoccupied university and law enforcement officials.[28]

Law enforcement groups clearly overreacted in some cases and in others violated the laws they were sworn to protect. It's now known that the FBI conducted a deliberate campaign of disinformation against the Ohio State chapter of SDS out of its Cincinnati office. The efforts included posting notices of nonexistent meetings and sending packets of derogatory material to parents of SDS members.[29]

STUDENT GOVERNMENT STRUGGLES

Recognizing that many of the university's problems stemmed from state policies, student government leaders worked with their counterparts across Ohio to develop a legislative agenda. It included reducing the voting age from 21 to 19, putting student representatives on university boards of trustees, and securing sufficient state funding to keep tuition down. They even hired a former legislator as a part-time lobbyist (at $600 a year); still, they were unable to move recalcitrant legislators.[30]

Elected student leaders had a little more success closer to home when they finally convinced the Ohio State trustees to approve a tougher fair housing policy. They also managed to overturn restricted hours for sophomore women. But they failed to get rid of the Dorm Rule, failed to clarify the new Disruption Rule, and failed to gain amnesty for the so-called Black 34 or for David Green, the assistant professor who had been fired the previous year for his antiwar stance. In the campuswide Undergraduate Student Government elections in the spring, the University Party won another decisive victory. Tim Sheeran and running mate W. Bruce Achenbach, both sophomores, captured 51.5 percent of the votes for president in a field of five candidates. The University Party won 22 of 25 assembly seats. Only 3,821 students voted out of more than 28,000 eligible, prompting Sheeran to remark after the election: "From this turnout, I'm not convinced that I'm the leader of the students."[31]

YOU'VE COME A LONG WAY

While lacking the theatrics associated with some of the other changes going on at the time, the evolution of accepted roles for women continued to pick up momentum. A line used to advertise Virginia Slims cigarettes became the catchphrase of the day: "You've come a long way, baby." The approval of extended hours for sophomore women in January and the loosening of visitation restrictions on members of the opposite sex in residence halls meant that in loco parentis was on its last legs. Discussion now moved to broader issues of concern to campus women.

The first public statement of an organized women's liberation movement on campus came from junior Barbara Helm, who wrote a

10.3. The first women to enroll in ROTC at Ohio State turn out for drill on a January day in 1969. (*Lantern*)

February 3, 1969, opinion piece for the *Lantern* titled “Free Women.” Helm argued for opening up more professions to women, removing restrictions on abortions, dividing housework and child-care chores more equally, and hiring more women faculty. In a period where inflated rhetoric was the rule, she stressed reason. “It is not a matter of superiority or revenge,” she concluded, “but of recognition of the need for women as contributors and leaders, and a respect for the delightful differences between the sexes without typecasting people into preconceived roles. Human first; women second.”[32]

In fact, changes were already taking place. Ohio State now had its first woman resident in aerospace medicine, Sarah Nunneley, and its first woman asphalt tester, Carole Bernardo. An all-woman research team headed off on an Antarctic expedition, and leader Lois M. Jones, a graduate student from Columbus, would be the first woman to reach the South Pole. The first women to participate in ROTC drill with male cadets did so in January. And a public call went out for women to be admitted to the last bastion of male exclusivity, the Ohio State Marching Band. Four years later the first women would join the band.[33]

THE UNIVERSITY: NO. 1 IN ALL FIELDS

On Thanksgiving weekend 1968, Governor James Rhodes unveiled an audacious plan to restructure education in Ohio. He announced he would ask the Ohio General Assembly to consider changes in the law that would turn over governance of higher education to eight regional authorities. Each would be headed by a board appointed by the governor. Each region would include a campus of up to 40,000 students (presumably Ohio State in the central region), at least one two-year technical college, and a research center similar to Ohio State's Transportation Research Center. The proposal also called for the state's 646 school districts to be consolidated into 88 countywide districts and for governance of both K–12 and higher education to eventually be merged into one cabinet-level department. The plan was part of a larger program that Rhodes claimed would make Ohio No. 1 "in the nation in all fields."[34]

Reaction was initially guarded, as neither legislators nor education leaders had been briefed beforehand. It didn't take long for opposition to surface. Provost Corbally was among the first to speak out, saying that Ohio State's unique status meant it "serves the whole state, not just a piece of the state." President Fawcett said some elements of the proposal were "utterly impossible." Once educators realized there was no additional money attached, criticism intensified. In what was described as a "tense" meeting between the Board of Regents and university presidents in January, the gloves came off. The proposed increase in the budget for the next biennium was so small, the regents acknowledged that tuition increases of 47 percent might be necessary. William Jerome, president of Bowling Green State University, called the whole thing "a mass mess." Ohio State's Arts and Sciences Council, a student group, labeled it "a disaster for the seventies."[35]

Rhodes quickly changed direction. In his February 5 State of the State address, he called for a two-year freeze on resident tuition for all of Ohio's public universities. How would he pay for it? The governor, who up to this point had opposed any new taxes, announced he would support a vendor excise tax on business to fund his plan. Fawcett and the other university presidents expressed cautious support.[36]

The excise tax immediately ran into opposition from the powerful Council of Retail Merchants, which had killed a similar proposal two years earlier. Rhodes beat a quick retreat and said it was up to the legislature to find a solution. John Millett, chancellor of the Board of Regents, warned university presidents there was little hope for additional money, but said he supported legislation that would give the regents more control over university spending.[37]

All this led to a series of confusing and contentious hearings throughout the spring where the university presidents tried to cope with the double whammy of less state support and more state control. In the end the legislature opted for preserving the status quo. It abandoned Rhodes's plan, watered down the regents' financial management proposals, and provided a modest increase in appropriations sufficient to head off a 47 percent tuition increase. Still, no one was really happy. At their August meeting the Ohio State trustees approved Fawcett's recommendation for a budget that called for a 17.6 percent tuition increase, from $170 to $200 per quarter. Room and board fees were increased by $12 per quarter. Fawcett described the increases as barely enough to keep up with rising inflation and growing enrollments. Student leaders blamed the legislature for failing to provide adequate funding.[38]

INSTRUCTION: A MIXED BAG

Despite the constrained funding environment, the university was able to make some improvements in the delivery of instruction. The honors program continued to grow and now boasted a thousand participants. The South Campus Student Association worked with university officials to inaugurate a living-learning program that would bring faculty into the residence halls to teach three basic undergraduate courses beginning in the fall of 1969. The College of Biological Sciences tested a new automated lab course designed to let students learn at their own pace. The experiment was so successful, the college decided to expand it to include all introductory biology courses in the fall of 1969.[39]

Ohio State students won five prestigious Woodrow Wilson fellowships, fewer than at most of their peer institutions but a much better showing than in previous years. The university also graduated its first major in Japanese and awarded its first degree in surgical equipment management, which trained people to manage high-tech devices such as kidney dialysis machines. It approved a four-year degree in engineering and three graduate programs in public administration. The School of Natural Resources was started, as was a new building for the rapidly growing School of Nursing.

Ohio State continued to attract better-prepared students. The registrar announced in late March that 31 percent of the incoming freshman class had placed in the top tier of ACT scores, compared to 25 percent the year before. Only 6 percent placed in the lowest category, down from 9 percent the previous year. When asked why they had chosen Ohio State, 68 percent of incoming freshmen mentioned the faculty and 65 percent cited the academic programs. Only 13 percent mentioned athletics.[40] Nevertheless, stubborn problems remained. The university declared the students loved TV courses, but *Lantern* interviews painted a much different picture. Money shortages prevented hiring enough faculty to reduce class sizes, and a new problem was developing regarding closed courses.[41]

RESEARCH: THE PARTY'S OVER

The slowdown in federal research funding was now being felt on campus. In the budget year ending June 30, 1969, funding through Ohio State's Research Foundation fell 4 percent, from $16.8 million to $16.1 million. It was the first such decline after a decade of spectacular growth. The completion of the Apollo mission to the moon in July meant that particular source of funds would continue to decline. For example, a new radar telescope project was already threatened by a 20 percent cut in National Science Foundation funding.[42]

Some parts of the campus were able to adapt. The ElectroScience Lab turned its attention to the growing field of communications satellites. William W. Anderson, a professor of electrical engineering, experimented with using crystals to develop flat-screen TV displays. Other engineers applied space-age technology to automated cars and safer highways. The Slavic studies program pulled off a major coup when it lured the prestigious *Current Digest of the Soviet Press* and its funded staff of 18 away from Columbia University by offering more space and better printing capabilities. The biggest opportunities lay in medicine, where the emphasis evolved from space medicine to prevention and treatment. In October the College of Medicine announced a partnership with a local firm, David Ellis Industries, to develop the country's first mobile coronary care unit.

Decreases in federal funding were not the only challenges facing Ohio State research programs. The wave of unified public support for research spurred by Sputnik was now crumbling in the wake of Vietnam. Representative Mark Schinnerer (R-Lakewood) co-sponsored a bill in March that defined the faculty workweek as 40 hours, but with the proviso that at least 15 hours be spent in the classroom. Schinnerer, the only legislator holding a Ph.D. and a former superintendent of the Cleveland public schools, presumably would be more supportive of the creation of new knowledge. Apparently not. Introducing his bill, he explained: "Teaching, service and research comprise the principal commitments of faculty members. But teaching has been relegated to the position of least importance."[43]

Novice Fawcett and the other university presidents strongly opposed the measure, saying it would put Ohio at an enormous competitive disadvantage in attracting and retaining faculty and in supporting the state's economic growth. Chancellor Millett, a former college president himself, was only somewhat helpful. He told legislators that most faculty worked much more than 40 hours a week, but accused Ohio's universities of not policing their ranks. He said he opposed setting a standard through legislation, but then volunteered to take on the task if the legislature would delegate the responsibility to him. In the end the universities prevailed, but attitudes clearly were changing from the post-Sputnik days.[44]

LEADERSHIP CHANGES

On March 28 John Corbally announced he was leaving Ohio State to become president of Syracuse University. In his three years as provost Corbally had functioned as chief academic officer and chief operating officer. He usually was the one who talked to the press and met with students when there was a crisis or a major decision. He was one of the few administrators trusted by both President Fawcett and student leaders.

The university moved quickly to announce a successor. On July 31 Fawcett recommended to the board that political science professor James Robinson become Ohio State's chief academic officer. Robinson also directed the Mershon Center for Education in National Security and was a nationally recognized expert in public sector decision-making. At 37, he was the youngest person to be named a vice president at Ohio State. Faculty and student leaders were pleased with the appointment, which was approved unanimously by the trustees.

Fawcett also announced the appointment of Edward Moulton to the new position of vice president for administrative operations. Moulton, who went by Ned, began his career at Ohio State as an assistant professor of engineering and rose to associate dean of the faculty and head of the academic unit budgets. He left the university in 1966 to become president of the University of South Dakota; when he returned in 1968, Fawcett named him board secretary and assistant to the president, titles he retained in addition to his new vice presidential title.

The impending marriage of John Mount, vice president for student affairs, and Ruth Weimer, dean of students, meant changes in the Office of Student Relations. Because university policy prohibited married people from reporting to each other, Weimer stepped down and her assistant, 35-year-old Ken Bader, took her place. In response to continued low levels of state support, the university hired its first vice president for development. Robert G. Smith, 37, who had led successful fund-raising efforts at Colgate University, came on board January 1, 1969. After 21 years on Ohio State's board of trustees, former senator and governor John Bricker, 75, finished his term in May 1969 and was not reappointed.

As a result of these changes, Fawcett entered 1970 with a much younger management team to balance his more experienced hands, but neither youth nor experience would turn out to be a magic elixir in the troubled days ahead.

SOCIETY: BRING US TOGETHER

NOT A DIME'S WORTH OF DIFFERENCE

Divided and shell-shocked after the traumas of 1968, Americans yearned for healing and unity. First they would have to choose a new president who they hoped could lead them there. Many college-age voters, particularly those who had supported Kennedy and McCarthy, found all the choices unappealing. Former Alabama governor George Wallace, who ran as an independent, generated much of the early excitement. Wallace, who charged there wasn't "a dime's worth of difference" between the two major-party candidates, promised to crack down on protestors and other assorted troublemakers. However, Wallace's support began to erode after his running mate, Ohio State graduate and retired air force general Curtis LeMay, advocated using nuclear weapons in Vietnam.

The Democratic nominee, Vice President Hubert Humphrey, made one stop in Columbus for a press conference at Port Columbus airport on September 21. On October 1 he finally broke with President Lyndon Johnson's war policy and called for a halt to bombing in Vietnam. Voters seemed to like Humphrey's display of independence, and he started moving up in the polls.

At Ohio State the student government did not sponsor a straw poll as it had in 1960 and 1964, so it is hard to determine where most students stood. The *Lantern* randomly questioned 57 students on October 30 and found them slightly favoring Humphrey. However, when only those old enough to vote were counted (the voting age then was 21), Nixon held a slight lead. A *Columbus Dispatch* voting machine poll held on October 14 at University City Shopping Center near campus showed Nixon with a slight lead. The *Lantern,* which had remained neutral in 1960 and backed Johnson in 1964, raised some eyebrows when it came out for Nixon on October 30. The paper accused Humphrey of being a warmed-over Johnson, but saw in Nixon a "mellowed and tolerant" man who offered a "fresh approach to diagnosing and curing the nation's ills."[45]

Ironically, while it was the Kennedy and McCarthy activists who had generated excitement in the spring, Nixon seemed to capture the enthusiasm in the fall. Ohio State's Young Republicans, led by junior G. Timothy Marcks, focused on Franklin County, where they sent hundreds of volunteers out to knock on doors in more than 75 precincts. Marcks described it as "the largest effort in the nation."[46] Many of the same students turned out for a boisterous rally for Nixon when he made his only campaign appearance in Columbus on October 22. Standing on the Statehouse steps with Woody Hayes at his side, Nixon told the crowd of 10,000: "Ohio State plays rock 'em, sock 'em football and that's what we're gonna do."[47]

As citizens went to the polls on November 5, most opinion surveys showed a tight race. The popular vote was close, but Nixon captured 301 electoral votes, more than enough to win. He carried Ohio by 90,000 votes and Franklin County by 49,000 votes. Many former Kennedy and McCarthy supporters had thrown their energies behind Democrat John Gilligan, who was running for U.S. Senate but lost to Republican William Saxbe by 100,000 votes.

At his inauguration in January, Nixon struck a conciliatory tone. Referring to a sign he had seen held by a young woman in Deshler, Ohio, he promised to "bring us together." But the honeymoon turned out to be short-lived. Neither Nixon's opponents nor his supporters nor his internal demons were ready for reconciliation.

BRING US LAW AND ORDER

Fall quarter 1968 began with a stern warning from President Fawcett to would-be protestors. It didn't take long for the establishment to show it was serious. On November 4 the *Lantern* reported that two students arrested in the Hitchcock Hall recruiting protest in February—junior Michael Wright and sophomore William Ganz—had lost their student deferments and been reclassified as 1-A, available for induction by their local draft board. The students accused the university of snitching on them. The university and Selective Service officials denied the charge. A Selective Service spokesperson insisted his office learned about such things from newspaper accounts or "public spirited citizens" then passed on the information to the local draft boards to use at their discretion. The Selective Service had "no quarrel" with responsible dissent, the spokesperson said, but he also argued the 100,000 student deferments were not a right but a benefit to be granted only in the national interest. These actions by draft boards to punish protestors were eventually overturned by the U.S. Supreme Court as an abuse of power.[48]

Governor Rhodes and Chancellor Millett offered their own get-tough policy later the same month. Rhodes asked Millett to circulate a *Chicago Tribune* editorial to all university presidents in Ohio that called on university leaders to "expel troublemakers forthwith." Millett also reminded presidents who held the big club. "I think that the legislature is going to be influenced by what happens on our campuses," he warned, "and they will be influenced by what they read in news accounts and editorials." Millett was even blunter in private. He warned the presidents of "dire consequences" in the event of uprisings on their campuses.[49]

The forces of law and order now had a powerful ally in the Nixon administration. Nixon knew George Wallace had tapped real resentment among many middle-class voters, but Wallace also carried too much baggage as a segregationist to gain wider appeal. So Nixon honed a more subtle message that played off legitimate concerns and hidden resentments that resonated with many voters, particularly those who believed they played by the rules while others didn't.[50] At a speech before the U.S. Chamber of Commerce in April, Nixon got his biggest round of applause when he blasted protestors who espoused violence and called upon college administrators to "have the backbone to stand up against this kind of situation."[51]

Ohio's legislators recognized the political potency of the law-and-order message and were quick to double down. Six antidisruption bills were introduced in the first 60 days of the 108th General Assembly. One of them, sponsored by Senator Harry L. Armstrong (R-Logan), required college administrators to take action in the form of dismissal for any faculty, staff, or student who "directs, incites, encourages or participates in any activity which interferes or is likely to interfere with the orderly pursuit of educational programs or objectives."[52]

"Law and order must be carried out on the campuses of Ohio," said Armstrong, whose district included Ohio University, which had been the site of protests. Senator Robert Stockdale (R-Kent), whose district included Kent State University, said the legislation was necessary because there had not been "quick, forceful enforcement" of previous legislation. An exchange between Kent State president Robert I. White and Ohio House education chair Mark Schinnerer in April showed how deeply law-and-order verbiage framed discussions of education policy that spring. White appeared with other university presidents before the education committee to testify against Schinnerer's bill regulating faculty workweeks. White somewhat unartfully tried to invoke the law-and-order issue to his advantage. He told the committee that what he called "time-clock punching legislation" would alienate faculty and give "aid and comfort to those who favor violence over peaceful study." Unfazed by White's arguments, Schinnerer preferred to celebrate White's tough handling of demonstrations on his campus earlier that spring.[53]

If talk of law and order was meant to quell student unrest, students weren't buying it. Disorders that spring swept through 200 campuses and resulted in 2,300 arrests. At public hearings before the U.S. House Education Subcommittee in March, student leaders struck a defiant tone. Robert S. Powell Jr., president of the National Student Association (the group Ohio State undergraduates had voted not to join earlier in the decade), placed blame for the surge in violence on administrators and trustees for what he called the creation of "undemocratic and authoritarian institutions." David Hinshaw, a former University of Cincinnati student and now head of the presumably more mainstream Association of Student Governments, charged college administrators with defending a corrupt "old order." "You should understand that millions of middle class youths who have shared rather richly in our affluence not only do not prize it, but in fact consider it a positive handicap in the search for personal development and national integrity," Hinshaw said. Thus the rhetorical battle lines were drawn for what the following spring would be the worst spasm of domestic disorder since the Civil War.[54]

REVENGE OF THE COUNTERCULTURE

When the counterculture first pierced the national consciousness in mid-1967, both the Ohio State campus and the surrounding community reacted with skepticism and, in some cases, hostility. To the horror of their elders, by the middle of 1969 many young people at the university and elsewhere had embraced at least some elements of the movement, leaving behind the accepted values of suburban and small-town America they had grown up with.

The counterculture's symbolic epicenter at Ohio State was an eclectic collection of small shops such as Charlie's Guitar and Venus Tea Room that filled a one-block stretch of commercial real estate on 13th Avenue, across High Street from the Ohio Union. Known as Pearl Alley after a nearby cross street, it became the gathering place for a growing number of students and former students living in nearby apartments and rooming houses. They shared a lifestyle that differed from the traditional in their attitudes toward appearance, music, sex, and drugs. As one shop owner put it, "We just wanted to live the way we want to, with no outside intervention." That view was not shared by law enforcement,

10.4. Charlie's Guitar, which opened in April 1969, was one of several counterculture gathering places in Pearl Alley. (*Makio*)

and Pearl Alley became another symbol of the deteriorating relationship between the university youth culture and the Columbus police.[55]

The counterculture's distrust of established institutions spilled over into other venues. Switchboard, a nontraditional counseling and referral service for young people staffed primarily by volunteers, opened its doors in November 1968. It was followed by the Open Door Clinic and Huckleberry House for runaways. The 1968–69 school year also witnessed the birth of what became known as the underground press. *The People, Yes* billed itself as an alternative not only to the very establishment *Columbus Dispatch* and *Citizen-Journal,* but also to the *Lantern,* which it saw as becoming increasingly reactionary. *The People, Yes* claimed a paid readership of 2,000 and would soon be followed by *University Forum, Columbus Free Press,* and *Our Choking Times,* a paper put out by black students at Ohio State.[56]

BIG NAMES

Some big names visited campus during the school year, and for a while it looked like the university would land the biggest name of all. The White House announced in May that President Nixon would speak at commencement on June 7. Nixon reportedly wanted a friendly Midwestern venue in which to deliver a major address on student unrest. He was forced to cancel two weeks later because he had something more important to do that weekend: fly to Midway Island in the Pacific for a historic meeting with South Vietnamese president Nguyen Van Thieu to lay the groundwork for winding down U.S. involvement in the Vietnam War. Nixon offered instead his vice president, Spiro T. Agnew.[57]

Agnew landed with appropriate fanfare in a military helicopter on the grassy area south of Ohio Stadium. Accompanied by a phalanx of uniformed and plainclothes security, he spoke to some 4,000 graduates and 16,000 family and friends through intermittent rain. Agnew had been the president's primary attack vehicle, but he toned down his rhetoric somewhat in an address titled "A Time to Speak and a Time to Listen." However, Agnew couldn't resist questioning the masculinity of those who disagreed with him. "A society which comes to fear its children is effete," he said. "A sniveling, hand-wringing power structure deserves the violent rebellion it encourages. If my generation doesn't stop cringing, yours will inherit a lawless society where emotion and muscle displace reason."[58]

Local activists, including Students for a Democratic Society, sought to embarrass Agnew by organizing protests, but fell short. About 70 pickets demonstrated outside the stadium gates. They carried a Viet Cong flag and chanted antiwar slogans but were largely ignored by the crowd. About a dozen students in caps and gowns walked out when Agnew started to speak, then returned when he finished. Three young people who were not students were hustled out by police when they stood up to boo. Agnew received a standing ovation from the audience.

10.5. In the spring of 1969, Ohio State remained relatively quiet even as many other campuses were in turmoil. Shown here at an uneventful commencement ceremony are, left to right, university vice president Ned Moulton, comedian Bob Hope, U.S. vice president Spiro Agnew, and Provost John Corbally. (*Makio*)

The best line of the day came from comedian Bob Hope, who was on hand to receive an honorary degree. Referring to Agnew's gaffes during the election campaign, Hope quipped the vice president was "making a great comeback after last year's campaign." Hope also received a standing ovation.[59]

Other notables who came to Ohio State included counterculture poet Alan Ginsberg, who led a half-hour séance and chanting session in Hitchcock Hall and also spoke at the Ohio Union, where he described Columbus as a "hick-town police state as heavy as Prague." Rand consultant Daniel Ellsberg spoke to students in a Vietnam history course in May and criticized the U.S. effort to eliminate communists throughout Vietnam as unrealistic.[60] Two years later Ellsberg's growing dissatisfaction with the war led him to leak the highly classified documents that became known as the Pentagon Papers.

The most provocative and thoughtful address came from someone who was well known in Ohio but not nationally. Newly elected U.S. senator William B. Saxbe, who earned degrees from Ohio State in 1940 and 1948, spoke at the Law Day ceremony in May. The former state attorney general, a Republican, had defeated Democrat John Gilligan in the Senate race the past November, running a typical law-and-order campaign. But Saxbe, who would develop a reputation as a maverick, showed he already was thinking differently. He spoke of the need to preserve order, but then closed with this thought: "Our youth in one sense has become the defenders of traditional American values. As they grew up they were reared to believe in such things as Jefferson's idea of liberty, Lincoln's idea of equality, and Wilson's idea of a peaceful community of nations. Then they go to college or to work and look around them and all of a sudden they are seeing these ideas betrayed. And through their dissent, I think this is what they are protesting against. And I say again: let's listen to them."[61]

WOODSTOCK SUMMER

The 1960s were driven by massive contradictions—peace and war, order and disorder, change and resistance to change—which explains in part why the period was so volatile. The contradictions seemed to manifest themselves most dramatically in the hot months of summer. The last summer of the decade would be no exception.

Just before 11 p.m. EDT on July 20, 1969, 500 million people worldwide put aside their differences and watched as Ohioan Neil Armstrong became the first man to step on the surface of the moon. It took the efforts of thousands of people involved in the Apollo project, including scientists at Ohio State, to turn a dream into reality in the decade's most iconic moment. The *Lantern* asked several faculty members to comment. Their responses reflected the mixture of pride and ambivalence that permeated the period. Paul Underwood, an associate professor of journalism, said: "It would be impossible not to be almost overwhelmed by the happening of something which was undreamed of when I was a boy. The achievement is so immense and so fantastic that it seems almost improper to talk about whether we can afford it or not." James B. Kweder, an assistant professor of political science, spoke for those who saw things differently: "Insofar as we have to make a choice of the allocation of some very scarce resources right now, the first priority ought to be down here. There are people that are hungry down here; ill-fed, ill-clothed and ill-housed."[62]

Nearly three weeks after the moon landing, a grisly rampage in Los Angeles reminded everyone of the real tensions still loose in society. Over two August nights, Charles Manson and his cult of followers murdered seven people, including pregnant actress Sharon Tate. They were eventually caught, tried, and convicted, but as the sensational trial unfolded the association between nihilistic behavior, sex, drugs, and rock music scared many Americans who worried their children might succumb to similar temptations.

Another of the decade's signature events occurred on a farm in upstate New York. In mid-August nearly half a million young people gathered to celebrate the counterculture at the Woodstock Music Festival. Many Ohio State students were among them, including *Lantern* reporter Tom Burroughs, who observed: "After the shock of the fantastic size wore off, it did not take long for the people to realize that this occasion was something not of the ordinary." Woodstock participants and counterculture supporters believed they had accomplished something bigger than just entertaining themselves. They had overcome rain and mud—and the lack of food and water and sanitary facilities—by sharing as a community, without force and without violence. Although the spirit of Woodstock Nation was very real for the three days of the festival, its transference to the rest of society was not in the cards.[63]

Six thousand miles from upstate New York, another community of half a million young people listened to rock music, overcame poor sanitation, and in some cases dabbled in cheap drugs and cheap sex. They also learned to band together in a way few would experience again. Their job was to hunt down and kill suspected enemy combatants in the name of the government of the United States. Six months into the Nixon presidency there were still 500,000 American soldiers in Vietnam, and they were still dying at rate of more than a hundred a week as the war dragged into its fifth year.

CHAPTER 11

ROAD TO ARMAGEDDON

(1969–70)

On April 9, 1970, Armageddon came to Ohio State.

Armageddon was the name of a rock band sponsored by Campus Crusade for Christ. Its eight members played cover versions of popular hits plus some of their own compositions and talked about their personal relationship with Jesus Christ. It is not clear how many converts they found that night, but the concert progressed peacefully with no shouting of obscenities, no throwing of rocks or bottles, and no arrests.

Three weeks later the university careened into what some believed might be its own Armageddon, the worst period of violence in its hundred-year history.

11.1. Student Steven Piatt confronts Vice President John Mount at Prospectus '70 in April. Arrests at the job fair helped coalesce student protest groups. (*Lantern*)

STUDENTS: COALESCING

As the 1969–70 school year began, students were more concerned about access to football tickets than anything else. The national championship win the year before sparked increased demand, and rumors about a cutback in the student allocation sparked panic buying. Four thousand students waited up to six hours in a line that stretched from St. John Arena to the Lane Avenue bridge to buy tickets the first day they were offered. The rumors turned out to be false. All the student tickets, as well as all the others, were eventually sold. Woody's Warriors marched undefeated though their first eight games. Once again the season turned on the final game. The Buckeyes went into it ranked No. 1 and heavily favored over the Michigan Wolverines and their freshman coach, Bo Schembechler. Twenty-two thousand fans made their way up Route 23 to the Big House in Ann Arbor the weekend of November 22. They returned disappointed, on the short end of a 12–24 loss.

Meanwhile, the old problems didn't seem to want to go away. The Vietnam War dragged on, while the antiwar movement peaked. The draft lottery began, and Students for a Democratic Society took a pounding from law enforcement. More and more students found themselves closed out of courses, and the university fought with state officials over who was to blame for rising student fees. Still, the campus stayed quiet until spring, when all hell broke loose.

GIVE PEACE A CHANCE

By October 1969 Richard Nixon was into the 10th month of his presidency. Optimism about an early end to the Vietnam War was replaced by frustration amid continued heavy fighting. Casualties mounted—among them at least four Ohio State graduates killed between May and August alone.[1]

Antiwar leaders designated October 15 as Moratorium Day, a nationwide effort to cease business as usual, end the war, and bring the troops home. Stephen Stollmack, a researcher at Ohio State's Center for Water Resources, led the Columbus Moratorium Committee. Stollmack had worked on defense contracts as a systems analyst but had turned against the war. The committee quickly picked up support from faculty and students, including the Student Assembly, the legislative arm of the Undergraduate Student Government. Antiwar activists also drew a warning from the state legislature. Norm Murdock (R-Cincinnati), chair of the House Subcommittee on Campus Disorders, sent a letter to all university presidents in Ohio and their student body presidents cautioning them against violence.[2]

He needn't have worried. Moratorium events passed peaceably. They began on October 13 with a teach-in at the Ohio Union featuring U.S. congressman Allard Lowenstein (D-New York), the man who sparked the movement to dump Lyndon Johnson in 1967–68. About 500 people attended. Moratorium Day itself started with students reading a list of Ohio's war dead to date—about 1,500 names—from the steps of the Administration Building from 8 a.m. to 8 p.m. Students from the Columbus College of Art and Design led a march of about 500 from the Ohio State campus to the Statehouse, where they were joined by another thousand or so. The School of Social Work sponsored a teach-in at the United Christian Center that drew nearly a thousand participants.

Nationally, Moratorium Day generated widespread support, including a rally of 250,000 in the nation's capital. By and large the events went forward without violence. Leaders thought they were successful in reaching the silent majority they believed was opposed to the war. Energized, they planned an even bigger event, calling on people to converge on Washington, D.C., for a huge rally on Saturday, November 15.

At 5 p.m. on a rainy Thursday, a caravan of cars and five chartered buses left High Street and 15th Avenue headed for the nation's capital. Eight more buses and another procession of automobiles left later that evening. The passengers were among 1,300 central Ohioans—including students, teachers, housewives, and businesspeople—who along with like-minded people across the country believed the time had come when a massive but peaceful protest could end the war.[3]

An estimated 500,000 citizens turned out for the "March against Death," making it the largest war protest ever. It marked the high point of the antiwar movement.

Although the number of Ohio State participants was unprecedented compared to earlier protests, it was only a small portion of students and faculty and staff. The *Lantern* interviewed some students who stayed behind to learn why they did not participate. Though many expressed opposition to the war, they had various reasons for not going to Washington. Senior Jan Sanislo was typical. He said he was against the war, but planned to attend the football game against Purdue instead. He added that he would have done so even if the march were being held in Columbus.[4]

Two weeks later President Nixon delivered a nationally televised address regarded as one of the best of his long career. He maintained he was working for an end to the war in a thoughtful and reasonable way and called for the support of the silent majority of Americans who agreed with him. A Gallup poll done after the speech showed 77 percent approval. In December the president announced that an additional 50,000 troops would be withdrawn from Vietnam by the following April.

At the same time Nixon moved forcefully to end the unpopular draft. He delivered on a campaign promise when at 8 p.m. on Monday, December 1, the nation conducted its first draft lottery in 27 years. Students tuned in on TVs and radios at lottery parties across campus to find out where they stood among the 890,000 eligible males between the ages of 18 and 26. All 366 birthdates would be selected in random order. Those pulled first were certain to be drafted. Those pulled last were certain not to be. The status of those in between would be determined later.[5]

At the Delta Tau Delta fraternity house, members pitched in a few bucks each to create their own lottery. The person with the lowest draft number would win $100. The lucky individual turned out to be junior John Mossbarger, whose birthdate of September 7 was the eighth picked. Mossbarger said he wasn't too concerned because he planned to go to veterinary school. That meant he could get a deferment until he graduated, then enter as a veterinarian instead of a rifleman. The reactions of others varied. "I don't like it," junior Jay Shulman said when he found out he was 24th. "I'll get drafted in June when I graduate, and I planned to go to law school. I don't know what I'll do now. I'm as good as gone." Junior John McMahon, whose April 24 birthday made him second on the list, remarked, "If I have to, I'll serve. I'll be proud to do it."[6]

Nixon also engineered the retirement of Selective Service director Lewis Hershey, who had become a hated symbol to young people. Rumors surfaced that Woody Hayes, who had military experience and

11.2. John Mossbarger is surrounded by Delta Tau Delta fraternity brothers after "winning" the draft lottery on December 1. (*Lantern*)

was close to Nixon, might be the new director, but that was quickly denied.[7] Overall, war supporters and critics alike agreed the lottery was an improvement over the arbitrary system it replaced.

By the beginning of 1970 the antiwar movement had started to lose steam and split into factions, both nationally and on campus. Stephen Stollmack announced he was stepping down as chair of the Columbus Moratorium Committee, citing "personal reasons." Another officer, public relations chair Richard Stafford, had already announced his resignation. Stafford, a professor of psychology, objected to the committee's allowing members of Students for a Democratic Society to join who lacked a commitment to nonviolence. The new chair, Joel Ann Todd, held a press conference on April 9 to deny rumors of a split between the committee and an older group, the Student Mobilization Committee. Todd, a graduate student in political science, had turned against the Vietnam War while an undergraduate at Miami University.[8]

On April 20 Nixon announced that another 150,000 troops would be withdrawn from Vietnam over the next year, bringing the total to 225,000. And now, for the first time, American casualties were going down instead of up. The day before, the National Moratorium Committee announced it was closing its Washington, D.C., office and leaving local groups to carry on. It appeared the war over ending the war was over, and Nixon had won.

SDS UNDER FIRE

Students for a Democratic Society had had a difficult year at Ohio State in 1968–69, and the next year would be even worse. The members' immediate concern was hanging on to university recognition, which gave them access to space and publicity. It also required them to have a faculty adviser. After going through two advisers in 16 months, they lost university recognition again. This cost them a campus meeting room on the eve of an October 7 statewide meeting they were hosting. They managed to find space off campus, but the confusion was an obvious embarrassment. At the same time, they were pushed off center stage—if they were ever there—by the more moderate members of the Columbus Moratorium Committee.[9]

A series of congressional hearings in October provided further embarrassment. The U.S. House Investigations Subcommittee spent four days focusing on SDS activities in Columbus. It generated a number of lurid disclosures, including allegations by two teenagers who claimed that SDS tried to recruit them to firebomb the Lazarus department store downtown.[10] The big blow came shortly after the first of the year when Columbus police finished a nine-week investigation regarding local runaways. Over the next month they arrested 35 adults in the campus area for harboring juveniles and, in many cases, for drug-related charges. Police claimed 36 teenagers, mostly girls and some as young as 13, were exploited by adults living commune-style in situations where drugs and sex were plentiful. Those arrested included both students and nonstudents, among them several individuals associated with SDS.[11]

One of the students, freshman Michael Jaschik, was listed as president of the local SDS chapter. He and the others said they had done nothing more than offer temporary shelter to kids from troubled homes, some of whom claimed they would be beaten if they returned. "The police look at the Manson case out West and think that what's happened around the University is a parallel," one unidentified arrestee told the *Lantern*. "To them, more than two unrelated people in a house is a commune. If any male there has long hair, he's a dirty filthy hippie, like Manson, [and] he's bound to end up murdering someone or corrupting younger kids."[12]

All this resulted in a campus without much in the way of leadership on the left. SDS was under siege. The Free Student Federation and Students for Liberal Action were long gone. The Black Student Union had disappeared after the 1968 lock-in. The Vietnam War was winding down, and law and order ruled the campus. While conflict continued elsewhere, Ohio State was an oasis of calm, or so it seemed.

THE EMERGENCE OF AFRO-AM

On the morning of March 9, the Monday of the last week of winter quarter classes before finals, a group of black students requested a meeting with Vice President John Mount for that afternoon. Mount met with the delegation of a dozen students who said they represented about 200 members of a new organization called Afro-Am. They presented Mount with a list of 19 "concerns" and asked for a response by no later than noon that Friday. The concerns included some general items, such as more scholarships for black students and lower fees for all students. The group also called for specific actions, such as bringing an additional 2,500 black students onto campus by autumn quarter 1970, just six months away. Mount told the students the university would take their proposals under consideration, and the delegation left without further incident.[13]

Between Monday and Friday administrators worked on a detailed response supporting some but not all of the actions. As the Friday deadline approached, speculation grew about what would happen at noon that day. Afro-Am had planned a demonstration in front of the Administration Building. Administrators had picked up on an unconfirmed rumor that the students were going to bring bricks with them. An Afro-Am spokesperson later confirmed they were told to bring bricks—not to throw, but to construct a symbolic "bridge of understanding" in front of the building. Photos published in the *Makio* do show them being used that way, but the idea of students carrying bricks to a demonstration surely was not reassuring to university officials.[14]

The administration decided to have the building locked down as a precaution, with security on call. A delegation of a dozen students was admitted to the building at noon as planned. The students met with Mount for about 15 minutes, but didn't come to an agreement. Mount asked the students to sign a roster identifying themselves. Recalling that such a document was used to identify the black students for prosecution in the April 1968 lock-in, they refused. The talks went downhill from there. The students left Mount's office in an orderly manner, but as they exited the building they held open the doors so that 75 to 80 other students could get in. This second group marched up to Mount's office on the second floor and, according to university sources, broke the glass in his door as well as the glass on a sign in the lobby. Others scattered papers from the registrar's office on the floor. Mount came out of his office and tried to warn the students they were in danger of violating the Disruption Rule, but he was shouted down and cursed. He decided to summon the highway patrol to clear the building. The students left before the patrol arrived.

Meanwhile, four unidentified black males reportedly entered an office in Derby Hall, pressed a receptionist's head down on her desk, overturned a key punch machine and a file cabinet and scattered key punch cards, then left. At 2 p.m. the university decided to request an injunction against six leaders of Afro-Am and 150 unnamed others. Municipal judge Thomas Moody granted the injunction an hour later. Also that afternoon, small fires were reported in campus buildings, as well as a bomb threat and scattered false fire alarms.[15]

With finals week coming and then spring break, nothing else happened until after classes resumed in April. On April 7 the *Lantern* reported that two leaders of Afro-Am—senior William T. Kilgore and sophomore Jerry Roberts—would be charged under the Disruption Rule. Kilgore described himself as the head of the Columbus chapter of the NAACP, but the national NAACP denied any connection. Kilgore was one of the 34 students originally charged in the 1968 lock-in, but charges against him had been dropped.[16]

Loss of a Voice for Moderation

In the midst of turmoil Ohio State lost a badly needed link to the African American community. William Conley had been appointed minority affairs coordinator by Vice President John Mount in the wake of the Black Student Union efforts in 1968. Since then he had worked tirelessly to build bridges between the university and its black students.

In April 1970 Conley was convicted in municipal court of receiving $880 worth of stolen stereo equipment and concealing it in his office. His secretary told university officials Conley accepted the property as collateral for a loan to a needy student, something he did often. She even produced a receipt. The person in question, however, was not a student but a convicted burglar, and the goods had been stolen.

The dean of the College of Humanities wrote Mount a letter describing Conley as a "force for intelligent moderation," and the municipal judge downgraded the charges from a felony to a misdemeanor, but that was not enough. Mount suggested that Conley resign to spare himself further embarrassment, which he did. His resignation left a void when the university could least afford it.[1]

1. Roger J. Mezger, "Conley to Resign June 30," *Lantern,* April 20, 1970, 1; Report of Interview, Mrs. Mildred P. Parks, Secretary to Mr. William Conley, January 29, 1970, and Letter from Charles L. Babcock, Dean, and Paul J. Olscamp, Associate Dean, to John Mount, February 3, 1970, in Vice President for Academic Affairs, William E. Conley (Archives: RG 5/a/28).

Jerry Roberts was identified as the vice president of Afro-Am. The first black person to graduate from an all-white high school in Birmingham, Alabama, Roberts had transferred to Ohio State from the State University of New York system because his father was an alumnus. Like many of his African American counterparts, he immediately felt isolated. He later recalled: "When I came to this university in 1969, I had to attend an orientation session. During the meeting there was nothing I felt that related to the interests of black people . . . we were asked to go on hay rides, beer blasts . . . that's not the norm of culture in the black community."[17]

Over the next two weeks protests erupted on campus while Roberts, Kilgore, and their attorney sparred with the university over arrangements for their disciplinary hearings.

A NEW COALITION

During the second week of spring quarter, voters elected their student government officers for the next year. Some 7,550 students turned out, nearly double the number of the year before. The election results did not show a more radicalized student body, but they did show a more fragmented one. The team of junior Steve Kling and sophomore L. Lee Walker led a field of six, giving the University Party its fourth-straight victory. But they won by only 98 votes over the upstart United Student Organization, a more conservative party. A raft of more liberal minor parties split the remainder of the vote. The University Party captured only eight seats in the Student Assembly, instead of 24, as in the previous year. The rest were split among other parties.

The following week about a hundred students in the School of Social Work staged a walkout to protest what they believed was a lack of student involvement in the school's decision-making. They wanted students to occupy half of all seats on key committees.[18] On April 20 another group of about 100 students gathered to protest Prospectus '70, a student-organized jobs fair at the Ohio Union. The demonstration was sponsored by the Columbus Moratorium Committee and the Third World Solidarity Committee.[19] After rallying on the Oval the protestors marched to the Ohio Union chanting, "Big firms get rich, while G.I.'s die." When university officials asked them to leave, they did so.[20]

The same group came back the next day, led by six individuals in hooded black robes carrying a coffin with a replica pig's head in it. They reentered the jobs fair chanting and ringing a cow bell. They attempted to present the pig's head to FBI recruiters, who declined. Wendell Ellenwood, director of the Ohio Union, asked them to leave. They refused. John Mount was summoned to the scene and told them to disperse, adding that they were in danger of violating the Disruption Rule. Mount was shouted down. One student, junior Steven Piatt, started shouting obscenities in his face. At that point 60 uniformed highway patrolmen and university police officers were called in. Lorraine Cohen of the Columbus Moratorium Committee jumped on a table and encouraged the protestors to leave. Members of the Green Ribbon Commission—the group of faculty mediators—also tried to get them to leave. Most did, but in the ensuing confusion five students and one university employee were arrested.[21]

The next day, April 22, as the university celebrated Earth Day, a group called the Ad Hoc Committee on Student Rights emerged, identifying itself as a coalition that included representatives of the Columbus Moratorium Committee, the Student Mobilization Committee, the Third World Solidarity Committee, social work students, and Afro-Am. It presented a list of 11 demands to the university administration, included amnesty for all those who had been arrested so far.[22] The origins of this group remain unclear, but the coalition between white antiwar activists and black activists that professors Enrico Quarantelli and Russell Dynes had warned about almost two years earlier was now a reality.[23]

The Student Assembly voted the next evening to oppose the Disruption Rule and condemn the "brutal tactics used in apprehending those arrested." The reference to brutal tactics was in response to reports that one of the students arrested in the Ohio Union incident had been denied medical treatment after being sprayed in the eyes with mace. Delegates rejected a motion to provoke an immediate confrontation by conducting an unauthorized meeting and rejected another motion to censure the *Lantern* for allegedly biased coverage.[24]

The Ad Hoc Committee picked up on the theme of stifling dissent at a rally on the Oval at noon on Friday attended by about 300. The Third World Solidarity Committee circulated literature that charged: "Every time the university's disruption rule has been invoked, it has been used to disperse groups of students who fundamentally disagree with university policies." Lorraine Cohen told the crowd that after the first person was arrested at Prospectus '70, five others were singled out at random for arrest, even though they were in the process of leaving peacefully.[25]

(Information subsequently made public supported the accusation of selective enforcement. At a disciplinary hearing eight months later, an Ohio State policeman testified he was ordered to arrest students for trespassing and resisting arrest, even though those he arrested made no effort to resist. John Mount, who had witnessed the whole chain of events, told Ohio State's Oral History Project years later that the university would have been better off letting the protestors leave on their own.)[26]

After calling for a student strike the coming Wednesday, the group on the Oval then marched to the Administration Building, where members demanded a meeting with President Fawcett. They were told Fawcett was unavailable, but that Provost James Robinson could meet with a delegation from the group. Some protestors wanted to force a confrontation by storming the building, but they could not generate much support and the idea was dropped. Instead, they agreed that either all of them would meet or none would. They then marched off to Stillman Hall to show their support for the students in the School of Social Work. After that, the group broke up.[27]

During that same week and the previous week, student protests turned into confrontations at two other universities in the state. Nine students were arrested at Ohio University for disrupting a ROTC class. At Miami University, 155 students were disciplined for trying to take over the Navy ROTC building.[28] Nonetheless, the weekend passed peacefully at Ohio State. Thousands enjoyed a Friday-evening concert in St. John Arena featuring the popular singing group the Fifth Dimension. Hundreds gathered on the Oval on Sunday to hear six rock bands perform as part of the Creative Arts Festival.

A delegation of seven students representing the Ad Hoc Committee did meet with Provost Robinson and two other administrators on April 27. Although both sides described the tone as cordial, they ended the meeting with no agreement.[29] That same day the two black students who had been charged with violating the Disruption Rule, William Kilgore and Jerry Roberts, walked out of their disciplinary hearing along with their attorney and faculty adviser to protest the hearing's not being open to the public. Fawcett sent a letter to the faculty later that day that said in part: "I believe it is a disservice to those students [who are willing to work within the system] and to members of the faculty and staff when a fraction of one percent of the student body can mount an issue that detracts from the central purpose of the institution and dissipates the energies of so many of us who are willing to work here. . . . I cannot and will not react to demands, instantly and often thoughtlessly developed, and which usually require instant yes or no answers. There are very few problems in higher education today that can be simplified to such an extent."[30]

Fawcett's letter stirred even more resentment. The following evening the Student Assembly gathered in a special meeting. The group took particular exception to Fawcett's statement that fewer than 1 percent of the students supported the Ad Hoc Committee's demands. The assembly voted unanimously to approve an "active, peaceful and nonviolent" boycott of classes in support of the committee. Assembly members made clear they opposed the Disruption Rule, opposed the arrests, and

A Buckeye Bernadette Devlin?

11.3. Lorraine Cohen, one of the leaders of the student strike, addresses supporters in front of Stillman Hall on April 28. (*Lantern*)

Lorraine Cohen grew up in East Meadows, New York, and started her college career as a music major at the State University of New York at Potsdam. She decided to come to Columbus for graduate school after meeting David Kettler, a political science professor at Ohio State, when he spoke on her campus. A graduate teaching assistant in political science, she was active with the Columbus Moratorium Committee and then became a spokesperson for the coalition Ad Hoc Committee on Student Rights.

Cohen considered herself a Marxist in that she believed American society needed a sweeping overhaul, but she also advocated nonviolence. She caught the attention of *Lantern* reporter Lou Heldman, who wrote that a "motorcycle-riding, mini-skirted graduate student may be stepping in to fill a leadership gap among campus activists that has been vacant since the mid-60's." He went on to describe Cohen as "soft-spoken" and "good-looking" and "Ohio State's answer to Bernadette Devlin," referring to the well-known Irish political activist.

Cohen fired off a letter to the *Lantern* to correct some "inferences" in Heldman's article that "might be misconstrued." She pointed out that how she looked, what she wore, and what she rode had nothing to do with the concerns she and her colleagues were trying to address. She corrected Heldman for referring to her as "the" leader of the group rather than "a" leader and took issue with what she said was his characterization of her as a disruptive force.

Cohen also attracted the attention of police, one of whom reportedly told Heldman that she represented a generation of more aggressive leaders at Ohio

State and other Ohio campuses. The university subsequently found Cohen and the other strike leaders guilty of violating the Disruption Rule. She was allowed to graduate at the end of summer quarter 1970, but with a notation of her transgression on her permanent record.[1]

1. Louis M. Heldman, "New Look in Leadership," *Lantern,* April 27, 1970, 3; Lorraine Cohen, "'A' Leader, Not 'The,'" *Lantern,* April 28, 1970, 3; "16 Found Guilty of Disruption," *Lantern,* September 30, 1970, 3; Lorraine Cohen interview.

supported the demands of Afro-Am, but did not support a violent confrontation. A *Lantern* editorial several days earlier had called the Prospectus '70 disturbance an "ego trip" by the protestors, but a later one aimed its severest criticism at what it called the administration's lack of candor in talking about problems.[31] Both sides had now staked out their positions and girded for a coming test of wills.

THE UNIVERSITY: CELEBRATING

March 22, 1970, marked the 100th anniversary of Ohio State's founding. The administration wanted to celebrate the occasion in a big way. After three years of planning and an investment of nearly a quarter of a million dollars, the commemorative events began in January with a student-oriented "Buckeye Cennebration" at the Ohio Union. A Centennial Queen was crowned, and celebrants enjoyed two dance bands; a 70-square-foot, 800-pound birthday cake with 100 candles; and all the ice cream they could eat.

Charter Day weekend, March 20–22, was the keystone event. (Because it occurred over spring break, students were not around to disrupt things.) The weekend began with a black-tie ball at the downtown Sheraton Motor Inn that featured the Sammy Kaye Orchestra. The high point turned out to be 76-year-old piano player Bill Dougherty, who brought all 800 guests to their feet by banging out "Across the Field," the official university fight song, which he had written back in 1915.

April featured the dedication of the Center for Tomorrow, a conference facility to support continuing education located just across the river from main campus. Also in April, the play *The Night Thoreau Spent in Jail,* written by alumnus Jerome Lawrence and Robert E. Lee specifically for the centennial, premiered. The university awarded a record 25 honorary degrees at commencement in June. The *Lantern* and the alumni magazine published commemorative editions. The Marching Band, the Men's Glee Club, and the University Chorus recorded two centennial albums. The photography and cinema department produced a documentary on the university's first 100 years. Alumnus and nationally known cartoonist Milt Caniff designed a commemorative medallion, and a centennial logo adorned everything that walked, crawled, or stayed put.

Reactions from students, who seemed otherwise preoccupied, were muted. *Lantern* reporter Jack Keis overheard one student who attended the Cennebration in January say, "There's a lot of stuff going on, but it just seems to be missing something." Keis interpreted this as meaning the era of big functions was over. "Some observers of campus life say that now and in the years to come the large student demonstration will become a thing of the past. The trend is toward a more personal type of concern through the individual and small groups," he wrote.[32] Keis was not far off in sensing where the next decade was headed, but his epitaph for big demonstrations turned out to be premature.

RESEARCH: MORE NEW FRONTIERS

Despite continued cutbacks in federal funding for research, Ohio State had a lot to celebrate. Scientists under the direction of T. Kristofferson, a professor of dairy technology, worked on perfecting low-fat dairy spreads. Physics professor K. Narachari Rao capped a 15-year effort to build a 40-ton spectrograph that would allow researchers to analyze ultraviolet and infrared light for industrial laser applications, as well as help astronomers view distant planets more clearly. Optometry professor Richard Hill tested plastics as a material for more comfortable soft contact lenses. In the College of Veterinary Medicine, researchers led by Richard Grismer began to isolate the virus that caused leukemia in cats, a process that would lead to the development of a vaccine.

The most dramatic discovery of 1969 took place more than 9,000 miles away. For nearly a decade, researchers from the Institute for Polar Studies had been trekking through Antarctica's frozen expanses to map uncharted territory, take ice core samples, and examine vegetation. On November 23 assistant professor David H. Elliot came across a field of fossils from the Triassic period of more than 200 million years ago. They included a jawbone from a reptile known as *Lystrosaurus.* Similar fossils from the same period had been found in South Africa and Australia; Elliot's discovery provided the strongest evidence yet that eons ago, Antarctica had been part of a Southern Hemisphere supercontinent.[33]

INSTRUCTION: CLOSED COURSE CRISIS

After a decade of dramatic growth, the head count of students at Ohio State was nearly double that of 10 years earlier. In the fall of 1969, 45,099 students crowded the Columbus campus. Increased enrollment meant more money and more national visibility—and was consistent with state goals—but it brought with it congestion, overcrowding, and other problems. Perhaps nowhere was that more evident than in the scheduling of courses.

Reconciling course supply with demand had been an issue at Ohio State since at least the turn of the century, but it had now metastasized into a full-fledged crisis. The number of students closed out of courses had skyrocketed to 11,000 from 7,000 the previous year. One student told the *Lantern* she had requested 19 credit hours three quarters in a row and each time had been able to get only 10. Another student told how he tried to game the system by signing up for 32 hours (the norm was 15), listing eight alternate courses, and including two notes from employers. He ended up being closed out of 22 hours. Many students couldn't even get courses they needed for graduation. One survey found at least 10 percent of students said they had to attend at least one extra quarter in order to get the required courses.[34]

Publicly, the university blamed growing enrollment, lack of state funds, and changes in student preferences. University budget director Ronald W. Brady pointed out that Ohio State's ratio of 23 students per faculty member was 28 percent higher than the average for all public universities in the Midwest. He blamed the low level of state funding, which in truth was only part of the problem. An analysis done by the budget office traced some problems to management decisions. For example, the psychology department, which accounted for three of the five most closed-out courses, had shifted resources from undergraduate education to graduate studies to support its research mission.[35]

The problem had gotten too big to ignore. In the spring President Fawcett created a committee of the Faculty Council to address the problem for fall quarter 1970.[36]

DRUG CRISIS

By 1969 the drug culture had imbedded itself into many young people's lives. Statistics were hard to come by, but by every indication the numbers across the country were large and growing even larger. The *Lantern* ran a story in the fall quoting a former dealer who claimed at least 40 percent of upperclassmen at Ohio State had used marijuana once or more. Several months later the paper conducted a survey as part of a series on drugs on campus. It polled 150 students at random who lived in the south campus residence halls, which meant they were predominantly freshmen and sophomores. Twenty-nine percent admitted to smoking marijuana (usually in the privacy of their rooms), and another 19 percent said they used other drugs such as speed and sedatives. Eighty percent of the respondents said they knew where in their dorm to get drugs if they wanted them. The figures were consistent with surveys done elsewhere at the time.[37]

University officials, who did not dispute the numbers, faced a major dilemma. They could ignore the law, which in Ohio treated marijuana possession as a felony, or enforce it and saddle thousands of students with felony arrest records. One frustrated resident adviser told the *Lantern* that staff members were aware students were doing drugs and had warned them of the consequences, but "it's bigger than us."[38]

Since 1966 Ohio State's informal policy had been to go easy on first-time offenders but take criminal action against sellers and distributors. This clearly was no longer sufficient. Ken Bader, the new dean of students, commissioned an internal task force that fall to look at the problem. The best the group could do was report back in February with a recommendation for a stepped-up education campaign and the creation of a university-wide task force that would enlist the support of faculty and other members of the campus community.[39] In May the College of Pharmacy announced a course for the fall on "the rational and irrational use of drugs." Billed as one of the first of its kind in the country, it would focus on "facts, not sermons," according to Christopher A. Rodowskas, one of three professors slated to teach the course.[40] More than 200 students signed up.

MONEY SQUABBLES

The debate over state funding intensified as the decade came to a close. The flash point turned out to be a $238,000 study ordered in 1968 by the General Assembly. The study, conducted by the Chicago firm of Warren King and Associates, concluded Ohio's public universities could save $32.7 million by standardizing business procedures such as registration and scheduling, library cataloging, and procurement. Reactions to the report showed how far apart the leadership of Ohio's public universities and the state's political leaders had grown.

Shortly after the report was released in January 1970, the 10 public university presidents, including Novice Fawcett, sent a 20-page letter to Ohio Board of Regents chancellor John Millett. They also shared the letter with legislative leaders. In it, the presidents said the report was part of a plot by the regents to assert "near monopoly control" over their universities. Fawcett later elaborated: "While there were many useful aspects of the report, the $32.7 million figure had no basis."[41]

Millett had first postured that the report was a legislative idea, not his, and that he didn't necessarily support it. But he then made clear he didn't back up the universities either, saying he had tried to get them to innovate but they wouldn't listen. "There should be a common voice of alumni, faculty and students, but the business of education is to disagree with everybody else—they don't know how to do anything in common," Millett said. Higher education was in the legislative "doghouse at the present," he added. A few days earlier a frustrated Millett had complained: "I am not a lobbyist for the universities, and I am not an errand boy. I spend half my time trying to get the universities out of trouble with the legislature."[42]

All this did not go unnoticed in the General Assembly. Representative Mark Schinnerer, the old nemesis of Ohio's state universities, chided the presidents: "In effect, the . . . report is telling legislators they don't know anything about the universities and should make no value judgments regarding state university operations. The report implies that the legislature should be limited to making appropriations, followed by complete silence on how the money should be spent. . . . You might be surprised to learn how nervous and unhappy the taxpayers are becoming about the state universities."[43]

In a reflection of how low the discourse had become, the *Lantern* ended up being the only adult voice in the room. It criticized the legislature for failing to provide funding support, the university presidents for putting turf protection ahead of innovation, and Millett for trying to play all sides of the issue rather than providing real leadership.[44] In the end the report went nowhere, appropriations stayed the same, and tuition and fees continued to increase.

Student governments at universities across Ohio figured out what was coming and tried to organize some countervailing pressure. Calling themselves Students for Reasonable Fees and Fair Taxes, they pointed out that Ohio was a rich state (fifth nationally in per capita income) but poor in support of higher education (46th per capita). They organized a march to the Statehouse on April 18 that drew 1,700 students from across Ohio. The group won praise from Columbus police for conducting an orderly rally, but not much else. When the marchers got downtown, they found the Statehouse locked and empty. (It was a Saturday.) *Lantern* reporters canvassed onlookers and found that while some approved of the march and others didn't, most of them supported more money for higher education but not a tax increase to make it possible.[45]

Also that spring Ohio State's trustees awarded Fawcett a 25 percent raise, to $50,000. This made him the highest-paid public official in the state, eclipsing Governor James Rhodes by $10,000. In fairness, Fawcett had not received a raise since 1963, but that didn't matter. Critics were quick to surface. Representative Fred Hadley (R-Pioneer) said, "They spend money and raise student fees and the parents blame the legislature."[46] Soon there would be plenty of blame to go around.

SOCIETY: CRACKING DOWN

In the third week of April the Ohio State community joined the rest of the country in a peaceful celebration of the earth's bounty. The beneficial impact of Earth Day would continue for years, but its immediate impact would be overshadowed by escalating violence fed at least in part by the inflammatory actions of elected officials sworn to preserve the public order.

GOING GREEN

In the polarized America of 1970, Earth Day provided a way for people to come together at a time when so much else seemed to be coming apart. U.S. senator Gaylord Nelson (D-Wisconsin) had floated the idea of Earth Day in a September 1969 address. Ohio State's student government jumped on board by early January. President Nixon gave it a boost when he made the environment one of his top priorities in his State of the Union message later that month.

The goal was to devote an entire day across the country to educating the public and building up support for preserving the environment. Eventually, 2,000 colleges and universities signed on, along with 7,000 high schools.

Earth Day at Ohio State began at a chilly 7 a.m. on April 22 with an address from Governor Rhodes before 150 students huddled at Browning Amphitheater. Rhodes was not known as a strong environmentalist, but he said he wanted to do something about air and water pollution. Then he reminded students about the need to create jobs. Nine formal events and 25 workshops followed throughout the day. Former astronaut John Glenn, who was running for the Democratic nomination for the U.S. Senate, drew the largest crowd, estimated at 700, for a talk on pollution. Earth Day closed with a late-night poetry reading at the Cockroach, a coffeehouse on East 15th Avenue.[47]

While students provided most of the energy behind Earth Day, the university stepped forward as well. At least 60 faculty members were working on projects to improve environmental quality that spring, including nine who were trying to save polluted Lake Erie. President Fawcett appointed a faculty task force to study more ways the university could get involved. The College of Biological Sciences developed a course called Environment Studies, available to all students on a pass/fail basis with no prerequisites. The new School of Natural Resources reported its enrollment for fall would increase from 180 to 300. The university also announced an initiative to use natural gas for heating rather than coal.

Before the school year came to an end, a core of students established themselves to continue the cause. The Earth Day Society gained formal university recognition, elected officers, and claimed 200 active members. President John McNeely declared: "We are bound together by the fact that we all love the earth."[48]

NIXON'S THE ONE

Although he won the presidency by a narrow margin, Richard Nixon was not one to accommodate his opponents. Instead, he chose to take risks to surprise and confuse them. Such was the case when in a nationally televised address on April 30, he announced he had authorized a cross-border military operation into supposedly neutral Cambodia. Just 10 days after announcing the success of Vietnamization—his effort to decrease U.S. involvement in the war—he now said it was necessary to expand the war to be successful. He described the operation in nearly apocalyptic terms: "We see mindless attacks on all the great institutions which have been created by free civilization in the last five hundred years. Even here in the States, great universities are being systematically destroyed. Small nations all over the world find themselves under attack from within and without."[49]

Opponents of the war saw this as a betrayal of the promise Nixon had made in a speech six months earlier. Three Ohio State experts contacted by the *Lantern* said the action would not shorten the war, as Nixon claimed. Richard Minear, who taught the course in Vietnam history, called it "foolish."[50] Campuses across the country erupted in protest. The response at Ohio State was muted, but at Kent State University, 120 miles to the northeast, a weekend of protests ended in a tragic confrontation between students and the Ohio National Guard.

LAW-AND-ORDER GOVERNOR

Governor Rhodes and President Nixon were not particularly close, even though they were both Republicans. Rhodes had backed Nixon's main rival, Nelson Rockefeller, in the 1968 presidential primary race. But when it came to law and order, they both sang from the same hymnal.

Limited to two four-year terms by Ohio's constitution, the lame duck governor found his influence ebbing as his second term went on. The voters had rejected his Ohio Bond Commission in 1967, and in 1969 the legislature rejected his plan to restructure education. In April of that year *Life* magazine ran a cover story implying that Rhodes had taken a bribe to pardon a convicted mobster. The story, while short on substantiating evidence, drew national attention. Then in November the *Cleveland Plain Dealer* got its hands on Rhodes's transcript from his time as an Ohio State student in 1932. It revealed that while the governor's official biography said he dropped out of the university for financial reasons, it failed to point out he had attended for only one quarter and was on academic probation for receiving two D's and two F's.[51]

Still, Rhodes remained popular enough to consider a run for the U.S. Senate in 1970. He first had to win the May primary against Ohio congressman Robert A. Taft Jr. of Cincinnati. Taft was the son of the revered Robert A. Taft, who served as Ohio's senator from 1939 to 1953, and the grandson of U.S. president William Howard Taft. Rhodes and Taft were both regarded as moderates, so policy differences were relatively few. One area where Rhodes sought to sharpen his difference with Taft was law and order. At a February press conference Rhodes announced a statewide initiative to combat a crime wave in areas surrounding urban campuses by using undercover liquor control agents and health department inspectors to help local officials. Even though the criminal activity had happened on his watch as governor for seven years, he blamed it on "conspirators out to overthrow the educational system." "I think it's organized," Rhodes said. "Four or five organizations basically are causing most of it. They are the same groups who are demonstrating around the Statehouse." When asked by a reporter to name these groups, he declined.[52] As the May 5 primary approached, the governor's law-and-order rhetoric would escalate with tragic consequences.

LAW-AND-ORDER MAYOR

Columbus mayor M. E. Sensenbrenner was the third leg of the law-and-order triangle of federal, state, and local officials, but not all his constituents felt good about that. The city's growing African American community, in particular, saw his stance as an attack on them. Tempers flared on January 31 when Columbus police shot and killed an unarmed 15-year-old boy fleeing from a burglary scene. Ohio State activists joined black community leaders to protest the shooting, which they characterized as the latest in a long history of "police genocidal activity."[53]

Six hundred people, including both critics and supporters of the police, jammed into City Council chambers on the evening of February 16. Sensenbrenner told them he hoped that "out of this meeting will come a respect for law and order," then went on to say, "We will not make changes just because some militant groups make demands to suit their own self-seeking interests." After listening to public testimony, which included a petition in support of the police, Sensenbrenner closed the meeting by reminding those present that "law and order is going to prevail in Columbus. Without the police department, we would have absolute chaos."[54]

Many Ohio State students had little use for the mayor's brand of law and order. They saw police harassing them for jaywalking and recreational drug use and on trumped-up charges of harboring runaways while real criminals seemed to run wild in the campus area. According to police department statistics, over the last five years rapes in the area had increased nearly fivefold, from nine a year to 43. Robberies had more than doubled, from 45 to 102, and burglaries rose from 290 to 660. Two murders at the end of February spread the most fear through the campus community. Graduate student William Sproat Jr. and a female companion were killed in Sproat's apartment on West Eighth Avenue. Sproat was stabbed 16 times; his friend was stabbed 18 times and assaulted. Their heads were crushed by a bowling ball. As the weeks passed, police still didn't have a suspect. It was yet another in a series of high-profile murders in the campus area that had not been solved.[55]

In fact, the rapidly growing area around campus had become a flash point. Over the last five years a large number of nonstudents, former students, and others had flocked there because of the liberated lifestyle it embodied. Students, street people, university administrators, elected officials, and law enforcement all circled each other warily as the troubled month of April drew to a close.

CHAPTER 12

CENTENNIAL CHAOS

(APRIL–AUGUST 1970)

As April passed into May in Ohio State's centennial year, what had been envisioned as a celebration of the university's success had turned into a test of its endurance. Not even a small army of National Guardsmen, highway patrol officers, city police, and deputy sheriffs could keep order. Finally, the campus was forced to shut down because of student protests for the first and only time in its history. When it reopened 12 days later the question on everyone's mind was, could Ohio State survive yet another round of violent confrontations?

12.1. Columbus police move to clear protestors from High Street on May 21. (University Archives)

STUDENTS: ON STRIKE

THE FIRST CONFRONTATION (APRIL 29)

Wednesday, April 29, dawned unseasonably warm and humid, just right to draw students outdoors. Given the call for a noon rally on the Oval by the Ad Hoc Committee on Student Rights, administrators thought it wise to place additional security on call, but out of sight. Around 11 a.m. black students carrying signs saying "On Strike; Close It Down" and "100 Years of Racism" showed up in front of campus buildings. The rally attracted a crowd of about 2,000. Strike leader Lorraine Cohen told the audience: "Apathetic students are finally getting together and showing their power together on this campus. For weeks and actually for two years, I have said the time is not right yet. Today the time is right. I didn't believe a violent confrontation was a way to achieve these demands and I still don't. We must set up a long-term program of action. We must have faith in each other and come out here day after day."[1]

Five other speakers representing other parts of the Ad Hoc Committee followed. The rally ended about 1 p.m. Organizers hoped that students would join the strike by not attending classes. Marshals selected by the committee fanned out across campus to keep things orderly, using walkie-talkies to communicate with each other. Some classes were temporarily disrupted when protestors tried to recruit supporters, but pickets did not attempt to block entrances and there were no violent confrontations. It was so quiet, President Novice Fawcett decided it was safe to fly to Syracuse University to participate in a function honoring its new president, former Ohio State provost John Corbally. He left at 2:30.

Forty-five minutes later police and protestors clashed at the intersection of Neil and 11th Avenues at the southwest corner of campus. The confrontation quickly escalated into a free-for-all that spread across campus. How and why this occurred is still a bone of contention 45 years later. University and police officials said protestors had planned to provoke a confrontation all along. Strike leaders maintained they did not seek a confrontation and blamed it on overzealous undercover officers. What is known is that at 2:45 p.m. small groups of demonstrators tried to block the entrances to the university at High Street and 15th Avenue and at Neil and Woodruff Avenues, but were not successful. At about 3:15 they moved on to the corner of Neil and 11th, where unidentified persons closed the metal gate on Neil. About 150 demonstrators then sat down in the middle of the street.[2]

The blocking of Neil at 11th prompted a phone call to university officials from Richard Meiling, the vice president for medical affairs. Meiling, a retired air force general, had a reputation for a somewhat "Teutonic" outlook, a colleague recalled. He demanded that the intersection, which was on one of the routes to the University Hospital emergency room, be cleared immediately or he would do it himself. Because Fawcett was gone, the senior official in charge, Provost James Robinson, called Vice Presidents Gordon Carson and John Mount together to decide what to do. The three agreed to ask the Ohio Highway Patrol, which was still on standby, to move in.[3]

The highway patrol responded with 10 plainclothes officers, presumably to avoid the more inflammatory appearance of uniformed police. The officers immediately scuffled with some of the protestors, while an estimated 2,000 spectators, many of them health sciences students still in their scrubs, looked on.[4]

The plainclothes officers called for backup, and a hundred uniformed highway patrolmen soon arrived. They carried nightsticks but were not in riot gear. They lined up at the intersection and tried to clear the protestors from the middle of Neil Avenue, first by arresting individuals who refused to move and then by charging into the crowd. Patrolmen, protestors, and spectators mixed it up in a melee that witnesses described as "very physical," with participants on all sides trading kicks, punches, and hammerlocks.[5]

After the highway patrol in turn asked for backup, 200 Columbus police in riot gear showed up and began firing tear gas to disperse the crowd. Most scattered, but 40 to 60 people threw rocks, bottles, and sticks at the police from both sides of the street. This went on for about 30 minutes until most of the crowd migrated north toward the central campus. Some of the protestors entered Derby and Denney Halls, breaking windows and furniture. Others attacked a highway patrol bus parked behind the Administration Building.

About 50 people had been arrested at that point. The roster of those hauled in reflects the confusion at the scene. Among those apprehended was Edward Boston of Afro-Am, who according to a *Lantern* reporter was urging students to clear the streets. Two others were plainclothes

Who Closed the Gate?

12.2. Protestors at the gate at Neil and 11th Avenues on April 29. The two individuals with short hair at the left and right of the two more unkempt individuals in the center of the photo were later identified as undercover highway patrolmen. It is not clear from the photo whether they were trying to open the gate or close it. (University Archives)

The clash between protestors and police at Neil and 11th Avenues on April 29 sparked a wider confrontation between students and law enforcement that eventually shut down the university. Authorities blamed protestors bent on causing trouble. Strike leaders blamed undercover police. The debate has continued unresolved for 45 years.

The war of words began just a few hours after the incident. At a press conference that evening, Vice President Gordon Carson said officials had received reports early that morning that rock throwing was planned. In an interview in the *Lantern* a year later, Columbus safety director James Hughes claimed city police knew three weeks in advance that there would be trouble at Neil and 11th on April 29.[1]

Strike leaders maintained they did not want a confrontation with police because they understood it would detract from their cause.[2] Instead, they said, undercover officers closed the gate to deliberately block the street and create an

1. Elise Schmetzer, "Fawcett Calls for Order," *Lantern,* April 30, 1970, 1; "Police Policies Vary at OSU, says Hughes," *Lantern,* May 25, 1971, 4.

2. Dan Bradley, Bill Crandell, Art Flesch, and Joel Ann Todd interviews.

excuse for a police response. Their case gained credibility at the trial of one of the arrested students six months later when a highway patrol photographer acknowledged that two undercover men appeared in a photo he took of protestors with their hands on the closed Neil Avenue gate. Highway patrol superintendent Robert M. Chiaramonte issued a statement the next day acknowledging the two men were his officers but claiming they were among 10 plainclothes officers sent to the scene to reopen the gate. The highway patrol released no additional information, and calls for an independent investigation were dismissed by state officials.[3]

While both scenarios are plausible, they are incomplete. They are plausible because it's now known that dirty tricks and illegal activity against protest groups by law enforcement took place across the country, including in Columbus, in the late 1960s. So did deliberate provocation of law enforcement by factions of the SDS and other militant protest groups. But these explanations are incomplete because they fail to fully explain what happened in this specific case.

For example, if authorities had such good intelligence of planned mischief, why did they let President Novice Fawcett leave campus at such a critical moment, and why didn't the highway patrol have riot gear available? We also know groups of protestors tried to block the intersections of High Street and 15th Avenue and High and Woodruff Avenue before coming to Neil and 11th, which suggests something more spontaneous. It is likely the police did have intelligence that something might happen at Neil and 11th, but didn't find it credible enough to act on. In fact, safety director Hughes referred to this intelligence as "scuttlebutt" in his interview with the *Lantern* a year later, so it is not out of the question that authorities pointed to the information after the fact to justify use of force.

It is also hard to believe the mischief at Neil and 11th was solely or primarily the work of undercover officers. The Ad Hoc Committee was a loosely organized coalition of groups unhappy with the university administration for a number of reasons. Although there is considerable evidence strike leaders tried to keep the demonstrations nonviolent, other students and nonstudents had their own axes to grind against the university and law enforcement. The closing of the gate may have provoked the confrontation at Neil and 11th, but the numbers involved mean more than just undercover officers participated.

The details of who closed the gate may never be known, but given the atmosphere of paranoia that built up that spring, the spark to ignite a confrontation could have come from anywhere.

3. Bonnie Schwartz, "Charges Dropped against Ronald Cade, Plainclothesmen's Strike Role Admitted," *Lantern,* October 30, 1970, 1; Les A. Somogyi, "Charges Denied by Chiaramonte," *Lantern,* November 3, 1970, 1.

agents working for the highway patrol who were booked for assault and battery but subsequently released.[6]

By 5 p.m. a crowd of about 2,500 had gathered on the Oval. Leaders of the protest urged them to disperse. Instead, they headed for the Administration Building. About 30 protest leaders, student marshals, and members of the faculty Green Ribbon Commission locked arms on the building steps and told the crowd to leave. People began throwing bricks and other materials at the building. They finally were dispersed with more tear gas and the arrival of 16 carloads of Columbus police in riot gear. Late that afternoon the university got a temporary restraining order from the Columbus Municipal Court against the strike leaders.

Skirmishes between demonstrators and police continued all evening. Windows were broken on campus and in businesses along High Street. When protestors sought refuge in fraternity houses or dormitories, pursuing police fired tear gas. Students claimed the gassing was indiscriminate; in any event it emptied the buildings and added to the crowd. Finally, at 9 p.m., Columbus mayor M. E. Sensenbrenner declared a curfew for the entire campus area. At a press conference later that evening President Fawcett announced classes would be held the next day as scheduled and that he had called Governor James Rhodes to ask for Ohio National Guardsmen to help keep order. "I will have no hesitancy in summoning and retaining sufficient security forces to preserve order," Fawcett said.[7]

Lieutenant Colonel James Abraham commanded the first National Guard unit on the scene that evening. Six hours earlier Abraham had been watching his daughter compete in a high school track meet. Now he was leading the first armed troops ever to enter the Ohio State campus for riot duty. Abraham commanded the 1/116th Infantry, also known as the Riot Battalion because of its extensive training and experience in civil disorders. Abraham could muster only 130 men on such short notice; nevertheless, with the help of Columbus police they were able to clear High Street.[8]

The day ended with 50 people reported injured, including 18 students, 25 police, and seven nonstudents.[9] With the National Guard on campus and the curfew and restraining order in place, the administration thought it had the tools to make sure order was restored the next day.

TEAR GAS UNIVERSITY (APRIL 30)

By 10 a.m. on April 30 the number of National Guardsmen on campus had grown to about 500, but the crowd of students on the Oval had swelled to 4,000. Many of them just stood and watched, but others chanted "pigs off campus" and "Sieg heil." The crowd didn't seem inclined at the moment to do anything more provocative. In fact, Abraham, the Guard commander, later recalled being more worried about the possibility of an accident provoking an incident. He had faith in the discipline and training of his men, but he realized that one overly excited soldier with a loaded weapon could spark a tragic chain reaction. Ohio National Guard policy required soldiers to carry loaded weapons for duty such as this, a move that would later draw criticism. However, Abraham had his own interpretation of the order. Each of his soldiers did have an eight-round clip loaded in his rifle, but he required the men to leave the chamber clear. In other words, the rifle could not be fired unless an order was given to chamber the round, click off the safety, then fire. Abraham had all weapons inspected to make sure they were in compliance even before the soldiers went online.[10]

University officials and Abraham's superiors feared they didn't have enough troops on hand to control the crowd if it grew or decided to move on them, so they ordered Abraham to clear the Oval. He objected, saying it would provoke a confrontation, but was ordered to move forward anyway. Because they were already heavily outnumbered, the National Guardsmen used the only nonlethal weapon at their disposal: tear gas. It turned out to be less than ideal. The tear gas did disperse the crowd, but only temporarily. Like a nest of hornets, the mob grew larger and more unruly when provoked, especially after the gas drifted into nearby buildings. Some started throwing the canisters back, so the guardsmen had to wear gas masks, making it harder for them to see and talk and therefore harder for their officers to control and maneuver.[11]

The gassing had the opposite effect on the students, many of whom were spectators rather than activists. According to reporters, it instilled "a spirit of camaraderie." Many students walked around with rags and buckets of water to help stricken comrades.[12] David Guldin, director of Stradley Hall on south campus, spoke for many of his fellow directors when he told the *Lantern* he believed 90 percent of the students were "just watching." The use of tear gas, Guldin said, "polarized the attitude

12.3. By the second day of the demonstrations, university officials realized the extensive use of tear gas was counterproductive. (University Archives)

of a lot of students who were mainly from the dormitories and turned them against the police."[13]

The outnumbered guardsmen got additional help later that afternoon from deputies from the Franklin County Sheriff's Office who were equipped with shields, rifles, and pepper gas. However, the deputies' aggressive behavior aggravated even more students. As they were chased off the Oval many of them drifted up High Street and clashed with Columbus police. Fugitives ran behind and into fraternity houses along 15th Avenue, and police fired tear gas after them.

Finally, Brigadier General George F. Graf, the National Guard senior commander on the scene, asked one of his company commanders to see what he could do to reduce tensions on the Oval. Captain Philip Wright, a 32-year-old Columbus firefighter, stripped off his gear—including his gas mask, pistol, and ammunition—and stepped onto an overturned garbage can that was serving as a podium. "Stay out here, stay together," he told the crowd. When someone shouted a question about the mayor's curfew, Wright responded, "Mayor Sensenbrenner doesn't control the Ohio State campus." The crowd roared its approval.

Wright then emphasized how important it was for everyone to remain calm. "Right now every commander of every unit is pulling back. I've got 'em back as far as I think I can get them. And I'll keep them back as long as we don't have violence," he said. With that, he turned over the microphone to one of the student strike leaders who had jumped up to stand next to him. Mike White, a freshman from Cleveland who would later become that city's mayor, was director of the west campus branch of Afro-Am. Wright and White linked arms, and the onlookers cheered. "You're beautiful, beautiful people," Wright told them. "[The administration is] not always going to be right and you're not always going to be right. But together you've got it." He jumped off the garbage can, gathered his equipment, and headed toward the Administration Building. Students surged around him, patting his back as he pushed through the crowd.

Colonel James Falk, who outranked Wright, summoned him to his jeep. "He had no authority to be out there," Falk told a gaggle of press people. "I just chonked his ass. He's here to be on duty, not to work as a PR man."[14] Wright was counseled privately by his superiors about his failure to secure his weapon and the danger of promising what he could not deliver, but he was not formally disciplined.[15]

In addition to protestors of various kinds, university officials and police had to worry about criminally inclined provocateurs, who were showing up in increasing numbers. At 7:20 p.m., three individuals were seen running from the Brown Hall Annex. Seconds later, the building erupted in an explosion believed to have been caused by a firebomb. The day ended with 400 arrests and 131 injuries.[16]

The faculty Green Ribbon Commission and student marshals took the next steps. The marshals, who wore orange armbands, were volunteers sponsored by the student government who worked with the Green Ribbon Commission to act as a buffer between the protesters and law enforcement. They convinced university officials to call off a sweep of the Oval by promising to keep a planned overnight sleep-in peaceful. The university relented, and a small group of protestors spent an uneventful night.[17]

That same evening, Thursday, April 30, President Richard Nixon announced he had authorized U.S. troops to invade Cambodia. Across the country, campuses erupted in protest. Ohio State remained calm for the time being, but at Kent State, the announcement triggered several days of protests that would end tragically.

PEACE IS AT HAND (MAY 1–4)

The next three days were relatively peaceful on the Ohio State campus. Picketing and rallies continued on Friday, but without confrontations. Hearings regarding temporary suspensions were held amid rumors that students would not be suspended because of pressure from the student government and the American Civil Liberties Union. Most social activities for the weekend were canceled, including a performance of *The Night Thoreau Spent in Jail* and the Medical Center's annual fund-raiser. Campus bars remained closed, and a 9 p.m. curfew kept people off the streets. Many students went home for the weekend. The National Guard began to pull out its troops, leaving just a small contingent behind.[18]

Both sides used the weekend to plan their next steps. The administration discussed how to take the initiative away from the strikers. The strikers, with some disagreement among themselves, talked about how to make their actions more effective. Absenteeism in classes had ticked up somewhat to 25 percent, but that was not unusually high considering the weather and other distractions.[19]

Sunday saw a flurry of activity by administrators. Vice President John Mount announced that Howard C. Williams, an African American professor of agricultural economics and rural sociology, would head an intensified effort to recruit more black students. Mount also pointed out that three of the 14 orientation leaders selected for the fall were black, compared to none previously, and said he was adding more black students to residence hall staffs. Provost Robinson announced that the new Division of Black Studies would receive $170,000 in funding to hire a director and six or seven faculty members. Mount and Robinson both said their efforts had been in the works for some time and were not in direct response to the Ad Hoc Committee demands.[20] Given the deliberate pace at which the university normally moved, there was probably some truth in this; however, the timing of the announcement left skeptics unconvinced.

Administrators also appeared to have backed off their decision to suspend students arrested during the disturbances for certain offenses without the benefit of a hearing. Instead, on Monday, May 4, they began the tedious process of holding hearings for 53 students who were facing charges more serious than trespassing or violating curfew. Twelve hearings took place the first day, with only one resulting in a suspension.[21]

This effort by the administration to accommodate critics created a split among students. Undergraduate Student Government leaders issued a statement Monday morning supporting the goals of the Ad Hoc Committee but saying it was time to declare victory and call off the strike. Joel Ann Todd of the Ad Hoc Committee accused the USG of undermining the committee's efforts and called instead for ratcheting up pressure on the university.[22]

Although the organized protests remained peaceful, an undercurrent of more violent behavior lurked in the shadows. Monday morning saw a rash of fire calls that produced 16 false alarms and one real fire in Lord Hall.[23] Columbus police reported that a woman matching the description of SDS Weatherman and bomb maker Cathlyn Platt Wilkerson had been seen in the area several days earlier. Wilkerson was wanted by the FBI on homicide charges related to a bombing in New York.[24]

THE SUM OF ALL FEARS (MAY 4–6)

Whatever chance remained of a peaceful resolution to the issues on the Ohio State campus that spring ended in a burst of gunfire at Kent State University on Monday, May 4. The previous Friday, a mob of students and nonstudents enjoying the spring weather had engaged in a melee in downtown Kent that caused thousands of dollars of damage to businesses. Kent's mayor asked for state help from Governor Rhodes.

Rhodes, who was still engaged in a tough fight for an open U.S. Senate seat, was trailing Robert Taft Jr. by seven to eight points in the polls going into the final days before the May 5 primary. Rhodes, always a strong closer, decided to double down on law and order. At a debate in Cleveland on Saturday, May 2, he accused Taft of having a "soft attitude on campus violence" because Taft had voted against a 1968 amendment in Congress to deny federal financial aid to any student involved in rioting. That same evening a person or persons unknown set fire to the old ROTC building on the Kent State campus, burning it to the ground. When firefighters arrived, they were harassed by a crowd of students and nonstudents.[25]

Rhodes helicoptered into Kent the next day, accompanied by Ohio's adjutant general, for a press conference with Kent's mayor and the Stark County prosecutor. Kent State president Robert White was not invited.

The show was all Jim Rhodes. Ignoring the prosecutor's advice to shut the campus down, Rhodes pounded the table and described student protestors as "the worst kind of people we harbor in America. I think that we're up against the strongest, well-trained, militant revolutionary group that has ever assembled in America. . . . We're going to eradicate the problem, we're not going to treat the symptoms." Ohio National Guardsmen tussled with students at Kent throughout the weekend. Then, at 12:24 p.m. on Monday, a group of guardsmen opened fire on an unarmed crowd of student protestors and bystanders at a campus rally, leaving four dead and nine wounded.[26]

News of the shooting "freaked out" students at Ohio State, striker Dan Bradley recalled. One press report described student reaction across the country as "silent, sullen, stunned."[27] A line had now been crossed, and no one knew where things would go from there.

About 2,000 protestors gathered on the Oval later that afternoon. They decided to move to the intramural fields near the hospital to demonstrate against the Army ROTC awards ceremony taking place there. Authorities responded by sending National Guardsmen to the scene. A column of five jeeps and six trucks unloaded several dozen armed soldiers, and six more trucks quickly followed, bringing their numbers to about 300. The guardsmen, later described as "visibly nervous," lined the east side of the field between the reviewing stand and the protestors. Rumors were flying that guardsmen as well as students had been killed at Kent State. The units at Ohio State operated under different commanders than the ones at Kent; nevertheless, they carried loaded weapons and had been authorized to use them. And while the Guard had weapons, the students had numbers. One miscalculation on either side could spark an even greater tragedy.[28]

An unidentified black man with a bullhorn approached the ROTC commander. Assisted by student marshals and members of the Green Ribbon Commission, the participants agreed to ground rules that allowed the protestors to demonstrate while the ceremony continued. Protestors danced through the ranks and shouted insults and obscenities at the cadets, but did not physically obstruct anyone. The cadets kept their discipline, and the episode ended without violence.[29]

After an uneasy but uneventful night, pickets were out early on Tuesday at the dining halls trying to shut down service. Some food service workers failed to show up for work. Others refused to cross picket lines.

12.4. Protestors surround the drum major of the Buckeye Scottish Pipers during the May 4 ROTC awards ceremony. Note the National Guardsmen lined up on the left. Their rifles are loaded. Cooler heads kept the incident from escalating into tragedy just a few hours after four students were killed by the National Guard at Kent State University. (*Makio*)

Those who did cross the lines were escorted by National Guardsmen. Later that morning some pickets attempted to block entrances to academic buildings for the first time. The National Guard swept through to push them out. Some classes were temporarily interrupted and some arrests were made, but there was no violence.[30]

About 3 p.m. protestors and the National Guard squared off in what was described in press reports as a "tense" face-off in front of the Administration Building.[31] Frank Garver, a 36-year-old air force veteran who'd returned to Ohio State as a student, was head of the student marshals. He later recalled linking arms with the other marshals and Green Ribbon Commission members to keep the Guard and the students separated. He watched bricks and rocks arch overhead, landing on the guardsmen who stared back at the students with their loaded rifles at the ready. "Without the crowd control measures," Garver wrote later, "there is no doubt in the mind of the author that more people would have been shot and probably some students killed." After this incident officials decided to temporarily withdraw the Guard from campus. The student marshals and the Green Ribbon Commission members again had to place themselves between the guardsmen and angry students while the soldiers pulled back to their trucks and withdrew.[32] President Fawcett asked for time on all three local commercial TV stations that evening to call for support in keeping the university open. He threatened to cancel all activities except classes if order could not be maintained.[33]

Later that same evening, members of the Green Ribbon Commission met for two hours with Provost Robinson at his home. They told him the full impact of the Kent State shootings had settled in and made the students much more likely to confront the National Guard. Worried that tensions had escalated to the point where they could no longer keep control, they recommended shutting down the university.[34] Several hours later, at 3 a.m., two students were arrested with gasoline, fuses, and a small container in the trunk of their car. Police charged them with possession of materials to make firebombs.[35]

Protestors continued to picket the food facilities on the morning of Wednesday, May 6, as the strike reached its eighth day. Some food service employees didn't show up for work. Strikers again tried to prevent students from entering classroom buildings and had to be cleared by National Guardsmen. Arrests increased. Tensions rose. At 11:30 a.m. Fawcett announced that a student recognition dinner scheduled for that evening had been canceled, as well as the ROTC review and the May Week celebration scheduled for the next day. He asked that all regularly scheduled classes meet to discuss the issues facing the campus.[36]

At noon that day a large group of demonstrators gathered around Denney Hall and blocked entrances. National Guardsmen with fixed bayonets pushed them back toward the Oval. A fire broke out on the second floor of Hayes Hall near the Administration Building. When Columbus firefighters responded, some protestors pelted them with rocks. A firebomb thrown into the College of Law building destroyed a faculty member's papers and personal possessions. It was one of more than 20 fires reported since the strike began.[37]

By 4 p.m. the crowd of protestors in front of the Administration Building had grown to 1,500. The National Guard tried to push them back toward the Oval, which produced a hail of bricks and rocks aimed at the building. Some protestors threw bags of urine and excrement at the guardsmen. At 5:30 Fawcett announced that after consultation with Governor Rhodes, he had decided to close the university until further notice. Students had until noon the next day, May 7, to leave campus. Some protestors jumped up and down, shouting, "We won!"[38]

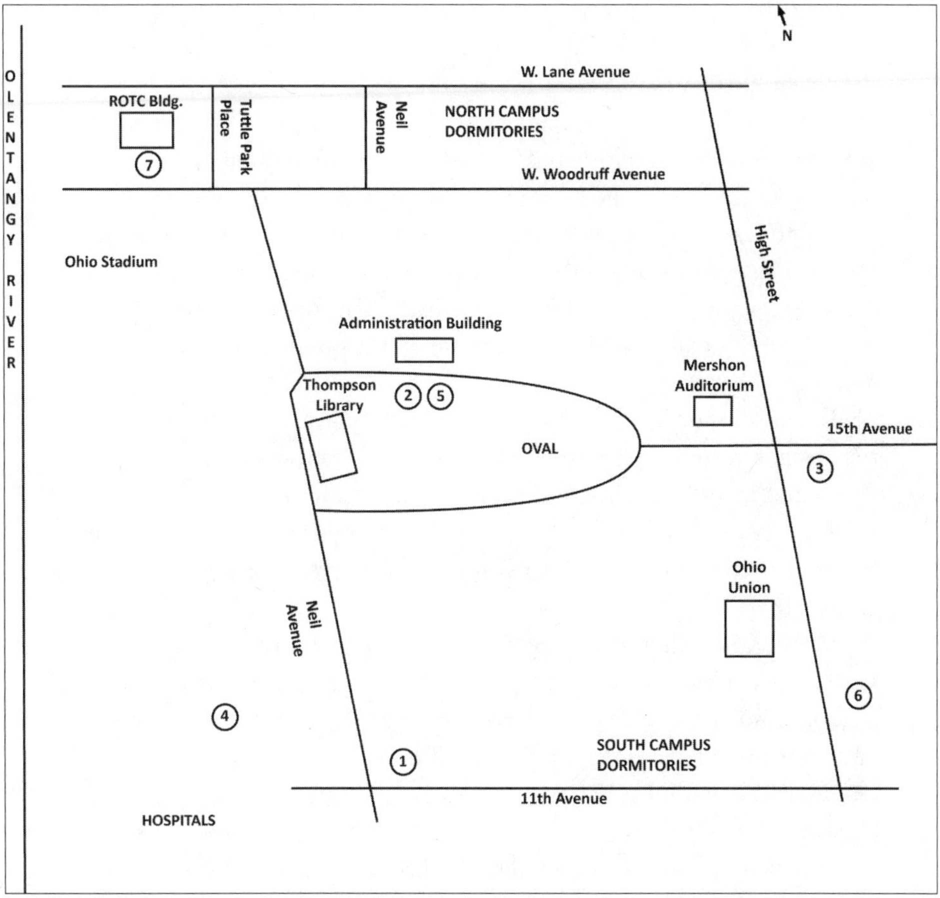

12.5. Confrontation flash points: April–May 1970

Key
1. Neil and 11th Avenues (4/29)
2. Administration Building (4/29)
3. High Street and 15th Avenue (4/29)
4. Intramural fields (5/4)
5. Administration Building (5/5)
6. High Street between 11th and 15th Avenues (5/21)
7. ROTC building (6/1)

THE UNIVERSITY: CHANGING STRATEGY

Closing the campus threw everyone involved into uncharted territory. Ohio State had been closed for more than one day only once in its hundred-year history—and then it was for a month during the 1918 flu epidemic.[39] The university had never been forced to close because of student protests. Despite what some demonstrators thought was a victory, some leaders of the strike recognized that a closed university was not helpful. Lorraine Cohen recalls believing the strike was over because it would be impossible to keep pressure on the administration with students gone from campus. Other strike leaders were concerned the police would use the hiatus when students weren't around to hunt them down and arrest them.[40]

Lantern reporter Mary Webster, who sympathized with the strikers, presented a solution. She offered an isolated farmhouse on land her family owned in rural Lodi, about a hundred miles north of Columbus, as a refuge. Several strike leaders spent the better part of two weeks there, but they used the time more to wind down than to develop a change in strategy.[41]

Meanwhile, other actors were beginning to assert themselves. A coalition of 13 campus groups calling itself the Majority Alliance announced it supported the goals of the strike but not the strike itself. A conservative group of veterans calling itself Citizens for Higher Education announced it would lobby the legislature to expel protestors and keep all state universities open.[42]

The closing of Ohio State did energize the faculty, who until now had largely remained on the sidelines. About 10 percent of the faculty continued to offer instruction at local churches and elsewhere during the strike. Political science professor Louis Nemzer observed that after a series of meetings during the 12 days the university was shut down, "there is more cohesion and more involvement by the faculty than I have seen in my 25 years at the university."[43]

The administration now had to decide whether the campus should reopen, and if so, under what circumstances. Nearly four weeks of instruction remained, not to mention graduation. Ohio State was not alone. Disorder that spring resulted in the closing of five other public universities in the state—Akron, Cincinnati, Kent, Miami, and Ohio—as well as hundreds of others across the country, including Brown and Princeton.[44]

OPEN OR CLOSED? (MAY 7–17)

In less than a week university officials were ready to meet with the Faculty Council to discuss reopening. The meeting on Tuesday, May 12, lasted five hours. The session began with an overview from Provost Robinson. His speech provided an unusually candid assessment of where the administration stood and what its strategy would be going forward, although with the *Lantern* not publishing, his comments were not widely distributed.[45] Robinson began by acknowledging that administrators had made mistakes. He highlighted as examples the arrest of the six students at Prospectus '70 and a slow response to the demands of the Ad Hoc Committee. He said the demonstrations on April 29 had quickly gotten out of control of the protest leaders, but that the administration had overreacted by arresting so many students and by its zealous use of tear gas.

Robinson said Ohio State was now engaged in what he called "tacit negotiation" with the protest leaders via intermediaries that both sides trusted in order to minimize misunderstandings. He acknowledged that the university would need to change the overall climate if people expected a better outcome after reopening. This included making some progress on legitimate grievances as well as improving security. He told the faculty there had already been substantial agreement in the negotiations regarding the establishment of a minority affairs office, a black studies program, and some other issues.

By the end of the meeting the Faculty Council had agreed to explore reopening the university and to deal with the academic issues that presented. Five hundred faculty members convened at nearby St. Stephen's Episcopal Church the next day to endorse a series of resolutions. "The dominant causes of the present crisis at OSU are local university issues," they declared. "Disregard for the concerns of the young has long seemed to many of our students to be characteristic of this university." They appointed what became known as the Faculty Committee of Five, a five-person group headed by economics professor Herbert Parnes to represent them in negotiations with students and the administration. Parnes showed up at the Student Assembly meeting a week later to encourage students to stick with the negotiations. "The strike leaders feel the changes are slow," he said, "but I feel they have been dramatic—not in accomplishment but in the change in the administration's realizing what must be done."[46] While these faculty members generally supported the goals of the strike, a second group of 400 faculty petitioned the administration to protect what they saw as the rights of the majority.[47]

The next step for the administration was to gain the concurrence of the board of trustees. That came on May 14. The trustees approved a staged reopening to be completed by Tuesday, May 19, but under conditions to minimize possible distractions. The conditions included limiting access to the campus by outsiders and a midnight to 6 a.m. curfew for as long as needed. Fawcett laid the conditions out in an open meeting attended by some 1,600 faculty and student leaders at Mershon Auditorium on Sunday, May 17.[48]

PARTICIPATORY DEMOCRACY (MAY 19–21)

When the campus reopened, vehicles were restricted and police checked IDs at all entrances. About 35 volunteers from the Majority Alliance passed out "Cool It" pamphlets and buttons. The administration issued a progress report that included the following actions:

- Removing the restraining orders of March 13 against Afro-Am and April 29 against the strike leaders.
- Recommending that the University Committee on Discipline—which had been created after the 1968 disturbances—refrain from further action until the Disruption Rule was reviewed.
- Creating a new minority affairs office.
- Moving forward with a black studies division.
- Finding a way to put more students on university committees.
- Declaring a Day of Reflection to honor the memory of students killed and wounded at Kent State and at Jackson State in Mississippi, where two were killed and others injured by police fire on May 14.[49]

The first mass student rally after the university reopened occurred at noon that same day. Strike leaders encouraged the 2,000 students present to attend their classes and participate in the Day of Reflection. Also that day, both Provost Robinson and Vice President Mount were admitted to the hospital, Robinson for fatigue and Mount for a serious upper respiratory infection.[50]

At a special Faculty Council meeting the next day, May 20, the delegates took additional steps to formalize their position to bring the crisis to an end. Vice President Ned Moulton introduced a resolution laying aside the Disruption Rule until it could be rewritten to make it clearer. The resolution passed unanimously.

The council also voted to recommend to the board of trustees changes in the academic calendar to address the nearly two-week closing. The changes would allow seniors to graduate on time and gave students the option to take any or all courses on a pass/fail basis. In addition, the council considered a resolution calling for student representation on all university committees. Agriculture dean Roy Kottman objected to the final resolution, arguing it ceded too much authority to students. Herbert Parnes spoke in favor of it, saying in an emotional address that he'd been "overwhelmed" by the maturity of the students he had dealt with: "The past week and one day have been the most moving and educational I have ever experienced." The motion passed easily.[51] After the meeting Salvatore M. Marco, a professor of engineering who chaired the University Committee on Discipline, resigned his position, saying that failure to immediately suspend suspected rioters would "destroy" the university.[52]

The main event of the week proved to be a mass meeting on Thursday, May 21, called by the Ad Hoc Committee to discuss the next steps. Some 6,000 to 12,000 students congregated on the Oval at noon. The effort to energize more moderate students was beginning to take hold. Steve Kling, newly elected Undergraduate Student Government president, counseled restraint. "Everything that has been gained, everything that can be gained, will be lost" should the strike continue, Kling said to a mixture of boos and applause. Then, for the first time, members of the audience began to challenge the more militant speakers. When William Kilgore and Mike White of Afro-Am called for a continuation of the strike, they also were met with both jeers and applause.

The faculty weighed in next. Physics professor Philip Jastram told the crowd: "Don't shut this place down when you have it going for you. When there is a lack of good faith [on the part of the administration] we will let you know. We are with you. For God's sake, keep this place

12.6. Football coach Woody Hayes calls on students to work together to overcome their differences at a May 21 rally on the Oval. (*Lantern*)

going." David Kettler, professor of political science, urged the group to think long term. "Don't blow this chance to build an organization [by making] a dramatic gesture," he cautioned. Even Woody Hayes got into the discussion. Hayes had appeared at earlier rallies, but only as an observer. Now students called for the football coach to say something. "You've got to win together. We can work out every problem on this campus if we will do it in a democratic effort," he said, drawing cheers and some boos. Professor Louis Nemzer spoke next. He pointed out the administration had already agreed to several of the students' demands, then added, "If the board of trustees does not ratify the proposals on Monday, not only will I support the strike, I will lead it."[53]

Columbus safety director James Hughes was on hand to observe the meeting. He later recalled: "We saw the finest session of participatory democracy in action that I have ever seen. . . . It was the only time I have ever in my life seen 12,000 people actually stand there and decide their future and fate. This was an amazing incident in group dynamics. . . . You could actually watch people's faces and see a change of attitude and mood throughout the campus."[54]

PARTICIPATORY MISCHIEF (MAY 21–31)

Most of the students went back to their regular routines after the May 21 rally ended, but some continued the protests.[55] A group of black students scuffled with white students over the flag in front of the Administration Building, while another group of about a hundred protestors headed to nearby Hagerty Hall and other buildings. Members of the Green Ribbon Commission tried to intervene, but the protestors blocked entrances anyway. After failing to provoke a response from authorities, they migrated to the corner of Neil and 11th Avenues and tried to block traffic. They again failed to draw a police response, so they marched to High and 15th. The crowd now numbered about 400. Some began breaking windows on both sides of High Street. This finally got a reaction. About 60 city police and county sheriff's deputies in riot gear swept down the street and cleared the group out.

Police and small groups of protestors skirmished all evening amid reports of snipers on rooftops. By the time order was restored 11 people (including two faculty members) had been injured, 149 had been arrested, and 160 windows and doors had been broken. Police blamed the High Street disturbance on local toughs. That evening Governor Rhodes ordered the National Guard back to campus.

The next morning the *Lantern* ran a front-page editorial condemning the violence of the day before and calling for the campus to remain open. This time officials made sure the National Guard would not be outnumbered. Five thousand guardsmen moved in to cordon off the campus. The weekend passed quietly as everyone waited to see what the university trustees would do at a special meeting on the morning of Monday, May 25.

The meeting began with the trustees unanimously approving President Fawcett's recommendation for the creation of a minority affairs office, as well as the Faculty Council's recommendations for revising the calendar for spring quarter and giving students the option to finish courses on a pass/fail basis.[56] But when it came to the Disruption Rule, Fawcett and the board clearly had their own ideas. Fawcett brought forward a proposal to replace the University Committee on Discipline (which had dissolved after its chair resigned) with a hearing officer or officers selected by the administration. Trustee M. Merle Harrod supported the proposal, saying he was speaking for "the 11 million people

12.7. At a May 25 rally on the Oval, political science professor Louis Nemzer pleads with a crowd estimated at 6,000 to keep the university open. (University Archives)

in this state who own this university" and that he was "unalterably opposed to amnesty and . . . capitulation." After a brief discussion the proposal passed unanimously.[57]

Student and faculty leaders, who were caught by surprise, were outraged. The discipline committee had included a student representative along with four faculty members and one administrator. Now both students and faculty had been taken out of the disciplinary process by administrative fiat. The noon rally that followed the board meeting drew about 6,000 students. They listened to Ad Hoc Committee members attack the proposal and threaten to restart the strike. The rally broke up after the Ad Hoc Committee announced it would wait until Afro-Am met the next day to decide what to do. The Faculty Council followed with a rally of its own where members continued to preach restraint. Professor Nemzer pleaded with the students: "When the university closes and violence begins, it will be our obituary."[58]

The National Guard remained ready but out of sight. Sylvester Del Corso, the overall commander, was on hand to observe the rally. He told reporters some of his men's families had received threatening telephone calls; a colleague said that the guardsmen themselves were "fed up" with riot duty and wanted to go home.[59] Also looking on that day was Lee Huebner, a Northwestern graduate who served as an aide to President Richard Nixon. Huebner was one of eight staffers who had been directed by the president to visit more than two dozen campuses across the country and report back on what students were thinking. The results of their work leaked out a week later. They reportedly found that "the non-political, middle-class students were just as suspicious of the Nixon administration as the anti-war radicals" and the students' "near unanimous criticism of [Vice President Spiro] Agnew was considered the symptom of a bigger problem: growing alienation from the administration and the political system."[60]

On the morning of May 26 the *Lantern* reported the university had offered the job of director of black studies to Charles Ross, an African American faculty member at the University of Chicago.[61] But negotiations with the administration broke down over insistence by the Ad Hoc Committee that meetings be moved to a church in the black community. Afro-Am charged the move was necessary because its members were being harassed by security forces whenever they stepped on campus. Undergraduate Student Government leaders began a fast and a vigil calling for the resumption of negotiations.[62]

That evening a group of 300 strikers who had been camped on the Oval deliberated about whether to stay there all night despite the midnight curfew. Strike leader Bill Crandell had heard reports that armed plainclothes officers were congregating on the Oval in growing numbers. He feared they would quickly commence mass arrests if students defied the curfew, and he pleaded with the campers to move rather than risk a confrontation that would distract from the strike and result in arrests or worse. After a heated debate among themselves, most of the strikers agreed to move to St. Stephen's Church.[63]

The 28-year-old Crandell had emerged as a visible strike leader during the second half of May. A native of Sylvania near Toledo, he started at OSU as a freshman in the fall of 1960. After graduation he served in the army, including a tour in Vietnam as an infantry platoon leader. He returned to Ohio State to pursue a master's degree in history. A few

12.8. Where's Novice? On May 27, strike leaders set up empty chairs opposite the Ad Hoc Committee's team outside the Administration Building to symbolize what they called administrators' unwillingness to negotiate. They are showing their student ID cards to prove they are not "outside agitators." It was effective guerrilla theatre; note the size of the crowd behind them. In fact, representatives of the administration and faculty were waiting at the Fawcett Center, but the students refused to meet with them there, citing differences over the location and the number of negotiators allowed at the table. (*Makio*)

months later he joined the newly established Vietnam Veterans Against the War and helped organize the Midwest, including the central Ohio chapter. Crandell got involved with the Ad Hoc Committee when activist Joel Ann Todd, who knew him from class, asked him to be a student marshal for the strike. Crandell and two dozen or so fellow veterans turned out to be an important part of the coalition, giving it both maturity and credibility.

The following day, May 27, the Ad Hoc Committee tried to use guerrilla theatre to generate support. Bill Crandell led what he called a "search party" to look for Fawcett, whom he said was missing in action from the negotiations. Bullhorn in hand, Crandell marched across campus to the Ohio Union, the south campus dorms, and the west campus dorms, attracting about a thousand followers along the way. They ended up in front of the Administration Building, where empty chairs were set up opposite the committee's negotiating team to symbolize the absent administration.[64]

That same day a delegation of 63 student government leaders from 12 Ohio universities met with Governor Rhodes and the two majority leaders, House speaker Charles Kurfess (R-Maumee) and Senate president Ted Gray (R-Columbus), at the governor's mansion. Melany Stinson, representing Ohio State's Panhellenic Council, reported the initial tone of the six-hour meeting was hostile, but the discussion became more constructive toward the end. All parties agreed to continue to stay in communication.[65]

Thursday, May 28, brought several developments. A group of students and one parent calling themselves Students for Majority Rights announced they had filed a lawsuit in Columbus Municipal Court seeking a restraining order against the strike leaders and a companion suit seeking one million dollars in damages.[66] And in another display of guerrilla theatre, about 150 protestors pelted the Administration Building with marshmallows and paper airplanes.[67]

As the campus settled into a quiet Memorial Day weekend, the last National Guard troops left but remained on call. Security was now in the hands of special-duty local police and county sheriff's officers hired by the university, as well as Pinkerton security guards.

DAZED AND CONFUSED (JUNE 1–13)

By the first week in June, the entire campus was showing signs of combat fatigue. James Robinson and John Mount were out of the hospital, but Robinson was still recuperating at home on the orders of his doctors. Staff in the south campus residence halls proposed letting students go home early. Students living off campus had difficulty getting to jobs and classes.[68] *Lantern* interviews showed many people had had enough. "I just don't care anymore," one student said.[69]

The Ad Hoc Committee was worried that time was running out. At a noon rally on Monday, June 1, it called for mass marches and the resumption of the strike. About 1,000 marchers accompanied by banners emblazoned with clenched fists headed off to the ROTC building, located in the northwest part of campus in what they called Militaryland,

Who Speaks for the Silent Majority?

The term "silent majority" entered the public consciousness when President Richard Nixon invoked it in a televised address in November 1969. Throughout the following spring, various players claimed to be speaking on behalf of the silent majority of Ohio State students. The administration said the activists represented only a small portion of the student body. The activists of the Ad Hoc Committee said the administration was out of touch with the majority of the students. Student government leaders said they were the legitimate voice of the students. Groups such as the Majority Alliance and Students for Majority Rights sprang up to seize the title of silent majority for themselves. They all realized that whoever prevailed on the issue would claim legitimacy in the continuing struggle for the political high ground.

Students and faculty conducted three referendums and three scientific opinion polls in May 1970 that provided additional insight into what students were thinking at the time. Although the methodologies were different, the outcomes among the surveys and referendums were remarkably consistent:

- Students were not of one mind on all issues and did not fit into neat groupings. Nevertheless, a majority did say they supported the strike, but they also opposed closing the university and blocking entrances to classroom buildings.
- Support for elements of the Ad Hoc Committee's demands varied. Doing more for black students had the greatest amount of support. Most students strongly opposed banning ROTC from campus.
- Support for various leadership groups differed considerably. A majority of students did not support the strike leaders, but an even larger majority (75 percent to 95 percent, depending on the poll) blamed or distrusted the university administration. Conversely, the faculty leadership, the Majority Alliance, and even student government had majority support.[1]

While it's important to remember that majority opinion is not necessarily the best informed, or the best measure of right or wrong, these results do confirm widespread discontent among the student body concerning Ohio State's position on many of the issues and very little trust or confidence in its ability or willingness to address them.

1. This is summarized in Committee of Inquiry, 116–24. See also "Majority Favors Strikers in Referendum," *Lantern,* May 20, 1970, 2; "Campus Referendum Results Show 57% of Voters Favor Student Strike," *Lantern,* June 9, 1970, 1.

a takeoff on Disneyland. The building was protected by locked metal gates. The marchers were able to push through the gates, but were met by members of the Green Ribbon Commission, who persuaded them not to force their way in. Instead, the marchers called for an Army ROTC officer to come out to answer their charges. When no one did, some protestors let the air out of the tires of cars parked nearby and broke off antennas. By now their numbers had dwindled considerably. The crowd marched to the Navy ROTC part of the building and got inside after tussling with a group of cadets, but found all offices and doors locked. The remaining protesters went back to the Oval hoping to recruit more marchers but disbanded after failing to do so. A second group of about 70 protestors then tried to block the entrance to Denney Hall for about an hour. At a rally later that afternoon, Bill Crandell and five others were arrested for their roles in the ROTC incidents, even though Crandell was not present at the protest in question.[70]

The Ad Hoc Committee announced the next day it was suspending all further activity due to what it termed "police suppression." Meanwhile, the negotiations, which had started back up, broke off again. This time Vice President Ned Moulton walked out after William Kilgore of Afro-Am objected to the provost's appointment of a white person to lead the search committee for the new director of minority affairs.[71]

After waiting 10 days to make a decision, Judge Thomas Moody granted the restraining order requested by Students for Majority Rights on June 8, with only four days of classes remaining.[72] Two days later, on June 10, a noon rally on the Oval to support the arrested strike leaders drew only 200 weary souls. *Lantern* reporter Bonnie Schwartz seemed to capture the mood of the day, calling the rally an "unfitting obituary" to a movement that had clearly lost its momentum.[73]

At their June 11 meeting the trustees showed that as far as they were concerned, they were still in charge. They approved the administration's recommendation for a 5 percent hike in tuition, from $200 a quarter to $210, and an 8.9 percent increase in room and board fees, from $338 to $368. University officials blamed the tuition increase on lack of state support, pointing out that in the 1961–62 school year, student fees were only 26 percent of the university budget; they now were 37 percent. At the same time, the share paid by the state had declined from 67 percent to 50 percent. To cap it off, the university announced that money for new programs would be less than the originally planned amount, in part

12.9. A graduate wearing an armband protesting the Vietnam War sits next to a ROTC member newly commissioned into the armed forces at spring commencement in 1970. (University Archives)

because of low state support and in part because of costs related to the spring quarter disruptions.[74]

After passing the budget the trustees sent back to the Faculty Council the changes President Fawcett had proposed to the Disruption Rule and approved instead Fawcett's proposal to appoint a university hearing officer to review the pending cases. Then, in a 3–3 tie, they failed to approve Fawcett's recommendation of the appointment of Charles Ross as director of the new black studies program, which required a majority vote. When asked why, a frustrated Fawcett, who was clearly surprised by the move, said he had "no idea." By this point no one was happy. The *Lantern* fumed that the trustees had succeeded in "further alienat[ing] an already tired and tense campus."[75]

On the muggy afternoon of June 12, 4,200 graduates and 20,000 friends and family members filed into Ohio Stadium under tight security. Everyone, including graduates, had to pass through metal detectors.

Officers armed with rifles dotted the top rows of the stadium. An eerie mist rose from the damp grass, giving the event what one student described as a "Kafkaesque" feel.[76]

Antiwar students with yellow armbands over their black robes sat next to ROTC cadets in full uniform, who would receive their commission into the armed forces that same day. By some estimates 30 percent of the graduates wore the armbands in an effort organized by graduate students Rich Levin and Stan Selinger and law student Mike Schwarzwalder.[77] The speaker, White House counselor Robert Finch, took a more conciliatory approach than Spiro Agnew had the year before. Students should be taken seriously, he said, "not because they are the future voters but because they help voice the nation's conscience."[78] The ceremonies concluded without incident. As students and parents headed home, they left behind a campus exhausted, divided, and unsure of what lay ahead.

SOCIETY: SUMMER OF REFLECTION

As the summer wore on, a polarized nation seemed to embrace a more reflective mood. Even elected officials began to tone down the inflated rhetoric a bit. On June 8 the Justice Department released guidelines for local law enforcement officials that called for minimum use of force against demonstrators.[79] A week later President Nixon announced the appointment of a commission to look into the Kent State shootings and other disruptions that spring, to be headed by Pennsylvania governor William Scranton. And on July 5 federal officials certified the 26th Amendment, giving 11 million people between the ages of 18 and 20 the right to vote in federal, state, and local elections.

In his heart Nixon still believed he had the political advantage. His top aide, John Halderman, wrote in his diary that the president "thinks now the college demonstrators have overplayed their hand."[80] And reactions from beyond the Beltway seemed to back him up. Letters supporting the Ohio National Guard's actions at Kent State poured in. A Gallup poll commissioned in mid-May by *Newsweek* found only 11 percent of Americans blamed the National Guard for the shootings, while 58 percent blamed the protestors.[81] Throughout the country a common refrain was "they should have shot more of them." Nixon's political allies looked forward to the fall elections, which they thought would produce a victory for them as the silent majority rallied to the call for law and order. In fact, attorney general and Nixon campaign strategist John Mitchell said as much at an informal luncheon with reporters on August 19: "If all those kids come off the campuses and campaign for candidate X, it might urge people to vote for the other candidate."[82]

On August 24 at the University of Wisconsin, home-grown radicals protesting the Vietnam War used a truck bomb to blow up the building housing the Army Mathematics Research Center. The blast killed a postdoctoral student and injured three others, setting off a nationwide manhunt. The senseless act strengthened the determination of people across the political spectrum to end the violence.

Although Governor Rhodes's poll ratings went up after his tough talk against campus violence in May, he lost his primary fight with Robert Taft Jr. by a narrow margin of 5,270 votes out of 940,000 cast. Rhodes quietly prepared to leave public office after more than three decades.[83] Meanwhile, the state's legislative leaders appointed a joint select committee to see what could be done about the rioting. Columbus mayor M. E. Sensenbrenner was not up for reelection until 1971, but even his law-and-order administration had already backed off a little. City safety director James Hughes announced that guns of the type officers had used to shoot an unarmed teenager in the back in January would be restricted to supervisors at the rank of sergeant and above. Hughes had also appointed a citizens committee of local attorneys to review the police department's controversial shoot-to-kill policy.[84]

While elected officials busied themselves positioning and repositioning, Ohio State's leaders had a more immediate problem. The board of trustees had severely undercut Fawcett's credibility with the African American community when it refused to approve Charles Ross's appointment at its June 11 meeting. Probably more than any other issue, the delays over starting a black studies program had frustrated black students. Advocates of the program had worked through the university process. The faculty and the administration had approved the director, who was academically qualified. How could Fawcett get students or anyone else to engage with him in good faith if he was going to be second-guessed by his own trustees?

In the end Fawcett decided to address the issue the same way he had handled a similar challenge with the Speakers Rule five years earlier. He got to work behind the scenes to finesse a re-vote. John Ketterer, who had helped him on the Speakers Rule issue and was now board chair, announced the trustees would convene in a special meeting on June 19 to reconsider Ross's appointment.

Only five of the nine trustees showed, but the missing included the three who had voted against Ross. Ketterer began the meeting by explaining how important the vote was. Fawcett then described how Ross's appointment had been appropriately vetted through the university process. All five trustees present voted yes, and the crisis was averted. Three days later Frederick Jones, who had voted against Ross on June 11 but missed the June 19 meeting, resigned in protest.[85]

DIVIDED UNIVERSITY

The riots had left in their wake 844 arrests, 19 pending discipline cases, 32 cases in civil courts, and more than $480,000 in property damage.[86] City and state officials were demanding the university pay for nearly a million dollars in overtime and other costs. Worst of all, even though the strike petered out at the end, most of the major issues that had provoked it remained unresolved.

How difficult it would be to put the pieces back together became clear when a subcommittee of the Ohio General Assembly's select committee came to campus August 5 to gather information. Twenty-five witnesses testified and gave wildly differing interpretations of what happened, why it happened, and what needed to be done.[87]

Fawcett testified first. "Certain popular explanations [for the unrest] put much reliance on the hypothesis that the strike and demonstrations resulted from students' inability to effect some significant changes from within the system," he said. He criticized the dissidents for resorting to demonstrations before they sought change through the system, observing that a "network of protests" seemed to be "neither accidental nor coincidental." He acknowledged that discipline alone would not relieve campus tensions and described a series of steps he thought would meet student needs "over time."

Betty Cashman, a parent from Columbus, testified next. She said her daughter, who would begin at Ohio State in the fall, "is not a communist, not a radical," but cared about society. "I can't guarantee she won't be involved in demonstrations here," she said, her voice breaking. "Can you guarantee me she won't be killed?" The audience, estimated at 300, gave her a standing ovation. But Constance Whistler, who identified herself as a student, told the subcommittee that law enforcement personnel were "very courteous and conducted themselves in an excellent manner."

Michael R. Johnson, a law student and Vietnam veteran, described seeing deputy sheriffs shoot a student later identified as Carol Mart in the back as she walked to class near the Faculty Club on April 30. Roger E. Clay, an assistant professor of genetics, testified that at least six other people that day were shot and injured seriously enough to require hospital treatment. Despite multiple witnesses attesting to the contrary, the Franklin County Sheriff's Office denied firing at students. Two other students told the subcommittee they were shot at while running away from Columbus police in an alley between Eighth and Ninth Avenues on April 29. The police denied having any officers in the area, or shooting any students. They blamed Black Panthers who they said were impersonating police in the area.[88]

Graduate student James Thompson blamed the "leftist leaning" *Lantern* for the disturbances. Sophomore Steve Abbott talked about the feelings of confusion and helplessness that had built up and fueled the riots.

After the hearings ended the legislative members went off to write their report. The university had seven weeks until classes started again to decide what to do. Looking back 40 years later at the spring and summer of 1970, author David Browne summarized the prevailing national mood this way: "Whatever hadn't already exploded in the two previous years let loose one last time, like a final blast of steam from a manhole cover. The cover flew into the air, crashed onto the street, and gradually rolled to a stop, and everyone seemed too exhausted to retrieve and replace it."[89]

EPILOGUE

LIVING WITH THE SIXTIES

The storm that roared through the Ohio State campus at the end of the 1960s was so sweeping, it took years for the effects to sort themselves out. During that time student attitudes shifted, the university struggled to reinvent itself, and society found itself transformed.

E.1. An unidentified student lets National Guardsmen know what she thinks of their presence on campus in 1970. The scene would have been unimaginable 10 years earlier. (University Archives)

STUDENTS: TEAR GAS OR FRISBEE?

In the spring of 1975 the *Lantern* ran a story on the changing attitudes of Ohio State students. It featured two photos—one of a long-haired young man on the Oval throwing a tear gas canister at a National Guardsman in May 1970, and the other of a long-haired young man on the Oval throwing a Frisbee in May 1975. "Students Turn from Riots to Games," proclaimed the headline.[1]

The outlook of college students did change over the course of the seventies. They became more conservative and career-oriented and less interested in political causes. The change was more gradual than revolutionary. In a landmark study, *When Dreams and Heroes Died: A Portrait of Today's College Student,* published in 1980, Arthur Levine pointed out that the students who saw themselves as moderates well outnumbered left-wing radicals in the late 1960s, and those who saw themselves as moderates outnumbered conservatives at the end of the 1970s. Ohio State's own polling in the early seventies also showed student attitudes evolving, but not radically. Over time, what made the critical difference was where the center stood.[2]

WELCOME BACK

As students headed to their first day of classes on September 29, 1970, they noticed significant changes in the physical environment. The smell of tear gas was gone, as were city police and National Guardsmen. Cars for everyone but faculty and senior administrators were banned from central campus. Three guard shacks stood at entry points near Neil and 12th Avenues, Neil and 19th, and 15th Avenue and College Road to keep unauthorized automobiles out. Fifty thousand bricks on sidewalks along 17th Avenue had been removed and replaced with asphalt. New mercury vapor lights dotted the area around Mirror Lake Hollow and the hospital. Rumors circulated that cameras now spied on students from the faces of several clocks in the Administration Building.[3]

Also on the first day of classes, the university released its long-awaited response to the demands made in the spring by the Ad Hoc Committee on Student Rights. The report, prepared by Vice President

Ned Moulton, accepted 22 of the 37 demands, all or in part. Many of the accepted demands involved recruiting more black students, staff, and faculty; improving conditions for women students; and placing more students on university committees. Other demands, such as lower student fees and amnesty for the students who'd been arrested during the spring strikes, were rejected.[4]

Initial reaction across campus was mixed. Ad Hoc Committee leaders such as Joel Ann Todd and Bill Crandell criticized the report for being vague in key areas. Charles Ross, the new head of the black studies program, chastised the administration for not doing enough to combat institutional racism. Faculty Council head W. Thomas Lippincott and Undergraduate Student Government president Steve Kling disagreed with some portions but found others encouraging. The *Lantern* noted progress, but said more action was needed and encouraged all involved to continue to work together.[5]

BLACK STUDENTS: FROM INVISIBLE TO VOCAL

Much of the energy behind the 1970 protests came from African American students and supporters frustrated with the failure of the state's largest public university to serve the needs of its black citizens. Fifteen of the 37 demands of the Ad Hoc Committee dealt with this issue. The spring confrontations did prod the university administration into more action, but overcoming a long history of discrimination and neglect was difficult.

By May 1971 the university could point to African Americans in seven senior administrative positions, where two years earlier there had been none. In just one year, from 1970 to 1971, the number of black faculty increased 67 percent, from 48 to 81.[6] Adding black administrators and faculty members opened up new opportunities for them, but also created new challenges. The activists who fought to create the positions in the first place wanted the black faculty and administrators who filled them to remain faithful to the cause and not become co-opted by the white establishment. The white administrators who appointed them wanted team players whom they could depend on to solve problems, rather than create new ones. Some of the new appointees were able to reconcile these expectations; others were not.

The most visible case involved Charles Ross, the man President Novice Fawcett had convinced his trustees to approve as head of the Division of Black Studies after they initially rejected him. Ross proved to be very much his own man. While black activists welcomed his willingness to challenge the white establishment, university officials found Ross was not attending to his duties as chair of an academic unit, such as preparing budgets and hiring and mentoring new faculty members. The final straw came when Ross was arrested for assault and battery against a Columbus police officer while participating in a protest at a local high school in June 1971. Ross's contract as head of black studies was up for renewal at that time, and while Fawcett decided not to renew it, Ross continued as a tenured associate professor of social work. Ross fought the arrest and the nonappointment and lost in both cases.[7] The university quickly appointed political science professor William E. Nelson to head the black studies division. Nelson would successfully serve in that capacity for 14 years. Ross, who continued to be popular in the black community, remained on the faculty until his retirement in 2006.

Ohio State's efforts to recruit and assimilate more black students stalled in the mid-1970s. Frustrated black students conducted a sit-in at the president's office in May 1975 to protest the lack of progress. By the end of the decade affirmative action had come under attack politically and legally, and only 26 percent of black students were graduating.[8] The university continued to struggle with a legacy of discrimination and neglect for the next three decades. By the fall of 2014 African Americans represented only about 5 percent of students and 4 percent of faculty.[9] Those percentages were twice what they had been in the 1960s, but at the same time black citizens made up 13 percent of the state's population. Many colleges and universities were continuing to struggle with improving access and ensuring success for African American students. One area where Ohio State was able to show significant progress was in graduation rates for black students, which, although still trailing that for white students, had improved to 72 percent by 2013.[10]

The efforts of black students to gain recognition opened the door for other minorities. Advocacy groups for Hispanic and gay students grew during the 1970s and 1980s. By the fall of 2014 more than 17 percent of all students on the Columbus campus were nonwhite, giving Ohio State a much richer mix of people more fitting to its international mission than 50 years earlier.[11]

BUCKEYE COEDS: HEAR US ROAR

The women's movement at Ohio State began with steady pressure on in loco parentis, particularly those elements that placed restrictions on women but not men. The administration and the Women's Self Government Association resisted changes at first, but by the middle of the 1960s the momentum was impossible to stop. Women's hours were abolished completely in 1971. Without any rules to enforce, WSGA abolished itself in 1975 and became the Association of Women Students, with an agenda of advancing opportunities for women. These changes occurred not because of mass demonstrations but because of pressure applied by women and their political allies through the university's governance system.

More than 200 women (and 10 men) attended the first organizational meeting for the Ohio State chapter of Women's Liberation at Page Hall in September 1970. They agreed to support two demands of the Ad Hoc Committee: university-provided child care and the establishment of a commission on women.[12] President Fawcett appointed the requested commission, which included women faculty, staff, and students. Seven months later the group reported that although women made up 35 percent of the university's administrative and professional workers, they included no high-ranking administrators, including vice presidents and deans. The commission also found a lack of women in many academic fields and significant pay differentials between men and women doing similar work.[13]

Ohio State began to make changes to address these and other issues, some more quickly than others. By May 1972 a university-sponsored day care center was taking care of 85 children at a church on Summit Street. That same year Governor John Gilligan appointed Ohio State's first black woman trustee, Patricia James of Cleveland. A women's studies office was established in 1975. Kathryn T. Schoen became the university's first female senior executive when she was appointed vice president for educational services in 1978. The next year W. Ann Reynolds became provost, making her the second-highest ranking administrator at the university. An academic program in women's studies was established in 1980. Karen Holbrook was named Ohio State's first woman president in 2002. By 2015 women comprised nearly half of all students in professional fields such as law and medicine.

In 2004, writing about the changing status of women as part of her thesis in history, doctoral student Renee Lansley described the transformation at Ohio State and elsewhere during this period as "one of the most overlooked revolutions on American campuses in the sixties."[14] The revolution transformed those campuses and in the end transformed society.

ROTC: DOWNSIZED

The administration rejected the strikers' demand that ROTC no longer count for academic credit. However, what the critics of ROTC and the Vietnam War were unable to do, the end of the draft did. ROTC enrollments plummeted on the heels of the first draft lottery in December 1969, from 5,137 in the fall of 1969 to only 1,757 a year later. They never recovered, even after the Vietnam War ended. ROTC remained on campus and returned to the Oval for Corps Day in 2008, but not in the numbers it enjoyed previously. ROTC enrollment on the Columbus campus totaled 418 in the fall of 2014 (including 84 women), compared to a peak of 6,917 in the fall of 1966.[15]

DISSENTERS OR DISRUPTERS?

Ohio State faced a quandary after the end of the strike: how to deal with the more than 300 students who'd been arrested. Activist students wanted amnesty. Most elected officials and many members of the voting public wanted the students expelled. The university decided to do some of both. The majority of the students had been arrested for curfew violations. Some were put on probation, and no further action was taken against others. The university did examine 96 cases for potential additional discipline under the Disruption Rule. Of those, 51 cases were dropped because of insufficient evidence and 45 were referred to hearing officers. Of the 45 referred, 29 students were found guilty and 13 not guilty. Charges were dropped for three.[16] Most of the strike leaders were thrown out of school.

Jerry Roberts and William Kilgore, the leaders of Afro-Am, were the first to be dismissed under the new Disruption Rule. They challenged the action in court, but lost. Jerry Roberts gained readmission a year later and graduated in 1973.[17]

As previously noted, Lorraine Cohen graduated that summer before the university could complete its hearing process, but she was banned from campus for a year and a notation put in her file.[18]

Although university officials knew there was no evidence Joel Ann Todd had incited violence, the hearing officer ruled she had contributed to the unlawful acts of others and she was dismissed for a minimum of four quarters.[19] She challenged the ruling in the U.S. District Court, and in March 1973 the court found the university had deprived her of her constitutional rights regarding free speech and freedom of assembly and ordered the university to reinstate her. Todd graduated in 1974.[20] In Bill Crandell's case, Vice President John Mount overruled the hearing officer's recommendation that he be expelled. He graduated with a Ph.D. in history in 1983.[21]

No faculty members were disciplined; however, political science professor David Kettler was singled out as a defendant by Students for Majority Rights, the group that asked for a restraining order against the strike leaders and a million dollars in damages. Kettler, who had advised many of the leaders, was outspoken and seemed to enjoy the limelight, but there was no evidence he advocated violence. The judge eventually dismissed Kettler from the suit, but the ensuing controversy probably cost him a job at Purdue University. He left Ohio State over the summer.[22]

The university would never again face student disruptions on the level of those that occurred in the spring of 1970. However, tough policies alone did not produce an immediate end to disruptive behavior. On the night of November 22, 1970, students celebrating a football win over Michigan went on a rampage that caused more than $70,000 in damage to storefronts along High Street. Twenty-eight students were arrested, and 70 people ended up in the University Hospital emergency room. Irate merchants blamed Columbus police and university officials for not acting soon enough to stop the destruction. Then in November 1971 a drug bust behind a fast food restaurant on High Street triggered a battle between street people and Columbus police that resulted in 200 arrests and $7,000 in property damages. It also produced a new flurry of charges of excessive force.

A group of 200 protestors, including 15 members of the Columbus chapter of Vietnam Veterans Against the War, protested Corps Day activities in May 1971. They shouted slogans but stayed outside the fence of the ROTC building and did not engage in any physical confrontations. Nevertheless, the university chose to prosecute the leaders under a Civil War–era statute prohibiting disruption of lawful meetings. One of the students charged, Art Flesch, a Vietnam veteran who had been active in the 1970 strike, appealed his conviction to the Ohio Supreme Court, which ruled in his favor after it struck down the statute on constitutional grounds.[23]

The final Vietnam War demonstrations took place on May 12, 1972, after President Richard Nixon ordered the mining of the harbor at Haiphong. Seventy-two students were arrested and 31 people injured when about 250 students sat down at the corner of High and 15th, then marched on the ROTC building. Once America's involvement in Vietnam finally came to an end in 1973, the anger dissipated. The campus chapter of Students for a Democratic Society had tried to reconstitute itself in 1971 after splitting from the more violent Weathermen faction, but was never able to generate much momentum. By mid-decade it had disappeared entirely. The university enjoyed years of relative tranquility without mass student disorder until post–football game behavior got out of hand in 2000–2001.

It is difficult to generalize whether the line between dissent and disruption on the Ohio State campus was clarified or obfuscated as a result of the tumult of the 1960s and early 1970s. The court decisions in the Joel Ann Todd and Art Flesch cases did put some clear limits on the university's ability to blame dissenters for the actions of others, but the Campus Disruption Act (HB 1219) passed by the Ohio General Assembly in the wake of the 1970 spring disturbances remains on the books to this day.[24]

Although the 1960s produced an ambiguous outcome regarding student dissenters, the limits on outside speakers removed in 1965 never returned. Over the next 50 years Ohio State hosted a variety of controversial speakers with no attempt on the part of the administration to exercise prior restraint; nor did any of the speakers incite a riot or other illegal activity. The discussion has now shifted to what constitutes hate speech.

STUDENT GOVERNMENT: EMPOWERED OR POWERLESS?

While the 1970 disturbances prompted reforms, they can also be looked at as a failure of the university's administrative and governance systems. Writing in May of that year, *Lantern* columnist Lou Heldman placed blame for the conditions that led to the unrest on remote trustees, tone-deaf administrators, and apathetic students. He also reserved criticism for members of the Undergraduate Student Government, accusing them of being too passive: "They never urged that buildings be picketed or persons be prevented from going to class. Instead they sat in meeting after meeting with smiling but intransigent administrators and sweated each small bit of progress. Well, the days of gentlemen sitting around a table and discussing issues reasonably are over. For at this university, there seems to be no power in reason, only threats."[25]

Heldman's argument, while provocative, is overly simplistic. Student government leaders were able to win some significant concessions from the administration prior to 1970 by working through the system—the most tangible concessions being the end of compulsory ROTC in 1961; the elimination of most in loco parentis rules in the midsixties; and, after many delays, the banning of housing discrimination in 1968. Student government leaders were not able to get the administration to modify the Speakers Rule until the Free Speech Front took up the issue in 1965.

It's not at all clear student leaders would have produced different outcomes simply by being more assertive. For example, the university rejected several of the Ad Hoc Committee's demands despite threats of more demonstrations, including ending academic credit for ROTC, granting amnesty for strikers, and setting quotas for admissions based on race. Heldman wrote that the strike brought Ohio State "to its knees"—also an exaggeration. The strike did put major pressure on the administration and led to the temporary closing of the university; but over the course of the spring, academic and research activity continued and the quarter was completed as the strike ran out of steam.

The strike leaders themselves were ambivalent in assessing what they had achieved and what they hadn't. It is true the strike numbers were swelled by previously apathetic students reacting against overzealous enforcement, but Bill Crandell described the additional supporters as "not very effective" in a *Lantern* interview a year later. "The police, and later the National Guard, were always doing something that enraged the crowd," he said. "It became too easy to simply hate the police. Too much energy was expended that way." Joel Ann Todd acknowledged: "Most of us weren't really sure what we were getting into. We never thought the response would be so great, and we were ill prepared for the numbers of people who supported the strike."[26]

Others saw the issues more broadly. L. Lee Walker, vice president of the Undergraduate Student Government, testified before a select legislative committee on August 8, just two months after the events. After reeling off a litany of things that students found frustrating—such as inadequate parking, the Dorm Rule, antiquated scheduling methods, and large classes—she concluded: "The disturbances here reflected the helpless frustrations of many students, not just a raving lunatic fringe bent on the destruction of the university. No amount of frustration should have resulted in the violence seen at Ohio State University spring quarter, and the violence was probably the result of a few, but the strike was able to continue due to the frustrations many students felt trying to affect the university and its policy."[27]

Former *Lantern* adviser Martha Brian and former reporter Mary Webster wrote in a 1978 retrospective: "What was happening at Ohio State was in many ways unique and unrelated to Kent State, directed more narrowly against the university itself."[28] Looking back 40 years later, former student government leader David Williams said: "I always thought that the politicization of campus had more to do with the registrar's office than with Cambodia. I really thought that the depth of the anti-war feeling was far less than the depth of anti-administration, anti-authority, anti-getting-continually-jerked-around feeling."[29] In fact, university leaders had been concerned the strike leaders would tap deep resentment around the issue of closed courses, for example.[30]

Lou Heldman himself seemed to come around to this view upon further reflection. Writing shortly after his first article, he concluded the depersonalization of the university as a result of relentless growth was a major culprit. "The lack of personal contact between administration, faculty and their constituent group, the students, has led to mistrust over the years that, in some cases, has turned to hatred."[31]

The Undergraduate Student Government elections in the spring of 1971 provide an interesting footnote. Initially, it appears the voters were more inclined to Heldman's analysis that student leaders needed to be more aggressive. They turned away from the more moderate leadership

E.2. Jerry Friedman, the first Undergraduate Student Government president elected in the wake of the 1970 riots, did not fit the profile of his more conventional predecessors. (*Lantern*)

of the University Party to elect independents Jerry Friedman and Jeff Yapalater. Friedman, with his long frizzy hair and full beard, and Yapalater, who wore his hair shoulder length, looked anything but buttoned down. Still, just a year after the strike, only 6,699 students voted. Friedman and Yapalater captured 1,995 votes to win a plurality in a field with seven other candidates. Friedman explained he didn't consider himself a freak or a radical, but offered this take on his approach to dealing with the administration: "With me in there it reminds them of last spring. This equalizes us and then we can talk." But instead of continuing to confront the administration, Friedman distanced student government from the establishment by creating independent student-oriented organizations such as a tenants union and a food co-op.[32]

The following year witnessed the first black USG president, former Afro-Am leader and future Cleveland mayor Mike White. White and his running mate, Matt Dowling, won under the banner of the new Student Coalition Party. They beat eight other candidates, drawing 4,055 votes out of a record turnout of 13,243. Although White had been a leader of the 1970 strike, he ran as a moderate seeking to improve communications between students and the administration.[33] By the mid-1970s student were back to electing more traditional student government leaders.

Campus conservatives began the 1960s in charge; they ended the decade marginalized and in disarray. By October 1970 only 20 people were attending the meetings of the local chapter of Young Americans for Freedom.[34] Nevertheless, some campus conservatives soldiered on,

E.3. Strike leader Mike White was the first black student to be elected Undergraduate Student Government president, in April 1972. White later became mayor of Cleveland. (*Lantern*)

among them future Ohio governor and U.S. presidential candidate John Kasich.[35] By the end of the decade they would be back, united and growing under the banner of Reagan conservatism. They would continue to remain a force on campus, but would never again dominate campus politics as they had in the early 1960s.

Ironically, the outcome of the strike strengthened student involvement in the system during the next decade. The university agreed to put students on all key committees, including the Council on Academic Affairs; it created the University Senate, which included representation for faculty, administration, and students; and it established a university ombudsman to help students and others deal with red tape. In 1988 Governor Richard Celeste signed a bill giving students nonvoting seats on state university boards of trustees. By the 1990s Ohio State was recognized by a team of outside reviewers for having one of the best systems of shared governance in the country.[36] In 2015 it became the first state university in Ohio to give its student trustees the right to vote.

In retrospect it is fair to say that the strike leaders succeeded in getting the administration's attention where earlier efforts had failed. To claim they brought Ohio State to its knees is too much. It would be more appropriate to say they gave the university a sharp kick in the shins. The strike leaders played the role of a catalyst. The subsequent changes wouldn't have occurred without them, but they alone were not sufficient to bring the ingredients together in the first place, nor were they sufficient to sustain the reaction once it started. For that they needed legitimacy in the form of support from a wider group of students.

The students who participated in trying to remake the university in the 1960s may differ on how successful they were, but almost all believe the effort was worth it. Many said it was one of the most fulfilling experiences of their lives.

THE UNIVERSITY: PICKING UP THE PIECES

At the beginning of the 1960s, society's expectations of its largest universities were clear: to strengthen national security by expanding federally sponsored research and bolster the economy by providing an advanced education for more young people. By any measure the universities succeeded in both endeavors during the following decade. But at the same time society changed dramatically, and expectations changed with it. The backlash against the Vietnam War, and the financial pressures generated, made sponsored research more of a burden than an asset. Skyrocketing enrollments strained instructional resources. And all those baby boomers shouting about ideas that differed from those of their elders triggered a reaction from the people footing the bill. Public universities such as Ohio State, with a lot of research and a lot of students, reached a crisis point.

University officials knew they had to be ready with a plan by the time school started in the fall of 1970. This involved not only how to respond to the Ad Hoc Committee's demands from the spring, but how to improve security, how to address other issues involving academics and housing, and how to communicate to a divided and shell-shocked university community.

At the end of August President Fawcett met with the Faculty Council to discuss the upcoming school year, particularly how Ohio State proposed to avoid a repeat of the previous year's catastrophe. He began by discussing how much education had changed during the 40 years he had been involved and how even more change lay ahead. The university needed to improve its responsiveness to its constituencies, particularly black Americans, he said. "When we help them we help everyone." Fawcett acknowledged that communicating was not enough, however, and that it might initially turn up more problems. He noted that legislators and others were watching the university and "growing more critical of practices like low teaching loads, limited office hours and tenure." He asked the faculty to help address these concerns in order to restore public confidence and concluded: "It is fair to say that universities, especially faculty like ours, are on trial, this year, in this country."[37]

In an open letter in the *Ohio State University Monthly,* Fawcett acknowledged that many alumni had called for the immediate dismissal of troublemakers. Others accused him of granting amnesty, or caving in to student demands. Fawcett assured readers that no amnesty had been granted, nor would it be. He said violators would be punished, but only after due process to separate the guilty from the innocent. He also said Ohio State had not capitulated to student demands, but in fact changes were needed in the way the university treated its students, particularly its black students. He reminded alumni that the days of in loco parentis were gone and that the university had to adjust accordingly. It was in some ways a tough message, but one his readers needed to hear. He used similar wording in a letter to parents.[38]

In November the Faculty Committee of Inquiry, which had been appointed by the Faculty Council to review the spring disturbances, issued a 265-page report.[39] The committee concluded the crisis represented a convergence of interests by a number of disparate groups who were unhappy with Ohio State. One group included black student activists who felt betrayed by the university's treatment of their colleagues; political activists outraged at the university's complicity with what they saw as an immoral war and a corrupt system; and more moderate activists who believed the university was moving too slowly in making needed reforms. A second, much larger group nominally was part of the silent majority of students who were generally unhappy about tuition increases on short notice, closed courses, crowded dorms, and limited contact with senior faculty. These students saw the university's response as unnecessarily slow, but it took some sort of action, such as tear-gassing, to prod them into doing something. They were joined by a growing group of former students, part-time students, and nonstudents who lived near campus and who wanted to be left alone but felt persecuted by law enforcement.

The Committee of Inquiry did not attempt to put numbers to these groupings. Although it is clear from contemporary news accounts and other evidence that the number of activists was small, the number of potential sympathizers under certain circumstances was in the thousands.

But the tough question was how or what the administration could do to restore some semblance of order so that the university's academic mission could continue when students returned in the fall.

The committee recommended a two-part approach that involved isolating the small number of true troublemakers while pursuing reforms to address legitimate student concerns. It called on Ohio State to recognize and protect dissent; strengthen efforts to bring more black students and faculty to campus; involve students more in the university governance process; and work on building a sense of community within the university. This was the strategy the university adopted.

Ohio State historian Rai Goerler has rated the 1970 spring disturbances and the response to them as one of the five most important turning points in the university's history because of the reforms they generated.[40] Those reforms began with a hard look at law enforcement.

LAW AND ORDER REVISITED

The first step in the new strategy was to figure out how to restore some degree of order without provoking more disorder. University and law enforcement officials both realized they had made mistakes in the spring of 1970. As one administrator recalled, "We were confronted with something we'd never faced before."[41] The Ohio Highway Patrol, which took great pride in its professionalism, recognized it had been caught unprepared for the intensity of the riots. National Guard officials reached similar conclusions. Over-reliance on tear gas was one factor.[42] Post mortems also identified a lack of coordination among law enforcement agencies.[43]

University officials and law enforcement had already begun to change tactics after the campus reopened in the spring. When National Guardsmen were called back later in May, they relied more on their greater numbers and less on tear gas. Instead of using troops to chase students off the Oval in an endless game of whack-a-mole, the Guard cordoned off the campus to keep potential troublemakers out. Inside the cordon, the university took a more restrained approach toward protests and deliberate provocations. For example, after a small group of demonstrators sat down at the corner of Neil and 11th Avenues on May 21, the university ignored them and they eventually left.[44]

The steps taken to improve security before classes resumed included restricting vehicles on campus, which would make it harder to deliver explosives or weapons in large numbers. The university also moved to make itself less dependent on outside police forces, whose presence had become inflammatory. During the spring disturbances campus police were too small in number and too limited in training to be much of a factor. Consequently, President Fawcett announced in the fall that he would more double the size of the campus security forces and change their emphasis from arresting transgressors to deterring and preventing crime. The university raised police salaries, upgraded training, and named its first public safety director, Donald G. Hanna.[45]

Over the next 12 months changes in key personnel signaled that a more flexible approach to dealing with students was forthcoming. At the end of August Fawcett announced that John Mount, who had replaced John Bonner as vice president for student affairs after the spring 1968 disturbances, would leave that position to become vice president for regional campuses and dean of University College. Critics had blamed Mount for ordering the police to make the controversial arrests at the Prospectus '70 jobs fair, an allegation he denied.[46]

Others believed Mount genuinely cared about students but was out of touch with how much attitudes had changed. Sharon West, vice president of the Women's Self Government Association, recalled how she and WSGA president Sue Packard would dress up for their monthly meetings with Mount in the spring of 1970, because they knew that's what he expected of them. He would explain to them how the strict rules his wife, Ruth Weimer Mount, had followed in her college days helped make her a better person. West and Packard would listen politely, then go and change into jeans and T-shirts before joining the protest of the day on the Oval.[47]

Fawcett announced that Ted R. Robinson, the university's director of admissions, would succeed Mount as vice president for student affairs. Robinson described his role as that of an advocate for the students and said he intended to move out of the Administration Building into a location more inviting to students. (It turned out to be the Ohio Union.)[48]

A year later, Gordon Carson, vice president for business and finance, announced he was leaving to become president of Albion College in Michigan. Carson was regarded as the most hard-line of the hard-liners.[49] Mount and Ned Moulton both believed the confrontation with the Black Student Union during the 1968 sit-in left Carson embittered toward protestors in general and black ones in particular.[50] In the wake of the Kent State shootings, Carson wrote a Toledo businessman that the "Communists have won every round" and the National Guard had been rendered "impotent." Carson's solution was to explore buying water cannons similar to those used by German police. He subsequently wrote he thought such cannons would help "check the barbarians who are now operating from within." Water cannons were not acquired, and Carson left shortly thereafter.[51]

Moulton stepped forward as the administration's main contact point with dissident students. In September 1971 he was promoted to executive vice president. The reorganization strengthened the hand of younger, more conciliatory players within the administration. But the university also set out on a course to deal proactively with other simmering issues.

INSTRUCTION: STUDENTS COUNT

By the spring of 1970 Ohio State officials realized they needed to do something about the ticking time bomb of closed courses. Due to an influx of targeted money and the efforts of the committee appointed to study the problem, the university did manage to cut the number of close-outs in half for the 1970–71 school year.[52] The arrival of the long-awaited computerized scheduling system that fall helped even more. Still, close-outs would continue to annoy students for the next three decades. In 2001 the university adopted a new budget system that made dollars more closely follow students; and in 2009 a truly integrated student information system streamlined scheduling even further and finally eliminated most long lines.

Officials also continued to pursue the strategy developed in the late 1960s of making a large university seem small. The primary vehicle was the honors program, which offered top students preferred scheduling and smaller classes with senior faculty. Although initiated under Novice Fawcett, the program expanded under President Edward Jennings in the 1980s. The living-learning program also grew steadily through the years. However, selective admissions proved to be the transformational breakthrough.

Fawcett and other university officials knew that making undergraduate admissions more selective would let Ohio State, like other large research institutions, focus on students who could benefit from a more academically demanding environment. But they were not able to overcome elected officials' concerns that the move would restrict access and make Ohio State an elitist institution. The growth of the university's branch campuses and of Columbus State Community College gave central Ohioans options they didn't have before. President Jennings was able to initiate a gradual move to selective admissions for the Columbus campus beginning in 1987. It took another 10 years to fully implement the concept.[53]

Not every initiative started in the Fawcett years was successful. The segregation of freshmen and sophomores into University College was eventually recognized as a failure, just as its critics had predicted. Jennings announced in 1984 that he would bring back all freshmen from across the river over the next four years. "[They] tend to land on west campus and stay there," he said. "They do not realize the enormous benefits available at Ohio State."[54] University College was abolished in 2001 and merged into the arts and sciences.

The decentralization of the arts and sciences never achieved the hoped-for synergies, and in 2009 the university went back to a centralized College of the Arts and Sciences under a strong dean, similar to what it had abandoned 40 years earlier.

The investment in TV courses didn't produce the benefits its advocates had expected. Thirty years later, the personal computer made technology-assisted learning much more flexible.

HOUSING: BEYOND SODOM AND GOMORRAH

Student preferences for housing changed dramatically in the sixties. Between 1960 and 1970 the number of students living in apartments soared from 1,600 to 6,600, with even more clamoring to get out of university housing into less restrictive environments.[55] Administrators knew they had to do something about the unhappy students. In January 1971 they announced a major initiative to improve residence hall experiences beginning the coming fall. The plans included reducing overcrowding on west and south campuses, offering more meal and living style choices, and upgrading staffing. John P. Nelson, a residence hall official at Purdue University, was recruited to lead the effort.

Officials also had to cope with unhappy parents. In early 1971 the disgruntled mother of a Lincoln Tower freshman sent an anonymous letter to the *Cincinnati Post* complaining about her daughter's bunkmate, who regularly shared the upper bed with her boyfriend. Citing a combination of promiscuous sex and illicit drug use, the mother described Lincoln and Morrill Towers as "Sodom and Gomorrah in the midst of a brilliant university." The "brilliant university" description was quickly forgotten, but the reference to the Old Testament sin pots of Sodom and Gomorrah caught on. Under a barrage of press inquiries, embarrassed officials promised an investigation and scrambled to explain why they couldn't control the private behavior of every student.[56] Over time the controversy faded away.

It took a while to overcome the negative image created by the rapid expansion of the 1960s, but by the 1990s students considered the residence halls attractive places to live—and leading the way were the once maligned river towers. After occupancy was reduced from 16 per suite to eight, the towers became the most desired housing on campus, even for upperclassmen.[57]

GREEKS: LESS INFLUENTIAL

The Greek system faced major challenges as well. In 1960 fraternities and sororities could claim 4,700 members, or about 25 percent of the undergraduate student body. While university enrollment doubled during the decade, Greek participation declined. More and more students saw Greek life as confining and no longer relevant. By 1970 Greeks accounted for no more than 12 percent of undergraduates, and many chapters were limping along financially. Greeks tried to improve their appeal by eliminating hazing and emphasizing service and scholarship. Participation stabilized but never regained the levels of the early 1960s. Today the university's 2,700 fraternity and sorority members account for about 6 percent of the undergraduate student body.[58]

RESEARCH PRIORITIES SHIFT

The relationship between undergraduate teaching and research was one of the most challenging paradoxes facing large public research universities during the growth spurt in the 1960s. It became even more complicated when student antiwar activists across the country called for an end to war-related research. Officials said no research at Ohio State involved chemical or biological weapons and no research directly involved the conflicts in Vietnam or Cambodia. Nevertheless, about a third of the $16 million in federal research done at Ohio State in 1969 was sponsored by the Department of Defense. It involved 850 faculty members out of 2,700 and 800 graduate students out of 8,000.[59] The Ad Hoc Committee pressed for further exclusions as a moral issue.

The university administration resisted on both principle and practical grounds. Although pressure in this case came from the political left, 1970 was not that far removed from the Speakers Rule days when the political right successfully pressured the university to limit so-called subversives on campus. Many members of the faculty joined with the administration to keep out unwelcome political influence as an academic freedom issue. In addition, there were practical difficulties in defining what military research was and was not. For example, Ohio State researchers were heavily involved in studying rocket propulsion, celestial navigation, and flight medicine, all of which had both military and nonmilitary applications.

After four months of fruitless negotiations, the University Research Council announced a policy that called for the review of research projects via an ill-defined management information system that was supposed to prohibit the development of "weapons or weapon systems whose intended effect is the destruction or degradation of human life."[60] Student activists and the *Lantern* criticized the policy as vague and toothless, but by then other forces—such as the thaw in the Cold War and reactions against war-related research due to Vietnam—were at work to accomplish much the same goal. At the end of the 1960s the Ohio State Research Foundation reported that Defense Department–funded research at the university had declined from a Cold War high of 64 percent in 1960 to 28 percent in 1970.

It would fall even more in the years ahead. Instead, research at Ohio State would continue to grow in medicine, instrumentation, education, and energy and the environment, so that by fiscal year 2014 the university's leading research funding sources were the National Institutes of Health and the National Science Foundation. The Department of Defense share had fallen to 3.5 percent, while overall, sponsored research at the university had grown to $983 million.[61] Meanwhile, Ohio State had made significant strides in involving more students in research as part of their undergraduate experience.

ACADEMIC REPUTATION SUFFERS

Throughout the 1960s leaders and supporters chafed at Ohio State's image as a large, impersonal, academically underachieving football school. The 1966 report from the American Council on Education reinforced that image, and the internal squabbling in its wake did nothing to improve the situation. A follow-up report from the same group in 1970 showed the university slipping even further.[62] Although during his years as president Novice Fawcett did lay the groundwork for some of the initiatives that would advance the university academically, he clearly understood a lot remained to be done. In one of his closing interviews Fawcett described how he had presided over a period of phenomenal growth, but said it would take another 10 to 15 years to deal with the challenges of "quality, balance and depth."[63]

Fawcett's analysis was correct, but his timetable turned out to be optimistic. While succeeding presidents took steps to improve Ohio State's academic reputation, momentum did not really begin to build until after selective admissions was instituted in 1987. It took another 10 years after that to put the associated programmatic changes in place. By the late 1990s the university's reputation had begun a steady climb that continues to this day.[64]

SOCIETY: INTO THE SEVENTIES

On the sunny afternoon of October 19, 1970, a black limousine with a motorcycle escort and a helicopter buzzing overhead sped up High Street from downtown Columbus. It turned left at 18th Avenue, then circled back on College Road before stopping in front of Page Hall at the southeast corner of the Oval. Curious onlookers watched as a man in a dark-blue suit got out of the car and awkwardly climbed onto the hood.

President Richard M. Nixon was in town that day for a rally at the Statehouse to support Republican candidates for governor and U.S. senator in the upcoming elections. He then decided, to the chagrin of his security detail, to make a spontaneous trip to campus. Such an appearance would have been out of the question just four months earlier. Surprised university officials had little time to prepare. Nixon later explained he wanted to come to Ohio State because he'd had to cancel as graduation speaker the year before, when his conference with the president of South Vietnam interfered.

A crowd of about a thousand gathered around. Nixon reminded the onlookers of his role in winding down the Vietnam War and the draft. He told students he was proud of the U.S. soldiers in Vietnam and "proud of you." The largely friendly crowd listened politely. A few students started chanting anti-Nixon slogans but were shouted down. The president shook hands for a while, then raised his hands over his head in his classic victory pose before getting back into the limo and heading off to the airport. Columbus police chief Dwight Joseph watched the proceedings from the edge of the crowd, along with some nervous Secret Service agents. He told a reporter the spontaneous visit "scared the hell out of me" because of security concerns.[65]

While Nixon's visit indicated a degree of normality had returned to the troubled campus, deep divisions remained and needed to be addressed—not least among them the lessons of the spring confrontations and how to avoid a repeat. Ohio State officials had gone through their own review process; others outside the university had done the same but reached sharply different conclusions.

THE POLITICS OF BLAME

The President's Commission on Campus Unrest reported its findings in September 1970. Nixon had appointed the commission in June in the wake of the shootings at Kent State and Jackson State. At a private kickoff meeting with chair William Scranton, governor of Pennsylvania, Nixon said, "Don't let higher education off with a pat on the ass." Nixon believed most university presidents were "without spine—frightened of

E.4. President Richard Nixon makes a surprise visit to campus in October 1970. (University Archives)

faculties and radical students."[66] Instead, the Scranton Commission gave a kick in the ass to the Ohio National Guard. While denouncing the activity of militant radicals at Kent State, the commission concluded the Guard's behavior was "unnecessary, unwarranted and inexcusable." It also called on the president to tone down the divisive rhetoric and bring the country back together. The Nixon administration, not wanting to offend its law-and-order constituency two months before elections, kept its distance from the report.[67]

Michael E. Geltner, an associate law professor at Ohio State, also took a look at the behavior of the Ohio National Guard for the American Civil Liberties Union. Geltner interviewed more than a hundred witnesses to the Kent State shootings. He was particularly critical of the Guard's senior leaders at Kent, whom he characterized as "hard-liners" whose hostility to the students permeated down to the enlisted ranks. By comparison, he found that "tremendous hostility" was not present at Ohio State.[68]

A week after the Scranton Commission report came out, Ohio's Joint Legislative Committee on Student Disorders released its findings. The committee focused not on the National Guard but on agitators and administrators at the state's public universities. It concluded most of the problems of the past spring involved campus issues and should be resolved by the university administrators. But if administrators were not willing to stand up to protestors, the committee made it clear it would step in to do so. Although committee members said they had given campus administrators the tools they needed, including a sweeping anti-riot law passed in July, they also recommended additional legislation stripping demonstrators of scholarship money.[69]

President Fawcett, apparently not wanting to antagonize legislative leaders, took the politically safe position of commending the committee for its "careful study" but went no further. Others on campus were less guarded. Financial aid director Rodney Harrison pointed out that "using financial aid as a mode of dismissal penalized only the needy students and not those who are affluent or on other financial aid." Ohio State's new director of black studies, Charles Ross, suggested that the legislature would be more productive if it focused on meeting its responsibilities for funding education. When Board of Regents chancellor John Millett, not usually one to defend campus protestors, said that 13,000 students could lose financial aid under the broad definition put forth by the committee, the proposal lost support.[70]

Columbus police also were involved in reviews that reflected opposing interpretations. The police department's Staff Services Bureau issued a 33-page report at the end of June, less than a month after the end of the strike. The report stated: "Perhaps the most disturbing specter to rise from this riot is the number of students actively engaged in fighting the police." It blamed most of the trouble on white and black militants, but also cited "the vast majority of responsible students and faculty [who] allowed the riot to occur by their apathy, inaction and silence." The report repeated the claim that police impersonators tear-gassed fraternity and sorority houses and committed other provocations, but offered no evidence.[71]

Ten months later a second study, this one commissioned by the Columbus Department of Public Safety, which oversaw the police division, reached a different conclusion. The study included a survey conducted by Dayton consulting firm Roy Littlejohn Associates. Interviewers talked to more than 1,500 students, police, and community members. They found that 70 percent of white students and 90 percent of black students believed the police did a "poor" or "very poor" job in the campus community. When asked if they saw the police as their friends, only 30 percent of white students agreed. Not one black student did. For their part the police officers interviewed said they felt caught in the middle of a dispute between students and administrators that was made worse by what they believed was "appalling" coverage by the local media. The report concluded that "strained relations between police and students, coupled with the police's relative lack of interest in communicating with this group, strongly suggest the possibility of a worsening conflict."[72]

The outside law enforcement officers who were called to the Ohio State campus in the spring of 1970 had riot training and special equipment but still found themselves nearly overwhelmed by the magnitude and intensity of what confronted them. Even though the vast majority of students did not physically assault them, many students deeply resented their presence. Nevertheless, students drew distinctions between the ways law enforcement agencies approached their work. While not happy to have National Guardsmen "invade" their campus, many students saw them as less hostile, at least until Kent State. "They were young people just like us," one student said.[73] Another, who also supported the protests, recalled baking cookies with her roommate and delivering them to appreciative guardsmen.[74] Ohio Highway Patrol officers did not rate cookies, but they were viewed as tough but disciplined. On the other hand, many students viewed the Columbus police as carrying a grudge against students. The highest level of disdain was reserved for Franklin County deputy sheriffs, who were seen as undisciplined and reckless.[75]

Still, law enforcement agencies did not operate in a vacuum. Some students and nonstudents deliberately tried to provoke violent reactions. Overstretched authorities also had to contend with reported snipers and both real and potential threats of arson and firebombings, especially with memories of the 1968 Lincoln Tower fire still fresh. Roger Meyer, area director of north campus residence halls, recalled spending most of his time making sure fireguards were present on every floor of every dorm 24 hours a day, seven days a week.[76] Police and highway patrol officers incurred injuries in record numbers. Sixty-four Columbus police officers had to be treated, including 18 who missed one to 20 days of work as they recuperated. Ninety-seven highway patrol officers were injured, with two requiring hospitalization. One National Guard unit reported 71 of its soldiers incurred some sort of injury in one day alone.[77] In addition, more than a hundred students were injured enough to require treatment. It is a tribute to most of the people on both sides of the barricades that no one was killed or gravely injured. The faculty members who participated in the Green Ribbon Commission deserve special recognition for their efforts. One student called them the "real heroes" of the spring's events.[78]

Sometimes a situation can get so lopsided, it forces the system to correct itself. Slowly but steadily reformers—both within law enforcement and outside it—began to press for changes. Ohio National Guard leaders continued to defend the Guard's actions at Kent State, but they also implemented a policy going forward that soldiers would no longer carry loaded military-style rifles into campus demonstrations. Instead, they would place more reliance on nonlethal ammunition such as wooden pellets and bird shot. In Columbus the courts and the voters forced a change in leadership for the police. And across the nation law enforcement began to adopt the concept of community policing, which called for enlisting citizens as allies rather than treating them as suspects. Slowly, the doctrine of minimal use of force began to take hold. But first there were political scores to settle.

Although Governor James Rhodes had narrowly lost his primary battle with Robert Taft Jr., Ohio Republicans still hoped to ride the law-and-order issue to victory in the fall 1970 elections. However, a scandal involving bad investments of state money with a large campaign contributor cost them dearly. Democrats swept all five statewide elected offices, including governor, where John Gilligan thumped Roger Cloud by more than 340,000 votes. Rhodes would make a stunning comeback in 1974, but Columbus mayor M. E. Sensenbrenner would not be so fortunate.

THOSE UNIVERSITY BASTARDS

After 18-year-olds gained the right to vote, a bipartisan coalition of activists led by former Ohio State student Alan Melamed and current student David Leland embarked on a campaign aimed at registering young voters in three of Ohio's most populous counties, including Franklin

Outside Agitators

Elected officials and Ohio State administrators were fond of blaming outside agitators of various stripes for whatever unrest plagued their domains. Columbus police chief Dwight Joseph claimed "large numbers" of such individuals were involved as the spring 1970 strike began. Three weeks later he continued to complain of "professional infiltrators and agitators." This rankled activists, who saw it as a way for university administrators to absolve themselves of responsibility.[1]

One way to quantify off-campus influence is to look at arrest records. While some people who were arrested should not have been, and others who should have been arrested weren't, the overall distribution should give a good approximation of the actual proportions involved. According to a university report in early May, 294 Ohio State students were among the 619 people arrested between April 29 and May 1, the period of the most intense confrontations. Of the others, 14 were identified as students from other universities and only four listed an out-of-state address.[2]

Claims of significant numbers of out-of-town agitators were never substantiated. Police sources said these individuals were hard to track because they used fake IDs or fictitious local addresses; however, their identities could easily have been determined after they were booked, fingerprinted, and photographed.[3]

Nonstudents living near campus and others from the Columbus area did play a more substantial role as the strike dragged on. During the High Street confrontation on May 21, a mixed bag of young people, including local gang members, battled Columbus police officers. Of the first 38 people arrested that night 15 were students; the rest were Columbus residents but not students. One of them had a firebomb.[4]

The spring strike clearly was organized and initiated by Ohio State students. The mayhem that followed included both students and local nonstudents. Political science professor Louis Nemzer, who dealt with students and administrators in trying to keep the university open, probably had it right when he told a reporter that outsiders were "inflaming old situations, not creating new ones."[5]

---

1. See, for example, Fawcett's statement on page 3 of his November 16, 1983, Oral History Project interview and university spokesperson Stephen Lance's statement in Milt Miller, "844 Arrest Tally Includes 258 on Campus," *Lantern,* September 30, 1970, 2C.

2. Charles Gambs, "Number of Arrests—Riots 4/29/70 et al.," May 7, 1970, in Vice President for Academic Affairs, Disruptions (Archives: RG 5/6/27).

3. "Arrest 'Outside' Students at OSU," *Citizen-Journal,* May 23, 1970, 6.

4. Charles Fenton et al., "Troops to Keep OSU Open, Fawcett Blames Outsiders," *Citizen-Journal,* May 22, 1970, 1.

5. Fenton et al., 1.

County.[79] While the youth vote did not have an immediate impact across the country, it made a big difference in Ohio's 1971 municipal elections. Columbus's law-and-order mayor, Democrat M. E. Sensenbrenner, was widely expected to coast to a third term. Just four years earlier he'd vanquished his Republican opponent by 46,000 votes out of 116,000 votes cast.

That fall younger voters helped boost turnout 25 percent over the 1967 total. Sensenbrenner's challenger, Municipal Court judge Thomas Moody, eked out a victory by a margin of 1,013 votes. Postelection analysis showed that black voters and residents of the university area shifted allegiances in significant numbers. For example, Moody carried the ward that encompassed the university area by a whopping three-to-one ratio. The area had gone for Sensenbrenner four years earlier. "Those bastards up at Ohio State ruined it," a disgruntled Sensenbrenner supporter complained on election night. "They're to blame."[80]

Ironically, it was Moody who issued the restraining order against the strike leaders in 1970 and who had been involved in sentencing students in the 1968 recruiting demonstrations. However, the young people and black residents who had been on the receiving end of Columbus police enforcement saw the low-key Moody as much less threatening than the aggressive Sensenbrenner. The lesson was not lost on Moody, who quickly replaced the leadership in the police department. Pressure from the courts helped as well.[81] Relations between the university and the police slowly began to improve as tensions from the sixties faded away.

Meanwhile, the economic growth generated by Ohio State and other research-based organizations such as Battelle Memorial Institute and Chemical Abstracts spurred ongoing growth in central Ohio, while other parts of the state that were more dependent on manufacturing continued to decline. Columbus became more cosmopolitan, more diverse, and more tolerant. By the 1990s the university and the city were engaging in more joint ventures that benefited both.[82]

THE END OF THE SIXTIES

Despite his best efforts Richard Nixon's plan to ride the law-and-order theme to victory in the 1970 midterm elections failed in Ohio and elsewhere. The presidential election two years later was a different story.

Nixon scored a stunning reelection victory over Democrat George McGovern, winning a popular-vote margin nearly as sweeping as Lyndon Johnson's in 1964.

American participation in Vietnam ended with the signing of the Paris Peace Accords in January 1973, shortly after Nixon's reelection. Between February and April 1973 the United States welcomed home 591 former POWs. Among them were former Ohio State students Alan P. Lurie, shot down in 1966; Paul Kari, missing since 1965; and William J. Breckner Jr., shot down in 1972. Lurie's wife, Mary, also an Ohio State graduate, told the *Lantern* that Nixon had gotten her tickets to the 1971 Rose Bowl but she had to attend without her husband, who was still in captivity at the time. "But he's going to the next one," she vowed.[83]

By the time Gerald Ford assumed the presidency in August 1974, he was able to declare that "our long national nightmare is over." Ford was referring to the Watergate crisis, but he could just as easily have been describing the events that plagued the late sixties and early seventies, including assassinations and the Vietnam War. The decade left many Americans cynical and the nation's core institutions in shambles. In a 1966 Harris poll higher education was ranked third among 11 institutions, behind only medicine and the military, in how much confidence respondents had in them. Sixty-one percent of those polled expressed "a great deal of confidence" in higher education leadership, compared to 73 percent and 63 percent for medicine and the military, respectively. By 1979 the same poll revealed a dramatic erosion in confidence. The rating of "a great deal of confidence" in higher education leadership fell to just 33 percent. Medicine and the military suffered similar declines, as did all levels of authority. This was reflected in declining public support financially and in other ways, and university leaders struggled for years to rebuild confidence within their institutions and with the public.[84]

SOCIETY REMADE

Many of the societal reforms associated with the sixties are still in place today, including the 18-year-old voting age and the all-volunteer military. Environmental policies boosted by Earth Day have been under attack, but most remain on the books. Affirmative action and voting rights also continue to be attacked both in the courts and legislatively, but a return to the pervasive limitations on minorities and women that characterized the 1950s does not seem likely. Police use of force to preserve the existing order remains an issue nationally, but has been replaced in many cases by community policing and other reforms designed to curb the excessive use of force.

Between 1968 and 1970 young people at Ohio State and elsewhere reflected a dramatic shift in attitudes toward issues such as sexual freedom, recreational drug use, and freedom of expression. What became known as alternative lifestyles continue to be controversial but also are much more widely accepted among the population as a whole. In perhaps the decade's greatest irony, the capitalist system that some sixties leftists tried so hard to overthrow has continued to thrive. The rights-based revolution of the sixties strengthened the concept of consumer choice, which in turn strengthened the appeal of capitalism throughout the world.[85]

Although their parents were rightfully known as the Greatest Generation for ending the Great Depression and winning the Second World War, members of the generation that came of age in the 1960s realized there was unfinished business on the way to making the country live up to its ideals. At some risk to themselves, they sought to reform the great institutions of higher learning. And they helped make the benefits of higher education available to many people who previously had been left out. In doing so they addressed much of what the Greatest Generation had promised, but had left undone.[86]

CONCLUSION

LIFE IN THE MIDDLE OF THE ROAD

In *The Megastates of America,* his 1972 profile of the 10 largest states, Neal Peirce dubbed Ohio "the middle-class society," or the purest reflection of values such as caution and steadiness.[1] The same might be said of the flagship university at the center of the state. How could a conservative, carefully modulated institution such as Ohio State go so far off the rails in the 1960s before figuring out how to get itself back on track?

Of course the university was, and is, larger than any one person. Yet people tend to personalize it in the form of its most visible symbols. When one person is president for a long time, especially during a period of intense tumult, the identification tends to be even more direct. The president is often credited for things he didn't do and blamed for things that were not his fault. Nevertheless, the legacy of Ohio State in the sixties is in many ways the legacy of Novice G. Fawcett.

C.1. A grim-faced Novice Fawcett with board chair John Bricker at a May 1968 press conference. (*Makio*)

RESISTANCE FROM ABOVE

As president, Fawcett answered first to a board of trustees, most of whom were not sympathetic to the changes sweeping through society in the 1960s. He also had to deal with state officials who decided on funding and other issues important to the university, but who were not supportive of student protests and were not shy about using the lever of funding to keep Ohio State in line.

When the trustees hired Novice Fawcett in 1956, they clearly wanted someone who could lead the university through the expansion they saw coming and do so in a way that did not create a lot of political problems for them. They got what they were looking for, at least initially. Between 1956 and 1972, when Fawcett retired, enrollment more than doubled, the value of campus buildings quadrupled, and the value of sponsored research contracts increased more than 10 times. The master plan that he initiated allowed Ohio State to grow in an orderly way while preserving green space and leaving room for future expansion. Fawcett also managed the corresponding growth in finances, despite unsteady state support, and left the university with a balanced budget and free of any financial misdeeds.[2]

Fawcett went out of his way to make sure he didn't surprise his trustees. They did not always return the favor, publicly rejecting his recommendations regarding the Speakers Rule in 1965, the remedy in the David Green case in 1968, and the hiring of the first head of black studies in 1970. His critics faulted him for not being more assertive with the board, particularly for not falling on his sword to defend academic freedom against the Speakers Rule in the 1961–62 controversies. But given the attitude and composition of the board at the time, it is difficult to see how that would have changed anyone's mind. Fawcett could have resigned in protest, but it was unlikely the board would appoint a successor who would oppose its position on the matter.

However, Fawcett was able to turn the board around on a number of critical points. He finessed a solution that got rid of the Speakers Rule for good in 1965, with minimal recriminations; and he engineered the approval of Charles Ross as director of the black studies program after the board had turned it down. Fawcett also protected the university in ways the public did not see. Probably the most critical incident was when the Faculty Council declined the 1961 Rose Bowl invitation.

The trustees were under enormous pressure from the community to overturn the unpopular decision. Working behind the scenes, Fawcett was able to keep the issue from even coming up in a public board meeting. Had the board reversed the Faculty Council, it would have humiliated the faculty and been a major blow to the university's academic reputation.[3]

Ideally, when a governing board does its job, it supports the president when he is on the right track and nudges him in a different direction when he starts to go astray. Instead, Ohio State's trustees for most of the 1960s did the opposite. Older, richer, whiter, and more conservative than most Ohioans, they were not sympathetic to what others saw as needed reforms. They often resisted Fawcett's attempts to involve people who historically had been on the fringes and pushed him further into a repressive strategy that contributed to the eruption that followed.

THE FIRE DOWN BELOW

Of all the issues Fawcett confronted in his 16-year tenure, his relationship with the students generated the most criticism. "Every progressive thing that has come from this university in the last ten years was student initiated. It is a shame that students have to do the thinking and planning for the administration," said Undergraduate Student Government spokesperson F. Eugene Garver, speaking to a special legislative committee in the summer of 1970.[4] Garver was exaggerating, but not by much. In many ways the students served as Ohio State's social conscience. Most of the reforms on campus—the end of compulsory ROTC, discrimination against black people, and restrictions on women and free speech—came from the efforts of activists both inside and outside student government. Administrative approval was necessary to make them reality, but that approval was often tardy or given only grudgingly.

Critics, especially the *Lantern,* consistently challenged Fawcett about his dealings with students. His answer was always the same: he met with students often, as much as his busy schedule would allow. He accommodated as many meeting requests as he could.[5] However, Fawcett seldom initiated dialogue on his own, nor was he fond of meeting with large groups of students directly. As a result the impressions of those who met with him varied a great deal. Some—usually those who were involved with him most directly—found him cordial and responsive to new ideas. Many others thought him aloof or out of touch.

Looking for a pattern over Fawcett's long tenure reveals a mixture of good intentions, self-restraint, paternalism, and hubris from both Fawcett and his lieutenants. During the first seven years of the 1960s, the administration took a fairly laid-back approach to protestors and protests. The Rose Bowl controversy and the jaywalking demonstration were allowed to burn themselves out with minimal arrests and property damage. Although Fawcett was dismissive regarding the Free Speech Front's position on the Speakers Rule, his decision to not expel protestors from the Administration Building by force, as had been done at Berkeley, contributed to a peaceful resolution of the issue.

By the spring of 1968 the administration had changed its approach. It cracked down on antiwar protests and on the participants in the Administration Building lock-in. In both instances small groups of students deliberately pushed toward a confrontation, but in the case of the Administration Building takeover the response was disproportionate to the transgression. Although Fawcett was under pressure from his board, these actions ruptured whatever rapport he had with the black community and sowed the seeds for what would follow.

Throughout his tenure Fawcett seemed to exhibit a certain disdain for anyone in the university who challenged his decisions. He made no secret of his dislike for Vice President Fred Heimberger and Alumni Association head Jack Fullen, who were vocal critics but also raised legitimate issues.[6] This pattern also was evident in his attitude toward student leaders. For example, when recognizing student leadership in the early and midsixties, Fawcett always looked to the more conservative, "responsible" students. Student government leaders and activists who pushed more aggressively for change were often marginalized by the administration. In 1967 the administration snubbed student body president Tim Neustadt and constitutional convention chair Alan Melamed in the nominations for the annual outstanding student awards. The omission was so obvious it drew a rare rebuke from the *Lantern*. Also, Fawcett's dismissive letter of April 27, 1970, in response to the student strike helped spark the Student Assembly to support the strike.[7]

After the 1970 spring disturbances Fawcett set up a committee of students to advise him on policy, but he deliberately excluded strike leaders and more moderate elected student government leaders. When asked why, he said: "I wanted a balanced viewpoint, people with institutional concerns—not political concerns."[8] He later backed off that statement, but it nevertheless reflected his continued aggravation. In a confidential memo to his cabinet in September 1970, Fawcett stated he would not back efforts to place students on the boards of Ohio's public universities. He wrote: "Because of what I learned on this campus in recent weeks and months, I am not giving my personal support to such involvement."[9] In other words, he would oppose giving additional voice to 48,000 students because of the actions of what he described as a small minority of them.

Fawcett's pique continued even after the immediate anxiety over the spring of 1970 had passed. In a 1972 interview with Barbara Walters on the *Today* show, he expressed frustration with students seeking to become more involved in decisions he believed they were not qualified to make. Even in a 1983 interview for Ohio State's Oral History Project, Fawcett continued to insist that the activists represented no more than 5 percent of the students, when the evidence showed majority student support for many of their positions.[10]

At a large university such as Ohio State, a capable team of lieutenants can go a long way in ameliorating lack of personal contact with the president. Fawcett's own lieutenants proved to be a mixed bag. He gave them a long leash, but that didn't always produce good results. Provost John Corbally was able to help Fawcett engage students in a number of ways. Executive Vice President Ned Moulton did, too, but Moulton confessed he thought Fawcett was too indulgent with some of his weaker subordinates.[11] Fawcett kept John Bonner as his executive dean for student relations for seven years even though Bonner did not have good relations with many student leaders. Fawcett finally replaced Bonner with John Mount, who many student leaders believed meant well but was fundamentally out of touch. Mount was reassigned after two years. Vice President Gordon Carson, who was strong on financial analysis but had a visceral dislike of student protestors, served for 15 of Fawcett's 16 years. Ironically, the administrator who did get removed rather quickly, minority affairs coordinator William Conley, was the one person who could have helped Fawcett most in dealing with disaffected black students at a critical time.

THE MAN IN THE MIDDLE

Those who knew Fawcett best described him as a warm and caring man who possessed both a commitment to principal and a sense of humor that the public rarely saw.[12] For example, daughter Jane recalled her father telling her he expected her to attend Columbus public schools even though they could afford to send her elsewhere because that was the right thing to do. *Lantern* columnist Lou Heldman, often a critic of the administration, expressed a similar view when Fawcett let his guard down in a pre-retirement interview in 1971. "Though we have often disagreed, I admire the dignity with which he has served and the grace he has projected in his bow from office," Heldman wrote.[13] But close friends and colleagues also described him as cautious and formal. Richard Weaver, who as assistant dean of men attended a number of social functions with Fawcett, recalled how he was polite and personable but always in control.[14] He'd hold a drink in his hand, for example, but sip it only occasionally. The line between dignified and aloof is sometimes blurry, and Fawcett's role became more difficult as tensions rose toward the end of decade.

Fawcett clearly was most comfortable with managing the physical aspect of the huge expansion of the university. While he did an exceptional job of it for the most part, he also faced challenges. Roger Meyer worked as an area residence hall director for Milton Overholt during this period. Overholt, the associate dean of student relations, often played golf with the president. Meyer remembers Overholt saying that Fawcett often complained he didn't have enough information to make good decisions, which is why he supported efforts to upgrade management information systems in the midsixties.[15] That also explains the university's interest in polling after the May 1970 strike.[16] Computers were no doubt helpful to those making decisions about buildings or finances or enrollment projections, but they could not tell an administrator when to sit down face-to-face with disaffected students or when to call in the police.

A comparison of how university presidents in the era coped with unrest shows that Fawcett was relatively insular in dealing with students. However, the connection between the presidents' actions (or inaction) and student unrest is less obvious. Some presidents were much more open to meeting with students on an informal basis. Some of them seemed to succeed in heading off more violent confrontations; others did not. Fred Harrington, president of the University of Wisconsin system, represented everything critics said Novice Fawcett did not. Harrington, a liberal, was a strong defender of academic freedom at one of the nation's most highly regarded campuses. Ohio State student leaders chose Harrington to speak at their 1962 symposium on the future of the university, where he warned against the dangers of an administration isolated from students and faculty. But eight years later Harrington found himself squeezed between campus radicals and very conservative legislators and was pushed out amid an ugly spiral of campus violence.[17]

The experiences of similar-sized campuses in states bordering Ohio were equally unpredictable. President Robben Fleming's engagement with students at the University of Michigan was widely credited with keeping that campus free of violence in the same period.[18] While the presidents of Michigan State and Penn State took a much tougher line against protestors, their campuses did manage to avoid the level of violent protest seen at Ohio State and Wisconsin.[19] On neighboring Indiana's bucolic Bloomington campus, the governor and the legislature took the hard line, but the administration was able to avoid a violent spring after the president and chancellor met with 4,000 students after the May 1970 Kent State shootings.[20]

Kent State president Robert White had earned praise from Ohio lawmakers for his crackdown on student protests in the spring of 1969, but a year later he lost control of his campus.[21] Phillip Shriver, president of Miami University, and Ohio University president Claude Sowle took pride in their ability to relate to their students. Protests on both campuses in the spring of 1970 fell short of the type of violence that swept Ohio State during that same time. Then, after the shootings at Kent State, Schriver and Sowle met directly with students en masse to plead for continued nonviolence. They were not successful, and both campuses had to shut down.[22]

Scholars who study this period have found that local issues were more important on each campus than any other influences. One study of unrest at Southern Illinois University concluded: "There is no dominant narrative that fits every case; what local stories tell us is that the supposed anomalies *are* the story."[23] What stands out about Ohio State is the unusually high level of violence that preceded the protests, even before Cambodia and Kent State. No other large institution in the country that spring faced the intensity or magnitude of the confrontations at Ohio State from April 29 to May 1.[24]

After the Kent State shootings on May 4, national and international events overwhelmed local issues, especially in Ohio, where students understandably took the tragedy personally. It is unlikely anything Fawcett could have done or said would have prevented an eruption at that point. But it is fair to conclude that before then, the approach taken by the president, the rest of the university administration, and law enforcement officers further antagonized an already alienated student body. Although Ohio State avoided a catastrophe the magnitude of Kent State's, Fawcett was less than successful in anticipating and addressing the changing expectations of the student population.

Fawcett saw himself as a middle-of-the-roader who could steer the university on an orderly course; but when the middle shifted more rapidly and dramatically than anyone had anticipated, he struggled to keep up. L. Lee Walker, vice president of the Undergraduate Student Government during the 1970–71 school year, described Fawcett this way: "As an administrator he was very capable, perhaps one of the best; but one problem he had was understanding what students wanted or needed."[25] Once jarred into action, and only after a great deal of unnecessary turmoil, he did make adjustments that proved to be beneficial and left the university positioned to be a better institution.

CHANGING OF THE GUARD

On March 7, 1971, Novice Fawcett announced he intended to retire at age 63. He had served the third-longest tenure in both Ohio State and Big Ten history. For the last two years he'd been battling health issues, not to mention the stress of the 1970 spring disturbances.

Harold Enarson took the reins as Ohio State's ninth president on September 1, 1972. His selection showed that even the board of trustees had finally recognized that times had changed. Enarson's biographer described the campus mood when the new president arrived as "strangely confused" and the attitude of the student body as "sullenly acquiescent." Enarson pledged to restore civility and self-confidence to the campus.[26]

Enarson, a native of Iowa, brought to the table two things Fawcett lacked. He was the first Ohio State president to have earned a Ph.D.

(his degree in government was from American University in Washington, D.C.), which reflected the desire of the faculty and the trustees to improve the university's academic standing after a period of nonstop physical growth. Furthermore, Enarson had a reputation of being able to connect with students. As president of Cleveland State University immediately before coming to Ohio State, he was credited with keeping that campus open while most other Ohio public universities were forced to shut down in the spring of 1970.[27]

Enarson would endure his share of controversies and failures in his seven years as president, but students, faculty, administrators, and trustees realized that they would have to resolve their differences and move forward. The Ohio State that emerged from the 1960s was more inclusive, more open, less restrictive, and less paternalistic than the institution at the beginning of the decade. Ultimately, the center held, not by repressing change but by embracing it in smaller doses—perhaps too slowly for some and too rapidly for others, but change nonetheless. This allowed the university to channel the energy of the sixties into a more constructive path that moved it closer to the fulfillment of its lofty promise. The outcome serves as a tribute to Ohio State's ability to adapt to a changing world. It should also serve as a warning of the dangers of institutional hubris.

NOTES

NOTES TO PROLOGUE

1. Raimund Goerler, *The Ohio State University: An Illustrated History* (Columbus: Ohio State University Press, 2011), 4–7.

2. Francis P. Weisenburger, *History of the Ohio State University: The Fawcett Years, 1956–1972* (Columbus: Ohio State University Press, 1975), 1–9.

3. Goerler, *Illustrated History,* 99–101.

4. Office of the Registrar, "Annual Report of the Registrar and University Examiner" (Columbus: Ohio State University, 1960), 68–72.

5. "The 'Soaring Sixties' at OSU," *Lantern,* February 25, 1960, 1.

NOTES TO CHAPTER 1

1. Women's Self Government Association, "About Buckeye Coeds, a Handbook for the Women Students, 1958–1959" (University Archives [hereafter Archives]), 2–3.

2. For an overview of women at Ohio State and other campuses in this period, see Renee Nicole Lansley, "College Women or College Girls? Gender, Sexuality and in Loco Parentis on Campus," Ph.D. thesis (Columbus: Ohio State University, 2004), 108–57.

3. Dorothy Sarna, "Rules for Women Are Concern of 'Standards,'" *Lantern,* October 25, 1960, 4.

4. Tom Hopkins, "Revised Apartment Rule Approved by CSA," *Lantern,* June 1, 1961, 1.

5. James E. Pollard, *Military Training in the Land-Grant Colleges and Universities* (Washington, D.C.: Association of State Universities and Land-Grant Colleges, 1964), 3–8, 28–29.

6. "ROTC Decision Is Delayed," *Ohio State University Monthly* (hereafter *OSU Monthly*), May 1961, 16.

7. "More and More Delays," *Lantern,* September 26, 1960, 2.

8. Tom Hopkins, "Senate Plans ROTC Demonstration," *Lantern,* April 21, 1961, 1; Phil Moots interview.

9. "Trustees List Alternatives for Students Who Drop ROTC," *Lantern,* June 19, 1961, 1.

10. "'Remove Restrictive Clauses . . . or Else,'" *Lantern,* January 5, 1961, 1.

11. John Mount interview, January 17, 2013.

12. "'Remember, Darling,'" *Lantern,* October 24, 1960, 2.

13. The first official attempt to count black students did not occur until 1967. See "Frustrated Black Students" in chapter 9.

14. Raimund Goerler, *The Ohio State University: An Illustrated History* (Columbus: Ohio State University Press, 2011), 160–62.

15. "Non-Discriminatory Policy Adopted," *OSU Monthly,* September 1960, 13.

16. "Fawcett Defends Police in Student Picket Case," *Lantern,* April 20, 1961, 1.

17. Judy Taylor and Denise Goodman, "Senate Scores Police Action against Von Braun Pickets," *Lantern,* April 7, 1961, 1.

18. "Fawcett Defends Police in Student Picket Case," *Lantern,* April 20, 1961, 1; Letter from Milton Overholt to Charles Gambs, April 5, 1961, in Office of Student Affairs and Executive Dean, Picketing, Students, 1961–62 (Archives: RG 9/a/17).

19. "Police Get Training on Handling Pickets," *Lantern,* April 26, 1961, 1.

20. Francis P. Weisenburger, *History of the Ohio State University: The Fawcett Years, 1956–1972* (Columbus: Ohio State University Press, 1975), 148–53; Educational Affairs Committee, Student Senate, "The Speakers' Rule Controversy at Ohio State," 1965 (Archives).

21. Randy Wright and Ben Kline, "U.S. Could Never Win War with Russia, Mandel Says," *Lantern,* April 14, 1961, 1.

22. "Guthrie Says Student Apathy Declining on College Campuses," *Lantern,* April 4, 1961, 1.

23. "Gone Is the Apathy," *OSU Monthly,* May 1961, 12.

24. William Fulwider, "OSU Students Free to Voice Controversial Opinions," *Dispatch,* April 2, 1961, 27A.

25. Hugh Davis Graham and Nancy Diamond, *The Rise of American Research Universities: Elites and Challengers in the Postwar Era* (Baltimore: Johns Hopkins University Press, 1997), 43–44, 83.

26. Bernard Berelson, *Graduate Education in the United States* (New York: McGraw-Hill, 1960), 280–81.

27. "Ohio State Research Grows," *Lantern,* May 26, 1961 (progress edition), 7.

28. Goerler, *Illustrated History,* 120–21.

29. "OSU Is Fifth in Enrollment," *Lantern,* December 5, 1960, 5.

30. Bram Dijkstra, "Students Criticize Teaching on Campus," *Lantern,* November 9, 1960, 2.

31. "951 Students Dropped for Low Grades," *Lantern,* January 9, 1961, 1.

32. Cited in "Scholastic Standards Are Effective," *OSU Monthly,* February 1961, 7.

33. "Trustees Bar Low Freshmen in Fall," *Lantern,* October 11, 1960, 1.

34. Gary Reynolds, "'Baby Boom' to Hit OSU Says Dean," *Lantern,* February 25, 1960, 7.

35. Judy McCluskey, "Cottrell Lists Important 'Ifs' in Education Future," *Lantern,* February 25, 1960, 3.

36. "Nixon Beats Kennedy in Big 10 Vote," *Lantern,* November 2, 1960, 1.

37. Judy Taylor, "Resolution Asking Unbiased Campaign Reports Defeated," *Lantern,* October 28, 1960, 1.

38. "The Kennedy Victory—What It Means," *Lantern,* November 10, 1960, 1.

39. "Boorstin Warns of 'Pseudo World,'" *Lantern,* October 31, 1960, 8.

40. Randy Wright, "1000 Hear Kettler, Lewis Debate Validity of Operation Abolition," *Lantern,* June 1, 1961, 1.

41. Bruce Fields, "Van Alstyne, Gregg Debate Birch Society," *Lantern,* June 2, 1961, 1.

42. "Ohio State without Civil Defense Plans; Campus Would Follow Those for County," *Lantern,* August 24, 1961, 1.

NOTES TO CHAPTER 2

1. James E. Odenkirk, "The Eighth Wonder of the World: Ohio State University's Rejection of a Rose Bowl Bid in 1961," *Journal of Sports History,* Fall 2007, 390–91.

2. John Lombardo, *A Fire to Win: The Life and Times of Woody Hayes* (New York: St. Martin's Press, 2005), 5.

3. Odenkirk, "Eighth Wonder," 391.

4. Odenkirk, "Eighth Wonder," 393.

5. "Hayes Defends Scholarship Rule Change," *Lantern,* October 2, 1961, 1.

6. Len Downie, "Faculty Approves Big Ten Proposal," *Lantern,* October 11, 1961, 1.

7. Len Downie, "Council Rejects Bowl Bid" and "Armitage, Fox Lead Opposition to Bowl as Faculty Discusses," *Lantern,* November 29, 1961, 1.

8. "Must Follow Rules—Hayes," *Lantern,* November 29, 1961, 1.

9. Ron Shafer and Steve Nidetz, "Futile Protest Becomes Unruly," *Lantern,* November 30, 1961, 1.

10. Ray Paprocki, "Inside the Wolfe Empire," *Columbus Monthly,* April 1986, 39.

11. Neal R. Peirce, *The Megastates of America: People, Politics, and Power in the Ten Great States* (New York: W. W. Norton, 1972), 330. The *Dispatch* editorial view mellowed somewhat over the years, especially after the *Citizen-Journal* folded in 1985. But as the dynamics of the newspaper industry changed, the paper began losing money. It was sold by the Wolfe family in 2015 to New York investors, ending 110 years of local ownership.

12. Jack Fullen, "Beneath the Bowl: Some Facts You Must Know," *OSU Monthly,* February 1962, 1.

13. Ned Stout, "Fullen-Hayes Feud Hits High Note Over Rose Bowl," *Dispatch,* December 3, 1961, 2B.

14. Frank J. Tate, "The Football Furore," *OSU Monthly,* January 1962, 24.

15. Ron Shafer, "Hayes, Fullen Resume Long-Standing Feud," *Lantern,* December 4, 1961, 1.

16. W. M. Kiplinger, "Open Letter to the OSU Faculty," *Lantern,* January 9, 1962, 2.

17. Len Downie, "Scarlet 'n' Gray," *Lantern,* November 30, 1961, 5.

18. "Council Gives Okay to Bowl Participation," *Lantern,* October 10, 1962, 1.

19. "Main Track Wins," *OSU Monthly,* June 1963, 4.

20. Paul Denison, "Hayes Explains Football's Role at University," *Lantern,* April 4, 1962, 1.

21. Gayle Miller, "Eisenberg Elected President, 6 Other WSGA Posts Filled, *Lantern,* February 15, 1962, 1.

22. Niki Schwartz interview.

23. Elizabeth Burns, "Fee Hike Arouses Variety of Opinion from Students," *Lantern,* April 26, 1962, 5.

24. "Apathy," *Lantern,* April 20, 1962, 2.

25. "Bonner Is Named Dean of Students," *Lantern,* June 19, 1961, 1; Len Downie, "Dean Bonner Reports on Radio Quotes," *Lantern,* November 16, 1961, 1.

26. "All Fraternities End Bias Laws Here," *Lantern,* September 26, 1961, 1.

27. "Luce Decision Rocks Campus," *OSU Monthly,* May 1962, 20.

28. Len Downie, "Lock-Out of SLA Talk Ordered by President," *Lantern,* April 26, 1962, 1.

29. President's Action Evokes Commentary," *Lantern,* April 30, 1962, 1.

30. Ron Shafer and Len Downie, "Faculty Supports Fawcett's Act," *Lantern,* May 15, 1962, 1; "Longest Faculty Meeting in History," *OSU Monthly,* June 1962, 12.

31. Shafer and Downie, "Faculty Supports Fawcett's Act"; "Trustees Support Fawcett; Two Profs Propose New Rule," *Lantern,* May 21, 1962, 1.

32. "The Ohio State of Tomorrow," *OSU Monthly,* December 1961, 6, and January 1962, 6.

33. "Report to the Campus: Major Actions by the Board of Trustees on Feb. 16, 1962," *Lantern,* February 19, 1962, 3.

34. Len Downie, "Fawcett Asks Discussion of Trimester Possibility," *Lantern,* December 6, 1961, 1.

35. "Ideals vs. Reality," *Lantern,* February 21, 1962, 2.

36. Phil Moots, "Student Senate's Purpose and Goals," *OSU Monthly,* November 1961, 24.

37. Nancy Stenger, "Students Show Dissatisfaction with Registrar Course Policy," *Lantern,* November 2, 1961, 1.

38. Pearlann Gulden, "Math Department Gives TV Classes Trial Basis," *Lantern,* January 12, 1962, 7.

39. Judy Wile, "'To Kill a Cockroach' Takes Forty Times Man's X-Ray Dose," *Lantern,* August 2, 1962, 5.

40. Peggy Jo Leech, "Bonner Says to Battle Reds with Faith in God, Country," *Lantern,* October 24, 1961, 1.

41. Jane Schneider, "Soviet Fallout Here Zero, for a Change," *Lantern,* October 19, 1961, 1.

42. Doris Searcy, "Base U.S. Foreign Policy on Strength—Goldwater," *Lantern,* November 21, 1961, 1.

43. "Grow with Your World," *Lantern,* June 18, 1962, 2. Dylan's memorable lyric—"It'll soon shake your windows and rattle your walls, for the times they are a-changin'"—was not written until a year later, so it could be said Bob Dylan was channeling Curtis LeMay.

NOTES TO CHAPTER 3

1. "Few Students Expelled for Bad Behavior," *Lantern,* November 1, 1962, 6.

2. Angus Johnston, "A Brief History of NSA and USSA," at usstudents.org/about/history.

3. "NSA," *Lantern,* October 26, 1961, 2.

4. "Senate Head Favors End of NSA Ties," *Lantern,* September 28, 1962, 1; Jim Gross interview.

5. Chris Jindra, "CIA Help Confirmed to U.S. Student Group," *Lantern,* February 15, 1967, 1; Johnston, "Brief History," 3–5.

6. Jud Shelnutt, "Battle Predicted in Winter Elections," *Lantern,* November 13, 1962, 1.

7. John MacDonald, "Survey on Campus Politics Indicates Student Apathy," *Lantern,* February 22, 1963, 1.

8. "Religion Is Popular Here," *Lantern,* November 2, 1962, 4; Martha G. K. Newton, "Religious Groups Here Give Counsel, Aid," *Lantern,* December 7, 1961, 7.

9. Patty Hartley, "Religion Vies with Activities for Time," *Lantern,* February 15, 1963, 4.

10. "Adopt Faculty Committee Speaker Rule Proposal," *Lantern,* January 2, 1963, 1; "The Speaker's Rule: The Question Continues," *OSU Monthly,* December 1962, 9.

11. "Bill Offered to Ban Reds as Campus Speakers," *Lantern,* March 26, 1963, 1.

12. Chuck Bell, "Speaker Rules Vary at 'Big Ten' Schools," *Lantern,* November 15, 1962, 1; "OU Held Free of Speaker Problem," *Lantern,* April 2, 1963, 1; "Leadership," *Lantern,* May 10, 1963, 2.

13. John Andrus, "Academic Atmosphere Called Unsatisfactory by 15 Resigning Ohio State Faculty Members," *Lantern,* May 31, 1963, 1.

14. "President States Faculty Turnover Is Lower," *Lantern,* June 17, 1963, 1.

15. Lee Berton, "Wall Street Journal Explores Speaker Controversy in Ohio," *Lantern,* August 15, 1963, 2 (reprint of August 6, 1963, *Wall Street Journal* story).

16. "University's Changing Role Seen as Problem in Sixties," *Lantern,* December 3, 1962, 3.

17. "Undergrad Reorganization Program Studied by Faculty," *Lantern,* June 18, 1962, 1.

18. Irv Haas, "Automation's Magnet Puts Accums on Grade Reports," *Lantern,* August 15, 1963, 5.

19. "University First in State with Chinese Curriculum," *Lantern,* November 6, 1962, 6.

20. "'Time Lag' Theory Is Topic of Textbook," *Lantern,* November 2, 1962, 5; "Everett M. Rogers" at plexusinstitute.org.

21. "State University Problems Discussed at Weekend Meet," *Lantern,* January 14, 1963, 1.

22. "Ohio's New Governor," *OSU Monthly,* December 1962, 3; Richard G. Zimmerman, "Rhodes's First Eight Years, 1963–1971," in Alexander P. Lamis, ed., *Ohio Politics* (Kent: Kent State University Press, 1994), 59–69.

23. "President's Report Calls for $$$ to Meet Changing Needs," *Lantern,* November 30, 1962, 3.

24. "Austerity Program Affects Campus," *OSU Monthly,* February 1963, 12.

25. Memo from John Mount to Novice Fawcett, "Report on Telephone Calls to Members of the Board of Trustees," January 16, 1963, in Budget Reductions (Archives: RG 3/i/8).

26. Fred Delaney, "Fawcett Says Bill Is Inadequate," *Lantern,* March 28, 1963, 1.

27. "Thompson Says Facilities Are Inadequate for Future Students," *Lantern,* February 28, 1963, 9.

28. Zimmerman, "Rhodes's First Eight Years," 72; Joseph Rice, "Rhodes to Sign Regents Bill," *Lantern,* June 17, 1963, 1.

29. "Dr. Lott's Talk Cited Blockade as Possible," *Lantern,* October 23, 1962, 1.

30. "Comment Here Is Evidence of Grave Concern," *Lantern,* October 23, 1962, 1.

31. "Student Reaction Mixed on Cuba," *Lantern,* October 25, 1962, 1.

32. "Fawcett Reassures Campus . . . Says OSU Is Calm, Ready," *Lantern,* October 25, 1962, 1.

33. For more about Ohio State during the Cuban Missile Crisis, see William Shkurti, "Searching the Skies over Fifteenth and High," *Timeline,* October/December 2014, 36–53.

34. "'OSU Strong' Fawcett Tells Symposium," *Lantern,* February 8, 1963, 1.

35. "Lawrence Tells OSU Seniors to Continue Study," *Lantern,* June 17, 1963, 6.

NOTES TO CHAPTER 4

1. Phil Cline, "The North Complex Story: From 4 to 1200 in 3 Years," *Lantern,* March 31, 1964, 9.

2. "WRHC Asks: How Cold Is Too Cold?" *Lantern,* November 20, 1963, 3.

3. "Progressive," *Lantern,* February 5, 1964, 11.

4. "Rule on Slacks 'Accepted' with Rap at Procedure," *Lantern,* February 18, 1964, 1.

5. "Let Dorm Coeds Make Their Own Decisions," *Lantern,* February 19, 1964, 2.

6. "WSGA OK's Private Visit, Urges Girls to Wear Well," *Lantern,* February 27, 1964, 1.

7. Fritzi Ayle, "No Alcohol or Guns for Coeds, but Apartments Have Other Benefits," *Lantern,* January 7, 1964, 10.

8. Judy Eckert, "Hey Women! You're Better, (It Says Here)," *Lantern,* April 17, 1964, 1.

9. Nancy Logue, "Panel Agrees Medicine Has Its Problems," *Lantern,* April 22, 1964, 11.

10. Joan Leitzel interview.

11. Raimund Goerler, *The Ohio State University: An Illustrated History* (Columbus: Ohio State University Press, 2011), 160–61.

12. "Housing Bias Charged by Civil Rights Pickets," *Lantern,* October 10, 1963, 1.

13. "Police Arrest Sit-Ins during Bias Protest," *Lantern,* November 19, 1963, 1.

14. "OSU Will Not Discipline Seven Convicted of Trespassing in Buckeye Property Sit-In," *Lantern,* January 6, 1964, 12.

15. "Students for Human Rights Disbands; New Group Forms," *Lantern,* January 16, 1964, 12.

16. As an aide in the Nixon White House, Huston designed the illegal surveillance plan known as the Huston Plan.

17. Thomas Gaumer and Jean Heller, "NSA Is Rejected 2 to 1," *Lantern,* November 21, 1963, 1.

18. Keith McKnight, "But Suddenly It Was a Day Like No Other," *Lantern,* November 25, 1963, 5.

19. McKnight, "But Suddenly."

20. "'Nothing Solved This Way,'" *Lantern,* November 25, 1963, 3.

21. Mabel Freeman interview; McKnight, "But Suddenly."

22. McKnight, "But Suddenly."

23. Steve Nidetz, "Michigan Game Rescheduled for Saturday," *Lantern,* November 25, 1963, 11.

24. Thomas Buckham, "Game Postponed, but—'No One Really Cared,'" *Lantern,* November 25, 1963, 11.

25. Leonard Downie Jr., "Experts See Few Policy Changes," *Lantern,* November 25, 1963, 6.

26. Stan Darling interview.

27. "That School up North," *Dispatch,* November 28, 2014, 20A.

28. "Thanksgiving 1963," *Lantern,* November 27, 1963, 2.

29. "Ohio State Students Awed at Site of Kennedy Grave," *Lantern,* December 2, 1963, 1.

30. "Police Strict in Enforcing Jaywalking," *Lantern,* February 12, 1964, 1.

31. "Coed's Jaywalking Fine Is Suspended," *Dispatch,* February 12, 1964, 1B.

32. Jean Heller, "People, Place Frighten Her," *Lantern,* February 12, 1964, 1; "Coed's Jail Trip Lantern's Page 1," *Citizen-Journal,* February 13, 1964, 1. Heller would twice be a Pulitzer Prize finalist for her coverage of the Tuskegee syphilis experiments and the Iraq war.

33. James W. Babcock, "Chant Prods Rioters," *Lantern,* February 13, 1964, 3; Bob Pendergast, "Coed's Arrest Sparks March," *Citizen-Journal,* February 13, 1964, 1.

34. Jean Heller, "Six Arrested, $1,000 Damage Done in 7-Hour Jaywalking Demonstration," *Lantern,* February 13, 1964, 3; "Bonfire Damaged High Street Corner; Student March Toll Reaches $11,500," *Citizen-Journal,* February 15, 1964, 1.

35. "Investigation of Jaywalking Incident Asked," *Lantern,* February 14, 1964, 1; Martha Brian, "OSU Officials Study Factors in Flare-up," *Dispatch,* February 13, 1964, 6A.

36. "Scholer Denies Ohio State Coed Wrongfully Treated in Arrest," *Dispatch,* February 13, 1964, 1B.

37. "Taxpayers to Foot $12,000 Bill in Rioting," *Dispatch,* February 16, 1964, 3A; "Time to Stop and Think," *Citizen-Journal,* February 14, 1964, 14.

38. "Question: When Is a Demonstration a Riot?" *OSU Monthly,* March 1964, 12.

39. John Bonner, "Report to the President, Mass Student Demonstration February 12, 1964," March 4, 1964, in Riot, Feb–Mar 1964 (Archives: RG 3/i/43).

40. "Jay Walking? Better Pay Up!" *Citizen-Journal,* February 15, 1964, 1.

41. "Fawcett Says Issue 1 Means Growth for Us," *Lantern,* October 12, 1963, 1.

42. Larry L. Rummell, "600 Frosh Say Instruction Is Inadequate," *Lantern,* January 22, 1964, 1.

43. Ladd Neuman and Daly Smith, "Instructors Criticize Freshman Behavior," *Lantern,* February 3, 1964, 11.

44. Pamela Van Nostran, "Big Dilemma: How to Make Educational TV Interesting," *Lantern,* November 21, 1963, 7.

45. Larry L. Rummell, "Frosh Senate Seeks Investigation of Quality of Graduate Assistants," *Lantern,* February 13, 1964, 7.

46. Keith McKnight, "OSU Lacks 'Teaching Art' Armitage Says," *Lantern,* March 6, 1964, 1.

47. James W. Babcock, "Faculty Council Asks for Changes," *Lantern,* May 13, 1964, 1.

48. "Fawcett Relates Plan for 2-Year College on Main Campus," *Lantern,* May 25, 1964, 1.

49. Tom Seslar, "Friend of Students, Faculty to Retire," *Lantern,* May 25, 1964; 1; Novice G. Fawcett interview, Oral History Project, November 16, 1983, 11.

50. Francis P. Weisenburger, *History of the Ohio State University: The Fawcett Years, 1956–1972* (Columbus: Ohio State University Press, 1975), 195.

51. Goerler, *Illustrated History,* 77–79; "OSU Extension: A Brief History," extension.osu.edu.

52. John Kean, *India: A History* (New York: Atlantic Monthly Press, 2000), 524.

53. Clark Kerr, *The Uses of the University* (Cambridge: Harvard University Press, 1963), 49.

54. "Sexual Love May Frustrate Identity," *Lantern,* December 4, 1963, 1.

55. Pam Hollister, "Tillich Ponders an Ancient Conflict: Is Morality Unchanging or Relative?" *Lantern,* January 30, 1964, 1.

56. "Rustin Cites Difficulties in Negro Affairs," *Lantern,* February 3, 1964, 1.

57. John A. MacDonald, "Wallace Invited to Speak at Mershon on Thursday," *Lantern,* February 7, 1964, 1.

58. Jean Heller, "Wallace Considering Running in Primaries of Three States," *Lantern,* February 14, 1964, 1.

59. "Town and Gown," *OSU Monthly,* March 1964, 28.

60. "We Live Here, Too," *Lantern,* October 17, 1963, 2.

61. "A Funny, Funny Town," *Lantern,* October 31, 1963, 2.

62. "60 Faculty Members to Present 'Alternative Views' on Issues," *Lantern,* January 10, 1963, 1; Committee for the Study of Alternatives, "Alternatives: The 'No Problems Here' Approach" (advertisement), *Lantern,* January 24, 1964, 8.

63. "Sensenbrenner, Maynard Edward 'Jack,'" at www.ourcampaigns.com/CandidateDetail.html?CandidateID=17538.

64. U.S. Bureau of the Census, Table 36, Ohio—Race and Hispanic Origin for Selected Large Cities and Other Places: Earliest Census to 1990, at census.gov/population/www/documentation/twps0076/OHtab.pdf.

65. "Columbus Is Called 'City of Prejudice' at Rights Rally," *Lantern,* January 20, 1964, 1.

66. Sandor M. Polster, "Civil Rights Rally Is Today," *Lantern,* May 18, 1964, 1.

67. Sandor M. Polstor and Robert Sheppard, "Student Senate Ayes (Softly) Rights Rally," *Lantern,* May 15, 1964, 1.

68. Pam Hollister and John D. Huddy, "1000 Rally for Civil Rights," *Lantern,* May 19, 1964, 1.

69. Larry Rummell, "Campus Supports Johnson," *Lantern,* August 6, 1964, 1.

NOTES TO CHAPTER 5

1. Marci Hilt, "Baby Boom Hits Ohio State," *Lantern,* September 28, 1964, 1.

2. "Sugar to Spice," *Lantern,* February 12, 1965, 4.

3. Sue Forman, "WSGA Urges Protection for Coeds at Night," *Lantern,* October 15, 1964, 1.

4. "Crime Tops Mean Rate," *Lantern,* January 28, 1965, 2.

5. Sherryl Woods, "Student Petitions Bring Better Street Lighting," *Lantern,* May 3, 1965, 1.

6. Tom W. Seslar, "Racial Barriers Prevalent within OSU Greek System," *Lantern,* December 4, 1964, 1.

7. John D. Huddy, "The Greek Problem," *Lantern,* December 9, 1964, 4.

8. Samuel B. Huff and Pat Dickelman, "Betterment or Burial?" *Lantern,* May 27, 1965, 3.

9. "Years Change Sundial Format," *Lantern,* May 17, 1965, 3.

10. "'Jovial Bob' Enters Race," *Lantern,* February 24, 1965, 1.

11. "Miami President Selected Director of Regents Board," *Lantern,* March 5, 1964, 11.

12. Pam Hollister, "Regents Would Make OSU Graduate Center," *Lantern,* April 23, 1965, 1.

13. "Regents Unveil Proposed Master Plan," *OSU Monthly,* June 1965, 8.

14. "Open Admission Is Aim," *Lantern,* July 9, 1965, 3.

15. "Regents Unveil Proposed Master Plan."

16. Joe Walsh, "Ohio: Old Laissez-Faire Attitude in Linking Education, Research and Industry Undergoing Change," *Science,* July 31, 1964, 468–70.

17. Tom Seslar, "Rhodes Tells Money Plans," *Lantern,* February 16, 1965, 1.

18. Thomas G. Buckham, "Research Expenditure at OSU Increasing," *Lantern,* October 21, 1964, 2.

19. "Four OSU Students End Six-Week Test," *Lantern,* February 24, 1965, 1.

20. Donna J. Plesh, "Poison Prolongs Life," *Lantern,* October 15, 1964, 5.

21. Patricia A. Williamson, "New Bulletin Draws Conflicting Opinions," *Lantern,* September 28, 1964, 4.

22. Irv Haas, "60% of Frosh Class Won't Get Diplomas," *Lantern,* March 30, 1965, 7; "Student Dismissals Up for Fall Quarter," *Lantern,* January 20, 1965, 1.

23. Hap Cawood, "Poor Wilson Showing Explained by Armitage," *Lantern,* April 6, 1965, 1.

24. Dean W. Schott, "Changes in Survey Course Requested by Arts Freshmen," *Lantern,* May 21, 1965, 5.

25. "Let's Get Professors Back in the Classroom," *Lantern,* March 2, 1965, 1.

26. "Students, Faculty React to Dr. Weaver's Speech," *Lantern,* February 26, 1965, 1.

27. Thomas G. Buckham, "Council Backs Plan for General College," *Lantern,* December 9, 1964, 1.

28. Daly Smith, "Trustees Create Columbus Branch," *Lantern,* March 12, 1965, 1.

29. Jack Fullen, "Berkeley—A Beacon," *OSU Monthly,* July 1965, 1.

30. John Mount interview, July 26, 2012; Edward Moulton interview, Oral History Project, 16.

31. Sue Stine, "OSU Expansion to Cost Millions," *Lantern,* February 5, 1965, 1.

32. Thomas G. Buckham, "Skyscrapers to Rise Soon," *Lantern,* November 9, 1964, 1.

33. See, for example, Oral History Project interviews with Christine Conaway, 4; Edward Moulton, 14–15; John Herrick, 12–14; and G. Robert Holsinger, 11–13. Bonner went so far as to send Carson a memo arguing for smaller scattered facilities instead of two big towers; see John Bonner, "Report to the Board of Trustees, River Tower Residence Hall," November 15, 1963, in Office of Business and Finance, Carson, Housing—River Dorm Planning, 1963 (Archives: RG 6/a/19).

34. Letter from Novice Fawcett to Gordon Carson, June 6, 1968, in Office of Business and Finance, Carson, Housing—River Dorm Planning, 1963 (Archives: RG 6/a/19).

35. Ernest Leggett, "The Dormitory Problem," December 10, 1963, in Office of Business and Finance, Carson, Housing—River Dorm Planning, 1963 (Archives: RG 6/a/19); "Housing to Cost Millions," *Lantern,* November 9, 1964, 1.

36. Judy Eckert and Dave Hopcraft, "Crowd Sprinkled with Buckeyes," and Pam Hollister, "Goldwater Charms Columbus Crowd at Vets Memorial," *Lantern,* October 1, 1964, 1.

37. Pam Hollister, "Compassion, Weakness Not the Same, Says Humphrey," *Lantern,* October 7, 1964, 1.

38. "Johnson to Push Hard for Program in Congress," *Lantern,* November 9, 1964 (election supplement), 8.

39. Tom Seslar, "Demonstrators Protest U.S. Policy in Vietnam," *Lantern,* February 22, 1965, 1.

40. "Shun Asia War, Dulles Urges," *Lantern,* April 2, 1965, 1; "Loss of Vietnam Will Imperil Rest of Asia, Army Head Says," *Lantern,* April 21, 1965, 1.

41. "Mock Discussion Shows Inevitability of War," *Lantern,* May 24, 1965, 2.

42. "Student Deferments Harder to Get Now," *Lantern,* August 5, 1965, 8.

43. Paul Yalsovac, "Negro Leaders See Columbus as Ripe for Racial Outbursts," *Lantern,* August 26, 165, 1.

NOTES TO CHAPTER 6

1. This account is drawn from W. J. Rorabaugh, *Berkeley at War: The 1960s* (New York: Oxford University Press, 1989), 19–40, and *California Monthly,* Free Speech Movement Chronology, at bancroft.berkeley.edu/FSM/chron.html.

2. Rorabaugh, *Berkeley,* 31.

3. "Significant Step," *Lantern,* February 22, 1965, 4.

4. Daly Smith and Thomas G. Buckham, "Trustees Invite Speakers' Rule Talks," *Lantern,* April 14, 1965, 1.

5. Emily Foster, "The Free Speech Movement at Ohio State," *Columbus Monthly,* December 1984, 53; Dennis Knepley interview.

6. Linda Bell, "Students Seek Rule Change at Free Speech Front Rally," *Lantern,* April 15, 1965, 1.

7. Jeff Schwartz interview. See also Jeff Schwartz interview, Oral History Project, 12.

8. Leonard Downie Jr. and Paul Denison, "Sit-in Drew Students, Faculty, the Curious," *Lantern,* April 26, 1965, 4.

9. Tom W. Seslar, "Speakers Rule Protestors Conduct All-Night Sit-In," *Lantern,* April 29, 1965, 1; Leonard Downie Jr., "FSF Says Future Action Is Up to Administration," *Lantern,* April 30, 1965, 1.

10. "FSF Tells Rally of Plan to Bring Aptheker," *Lantern,* May 10, 1965, 1.

11. "Herbert Aptheker: Biographical Facts," *Lantern,* April 23, 1965, 6.

12. Daly Smith, "Aptheker Speaks to Student Group," *Lantern,* May 11, 1965, 1.

13. "Report to the Campus: Actions by the Board of Trustees on May 13, 1965," *Lantern,* May 14, 1965, 3.

14. Hap Cawood, "428 Faculty Members Ask Trustees to Abolish Rule," *Lantern,* May 14, 1965, 1.

15. John D. Huddy and Ladd A. Neuman, "Aptheker's Visit Called Rehearsal by FSF Leader," *Lantern,* May 24, 1965, 1.

16. "FSF Rival Factions Clash over Aptheker's Silence," *Lantern,* May 24, 1965, 6; Sherry Woods, "Marxist Won't Return This Term, FSF Says," *Lantern,* May 25, 1965, 1.

17. Sue Stine, "FAC Drafts New Rule to End Speaker Veto," *Lantern,* June 1, 1965, 1; "Good Sign," *Lantern,* June 4, 1965, 4.

18. Carole Edwards, "Attorneys, Businessmen Guide University," *Lantern,* July 15, 1965, 1.

19. Richard O. Davies, *Defender of the Old Guard: John Bricker and American Politics* (Columbus: Ohio State University Press, 1993), 216–20.

20. Federal Bureau of Investigation, "Memo from M. A. Jones to Mr. DeLoach, Subject: Former Senator John Bricker (Ohio)," December 21, 1965. This was obtained from the FBI through a Freedom of Information request (courtesy of David Kettler).

21. John W. Bricker, "The Centennial of Ohio State," *Ohioana Quarterly* (Fall 1970), 75–77.

22. Richard G. Zimmerman, *Plain Dealing: Ohio Politics and Journalism Viewed from the Press Gallery* (Kent: Kent State University Press, 2006), 39.

23. William K. Gale, "New Trustee Sought as Dargush Quits; His Appeal Denied," *Lantern,* October 12, 1965, 1.

24. "Campus Subversion Demands a Stiffening of Discipline," *Dispatch,* May 23, 1965, 46A.

25. "Majority at Polls Hit Rule," *Lantern,* May 10, 1965, 1; "Faculty Surveyed by Tau Beta Pi," *Lantern,* July 15, 1965, 4.

26. "Report to the Campus: Actions by the Board of Trustees on July 8, 1965," *Lantern,* July 9, 1965, 5.

27. "Speakers' Rule Retained," *OSU Monthly,* September 1965, 4.

28. Richard Stelling and Ladd Neuman, "Faculty Foresees Teacher Exodus"; Charles Fenton, "Leaders Voice Dismay, Senate to Map Action"; Barry Shiller, "Students Shocked by Rule Decision"; *Lantern,* July 9, 1965, 1.

29. "Newspaper Reaction," in Office of the President, Speakers Rule Controversy, Aug–Dec 1965 (Archives: RG 3/i/44).

30. Penelope A. Bazler et al., Letter to the OSU Board of Trustees, September 8, 1965, in Secretary of the Board, Post 1958: Speaker's Rule, 1965 (Archives: RG 2/6/15).

31. Speaker's Rule—Correspondence after Board of Trustees Meeting of 8 July 1965, in Office of the President, July–Sept 1965 (Archives: RG 3/i/44).

32. This account is taken from "Report to the Campus: Actions by the Board of Trustees on September 14, 1965," *Lantern,* September 29, 1965, 17; "Speaker's Rule Is Revised," *OSU Monthly,* October 1965, 4.

33. Harry Franken, "Shocknessy Mum on Speaker's Rule," *Citizen-Journal,* August 4, 1965, 11.

34. "OSU Insiders Believe Speakers Rule Changes Will Stand," *Citizen-Journal,* September 16, 1965, 40.

35. Homer Brickey and William H. Artis, "Speaker Rule Change Eases Campus Tension," *Lantern,* September 29, 1965, 1.

36. "Speaker's Rule Is Revised," *OSU Monthly,* October 1965, 4."

37. Memo from Novice Fawcett to John Ketterer, April 12, 1965, in Office of the President, Speaker's Rule, Board of Trustees, Sept 1951, April–Aug 1965 (Archives: RG 3/i/44). Attached to this memo is a proposal dated July 11, 1963.

38. "President Declines AAA Offer," *OSU Monthly,* October 1964, 4; Jane Fawcett-Hoover interview.

39. Evidence shows Fawcett for his own reasons wanted to get rid of the rule as early as the summer of 1963 (see note 37).

40. Letter from Novice Fawcett to C. William O'Neill, July 23, 1965, Correspondence after Board of Trustees Meeting of 8 July 1965, in Office of the President, July–Sept 1965 (Archives: RG 3/i/44).

41. Paul Yalsovac, "Corbally Tells How to Challenge Rule," *Lantern,* July 15, 1965, 1.

42. See discussion in Jeffrey H. Schwartz, "The Speakers Rule Controversy at Ohio State: A Case Study," master's thesis (New York: Columbia University, 1966), 86–97.

Even though Schwartz was a participant in these events, his thesis is well documented and consistent with other independent accounts. It is available at University Archives.

43. John Mount interview, July 26, 2012.

44. Novice G. Fawcett interview, Oral History Project, November 16, 1983, 2.

45. Schwartz, "Speakers Rule," 88–90; "OSU Insiders Believe Speakers Rule Changes Will Stand."

46. "'Limits' on Speakers' Criticized by Free Front Speech Leader," *Lantern,* September 30, 1965, 1.

47. Bill Gale, "Speech Not 'Emotional,' Says Head of Liberals," *Lantern,* October 15, 1965, 1.

48. Richard Stelling and Richard Rowley, "Aptheker Tests Speech Rule; Lifting of Restrictions Sought," *Lantern,* October 19, 1965, 1; "Revised Rule Given First Test," *OSU Monthly,* November 1965, 22.

49. Charles G. Fenton, "Wilkinson Speech Set for Monday," *Lantern,* November 19, 1965, 1; William Shofner, "HUAC Losing, Wilkinson Says," *Lantern,* November 23, 1965, 1.

50. "Former OSU Leftist Renounces Old Beliefs," *Lantern,* May 13, 1966, 2.

NOTES TO CHAPTER 7

1. Donna J. Plesh, "Schwartz, Former FSF Spokesman, Proposes 'Student Power' Program," *Lantern,* October 11, 1965, 1; Tom W. Seslar, "Union Wants Abolition of Student Government," *Lantern,* October 12, 1965, 1.

2. "SCP Quits Election, Backs Senate Reform," *Lantern,* February 15, 1966, 1; "The Accelerated Fall of Student Government," *Lantern,* February 17, 1966, 4.

3. David L. Hopcraft, "Neustadt Proposes Constitutional Convention," *Lantern,* February 22, 1966, 1; Tim Neustadt interview.

4. Barbara Dobranic, "Traditions Board Ability Challenged," *Lantern,* February 25, 1966, 1.

5. "Bonner Doubts Feasibility of FSF and BPP Plans," *Lantern,* March 1, 1966, 3.

6. "4,500 Lanterns Stolen from Campus," *Lantern,* March 2, 1966, 1.

7. William N. Curry, "Senate Reform Is Still an Issue," *Lantern,* March 31, 1966, 1.

8. William N. Curry, "Convention Declares Independence of Senate," *Lantern,* May 2, 1966, 1. Although Neustadt and Melamed both were from Shaker Heights, they were not close in high school. They would subsequently become political allies at Ohio State; Alan Melamed and Tim Neustadt interviews.

9. Mary V. Gordon, "Six BPP Officials Resign, Object to Leaders," *Lantern,* May 19, 1966, 1.

10. "Senate Structure Labeled 'Archaic,'" *Lantern,* May 20, 1966, 1.

11. "Six Vice Presidents Elected by BPP," *Lantern,* May 26, 1966, 1.

12. "Bonner Would Accept Veto-less CSA Role," *Lantern,* April 28, 1966, 8; Barbara Dobranic, "Student Committeemen Opposed by Faculty," *Lantern,* May 26, 1966, 1.

13. "1800 Coeds Sign Petition for No Hours," *Lantern,* May 18, 1966, 1.

14. "Two Coeds Claim WSGA Unrepresentative, Resign," *Lantern,* May 20, 1966, 8.

15. "The Ponderous Pace of Self Government," *Lantern,* May 20, 1966, 4.

16. "Six Vice Presidents Elected by BPP."

17. William Shofner, "NAACP Probing Bias in Housing," *Lantern,* November 24, 1965, 1.

18. William G. Shofner, "NAACP Unit Spurs Fight for Housing," *Lantern,* January 5, 1966, 1.

19. "Employment Settlement Announced by NAACP," *Lantern,* May 20, 1966, 1.

20. "Fawcett Discusses Greek Integration," *Lantern,* June 30, 1966, 1.

21. David L. Hopcraft, "FSF Committee to Continue 'Free Press' Probe on Campus," *Lantern,* January 27, 1966, 1.

22. Charles G. Fenton, "Students Have Complained about *Lantern,* Fawcett Says," *Lantern,* January 27, 1966, 1; David L. Hopcraft, "SATA to Ask How Lantern Is Produced," *Lantern,* February 2, 1966, 1.

23. "SATA, Where Are You?" *Lantern,* May 2, 1966, 2.

24. Vic Frost interview; Sherryl A. Woods, "Communications Topic at Student Breakfast," *Lantern,* April 20, 1966, 1.

25. "FSF Questions Fawcett," *Lantern,* May 19, 1966, 1.

26. David Hopcraft interview, Oral History Project, 5-6.

27. "Grad Student Enrollments Skyrocketing," *Lantern,* November 12, 1965, 1.

28. "OSU Ranks 13th Nationally in Spending for Research," *Lantern,* May 31, 1966, 5.

29. Robert A. McKnight, "National Education Study 'Centered' at Ohio State," *Lantern,* February 16, 1966, 3; "Ohio State to Get $10 Million Grant," *Lantern,* October 10, 1966, 1.

30. "Effects of Vietnam Weapons Studied," *Lantern,* June 1, 1966, 3.

31. "System Considered Best," *Lantern,* March 28, 1966, 3.

32. Shirley Christian, "Plan Aired for Sophs, Freshmen," *Lantern,* December 3, 1965, 1.

33. Chandley Murphy, "Faculty Council Backs General College Plan," *Lantern,* May 11, 1966, 1.

34. William Willis, "OSU Branch Termed Success by Officials," *Lantern,* June 2, 1966, 3.

35. "Armitage Says Change Is Good for Ohio State," *Lantern,* July 15, 1966, 9.

36. "Board of Trustees Create New College," *Lantern,* March 11, 1966, 1.

37. "Regents Considering 35,000 Student Limit," *Lantern,* November 10, 1965, 1.

38. "Admissions Policy Remains Same," *Lantern,* February 11, 1966, 1.

39. "Board of Regents Releases Master Plan for Ohio Education," *OSU Monthly,* July 1966, 4.

40. "Committee Plan Probes into Problems of Teaching," *Lantern,* April 29, 1966, 4.

41. "4 Departments Launch Training Programs," *Lantern,* August 11, 1966, 3; Letter from Meno Lovenstein to Fred Crossland, January 11, 1966, "Proposal for a Ford Foundation Grant," in Office of Academic Affairs, University Committee on Teaching, 1965-66 (University Archives: RG 5/a/19).

42. "Experiment Pulls OSU Together," *Lantern,* August 11, 1966, 1.

43. William G. Shofner, "Unexpected Problems Delay Course Revision," *Lantern,* May 10, 1966, 1.

44. William N. Curry, "Students Grade Staff in Commerce College," *Lantern,* January 31, 1966, 1.

45. "J-School Panel Set Up by Fuller," *Lantern,* February 10, 1966, 1.

46. Mike Lorz, "Trustees Approve $300,000 Mansion: Plan Passes by 7-1 Vote," *Lantern,* December 10, 1965, 1; "The Mansion," *Lantern,* December 10, 1965, 4.

47. "Hall Invites 9 Faculty Resignations," *Lantern,* April 15, 1966, 1.

48. "Nebraska Faculty Letter to Fawcett Praises Hall," *Lantern,* April 25, 1966, 6; "Conference Committee Issues Lantern Report," *Lantern,* April 28, 1966, 1; Bill Werth, "Faculty Group Reports on J-School Issue," *OSU Monthly,* July 1966, 22.

49. "Professor Criticizes Planning of Biological Sciences College," *Lantern,* April 25, 1966, 1.

50. "The Council on Instruction Report: Answers Popham Charges," *Lantern,* May 4, 1966, 4.

51. Shirley Christian, "Faculty Seeks Bigger Voice in Policy," *Lantern,* February 8, 1966. AAUP members accounted for about 18 percent of the faculty in the mid-1960s.

52. Eric Solomon, "Free Speech at Ohio State," *Atlantic Monthly,* November 1965, 119–23; John Harold Wilson, "A Teacher Comments," *OSU Monthly,* December 1965, 7.

53. Carol Siemon, "Fullen to Leave OSU in '67," *Lantern,* June 30, 1966, 7.

54. Barry McGuire. "Eve of Destruction." Universal Music Publishing Group. 1965.

55. For an excellent analysis of this period from a national perspective, see James T. Patterson, *The Eve of Destruction: How 1965 Transformed America* (New York: Basic Books, 2012).

56. "700 Hear Professors Give Views on Vietnam," *Lantern,* December 3, 1965, 1.

57. William N. Curry, "Vietnam Veteran Backs U.S. Policy," *Lantern,* October 26, 1965, 1; Susan Brendel, "Vietnam Fighting 'Just a Job,' Returned Army Captain Says," *Lantern,* November 5, 1965, 6.

58. "'Pacifists' Urge End of Draft," *Lantern,* October 14, 1965, 1.

59. "Protests Go beyond Reality," *Lantern,* October 15, 1965, 4.

60. The Encyclopedia of Cleveland History, ech.case.edu/cgi/article.pl?id=PJB; William N. Curry, "Student Pickets War," *Lantern,* November 12, 1965, 1.

61. Lee Hansen, "Blood Drive Ends, 1,297 Pints Given," *Lantern,* November 12, 1965, 1.

62. "Viet Roll Is Signed by Mayor," *Lantern,* November 18, 1965, 1.

63. "College Students: Next Draft Target?" *Lantern,* January 4, 1966, 1.

64. "1807 Men Take 3-Hour Draft Test," *Lantern,* May 20, 1966, 8.

65. "OSU Student Accused in Coed Abortion Case," *Lantern,* November 19, 1965, 1.

66. "OSU Police Deny Morals Crackdown," *Lantern,* November 23, 1965, 5.

67. Nancy L. Rydman, "Sex Education: Ohio State Lantern Special Report," *Lantern,* February 28, 1966, 3.

68. Leslie Ruggles, "Minister Cites Behavior Shift," *Lantern,* March 2, 1964, 1.

69. John Huddy, "Dope Not Hard to Find: Reporter Enters World of OSU Campus 'Sick,'" *Dispatch,* January 12, 1966, 1A.

70. Richard Stelling, "Eleven Arrested by Police in Narcotics Crackdown," *Lantern,* January 13, 1966, 1; "Judge Dismisses Cases against 8 for Narcotics," *Lantern,* January 28, 1966, 1; "Narcotics Suspect Left Note Indicating Suicide, Police Say," *Lantern,* February 17, 1966, 8.

71. "Local Press Invents 'Dope Ring' on Campus," *Lantern,* January 21, 1966, 4; Kenneth P. Mills, "Vice-Squad Chief Praises Majority of OSU Students," *Lantern,* January 18, 1966, 1

72. "Brutal Killings Bring Safety Suggestions from Dean Conaway," *Lantern,* July 15, 1966, 1.

73. William Artis Jr., "A Desperate Shout: Black Power," *Lantern,* July 22, 1966, 4.

74. William H. Hurley, "Picture Is Suggestive," *Lantern,* August 11, 1966, 4.

NOTES TO CHAPTER 8

1. "Senate Is Delayed by 27 Vacancies," *Lantern,* October 7, 1966, 1; Kathryn Mason, "Constitutional Convention Plagued with Problems," *Lantern,* January 11, 1967, 7; "FSF to Meet Despite Losing Its Recognition," *Lantern,* November 18, 1966, 1.

2. "Convention Commended by Melamed," *Lantern,* March 30, 1967, 1.

3. Catherine F. Smith, "Undergraduates OK Constitution," *Lantern,* April 13, 1967, 1.

4. William J. Willis, "Siegel Seeks Student Presidency," *Lantern,* April 17, 1967, 1.

5. "Former Editor to Be Candidate," *Lantern,* April 21, 1967, 1.

6. Phil Long, "Dress Rule Vetoed on South Campus," *Lantern,* November 16, 1966, 1.

7. Sue Reisinger, "Living Units Find Girls Not Using New Hours," *Lantern,* November 11, 1966, 5.

8. "OSU to Lift Junior, Senior Curfews," *Lantern,* February 7, 1967, 1.

9. Sue Reisinger, "Big Ten Schools Favor No-Hours Policy," *Lantern,* March 7, 1967, 1.

10. Chris Jindra, "WSGA Officer Wants No Hours," *Lantern,* May 24, 1967, 3.

11. "Coed Apartment Rules under Study by WSGA," *Lantern,* October 20, 1966, 1.

12. Sue Reisinger, "WSGA Told Press Blurred Hours Issue," *Lantern,* November 10, 1966, 1.

13. "Deans Conaway, Ross Plan to Retire," *Lantern,* February 20, 1967, 1; Chris Jindra, "Overholt, Miss Weimer Named Deans," *Lantern,* May 12, 1967, 1; Cheryl Meredith, "Student Relations Reorganization Ends Deans Posts," *Lantern,* May 24, 1967, 1.

14. Meredith, "Student Relations Reorganization."

15. "Report to the Campus: Actions by the Board of Trustees on June 9, 1966: Student Fees Are Increased," *Lantern,* June 20, 1966, 7; "Report to the Campus: Actions by the Board of Trustees on June 6, 1967: Dormitory Fees Increased," *Lantern,* June 19, 1967, 7.

16. Steven Lubar, "'Do Not Fold. Spindle or Mutilate': A Cultural History of the Punch Card," *Journal of American Culture,* Winter 1992, 45–55.

17. Michele Wilson, "Where the Cards Go," *Lantern,* January 21, 1966, 7.

18. "Games Students Play: The Scheduling Ratrace," *Lantern,* January 5, 1967, 4.

19. "Changing Schedules" (photo essay), *Lantern,* January 4, 1967, 1.

20. "Lack of Postage Money Delays Grades to 4,875," *Lantern,* March 28, 1967, 1.

21. Chandley Murphy, "River Dormitory: Not a Bad Place to Live," *Lantern,* December 1, 1966, 7.

22. Roberta Katherine Jones, "A Study of the Physical Facilities at Morrill Tower, The Ohio State University, as Assessed by the Student Residents and Staff," master's thesis (Columbus: Ohio State University, 1967), 80, 90–95, in Office of Business and Finance, Morrill Tower (Archives: RG 6/a/23).

23. William Benham, "River Dorms' Completion Is Marked by Open House," *Lantern,* August 10, 1967, 1.

24. "Beauty and the Beasts," *Lantern,* August 10, 1967, 4; Jones, "A Study of the Physical Facilities at Morrill Tower," 94.

25. Bob Ross, "Undergrad Dorm Rule to Remain Unenforced," *Lantern,* January 25, 1967, 1; "Half of Voters Wrote Dorm," *Lantern,* April 17, 1967, 1.

26. Jane Blackburn, "War Hikes ROTC Rolls," *Lantern,* April 25, 1967, 5.

27. Susan Frey, "Vietnam Teach-in Protests the War," *Lantern,* November 7, 1966, 1; "Anti-War Marchers Hit Capitol," *Lantern,* November 7, 1966, 1.

28. Helene E. Chalfin, "50 Participate Friday in 1-Hour Peace Vigil," *Lantern,* February 13, 1967, 8.

29. "Students Discuss War in Vietnam," *Lantern,* January 12, 1967, 8.

30. David Haglund, "Peace Group Plans Songs, Silent Vigil for Corps Day," *Lantern,* May 4, 1967, 1.

31. "ROTC Review Interrupted by Demonstration," *Lantern,* May 5, 1967, 1.

32. Chris Jindra, "Marchers Queried," *Lantern,* May 9, 1967, 6.

33. "Anti-War Group Revamps Agenda," *Lantern,* August 17, 1967, 2.

34. Allan M. Cartter, *An Assessment of Quality in Graduate Education* (Washington, D.C.: American Council on Education, 1966), vii, 10–77.

35. Committee for the Study of Alternatives, "The Image of Greatness" (advertisement), *Lantern,* November 18, 1966, 3.

36. "Is Quality or Quantity a Measure of Growth?" *Lantern,* January 6, 1967, 4.

37. "Alternatives Ad Draws Reply," *OSU Monthly,* December 1966, 16.

38. "Again We Say: Let's Face the Truth," *Lantern,* January 27, 1967, 4.

39. "Plain Dealer Eyes 'Lag and Complacency,'" reprinted in *Lantern,* November 29, 1966, 4; Don E. Weaver, "Brighten the Corner Where You Are," *Citizen-Journal,* February 4, 1967, 14; Neil Hulsman, "Mall Calls OSU Critics 'Ignorant,'" *Lantern,* May 9, 1967, 1.

40. Committee for the Study of Alternatives, "The Board of Trustees" (advertisement), *Lantern,* January 27, 1967, 3.

41. Committee for the Study of Alternatives, "Toward the Improvement of Ohio State" (advertisement), *Lantern,* April 7, 1967, 2.

42. Stuart Spiegel, "Opinions Given of OSU," *Lantern,* May 25, 1967, 7.

43. James H. Endsley, "Ohio State May Eliminate Arts, Commerce Colleges," *Lantern,* December 5, 1966, 1.

44. Mary V. Gordon, "Arts Faculty Wants Strong, Lasting Plan," *Lantern,* January 18, 1967, 1.

45. John E. Corbally, "Let's Move Ahead," reprinted in *OSU Monthly,* March 1967, 4.

46. "A Logical Proposal for Reorganization," *Lantern,* April 17, 1967, 4.

47. Carole L. Siemon, "Reorganization Plan Approved," *Lantern,* May 10, 1967, 1.

48. James H. Endsley, "Faculty Status Is Key to Council Reorganization," *Lantern,* March 7, 1967, 1; "Faculty Council Reorganizes," *OSU Monthly,* April 1967, 12.

49. "Transport Research Slated at New Graduate Facility," *Lantern,* October 7, 1966, 12; "Transportation Research Center," *OSU Monthly,* January 1967, 5.

50. Letter from Meno Lovenstein to John Corbally, February 5, 1967, in Office of Academic Affairs, University Committee on Teaching (Archives: RG 5/a/24).

51. Ned Artman, "College Project Seeks 'Best of Two Worlds,'" *Lantern,* November 21, 1966, 3.

52. "The Budget: MORE—than ever or LESS—than needed," *OSU Monthly,* October 1967, 4.

53. "Reams Warns of Cost Rise," *Lantern,* October 20, 1966, 1.

54. John Mount (August 6, 2013) and Jane Fawcett-Hoover interviews.

55. Mike Flynn, "Rhodes Tops Reams in Lantern 'Voter' Poll," *Lantern,* November 7, 1966, 1.

56. Rick Kerger and Richard A. Bashor, "Rhodes Gives Priority to Education," *Lantern,* March 1, 1967, 1.

57. Richard G. Zimmerman, "Rhodes's First Eight Years, 1963–1971," in Alexander P. Lamis, editor, *Ohio Politics* (Kent: Kent State University Press, 1994), 73–74.

58. Chris Jindra, "Fawcett Endorses Bond Plan," *Lantern,* April 17, 1967, 1.

59. Bill Willis, "Senate Opposes Rhodes' OBC Plan," *Lantern,* April 21, 1967, 1.

60. Christine Jindra, "Bond Plan Passage Is Vital, Fawcett Says," *Lantern,* April 24, 1967, 1.

61. David Gollust, "Bond Commission Is Crushed," *Lantern,* May 3, 1967, 1.

62. "OBC Defeat Called Setback for OSU," *Lantern,* May 22, 1967, 1.

63. Zimmerman, "Rhodes's First Eight Years," 75.

64. "Picket at Larry's Continues," *Lantern,* March 30, 1967, 1.

65. Paul Cosner, "Charbert's Gives 'Boot' to Long-haired Customers," *Lantern,* July 13, 1967, 1.

66. Ronald E. Simon, "7 Student Arrests Made over Weekend," *Lantern,* May 29, 1967, 1.

67. Bruce Vilanch, "Underground Movies 'Inane, Insipid, Bare,'" *Lantern,* February 7, 1967, 3.

68. Carole L. Siemon, "The Hippie Culture—Why?" *Lantern,* May 16, 1967, 4.

69. "Profile Rates Freshmen High," *OSU Monthly,* June 1967, 21. "High" refers to academic achievement, not drug use. Activists at Berkeley had a similar profile. See W. J. Rorabaugh, *Berkeley at War: The 1960s* (New York: Oxford University Press, 1989), 34.

70. Kerry Lehtinen and Phil Long, "Prominent Theologian Is Bludgeoned to Death," *Lantern,* October 18, 1966, 1.

71. Sue Reisinger, "Senior Coed Attacked after Escort Arrested by Police for Jaywalking," *Lantern,* August 17, 1967, 1.

72. "The Tarnished Badge," *Lantern,* August 17, 1967, 4.

73. "Medal Winners, Singer Are Honored at Game," *Lantern,* November 21, 1966, 1.

74. David A. Gollust, "Goldwater Urges Firm War Policy," *Lantern,* March 8, 1967, 1.

NOTES TO CHAPTER 9

1. Jeffrey A. Tannenbaum, "Assembly Is Opposed to Constitutional Revision," *Lantern,* November 17, 1967, 1.

2. Mary Lou Ringle, "Solkov Raps Constitutional Revisions," *Lantern,* December 5, 1967, 1.

3. Chris Jindra, "Constitution Nearing Discussion by Trustees," *Lantern,* January 3, 1968; Board of Trustees, Minutes of April 11, 1968, meeting, 562, at trustees.osu.edu/assets/files/minutes/Archive%20minutes/1966–1968.pdf.

4. Carole Morton, "Hours Rule Has Little Effect on Dating," *Lantern,* November 29, 1967, 6.

5. "CSA Okays Beer Plan for Dorms," *Lantern,* May 31, 1968, 1; "Union, Faculty Club OK'd as Oases on Arid Campus," *Lantern,* July 12, 1968, 1.

6. "Union Requests May Create Increase in University Fees," *Lantern,* October 3, 1967, 1.

7. "Students Riot," *Lantern,* October 5, 1967, 1; "Strike One," *OSU Monthly,* November 1967, 4.

8. Contemporary press reports described D Platoon as a specially trained riot squad, but in a subsequent *Lantern* interview, Columbus safety director Frederick Simon maintained D Platoon members received no special training but instead were charged with providing support to the regular shifts (A, B, and C Platoons); Kathleen M. Cain, "Students Sense Isolation from Columbus," *Lantern,* May 13, 1968, 6A. Dewey Stokes, who served as a member of D Platoon, expressed the same interpretation in an interview.

9. James Endsley, "Police Arrest 16 in Strike Fracas," *Lantern,* October 6, 1967, 1.

10. Charles Gambs, "Report of Arrests during Strike," October 10, 1967, in Office of Student Affairs, Executive Dean, Discipline 1967–68 (Archives: RG 9/a/10).

11. James H. Endsley, "Reporters, Officials Meet to Discuss Riot Incident," *Lantern,* October 10, 1967, 1, and "Student Plans to Sue Police," *Lantern,* October 9, 1967, 1.

12. Endsley, "Reporters, Officials."

13. Mary Lou Ringle, "Union Agrees on Pact, Ends Strike," *Lantern,* October 10, 1967, 1.

14. "Mayor Vows Action in Brutality Charges," *Lantern,* October 23, 1967, 7.

15. Kathy Mikol, "AAUP Criticizes Police Judgment in Oct. Fracas," *Lantern,* February 9, 1968, 1; "Ex Student Awarded $21,255," *Dispatch,* December 17, 1970, 46A.

16. Ron Bishop and Jerry D. Shriver, "Clash in '67 Foretold OSU Protests," *Lantern,* October 6, 1977, 1.

17. Jeffrey A. Tannenbaum, "Antiwar Demonstrators Protest Navy Recruiting," *Lantern,* December 8, 1967, 1.

18. Joseph L. Wagner, "Sensenbrenner Blasts Antiwar Demonstrators," *Lantern,* December 8, 1967, 1; Louis M. Heldman, "Recruiters Cancel Visit," *Lantern,* January 11, 1968, 1.

19. "Students Block Aisle in Protest," *Lantern,* January 24, 1968, 1.

20. Gary Stull, "Fight Halts Demonstration against Marine Recruiting," *Lantern,* January 25, 1968, 1.

21. Gary Stull, "13 Arrested in Recruiting Protest," *Lantern,* February 1, 1968, 1; Memo from Charles Gambs to John Bonner, "Protest Demonstrations, Anti-U.S. Naval Recruiting," February 1, 1968, in Office of Student Affairs, Executive Dean, Discipline 1967–68 (Archives: RG 9/a/10).

22. Kay Burtscher, "CSA Recommends Recruiter Resolution," *Lantern,* January 29, 1968, 1.

23. Gary Stull, "11 Protestors Arrested at Hitchcock 'Mill-In,'" *Lantern,* February 8, 1968, 1.

24. "Marchers Denounce Recruiting," *Lantern,* February 13, 1968, 1; "Dorm Residents Protest Peace Group," *Lantern,* February 16, 1968, 1.

25. "189 Faculty Members Ask Fawcett to Drop Charges," *Lantern,* February 16, 1968, 1.

26. "13 Members Are Named to Rights Review Group," *Lantern,* February 21, 1968, 2.

27. C. William Ashley, "1,000 Students Assemble as Rally Quietly Fizzles," *Lantern,* April 11, 1968, 1; "The Day—that nothing happened," *OSU Monthly,* May 1968, 10.

28. Chris Jindra, "Adams Incites Crowd: 'We'll Burn Lanterns,'" *Lantern,* April 29, 1968, 5.

29. John D. Hofheimer, "Hamilton Hall Trespasser Convicted," *Lantern,* April 19, 1968, 1, and "Nine Students Sentenced in Trespass Case," *Lantern,* May 31, 1968, 1.

30. "ROTC March Moved to New Site," *Lantern,* May 2, 1968, 1.

31. Roger A. Myers, "100 Students Protest Rules for Recruiting," *Lantern,* May 22, 1968, 1.

32. "Crude Stunt Hurts Respectable Protests," *Lantern,* January 8, 1968, 4; "University, Protestors Looked Silly Wednesday," *Lantern,* February 5, 1968, 4.

33. "Census Lists Non-White Distribution," *Lantern,* December 5, 1967, 1.

34. See, for example, Greer C. Stanford-Randle, "The Black Student Movement at the Ohio State University," Ph.D. thesis (Atlanta: Georgia State University, 2010), 81, at scholarworks.gsu.edu/aas_theses.

35. "Developing Dialogue," *OSU Monthly,* March 1968, 4.

36. Kay Burtscher, "Students Want Changes in Counseling, Teaching," *Lantern,* February 2, 1968, 1.

37. Neil Huelsman, "Negroes Want Voice on Campus," *Lantern,* February 2, 1968, 1.

38. John D. Hofheimer, "Rioting Called for in Demonstration," *Lantern,* April 8, 1968, 1; "Correction," *Lantern,* April 12, 1968, 8.

39. "Police Hear Complaints of Alleged Bus Incident," *Lantern,* April 26, 1968, 1.

40. This account is taken from Report of the University Discipline Hearing Committee, "Administration Building 'Lock-in,' April 26, 1968," revised June 26, 1968, in Office of the President, Student Demonstration 1968 (Archives: RG 3/i/66), and Christine Patronik, "Students Were Set for Extended Siege," *Lantern,* April 29, 1968, 1.

41. Memo from John Corbally to Charles Gambs, "Events on Friday, April 26, 1968," May 6, 1968, in Office of the Vice President and Provost, Demonstrations 1968 (Archives: RG 5/a/24); John E. Corbally interview, Oral History Project, 11–13.

42. Duane St. Clair, "OSU Trustee Asks Siege Student Dismissal," *Dispatch,* April 28, 1968, 1A; C. William Ashley, "Accord with Negroes Is Challenged," *Lantern,* April 29, 1968, 1.

43. "OSU 'Kidnap' Victims Said to Fear for Lives," *Dispatch,* April 30, 1968, 1A.

44. Report of the University Discipline Hearing Committee; Corbally interview, Oral History Project, 13.

45. Corbally interview, Oral History Project, 13; "OSU Veep Denies He'll Quit," *Dispatch,* May 2, 1968, 1A.

46. John D. Hofheimer, "Trustees Authorize Takeover Inquiry," *Lantern,* May 1, 1968, 1.

47. Ned Stout, "OSU Alumni Disturbed by 'Soft Line,'" *Dispatch,* May 3, 1968, 1B; UPI, "Solon Requests Special Session," *Dispatch,* April 27, 1968, 12; C. William Ashley, "BSU Siege Violates Civil Rights—Devine," *Lantern,* May 16, 1968, 1; "Columbia, OSU Study Requested," *Lantern,* May 2, 1968, 1.

48. Ashley, "Accord with Negroes Is Challenged"; "Blacks Gain Frat Support," *Lantern,* May 8, 1968, 1.

49. Peter H. Eichstaedt, "Negro Hired as Assistant in University College," *Lantern,* May 10, 1968, 1; Roger Myers, "Negro Graduate Joins Student Relations Staff," *Lantern,* July 16, 1968, 1.

50. Corbally interview, Oral History Project, 13.

51. "34 Negro Students Are Facing Trial over April 26 Lock-in," *Lantern,* June 18, 1968, 1; Roger Myers, "Expulsions Bring Protest by BSU," *Lantern,* July 11, 1968, 10.

52. Ralph Hammock, "Disorder Rules Set by Board," *Lantern,* July 12, 1968, 4; "Faculty Group Recommends Rules for OSU Disruptions," *Lantern,* May 1, 1968, 1.

53. Sam Stein, "Bonner, Mount to Switch Positions," *Lantern,* July 12, 1968, 1; "New Policy Indicated," *Lantern,* July 18, 1968, 4.

54. Myers, "Expulsions Bring Protest."

55. Robert C. Ross, "Vacancies Abound in Campus Dorms," *Lantern,* October 27, 1967, 1.

56. Bill Benham, "Architect Calls River Dorms 'Mistakes,'" *Lantern,* August 24, 1967, 1.

57. Gary Stull, "UCB Professor Raps OSU Housing," *Lantern,* November 13, 1967, 1; Michael L. Drake, "Editor Praises Tower Dorms," *Lantern,* November 15, 1967, 5.

58. C. William Ashley, "OSU to Enact Dorm Rule for Sophomore Men," *Lantern,* April 15, 1968, 1.

59. "Fire Probe Sought by Tower Residents," *Lantern,* May 22, 1968, 1.

60. Christine Patronik, "Three-Way Investigation Launched after Fatal Blaze Strikes Dormitory," *Lantern,* May 23, 1968, 1.

61. "Tragic Fire Must Bring Changes," *Lantern,* May 23, 1968, 4.

62. John Arnold, "Students Vow Action if Demands Ignored," *Lantern,* May 24, 1968, 1; John Zink, "Administrator Is Censured for 'Contemptible Attitude,'" *Lantern,* May 24, 1968, 1.

63. Christine Lingard, "Dormitory Blaze 'Deliberately Set,'" *Lantern,* May 29, 1968, 1.

64. Richard Bletzacker, "Some Views on the Design Safety Features of Lincoln and Morrill Towers," May 29, 1968, in Office of the President, Lincoln Tower Fire (Archives: RG 3/i/66).

65. David Work, "Fire: Administration Not to Blame," *Lantern,* May 29, 1968, 4.

66. Ralph Hammock, "Freshman Arrested in Tower Fire," *Lantern,* May 31, 1968, 1.

67. Carl Peterson, "Ohio State University: The Morrill and Lincoln Fires," Boston: National Fire Prevention Association, July 11, 1968, in Office of the President, Lincoln Tower Fire (Archives: RG 3/i/66).

68. "West Dormitories Made Safer by Water Sprinkler System," *Lantern,* July 12, 1968, 4.

69. "Leeb Is Freed 'Unconditionally,'" *Lantern,* March 9, 1971, 1.

70. David Lore, "Death in Dorm Fire Climaxes Frustrations," *Dispatch,* May 23, 1968, 1B.

71. Jeffrey A. Tannenbaum, "Kerr Calls for Reform," *Lantern,* November 15, 1967, 1.

72. Bill Benham, "Computer Scheduling Held Up," *Lantern,* March 8, 1968, 3.

73. "Students Get Better Start in U. College," *Lantern,* February 16, 1968, 1.

74. Gideon Frankel, "University College: Location Poor," *Lantern,* May 14, 1968, 4.

75. C. William Ashley, "Prof Burns Draft Card during Class," *Lantern,* April 8, 1968, 1; John Bender, Ira Sully, and Jack Cooley interviews. The author was a student in David Green's History 671 course that quarter.

76. Brian J. Patterson, "Green Raps U.S. Racism; Photographer Attacked," *Lantern,* May 1, 1968, 8.

77. Memo to members of the university faculty from Robert Fisher et al., "Report of the Special Faculty Hearing Committee with Regard to David E. Green," July 12, 1968, in Vice President for Academic Affairs, Green (David) Case (Archives: RG 5/a/25).

78. Roger Myers, "Board of Trustees Fires Green," *Lantern,* July 12, 1968, 1.

79. Mimi Deaton, "Was Dismissal Justified? Poll Reveals Student Split," *Lantern,* July 12, 1968, 4.

80. Letter to Novice Fawcett from Steve Breyfogle, April 23, 1968, in Vice President for Academic Affairs, Green (David) Case (Archives: RG 5/a/25).

81. Gail Harrison, "AAUP Lifts 7-Year Censure," *Lantern,* June 27, 1980, 2.

82. Committee for the Study of Alternatives, "Rhetoric vs. Reality" (advertisement), *Lantern,* May 24, 1968, 5.

83. "Memo from Mall," *OSU Monthly,* July 1968, 56.

84. Jeffrey A. Tannenbaum, "View from Here: Student Power?" *Lantern,* April 19, 1968, 4.

85. Letter from Russell Dynes and E. L. Quarantelli to John Bonner, July 25, 1968, in Office of the President, Student Demonstrations 1968 (Archives: RG 3/i/66).

86. Louis M. Heldman, "Grad Deferments Slashed; Effects Seen as Uncertain," *Lantern,* February 19, 1968, 1; Ruth Gerbec, "Draft Threatens Only New Grads," *Lantern,* February 23, 1968, 1.

87. These statistics showed that fewer than one-third of males who turned 18 during the Vietnam War era (1964–73) served in the military. Of them, fewer than one-third served in Vietnam, and of them, only between one-quarter and one-half spent significant time exposed to enemy fire. Lawrence M. Baskir and William A. Strauss, *Chance and Circumstance: The Draft, the War and the Vietnam Generation* (New York: Vintage Books, 1978), 5.

88. "Grads View New Draft Plan," *Lantern,* February 23, 1968, 3.

89. See, for example, "The Student and the Draft," *Lantern,* January 3, 1968 (special edition).

90. "93.6% Read Lantern," *Lantern,* July 2, 1968, 1.

91. "More Students May Take Vietnam History Class," *Lantern,* March 27, 1968, 1.

92. "War Kills Ex-Student" in "Campus News Wrap Up," *Lantern,* March 1, 1968, 3.

93. "Letters: Soldier Wants Letters," *Lantern,* June 27, 1968, 4; "Soldier Killed in Action; Coed's Letter Returned," *Lantern,* August 22, 1968, 1.

94. Gary Stull, "Local Group Backs RFK for President," *Lantern,* November 30, 1967, 1.

95. For more about the turbulent politics of 1968, see James T. Patterson, *Grand Expectations: The United States, 1945–1974* (New York: Oxford University Press, 1996), 678–709.

96. Kay Burtscher, "350 Jam Opening Meeting of RFK's Campus Campaign," *Lantern,* March 29, 1968, 1.

97. Eileen Slutsky, "OSU McCarthyites to Begin Campaign," *Lantern,* April 2, 1968, 1.

98. "Classes Cancelled in King's Memory," *Lantern,* April 9, 1968, 8.

99. C. William Ashley, "Glenn, Hilsman Recruit RFK Supporters," *Lantern,* April 25, 1968, 1; "Newman Draws Capacity Crowd," *Lantern,* April 26, 1968, 1.

100. "Robert F. Kennedy: Leader of Youth," *Lantern,* June 18, 1968, 4.

101. David Haglund, "Gregory Raps War, Racism," *Lantern,* January 24, 1968, 1.

102. David Haglund, "To Control Racism in U.S., Eliminate Ghettoes—Bunche," *Lantern,* March 6, 1968, 1.

103. "'New' Blacks Will Alter System, Militants Say," *Lantern,* April 24, 1968, 1.

104. "Gentry of Radicals Needed to Preserve What We Have," *OSU Monthly,* July 1968, 4.

NOTES TO CHAPTER 10

1. Chris Jindra, "University No Soapbox—Fawcett," *Lantern,* September 25, 1968, 1; David Eppley, "Protests Ruled Out if Inside," *Lantern,* September 26, 1968, 1.

2. Peter Eichstaedt, "Report Proposes Code of Discipline," *Lantern,* September 26, 1968, 1.

3. Nancy Popa, "Student Ticket Sales Decline," *Lantern,* November 1, 1967, 2; "Football Dominance Is Part of the Past," *Lantern,* October 12, 1967, 4.

4. Dick Nethers, "The Bucks Are Dying," *Lantern,* November 1, 1967, 2; Robert Cantwell, "Say It Isn't So, Woody," *Sports Illustrated,* September 11, 1967, 104.

5. Karen Gartley, "Students Take to Streets to Celebrate Buckeye Win," *Lantern,* October 14, 1968, 2.

6. Kay Burtscher, "Happy Pandemonium Rose on High after Buckeye Win," *Lantern,* November 25, 1968, 1.

7. "That Game!" *OSU Monthly,* December 1968, 4; Christina Walker, "'Victory Party' Costs $7,000," *Lantern,* November 25, 1968, 7. Cost estimates varied depending on whether or not police overtime was included.

8. Cynthia Friedman, "Hughes Considers Use of 'D' Platoon," *Lantern,* January 15, 1970, 1. James J. Hughes Jr., the official quoted here, replaced Fred Simon as Columbus safety director in 1969.

9. "Rose Bowl, 1969," *OSU Monthly,* January 1969, 1.

10. See, for example, "Negro Lot Improving," *Lantern,* October 4, 1968, 7; Amy Richards, "Black Artist Will Sign Posters at Ohio Union," *Lantern,* March 27, 1969, 1; Vicki Schmitz, "OSU to Help 60 Get Job Training," *Lantern,* May 21, 1969, 2.

11. Donald L. Cook, "Report Cites Black Housing Bias," *Lantern,* November 19, 1968, 1.

12. Jay R. Smith, "Prompt Housing Action Pledged," *Lantern,* May 9, 1969, 1.

13. Sandra J. White, "Reindictments Filed in Cases against 34," *Lantern,* January 23, 1969, 1.

14. Mark Weaver, "'Behind the Scene' Pressure Applied in Court Decision of 32," *Lantern,* August 14, 1969, 1.

15. Rick Pilsbury, "Riot Was Justified, Say City Residents," *Lantern,* August 21, 1969, 8.

16. James T. Patterson, *Grand Expectations: The United States, 1945–1974* (New York: Oxford University Press, 1996), 624–25; Tom McAvoy, "SDS Attracts Radical Left," *Lantern,* January 23, 1969, 1.

17. "SDS," Student Organizations (Archives: RG 44/14/17).

18. Roger Myers, "Divided SDS Reacts to 'Slow' System," *Lantern,* January 28, 1969, 3.

19. "SDS Losing Ground," *Lantern,* March 27, 1969, 5.

20. Patrick Heydinger and Norman E. Cox, "Students Clash over ROTC as Cadets Receive Awards," *Lantern,* May 9, 1969, 1.

21. "Green Ribbons 'Cool It,'" *Lantern,* May 9, 1969, 1.

22. Robert H. Dorn, "ROTC Change Wanted, Student Survey Shows," *Lantern,* May 20, 1969, 1.

23. Sue Whitmyer, "YAF Presents 7-Point Program," *Lantern,* July 24, 1969, 1.

24. "SDS Go Home," *Lantern,* May 5, 1969, 3; Bob Tamasy, "Roberts Opposes SDS Objectives," *Lantern,* January 30, 1969, 1.

25. Thomas Burroughs, "Will the Real SDS Please Stand Up?" *Lantern,* July 3, 1969, 4; Patterson, *Grand Expectations,* 716–17.

26. Federal Bureau of Investigation, "New Left Activity—Ohio State University Columbus Ohio (OSU)," July 16, 1968, 1, at vault.fbi.gov/cointel-pro/new-left/cointel-pro-new-left-cincinnati-part-01-of-01/view.

27. Dewey Stokes interview. Stokes was a member of the undercover unit.

28. Confidential memo from Charles Gambs to John Mount, "Report of Anticipated Violence, April 4, 1969," April 3, 1969, in Office of the Vice President of Student Affairs, Charles R. Gambs, 1968 (Archives: RG 9/a/30); Patterson, *Grand Expectations,* 716–17.

29. Memo to Director FBI from SAC Cincinnati, "Subject: CONTELPRO—New Left Status Report, 1/1/69–2/28/69," March 4, 1969, 4–5, at vault.fbi.gov/cointel-pro /new-left/cointel-pro-new-left-cincinnati-part-01-of-01/view.

30. "Students to Lobby; Hire Professional," *Lantern,* January 13, 1969, 1; Jay Shaffer interview.

31. Amy Richards, "Beer and Victory Unites Old Rivals," *Lantern,* April 10, 1969, 1.

32. Barbara Helm, "Forum: Free Women," *Lantern,* February 3, 1969, 4.

33. Mary Beschenbossel, "Coed Studies Space Medicine," *Lantern,* May 29, 1969, 5; Larry L. Burris, "Coed Does a Man's Job," *Lantern,* March 3, 1969, 3; "Women Headed for Antarctic," *Lantern,* July 3, 1969, 2; Charles Hazard, "Man's World Invaded—Coed Joins ROTC Drill," *Lantern,* January 28, 1969, 1; "Coed Marching Band," *Lantern,* January 17, 1969, 4.

34. Howard Huntzinger, "Rhodes Plan Offers 'Solution for the Seventies,'" *Dispatch,* November 28, 1968, 1A.

35. "Changes Proposed for Higher Education Draw Varied Reactions," *OSU Monthly,* January 1969, 10; Fred Kocher, "Fawcett Questions Rhodes' Proposal," *Lantern,* December 5, 1968, 1; Cheryl Meredith, "Regent's Budget Could Mean Fee Hike," *Lantern,* January 13, 1969, 1; "A Disaster for the Seventies," *Lantern,* January 27, 1969, 4.

36. Robert J. Tamasy, "Fee Freeze Favored," *Lantern,* February 6, 1969, 10.

37. C. William Ashley and Robert J. Caldwell, "Millett Sees Little Hope for More Education Aid," *Lantern,* April 21, 1969, 1.

38. Thomas Burroughs, "Trustees Juggle Fees; Total Stays at $200," *Lantern,* August 14, 1969, 1.

39. Betty Willis, "Biology Plans Course Change," *Lantern,* July 10, 1969, 14.

40. Jay R. Smith, "Ohio State Freshmen Top National Average on ACT," *Lantern,* April 1, 1969, 8.

41. Harry Kingdom, "Students Say TV Courses Less Effective," *Lantern,* February 27, 1969, 5.

42. Mary Beschenbossel, "Budget Cut May Affect Telescope Construction," *Lantern,* April 2, 1969, 5.

43. "Bill Seeks to Set Classroom Hours for Faculty," *OSU Monthly,* April 1969, 4.

44. Robert J. Caldwell and C. William Ashley, "Faculty Bill Compromised," *Lantern,* May 7, 1969, 9.

45. "A Time for Rebirth," *Lantern,* October 30, 1968, 4.

46. "YR's to Canvass," *Lantern,* October 14, 1968, 3.

47. Stuart Meck and Carol Hassell, "Nixon Cites Strategy: Succeed like Bucks," *Lantern,* October 23, 1968, 1.

48. Jennie Buckner, "Student Protestors Lose II-S Deferments," *Lantern,* November 4, 1968, 1.

49. "'Get Tough,' Say Regents and Rhodes," *Lantern,* November 27, 1968, 1; Confidential memo from Novice Fawcett to Cabinet, "Report on Meeting in the Office of the Board of Regents on March 11, 1969," in Office of the President, President's Memorandums: 1970–72 (Archives: RG 3/i/76).

50. Rick Perlstein, *Nixonland: The Rise of a President and the Fracturing of America* (New York: Scribner, 2008), 277–79.

51. "Nixon Blasts Protestors," *Lantern,* April 30, 1969, 8.

52. C. William Ashley, "Student Disorder Target of Senate," *Lantern,* March 27, 1969, 1.

53. Robert J. Caldwell and C. William Ashley, "Presidents Hit Regent Bill," *Lantern,* April 23, 1969, 1.

54. "More College Riots?" *Lantern,* March 27, 1969, 7.

55. Nancy Newman, "University Dropouts Linger on Campus in Varied Jobs," *Lantern,* January 17, 1969, 5; Iris Galan, "'Pearl Alley' Shops Harassed Often," *Lantern,* July 31, 1969, 2.

56. Christina Walker, "Varied Response Greets Second Campus Paper," *Lantern,* November 14, 1968, 6.

57. Jay R. Smith, "Planning Begins for Nixon Visit," *Lantern,* May 12, 1969, 1.

58. "A Time to Speak and a Time to Listen," *OSU Monthly,* July 1969, 3.

59. Leanne McLaughlin, "Graduation '69—Spiro Style," *Lantern,* June 17, 1969, 1; "University's Largest Commencement," *OSU Monthly,* July 1969, 1.

60. "Speakers Cover Spectrum of Politics, Poetry," *Makio,* 1969, 209; Barbara Moyse, "US Aims Called Unrealistic," *Lantern,* May 29, 1969, 5.

61. "Let's Listen to Them," *OSU Monthly,* June 1969, 13.

62. Sue Whitmeyer and Thomas Burroughs, "Faculty Comments on Moon Landing," *Lantern,* July 17, 1969, 1.

63. Thomas Burroughs, "500,000 Try 3-Day Peace," *Lantern,* August 21, 1969, 1.

NOTES TO CHAPTER 11

1. "Alumni Who Lost Their Lives in Vietnam," in Francis P. Weisenburger, *History of the Ohio State University: The Fawcett Years, 1956–1972* (Columbus: Ohio State University Press, 1975), 275–77; "Vietnam Veterans Memorial," thewall-usa.com.

2. Robert J. Caldwell, "Disorders May Threaten OSU, Warns Legislator," *Lantern,* October 10, 1969, 1.

3. Mary Webster, "DC Caravan Departs," *Lantern,* November 14, 1969, 1.

4. Shirley Brownell, "Fans to Skip Protest," *Lantern,* November 14, 1969, 15.

5. As it turned out most of the middle category of students and some of the first category were not called up because manpower requirements declined significantly as the war wound down.

6. Mary Webster, "Lottery Prompts Varied Reactions," *Lantern,* December 2, 1969, 1.

7. "White House Denies Offering Post to Hayes," *Lantern,* December 4, 1969, 1.

8. Mary Webster, "Stollmack Leaves CMC Position," *Lantern,* January 15, 1970, 10, and "CMC Denies Split in Peace Movements," *Lantern,* April 10, 1970, 14; Joel Ann Todd interview.

9. "SDS," in Student Organizations (Archives: RG 44/14/17); Betty Garrett, "Vietnam Vigil Leader Denies SDS Involved," *Citizen-Journal,* October 11, 1969, 2.

10. "Teens Charge SDS," *Lantern,* October 21, 1969, 1.

11. Joe Gillette, "Runaway, Commune Probe Continues," *Citizen-Journal,* January 27, 1970, 2; Mary Zimmer, "Area Arrests Climb," *Lantern,* January 28, 1970, 1.

12. Mark Weaver, "Arrested Consider Police Invasion Illegal," *Lantern,* February 2, 1970, 1; Mark Weaver, "Jaschik Blasts Media," *Lantern,* January 29, 1970, 12.

13. Jody Ross, "Black Students Present 19 'Concerns' to Mount," *Lantern,* March 10, 1970, 1.

14. *Makio,* 1970, 171.

15. "Friday March 13," in "Diary of a Dilemma," *OSU Monthly,* June 1970, 7.

16. Jay R. Smith, "Blacks Identified in Disruption Charges," *Lantern,* April 7, 1970, 1.

17. Martha Brian and Mary Carran Webster, "The Campus Radicals: Where Are They Now?" *Columbus Monthly,* June 1978, 44–45.

18. Robert Garrison, "School of Social Work Hit by Walk-Out," *Lantern,* April 21, 1970, 1.

19. Even though it was a university-recognized student organization, the Third World Solidarity Committee did not leave behind much of a footprint. It listed John Behling, associate professor of social work, as its faculty adviser. Behling also advised the Ohio State chapter of SDS for a time. "Third World Solidarity Committee," in Student Organizations (Archives RG 44/14/17).

20. Bonnie Schwartz and Michael B. Lafferty, "Protest Disrupts Exhibit," *Lantern,* April 21, 1970, 1.

21. Jay R. Smith, "Six Arrested at Prospectus '70," *Lantern,* April 22, 1970, 1; Memo from Charles Gambs to John Mount, "Third World Solidarity Committee Demonstration against War Profiteers and Military Recruiters at Prospectus '70—Tuesday, April 21, 1970," April 22, 1970, in Student Affairs, Office of the Vice President, Disruptions-Demonstrations, April 20, 21, 1970 (Archives: RG 9/a/29).

22. Bonnie Schwartz, "Students to Rally against Union Arrests," *Lantern,* April 24, 1970, 1.

23. Former *Lantern* reporter Mary Webster recalled that a flier was sent to various disaffected groups inviting them to a meeting at a private home or apartment in the neighborhood east of High Street. The meeting resulted in the agreement to form the coalition. Former strike leader Joe Hyler believed Afro-Am initiated the meeting, but other participants were not able to recall who started the process. Mary Webster and Joe Hyler interviews.

24. Linda Hershey, "Assembly Opposes Disruption Rule," *Lantern,* April 24, 1970, 1.

25. Bonnie Schwartz, "Group Asks Student Strike," *Lantern,* April 27, 1970, 1.

26. "Hearings Reveal Prospectus '70 Arrest Orders," *Lantern,* December 11, 1970, 1; John T. Mount interview, Oral History Project , October 20, 2003.

27. Schwartz, "Group Asks Student Strike."

28. "OU and Miami U Protests Continue," *Lantern,* April 24, 1970, 6.

29. Robert Westwood, "Administrators, Students Argue Demands," *Lantern,* April 28, 1970, 1.

30. "Fawcett Reviews Student Demands," *Lantern,* April 28, 1970, 1.

31. Bonnie Schwartz, "Assembly Calls for Peaceful Boycott," *Lantern,* April 29, 1970, 1; "Protest vs. Walkout," *Lantern,* April 24, 1970, 3; "Demonstration Dilemma," *Lantern,* April 29, 1970, 3.

32. Jack Keis, "Centennial Shows Luster," *Lantern,* January 12, 1970, 7.

33. "Most Important Fossil Found on Continent Antarctica," *OSU Monthly,* January 1970, 6.

34. Leslie Zoslov and Robert Rhees, "Course Closeout High," *Lantern,* June 10, 1970, 1; Warren Gould, "10% Delay Graduation a Quarter Due to Close-Outs, Poll Shows," *Lantern,* March 5, 1971, 3.

35. "Scheduling: Choice vs. Resources," *Lantern,* April 2, 1970, 1; Memo from Ron Brady to Novice Fawcett and James Robinson, "Closed Courses," October 20, 1969, in Vice President for Student Affairs, Closed Courses (Archives: RG 5/a/28).

36. Dick Crump and Ronald Ishoy, "Hard Reality of Scheduling Woes Clashes with 'Development' Ideal," *Lantern,* June 9, 1970, 4.

37. Michael Tschappat, "Former Pusher Predicts Hard Drug Use Increase," *Lantern,* October 7, 1969, 1; Margaret T. McClure, "Survey Shows Dorm Drug Usage Common," *Lantern,* March 9, 1970, 1.

38. Bonnie McClure, "2 Drug Arrests Made after Dormitory Fire," *Lantern,* February 16, 1970, 1.

39. Memo from Kenneth Bader to Rod Swearingon, "Drug Committee Report," February 11, 1970, in Office of Student Affairs and Associate Dean of Students, Drug Committee, 1969–70 (Archives: RG 9/c-3/2).

40. Charlotte Gibb, "Drugs Course Will Be Taught," *Lantern,* May 27, 1970, 4.

41. Vince Doria, "Fawcett Opposes Warren-King Study," *Lantern,* January 16, 1970, 1.

42. Jody Ross, "Millett Will Oppose Warren-King Report," *Lantern,* January 14, 1970, 1, and "Regents Have 'Near Monopoly Control,'" *Lantern,* January 12, 1970, 1 .

43. Robert J. Caldwell, "Management Report Labeled 'Snow Job' by Official," *Lantern,* February 27, 1970, 1.

44. "Man for All Seasons" and ". . . Furthermore, What Gives?" *Lantern,* January 19, 1970, 3.

45. Mary Webster and Lee R. Jenkins, "Students March to Protest Fees," *Lantern,* April 20, 1970, 1; Michael B. Lafferty, "Tax Payers Comment," *Lantern,* April 20, 1970, 12.

46. Melanie Menrath, "While You Were on Vacation," *Lantern,* March 31, 1970, 13.

47. Mary Webster,"Rhodes Opens Earth Day," *Lantern,* April 23, 1970, 4; "Glenn's Earth Day Talk Centered on Pollution," *Lantern,* April 23, 1970, 4.

48. Richard Markel, "Every Day Is Earthday for Campus Club," *Lantern,* June 9, 1970, 2.

49. Rick Perlstein, *Nixonland: The Rise of a President and the Fracturing of America* (New York: Scribner, 2008), 477–79.

50. Margy McDermott, "Professors Criticize Drive into Cambodia," *Lantern,* May 6, 1970, 2.

51. Richard G. Zimmerman, "Rhodes's First Eight Years, 1963–1971," in Alexander P. Lamis, editor, *Ohio Politics* (Kent: Kent State University Press, 1994), 78–79.

52. Marianne Zegers, "Rhodes 'Cracking Down' on Campus-Area Crime," *Lantern,* February 11, 1970, 1.

53. "Opposition Voiced over Police Shootings," *Lantern,* February 4, 1970, 1.

54. John Ewing, "Council Hears Both Sides," *Lantern,* February 17, 1970, 1.

55. "Serious Crimes Rise in the University Area" and "Unsolved Murders Mount," *Lantern,* August 6, 1970, 4.

NOTES TO CHAPTER 12

1. Bonnie Schwartz, "Student Rioters Battle Police," *Lantern,* April 30, 1970, 1.

2. "Chronology of Day's Events," *Lantern,* April 30, 1970, 9.

3. Jay R. Smith, "Officials React to Strikers," *Lantern,* April 30, 1970, 9. The "Teutonic" observation is from Ron St. Pierre interview; Meiling's threat to remove the protestors himself is from John Mount interview, August 6, 2013.

4. Robin Wallis, "Conflict Follows Closing," *Lantern,* April 30, 1970, 10.

5. Dan Bradley, Jerry Friedman, Blaine Lilly, Don Slemmer, and Ron St. Pierre interviews.

6. Wallis, "Conflict Follows Closing."

7. "Chronology of Day's Events."

8. James Abraham interview.

9. Robert Westwood, "50 Injured in Campus Riot," *Lantern,* April 30, 1970, 9.

10. LTC James M. Abraham, "Commander's Confidential Report on Aid to Civil Authority at Ohio State University (Columbus, Ohio), 29 April to 2 May 1970," 5, 44 (Archives).

11. Abraham, "Commander's Confidential Report," 9–13.

12. Bonnie Schwartz, "Violence, Gas, Fire Bombs," *Lantern,* May 1, 1970, 1; Brian Patterson, "Many Were Gassed," *Dispatch,* April 30, 1970, 8A.

13. Elise Schmetzer, "Dorm Directors Comment," *Lantern,* May 1, 1970, 10.

14. "Guardsman Cheered," *Lantern,* May 1, 1970, 13.

15. "Captain Called Down on Guard Role at OSU," *Dispatch,* May 5, 1970, 8A.

16. Schwartz, "Violence, Gas, Fire Bombs."

17. "Students Allowed to Stay; Planned to Sleep on Oval," *Lantern,* May 1, 1970, 13.

18. Bonnie Schwartz, "Campus Calm Restored," and Ken Bandy, "Student Marshals Help to Keep Campus Cool," *Lantern,* May 4, 1970, 6.

19. Robert Smith, "Follow-up to WOSU-TV Broadcast, Friday May 1, 1970," 13, in Dean of Students, Campus Disorders, 1970–72 (Archives: RG 9/c/1).

20. "Mount Announces Black Recruiting," *Lantern,* May 4, 1970, 1; "Black Studies to Get $170,000," *Lantern,* May 5, 1970, 1.

21. "UCD Schedules Hearings Today, May End Temporary Suspensions," *Lantern,* May 4, 1970, 1.

22. "Strike Organizer Knocks Leaders," *Lantern,* May 6, 1970, 12.

23. "24 Fires Reported in 9 Days," *Lantern,* May 19, 1970, 12.

24. Louis M. Heldman, "Woman Linked to Bombings Reported in Columbus Area," *Lantern,* May 4, 1970, 1. No further sightings were reported. It might have been a case of mistaken identity, or Wilkerson may have moved on.

25. Gene Jordan, "Rhodes Accuses Taft of Coddling Rioters," *Dispatch,* May 3, 1970, 1.

26. Richard G. Zimmerman, "Rhodes's First Eight Years, 1963–1971," in Alexander P. Lamis, editor, *Ohio Politics* (Kent: Kent State University Press, 1994), 80–81.

27. Dan Bradley interview; "Kent Shootings Kill Four," *Lantern,* May 5, 1970, 1.

28. Report of the Committee of Inquiry to the Faculty Council (hereafter Committee of Inquiry), "The Spring Events at Ohio State," November 10, 1970, 81–82 (Archives: Demonstrations vertical file).

29. Charles Fenton, "Protest Is Peaceful at OSU Ceremony," *Citizen-Journal,* May 5, 1970, 1; Ray Lambert, "ROTC Activity Disrupted," *Dispatch,* May 5, 1970, 2A.

30. Bonnie Schwartz, "Guard Clears Building Entrances," *Lantern,* May 6, 1970, 1.

31. Schwartz, "Guard Clears Building Entrances."

32. Frank Eugene Garver, "The Organizational Structure and Operating Procedures of the Student Marshals at the Ohio State University, Spring 1970," 6–7 (Archives: Demonstrations vertical file).

33. "Fawcett's Statement," *Lantern,* May 6, 1970, 1.

34. Committee of Inquiry, 87.

35. "24 Fires Reported."

36. "Wednesday, May 6," in "Diary of a Dilemma," *OSU Monthly,* June 1970, 15.

37. "24 Fires Reported."

38. Jay R. Smith, "A Student Strike Roundup: Our Tense, Explosive Spring," *Lantern,* May 19, 1970, 1.

39. University Archives, "School's Out," at library.osu.edu/blogs/archives/2014/01/10/schools-out.

40. Lorraine Cohen, Art Flesch, and Mary Webster interviews.

41. Mary Webster and Art Flesch interviews.

42. Susan Shifres, "Peaceful Campus Negotiation Objective of Majority Alliance," *Lantern,* May 20, 1970, 1; "Veterans Demand Legislation to Expel," *Lantern,* May 19, 1970, 13.

43. Robin Willis, "Faculty's Role Changing; Result of Demonstrations," *Lantern,* May 20, 1970, 4.

44. Robert Westwood, "Students Protest Campus Slayings; Three State Universities Are Closed," *Lantern,* May 19, 1970, 13.

45. Text of "Remarks of James A. Robinson, Vice President for Academic Affairs and Provost, to Executive Session, Faculty Council, May 12, 1970" (courtesy of Pam Conrad), and Committee of Inquiry, 93–96.

46. Committee of Inquiry, 103.

47. Committee of Inquiry, 90–91.

48. "Thursday, May 14," and "Sunday, May 17," in "Diary of a Dilemma," *OSU Monthly,* June 1970, 16.

49. "Negotiations Progressing," *Lantern,* May 19, 1970, 1.

50. Mary Webster, "Procedure Set for Reopening," *Lantern,* May 20, 1970, 1.

51. "Faculty Council Proposes Grading System Changes," *Lantern,* May 21, 1970, 1.

52. "Discipline Chairman Resigns in Protest," *Lantern,* May 21, 1970, 1.

53. Bonnie Schwartz, "Scuffles Break Out after Rally," *Lantern,* May 22, 1970, 1.

54. Committee of Inquiry, 113.

55. Mary Webster and Robin Wallis, "Campus Is Open Despite Violence," *Lantern,* May 22, 1970, 1.

56. Students took 57,334 courses on a pass/fail basis (technically pass/nonpass) that spring quarter, or about one-quarter of the total number offered. "P/NP Courses High for Spring Quarter," *Lantern,* July 9, 1970, 2.

57. "Board Passes Proposals," *Lantern,* May 26, 1970, 1.

58. "Board Passes Proposals."

59. Robin Wallis, "Del Corso Views Student Rally; Comments on Campus Disorder," *Lantern,* May 26, 1970, 8.

60. Linda Hershey, "Nixon Aide Aims Talks at Campus Disturbances," *Lantern,* May 26, 1970, 8; "Campus Aides Say Nixon Losing Support of Youth," *Lantern,* June 9, 1970, 8.

61. Robert Oster, "Black Studies Head Selected," *Lantern,* May 26, 1970, 1.

62. Roger J. Mezger, "Negotiations Stall While Factions Fight over Neutral Bargaining Site," *Lantern,* May 27, 1970, 1.

63. Bonnie Schwartz and Mary Webster, "Strikers Leave Oval, Move to St. Stephen's," *Lantern,* May 27, 1970, 1; Bill Crandell interview.

64. Bonnie Schwartz, "Strike Picks Up Greatest Support as 'Fast and Vigil' Begins on Oval," *Lantern,* May 28, 1970, 1.

65. "Governor Establishes Communication Line," *Lantern,* May 28, 1970, 1.

66. Mary Huntzinger, "Petition Calls for Striker Restraint," *Lantern,* June 1, 1970, 1.

67. "Marshmallow Brigade," *Lantern,* June 1, 1970 (photo), 8.

68. For more about how the turmoil affected the surrounding community, see Emily Foster, *The Ohio State University District: A Neighborhood History* (Charleston, S.C.: History Press, 2014), 67–74.

69. Mary Weekley, "Campus Atmosphere 'Hot,'" *Lantern,* June 3, 1970, 8.

70. Bonnie Schwartz, "Crandell, Five Others Arrested Following Strike, March Monday," *Lantern,* June 2, 1970, 1.

71. Robert Garrison, "Moulton, Kilgore Clash; Moulton Walks Out," *Lantern,* June 5, 1970, 1.

72. Roger Mezger, "Court Injunction Granted against Coalition Leaders," *Lantern,* June 9, 1970, 1. The suit was never decided and was dropped two years later.

73. Bonnie Schwartz, "Noon Rally Buries Spring Quarter Strike," *Lantern,* June 11, 1970, 1.

74. Harold M. Snyder, "State Pay Cut, High Enrollment Hike Fees," *Lantern,* September 30, 1970, 7C.

75. Roger J. Mezger, "Trustees Reject Ross, Approve Fee Hike," *Lantern,* June 12, 1970, 1; "Summer Justice," *Lantern,* June 12, 1970, 1.

76. Sharon West interview.

77. Sally Kinchy, "Cap and Gown May Contribute to Peace," *Lantern,* June 2, 1970, 1; Rich Levin interview.

78. Mary Webster, "Finch Addresses Guarded Rite," *Lantern,* June 23, 1970, 3.

79. "Nixon Sets Police Objective; No Firing against Rioters," *Lantern,* June 9, 1970, 8.

80. Rick Perlstein, *Nixonland: The Rise of the President and the Fracturing of America* (New York: Scribner, 2008), 497.

81. "A Newsweek Poll: Mr. Nixon Holds Up," *Newsweek,* May 25, 1970, 30.

82. "Election Backlash Foretold," *Lantern,* August 20, 1970, 2.

83. Zimmerman, "Rhodes's First Eight Years," 81.

84. Roberta Becker, "Police Remove Shotguns," *Lantern,* February 13, 1970, 1.

85. Roger J. Mezger, "Trustees Reconsider, Approve Ross," *Lantern,* June 23, 1970, 1; Francis P. Weisenburger, *History of the Ohio State University: The Fawcett Years, 1956–1972* (Columbus: Ohio State University Press, 1975), 181–82.

86. Milt Miller, "844 Arrest Tally Includes 258 on Campus," *Lantern,* September 30, 1970, 2C.

87. Unless otherwise indicated, this testimony is from Roger J. Mezger, "Unrest Observations Differ," *Lantern,* August 6, 1970, 1.

88. "Shootings Detailed for Subcommittee," *Lantern,* August 6, 1970, 1; Charles Fenton, "Officers Shot OSU Coed, Student Tells Legislators," *Citizen-Journal,* August 6, 1970, 1.

89. David Browne, *Fire and Rain: The Beatles, Simon and Garfunkel, James Taylor, CSNY, and the Lost Story of 1970* (Cambridge, Mass.: Da Capo Press, 2011), 298.

NOTES TO EPILOGUE

1. Mary Kropko, "Students Turn from Riots to Games," *Lantern,* May 2, 1975, 14.

2. Arthur Levine, *When Dreams and Heroes Died: A Portrait of Today's College Student* (Washington, D.C.: Jossey-Bass, 1980), 1–8; Nancy Freeman, "Freshmen Flunk

'Youth' Image," *Lantern,* November 25, 1970, 1; Dale Feneli, "Survey Shows Premarital Sex Lags in Midwest," *Lantern,* April 9, 1971, 1.

3. Milt Miller, "Campus Security Measures Tightened and Sophisticated," *Lantern,* October 2, 1970, 3; Joseph Boulware, "University Renovates Walks, Brick by Brick," *Lantern,* August 20, 1970, 5.

4. Mary Webster, "University Meets 22 Student Demands," *Lantern,* October 1, 1970, 1. The complete report is available at library.osu.edu/projects/spring-of-dissent /documents/response_student_demands.pdf.

5. Karen Lamoreux, "Demand Report Called Poor," *Lantern,* October 2, 1970, 1; "Progress: More Needed," *Lantern,* October 2, 1970, 4.

6. K. P. Devaney, "Too Few Blacks on Faculty," *Lantern,* May 3, 1971, 2; Sue Giller, "Rising Minority Role Discussed at Meeting," *Lantern,* April 23, 1971, 14.

7. Dale Van Lerberghe, "Fawcett Dismisses Ross," *Lantern,* July 1, 1971, 1; Francis P. Weisenburger, *History of the Ohio State University: The Fawcett Years, 1956–1972* (Columbus: Ohio State University Press, 1975), 182.

8. John B. Gabel, *The Jennings Years, 1981–1990* (Columbus: Ohio State University, 1992), 85–88.

9. Ohio State Institutional Research and Planning, "Statistical Summary, 2014"; Office of Human Resources, Planning and Analysis, "Diversity Data for Faculty and Staff, University Summary as of 9/30/13."

10. Ohio State Enrollment Services, "Retention and Graduation Rates for New First Year Students," September 18, 2014.

11. "Statistical Summary, 2014."

12. Ann Sheldon, "Women's Lib Sets Goals," *Lantern,* October 6, 1970, 2.

13. "Women's Affairs Office Recommended," *Lantern,* May 5, 1971, 1.

14. Renee Nicole Lansley, "College Women or College Girls? Gender, Sexuality and in Loco Parentis on Campus," Ph.D. thesis (Columbus: Ohio State University, 2004), 159.

15. Email from Mike Carrell, Ohio State Office of Military and Veterans Services, August 26, 2015.

16. Memo from Charles Gambs to Edward Moulton, "Final Status Report—Rules 51.03 and 51.05 Disruption Cases," September 16, 1971, in Novice G. Fawcett, Disruptions and Demonstrations: Campus Status Reports of Discipline Cases, Jan–Aug 71 (Archives: RG 3/i/80).

17. Martha Brian and Mary Carran Webster, "The Campus Radicals: Where Are They Now?" *Columbus Monthly,* June 1978, 48–49.

18. Letter from John Mount to Lorraine Cohen, September 17, 1970, in Office of the President, Disciplinary Cases: Appeals: 1970, (Confidential), (Archives: RG 3/i/79.

19. Letter from Kenneth Bader to John Mount, May 11, 1970, in Student Affairs and Office of the Vice President, Disruption, 1968–69 (Archives: RG 9/a/29).

20. Bonnie Chavin, "Court Orders Riot Charge Stricken from Coed's Files," *Lantern,* March 6, 1973, 1.

21. Kathy McClusky, "Mount Reverses Suggestion of Crandell's Suspension," *Lantern,* December 7, 1970, 1.

22. "Franconia College Hires David Kettler," *Lantern,* August 20, 1970, 8; David Kettler interview.

23. "ROTC Charges Filed," *Lantern,* June 22, 1971, 2; Art Flesch interview.

24. See, for example, Ohio University, "Official Notifications: Campus Disruption (Ohio House Bill 1219)," at ohio.edu/students/notifications/on_disrupt.cfm.

25. Louis M. Heldman, "'Year of Rededication,'" *Lantern,* May 25, 1970, 3.

26. William A. Payer, "Strike Leaders Look Back—and Ahead," *Lantern,* August 5, 1971, 9.

27. "University Will Continue to Adapt to Change," *OSU Monthly,* September 1970, 1.

28. Brian and Webster, "The Campus Radicals," 43.

29. David Williams interview, Oral History Project, 11.

30. Notes prepared by the provost's staff warned the issue was one "on which dissidents and taxpayers and legislature can unite against administration and faculty." Notes for Deans Meeting, July 7, 1970, in Vice President for Academic Affairs, Closed Courses, 1969–71 (Archives: RG5/a/28).

31. Louis M. Heldman, "Growth Causes Discontent," *Lantern,* June 8, 1970, 3.

32. Linda Halsey, "Friedman—'Shock Appeal,'" *Lantern,* May 12, 1971, 4; Jerry Friedman interview.

33. "Mike White Reports on Student Government Progress," *OSU Monthly,* May 1973, 7.

34. Bill Hummer, "YAF Chairmen Resign after Rift with State Chief," *Lantern,* October 23, 1970, 3.

35. Kasich ran for USG president as an independent in 1973 and finished third.

36. Malcom S. Baroway, *The Gee Years, 1990–1997* (Columbus: Ohio State University, 2002), 27.

37. "Report to the Faculty Council by President Fawcett, August 25, 1970," in Report to Faculty Council (Archives: Demonstrations vertical file).

38. Novice G. Fawcett, "This Will Be a Productive Academic Year," *OSU Monthly,* October 1970, 1; "President Writes to Parents," *OSU Monthly,* September 1970, 5.

39. Report of the Committee of Inquiry to the Faculty Council, "The Spring Events at Ohio State," November 10, 1970 (Archives: Demonstrations vertical file).

40. Raimund Goerler, *The Ohio State University: An Illustrated History* (Columbus: Ohio State University Press, 2011), 92–99.

41. Roger Meyer interview.

42. Tom La Rochelle, "Has Campus Tear Gas Lost Its Effectiveness?" *Citizen-Journal,* May 1, 1970, 2; Howard P. Shore, "The Ohio National Guard Operations during the 1970 Campus Riots," May 29, 1983, 32–36 (Archives: Demonstrations vertical file); Edward Q. Moulton interview, Oral History Project, 24.

43. "No One Force Held Strike Police Reins," *Lantern,* May 19, 1970, 12.

44. Bonnie Schwartz, "Scuffles Break Out after Rally," *Lantern,* May 22, 1970, 1.

45. Dale Van Lerberghe, "Safety Department Undergoes Change," *Lantern,* April 9, 1971, 7.

46. A *Lantern* editor wrote that three *Lantern* reporters on the scene witnessed Mount telling officers to arrest Stephen Piatt. Mount continued to deny this until his death in 2014, pointing out that after a three-year stint in the navy he was not overly sensitive to profanity. Leanne McLaughlin, "I Had Optimism—Mount," *Lantern,* October 2, 1970, 1; John Mount interview, August 6, 2013.

47. Sharon West interview.

48. Leanne McLaughlin, "Robinson Plans Student Contact; Wants to 'Mend Campus Bridges,'" *Lantern,* October 1, 1970, 1.

49. Louis Heldman, "Draining the Swamp," *Lantern,* March 1, 1971, 4; Lou Heldman interview.

50. Moulton, Oral History Project, 23, and John Mount interview, January 17 and August 6, 2013.

51. Letters from Gordon Carson to Philip Stevens, May 11 and May 15, 1970, in Office of Business and Finance, Vice President and Treasurer, Supplement, Water Cannons (Archives: RG 6/a/32). Stevens was a Toledo businessman with contacts in Germany.

52. Linda Halsey, "Closed-Course Woes Halved from Year Ago," *Lantern*, January 7, 1971, 1.

53. Goerler, *Illustrated History*, 99–103.

54. Gabel, *Jennings Years*, 168–70.

55. "Student Trend Shifts to Off-Campus Housing," *OSU Monthly*, December 1972, 10; "Where Students Live," *Lantern*, July 18, 1971, 9.

56. Mary Webster, "Investigation Pledged to Probe 'Sodom and Gomorrah' Charge," *Lantern*, February 5, 1971, 1.

57. Kim Niswander, "Towers Attract Upperclassmen," *Lantern*, October 30, 1990, 3.

58. U.S. News College Campus, "Ohio State University—Columbus, Student Life," at colleges.USnews.rankingsandreviews.com/best-colleges/ohio-state-6883/student-life.

59. Robert Westwood, "Military Research Comprises One-Third of Total," *Lantern*, June 1, 1970, 1.

60. Sue Giller, "Weapons Research Rejected by University in New Policy," *Lantern*, February 25, 1971, 1.

61. Office of Research, "Ohio State's Research Profile," at research.osu.edu/osu-research/profile.

62. According to David Webster's calculation, Ohio State dropped out of the top 25 in the 1970 study after finishing 22nd in 1966 and 18th in 1959; David S. Webster, *Academic Quality Rankings of American Colleges and Universities* (Springfield, Ill.: Charles C. Thomas, 1986), 137.

63. Sue Giller, "Fawcett Feels Decision Is Best for University," *Lantern*, March 8, 1971, 1.

64. Baroway, *Gee Years*, 44–47, 294; Ohio State Media Relations, "U.S. News: Ohio State Climbs in Latest Rankings" (press release), September 9, 2015.

65. "Surprise Visit Stuns Students," *Lantern*, October 20, 1970, 1.

66. Quoted in Tom Wells, *The War Within: America's Battle over Vietnam* (New York: Henry Holt, 1994), 448.

67. "Report of the President's Commission on Campus Unrest" (Washington, D.C.: Government Printing Office, 1970), 289; Rick Perlstein, *Nixonland: The Rise of a President and the Fracturing of America* (New York: Scribner, 2008), 523.

68. Rita Shade, "Kent/OSU—Why Different?" *Lantern*, May 6, 1971, 2.

69. "State Aid Cut Asked for Rioters," *Lantern*, October 6, 1970, 1.

70. Julia Osborne, "Views Differ Widely on Legislative Report," *Lantern*, October 6, 1970, 1.

71. Staff Services Bureau, "The University Riot: A Brief Report of Events That Occurred April 29 through May 29, 1970," Columbus Police Division, June 26, 1970, 15, 30, in Vice President for Academic Affairs, Disruptions (Archives: RG 5/a/27).

72. Tim Fought, "Safety Director Predicts Peace Despite Hostility toward Police," *Lantern*, April 29, 1971, 1.

73. Mike Veres interview.

74. Marlene Cohen interview.

75. Marlene Cohen, Pam Conrad, Lou Heldman, Jerry Friedman, Blaine Lilly, Mike Veres, Mary Webster, and Sharon West interviews.

76. Roger Meyer interview.

77. Staff Services Bureau, "The University Riot," 25; "Record Number of Patrolmen Injured," *Lantern,* May 19, 1970, 12; James M. Abraham, "Commander's Confidential Report on Aid to Civil Authority at Ohio State University (Columbus Ohio), 29 April to May 1970," 33 (Archives).

78. Art Flesch interview.

79. Nancy Morris, "New Voters Sought," *Lantern,* July 29, 1971, 2.

80. Tom Brennan, "Heavy Youth Vote Key for Moody," *Lantern,* November 3, 1971, 1.

81. Marilyn Durbin, "New City Police Chief Assumes Post Monday," *Lantern,* March 31, 1972, 1; "City Is Ordered to Hire 220 Minority Police," *Dispatch,* January 17, 1975, 1C.

82. Christian K. Zacher, *The Holbrook Years,* 2002–2007 (Columbus: Ohio State University Press, 2012), 43–44.

83. Mike Harden, "Ordeal Over for Alumni," *Lantern,* February 14, 1973, 1; David Flick and Joyce McKenna, "Former Student Is POW Returnee," *Lantern,* April 2, 1973, 1.

84. Levine, *When Dreams and Heroes Died,* 12.

85. See, for example, David Steigerwald, *The Sixties and the End of Modern America* (New York: St. Martin's Press, 1995), 186.

86. For an elaboration on this argument, see Leonard Steinhorn, *The Greater Generation: In Defense of the Baby Boom Legacy* (New York: Thomas Dunne, 2006).

NOTES TO CONCLUSION

1. Neal R. Peirce, *The Megastates of America: People, Politics, and Power in the Ten Great States* (New York: W. W. Norton, 1972), 299.

2. Francis P. Weisenburger, *History of the Ohio State University: The Fawcett Years, 1956–1972* (Columbus: Ohio State University Press, 1975), 69, 236.

3. Novice G. Fawcett interview, Oral History Project, June 17, 1985, 6, and John Mount interview, August 6, 2013.

4. "If Only They'd Listened," *Lantern,* August 13, 1970, 3.

5. See, for example, Jerry Morelli, "Fawcett's Door 'Was Open,'" *Lantern,* April 25, 1972, 2.

6. Novice G. Fawcett interview, Oral History Project, November 16, 1983, 11, and May 16, 1984, 9; and John E. Corbally interview, Oral History Project, 5.

7. "A Few Omissions," *Lantern,* May 9, 1967, 4; Bonnie Schwartz, "Assembly Calls for Peaceful Boycott," *Lantern,* April 29, 1970, 1.

8. "Fawcett Appoints Student Advisers," *Lantern,* October 13, 1970, 1.

9. Novice Fawcett, Memorandum to Members of Cabinet, "A Report on the Substance of the IUC Meeting in the Chancellor's Office Held This Afternoon," September 14, 1970, Novice G. Fawcett, Cabinet: President's Memorandums, 1970–72, Confidential (Archives: RG 3/i/76).

10. Margaret Tarter, "Fawcett Tells 'Today' Students Not Experts in Determining Policy," *Lantern,* August 17, 1972, 1; Fawcett interview, Oral History Project, November 16, 1983, 3.

11. Edward Q. Moulton interview, Oral History Project, 6.

12. Stan Darling, Jane Fawcett-Hoover, John Mount (August 6, 2013), and Richard Weaver interviews.

13. Louis Heldman, "The Man Is Leaving," *Lantern,* March 8, 1971, 4.

14. Richard Weaver interview.

15. Roger Meyer interview.

16. Nancy Freeman, "Team Begins Monthly Surveys to Find What Makes OSU Tick," *Lantern*, November 18, 1970, 3.

17. Edmund David Cronin and John W. Jenkins, *The University of Wisconsin: A History, 1945–1971* (Madison: University of Wisconsin Press, 1999), 509–10.

18. Bentley Historical Library, University of Michigan, "Robben Wright Fleming," at bentley.umich.edu/legacy-support/um/umpresid.php.

19. Kenneth J. Heineman, *Campus Wars: The Peace Movement at American State Universities in the Vietnam Era* (New York: New York University Press, 1993), 20–31, 249–54.

20. Mary Ann Wynkoop, *Dissent in the Heartland: The Sixties at Indiana University* (Bloomington: Indiana University Press, 2002), 83–112.

21. Heineman, *Campus Wars*, 26–41, 229–30, 245–49.

22. "Campus Crisis," in Walter Havinghurst, *The Miami Years, 1809–1984* (Oxford: Miami University, 1996), at lib.muohio.edu/my/miamiyearsXXVI.html; "Month of Campus Tension Results in Violent Closing," *Ohio University Alumni Journal*, August 1970, 1–2.

23. Robbie Lieberman and David Cochran, "It Seemed a Very Local Affair: The Student Movement at Southern Illinois University at Carbondale," in John McMillan and Paul Buhle, eds., *The New Left Revisited* (Philadelphia: Temple University Press, 2003), 11–27.

24. The Kent State shootings and the Wisconsin bombing both achieved greater notoriety because they involved loss of life, which fortunately was not the case at Ohio State. Nevertheless, in terms of numbers of arrests and associated mayhem, the Ohio State confrontations were much greater.

25. Jocelyn Dorsey, "Fawcett Graded High by Several Students," *Lantern*, March 8, 1971, 3.

26. Paul Underwood, *The Enarson Years, 1972–1981* (Columbus: Ohio State University, 1985), 15–16.

27. Underwood, *Enarson Years*, 10.

BIBLIOGRAPHIC NOTE

This book builds on the work of many others. Sources include locally published materials, including contemporary press reports; documents and other materials from the Ohio State archives; other published materials; and interviews with witnesses and participants.

LOCALLY PUBLISHED

The starting points for any examination of Ohio State in the 1960s are two books published by the University Press: Francis P. Weisenburger's *History of the Ohio State University: The Fawcett Years, 1956–1972* (1975) and Raimund Goerler's *The Ohio State University: An Illustrated History* (2011). Weisenburger's book, the ninth volume in a series of histories of the university's presidents, covers the decade from the viewpoint of the administration. While it is a good reflection of Novice Fawcett's perspective on the sixties, it lacks a feel for the changes in student behavior that drove much of the events.

Goerler's book is the best account of the university's development since its founding to the present day and is particularly strong in its examination of the role of students in the 1970 upheaval, the treatment of African American students, the development of the campuswide master plan, and the move to selective admissions. Because the book spans 140 years, it is by necessity limited to a high-level survey of events.

Much of the vivid detail reflected in *The Ohio State University in the Sixties* comes from the university's award-winning student newspaper, the *Lantern.* Because the changing culture of the 1960s included a willingness to challenge the existing authority, the *Lantern* was able to capture much of the energy of the period. Back copies are available online at digital.olivesoftware.com/Olive/APA/Ohio.

Using the *Lantern* as a source does have limitations. The paper is published only when classes are in session, and because it is a student laboratory newspaper, mistakes sometimes end up in print. Consequently, wherever possible I supplemented or corroborated *Lantern* coverage with other sources. The *Ohio State University Monthly,* as it was called at the time, is the official magazine of the university's Alumni Association and was especially helpful in this regard. For most of the 1960s the magazine was headed by Association secretary and former *Lantern* editor Jack Fullen, who held it to journalistic standards and was not afraid to take on controversial issues. A complete set of the magazines is available to the public at University Archives. Ohio State's yearbook, the *Makio,* provided additional information and many excellent photographs. University Archives has hard copies of the *Makio,* and it is available online at edu.arcasearch.com/usohosy.

Columbus's two daily newspapers of the period, the *Citizen-Journal* and the *Dispatch,* covered campus events as well. Issues from that time are not available online, but microfilm copies of both papers are available at the Columbus Metropolitan Library's main building on Grant Street. *Columbus Monthly* magazine also proved to be a valuable resource for specific topics, such as the Speakers Rule controversy and the 1970 demonstrations. Bound copies are available at the Columbus Metropolitan Library.

UNPUBLISHED MATERIAL

Documents in University Archives, some of which have not been made public until now, are a rich source of information on the thinking of various officials. The Novice Fawcett papers alone include 104 boxes of memos, reports, speeches, and letters. Similar materials from the files of the board of trustees and the academic affairs, student relations, and business and finance offices also are valuable. In addition, University Archives maintains records from various student organizations, including registration forms, rosters, and newsletters. Annual reports of the university registrar, student and staff directories, and course catalogs are available at the Archives reading room.

Papers prepared by students at Ohio State and elsewhere for academic credit provide valuable information on specific topics addressed in this book. They include Roberta Katherine Jones, "A Study of the Physical Facilities at Morrill Tower, The Ohio State University, as Assessed by the Student Residents and Staff" (1967, master's thesis); Renee Nicole Lansley, "College Women or College Girls? Gender, Sexuality and in Loco Parentis on Campus" (2004, Ph.D. thesis); Jeffrey H. Schwartz, "The Speakers Rule Controversy at Ohio State: A Case Study" (1966, master's thesis); Howard P. Shores, "The National Guard Operations during the 1970 Campus Riots" (1983, class paper); Greer C. Stanford-Randle, "The Black Student Movement at the Ohio State University" (2010, master's thesis); and William Joseph Vollmar, "The Issue of Compulsory Military Training at the Ohio State University, 1913–1973" (1976, Ph.D. thesis).

In addition, University Archives has prepared an excellent online exhibit titled "Spring of Dissent" that features a timeline, photos, eyewitness accounts, and various documents. It can be seen at library.osu.edu/projects/spring-of-dissent.

INTERVIEWS

Although memories are not infallible, they do provide insights often missing from written documents. Some interviews used for this book came from Ohio State's Oral History Project; others were conducted by me.

Oral History Project interviews have been conducted during the last 20 years by the Archives staff. Transcripts are available at kb.osu.edu/dspace/handle/1811/56913. Interviews that were used for this book are listed below, along with the date of the interview and the title most associated with the interviewee during the period covered here:

Richard H. Armitage, dean of the graduate school. May 28, 2002.

John T. Bonner Jr., executive dean for student relations. July 25, 2001.

Christine Y. Conaway, dean of women. November 15, 1984.

John E. Corbally, vice president for academic affairs and provost. March 7–10, 2002.

Robert M. Duncan, student (1940s, 1950s), municipal court judge. June 15, 2010.

Wendell Ellenwood, director of the Ohio Union. July 18, 2002.

Novice G. Fawcett, president. November 16, 1983; February 16, April 9, and May 16, 1984; June 17 and August 5, 1985.

William S. Guthrie, executive dean for student relations. December 7, 1983.

John Herrick, executive director of campus planning. November 8, 1983.

G. Robert Holsinger, secretary to the faculty. July 30, 1985.

David Hopcraft, student. June 22, 2010.

David Kettler, professor of political science. June 24, 2010.

Edward Q. Moulton, vice president for administrative operations. July 24, 1985.

John T. Mount, vice president for student affairs. October 20, 2003. (Forthcoming; release of Mount's interview was held until after his death at his request.)

Jeff Schwartz, student. November 16, 2012.

Niki Schwartz, student. January 8, 2013.

David Williams, student. June 28, 2010.

Between 2012 and 2015 I conducted interviews with more than 40 individuals for this book:

James Abraham, lieutenant colonel, Ohio National Guard. November 12, 2013.

John Bender, student, 1964–71. August 6, 2014.

Dan Bradley, student, 1969–71. August 28, 2013.

Lorraine Cohen, student, 1969–70. June 29, 2013.

Marlene Cohen, student, 1970–74. March 26, 2013.

Pam Conrad, student, 1967–71. April 25, 2015.

Jack Cooley, student, 1966–72. June 25, 2014.

Bill Crandell, student, 1960–64, 1968–70. August 6, 2014.

Stan Darling, student, 1961–65. October 27, 2012.

Jane Fawcett-Hoover, student, 1961–65. December 2, 2012.

Art Flesch, student, 1966–67, 1970–78. October 9, 2014.

Mabel Freeman, student, 1962–66. April 16, 2013.

Jerry Friedman, student, 1967–72. January 16, 2014.

Vic Frost, student, 1962–66. July 18, 2014.

Jim Gross, student, 1959–63. November 28, 2013.

Lou Heldman, student, 1968–72. March 27, 2015.

Becky Hines, student, 1970–72. September 4, 2015.

Joe Hyler, student, 1966–70. July 18, 2013.

David Kettler, professor of political science. June 16, 2013.

Dennis Knepley, student, 1963–67. February 10, 2015.

James Lawrence, student, 1958–62. June 19, 2013.

Joan Leitzel, assistant professor of mathematics. July 17, 2014.

Rich Levin, student, 1963–70. April 18, 2013.

Blaine Lilly, student, 1967–71. January 30, 2015.

Alan Melamed, student, 1963–67. February 26, 2014.

Roger Meyer, area director of north campus residence halls. December 12, 2013.

Philip Moots, student, 1957–62. May 31, 2012.

John Mount, vice president for student affairs. July 26, 2012; January 17 and August 6, 2013.

Tim Neustadt, student, 1963–67. April 22, 2014.

Randall Ripley, chair of the Department of Political Science. March 27, 2013.

Jeff Schwartz, student, 1961–65. August 12, 2012.

Niki Schwartz, student, 1957–63. September 7, 2012.

Jay Shaffer, student, 1966–70. March 5, 2015.

Tim Sheeran, student, 1968–71. March 23, 2015.

Lloyd Siegel, student, 1965–69. June 3, 2014.

Don Slemmer, Ohio Highway Patrol officer. December 10, 2014.

Ron Solove, student, 1964–70. May 8, 2013.

Dewey Stokes, Columbus police officer. May 15, 2014.

Ron St. Pierre, associate professor of anatomy. February 26, 2014.

Ira Sully, student, 1965–71. May 7, 2013.

Joel Ann Todd, student, 1969–70. August 23, 2013.

Mike Veres, student, 1967–71. April 14, 2013.

Richard Weaver, assistant dean of men. September 11, 2013.

Mary Webster, student, 1965–71. October 21, 2013.

Sharon West, student, 1966–70. June 18, 2013.

Tom Workman, student, 1962–69. December 6, 2013.

NATIONALLY PUBLISHED

Two individuals on campus during the 1960s have discussed their perspectives in national publications. Former USG president Jay Shaffer wrote about "Students in the Policy Process" in the *Journal of Higher Education Policy*, May 1970, 341–49, and former political science professor David Kettler coauthored a piece with Harry R. Blaine titled, "Law as a Political Weapon," in *Politics and Society*, September 1971, 479–526.

Several nationally published books provide context for events outside the university in the 1960s. James T. Patterson's *Grand Expectations: The United States, 1945–1974* (New York: Oxford University Press, 1996) is an excellent general history of the period. Rick Perlstein's *Nixonland: The Rise of the President and the Fracturing of America* (New York: Scribner, 2008) is a good exploration of the politics of law and order on the national scene. An informative source on the civil rights movement is Juan Williams, *Eyes on the Prize: America's Civil Rights Years, 1954–1965* (New York: Penguin, 1988). *Chance and Circumstance: The Draft, the War, and the Vietnam Generation* by Lawrence M. Baskir and William A. Strauss (New York: Vantage, 1978) is a classic study of the impact of the draft. Arthur Levine explores the psyche of college students in another classic, *When Dreams and Heroes Died: A Portrait of Today's College Student* (Washington, D.C.: Jossey-Bass, 1980). The best work on state politics in this period is Alexander P. Lamis, editor, *Ohio Politics* (Kent: Kent State University Press, 1994), particularly the chapters by Mike Curtin on Governor Mike DiSalle and Richard G. Zimmerman's chapter on Governor James Rhodes's first two terms. An updated account of Rhodes's governorship is also included in Tom Diemer et al., *James A. Rhodes, Ohio Colossus* (Kent: Kent State University Press, 2015). The chapter on Ohio in Neal R. Peirce's *The Megastates of America: People, Politics, and Power in the Ten Great States* (New York: W. W. Norton, 1972) also provides a good perspective on politics in the Buckeye state in the 1960s.

Kenneth J. Heineman's *Campus Wars: The Peace Movement at American State Universities in the Vietnam Era* (New York: New York University Press, 1993) delves into antiwar protests at four Midwestern public universities, but not Ohio State. W. J. Rorabaugh, *Berkeley at War: The 1960s* (New York: Oxford University Press, 1989); Mary Ann Wynkoop, *Dissent in the Heartland: The Sixties at Indiana University* (Bloomington: Indiana University Press, 2002); and Matthew Levin, *Cold War University: Madison and the New Left in the Sixties* (Madison: University of Wisconsin Press, 2013) all provide excellent accounts of the changes affecting those campuses in the 1960s.

INDEX

Note: Page numbers in italics refer to figures.